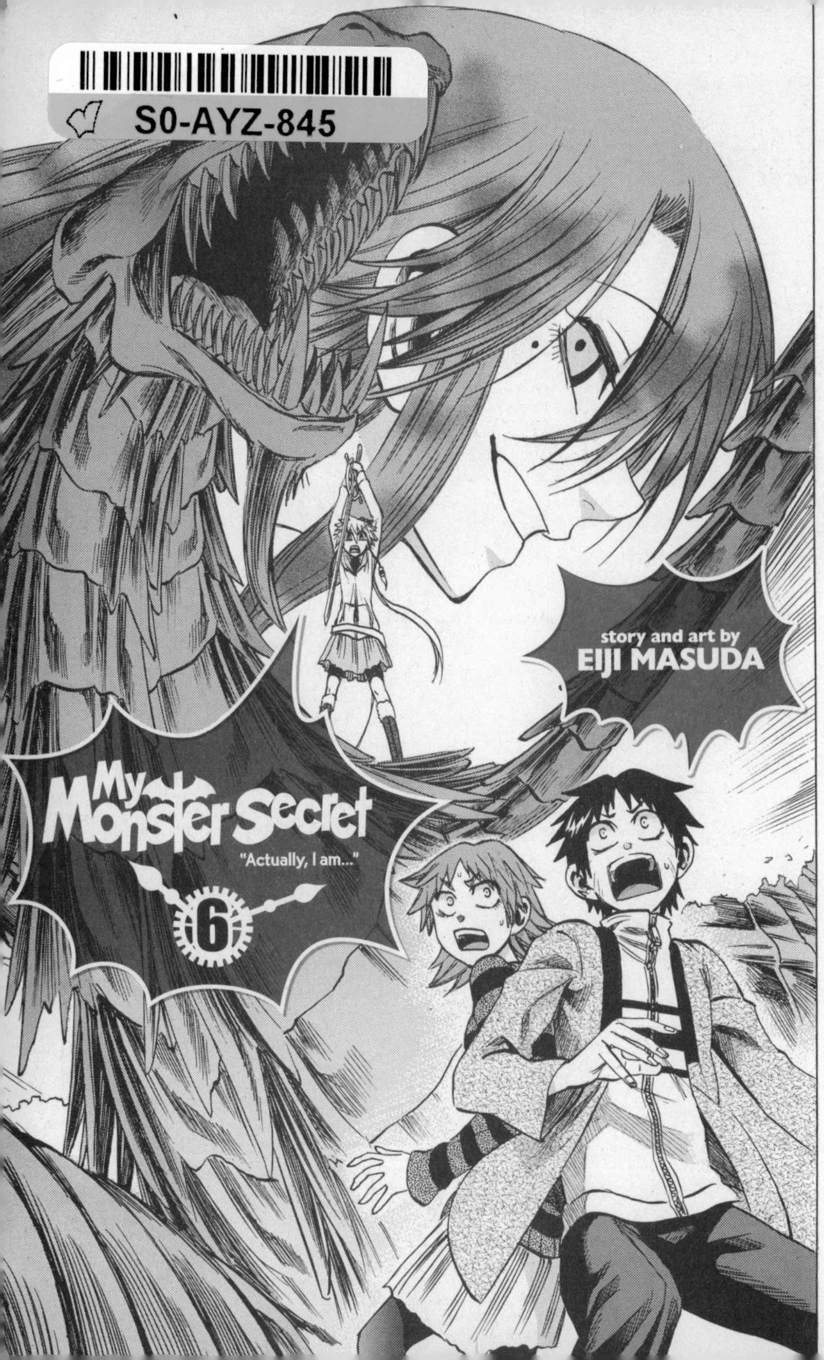
story and art by
EIJI MASUDA
My Monster Secret
"Actually, I am..."
6

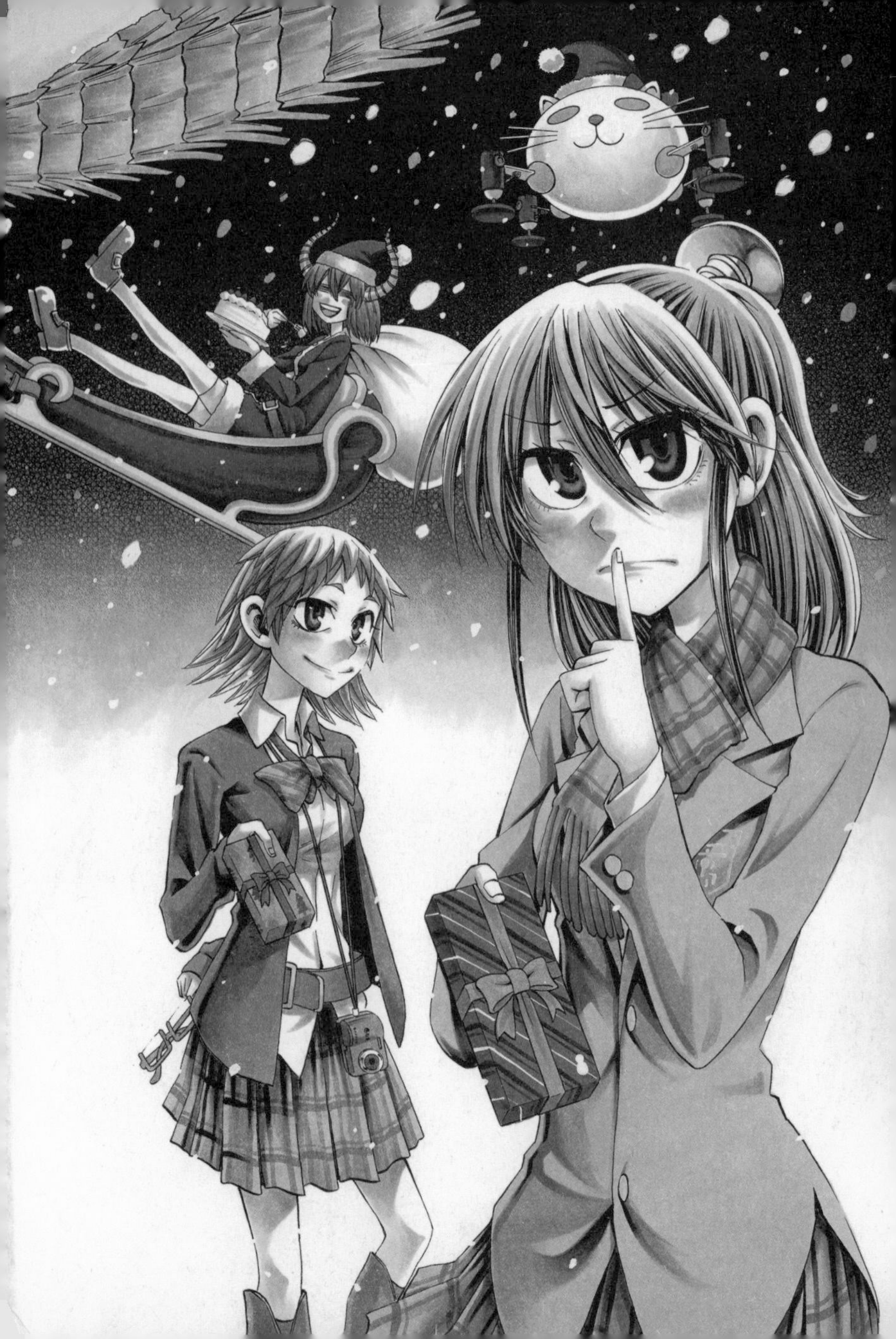

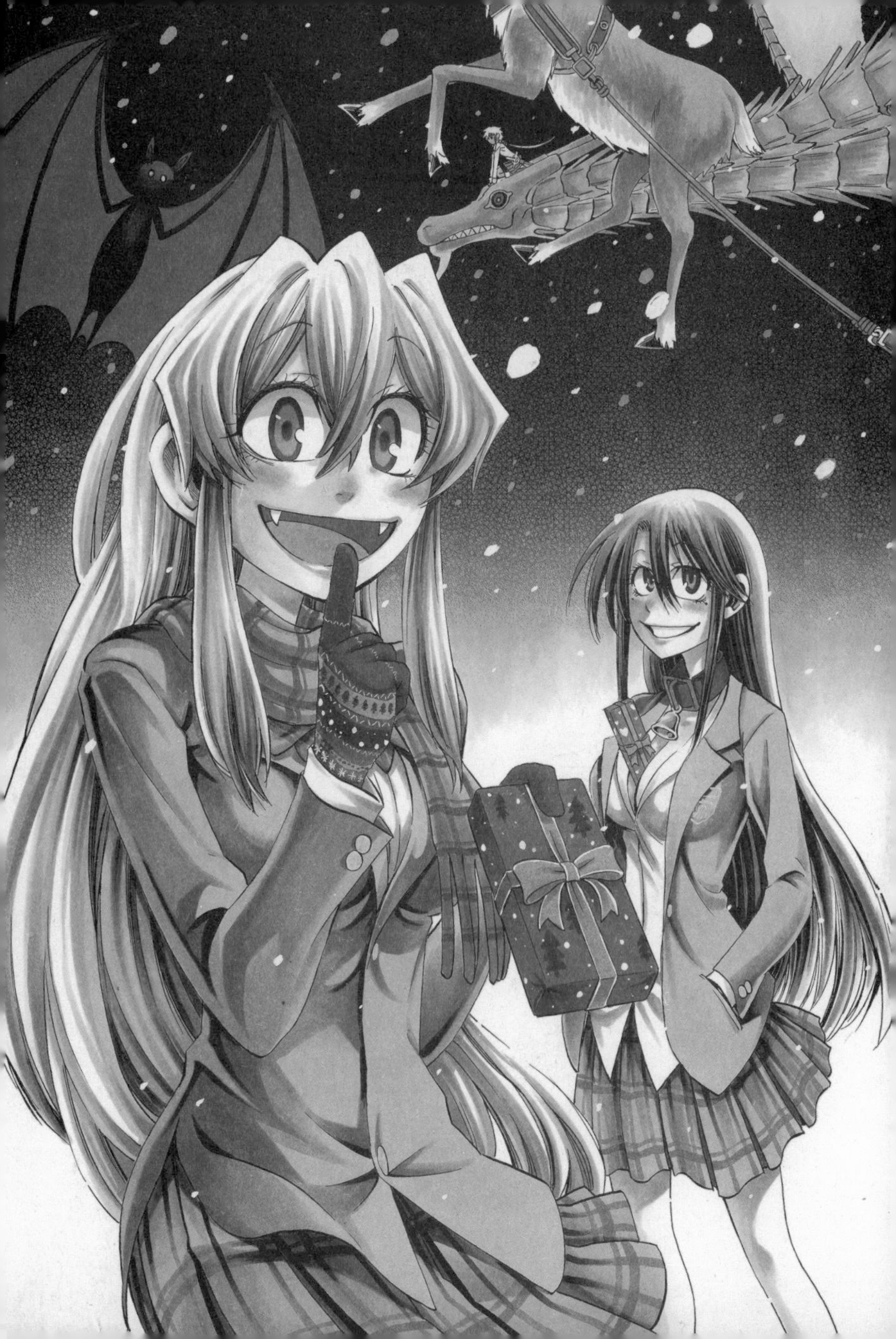

My Monster Secret
"Actually, I am..."

Story & Character

After school one day, **Kuromine Asahi** opened the door to his classroom to confess his love to his crush **Shiragami Youko**... and discovered that she's actually a vampire! His goal was to tell Shiragami that he loved her, but he instead resolved to keep her secret--as a friend. It means they can continue to go to school together, but their problems are only beginning...

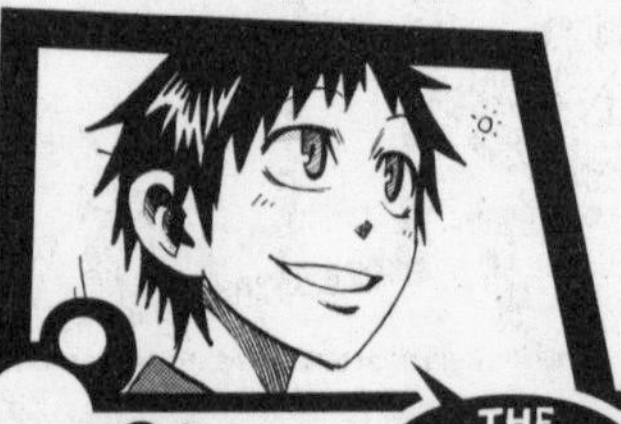

KUROMINE ASAHI
THE HOLEY SIEVE

The man with the worst poker face in the world, he's known as ***The Sieve With A Hole In It***...because secrets slide right out of him. Now he has to hide the fact that Shiragami-san--the girl he's in love with--is a vampire.

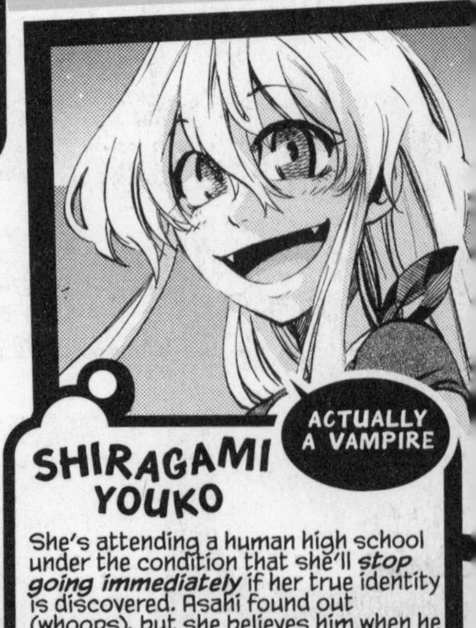

SHIRAGAMI YOUKO
ACTUALLY A VAMPIRE

She's attending a human high school under the condition that she'll ***stop going immediately*** if her true identity is discovered. Asahi found out (whoops), but she believes him when he says he'll keep her secret, and the two are now friends.

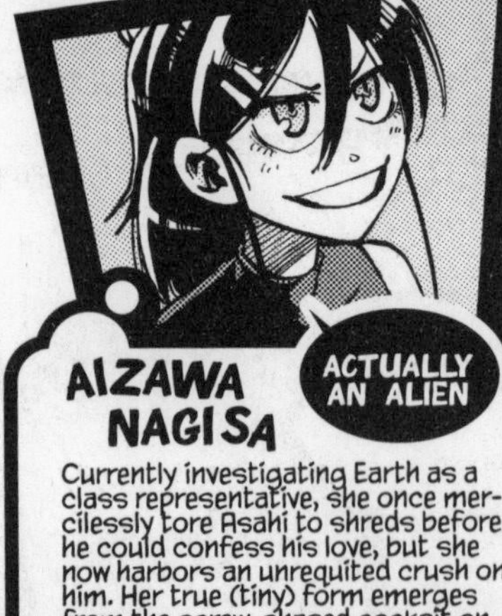

AIZAWA NAGISA
ACTUALLY AN ALIEN

Currently investigating Earth as a class representative, she once mercilessly tore Asahi to shreds before he could confess his love, but she now harbors an unrequited crush on him. Her true (tiny) form emerges from the screw-shaped cockpit on her head. Her brother **Aizawa Ryo** is also staying on Earth.

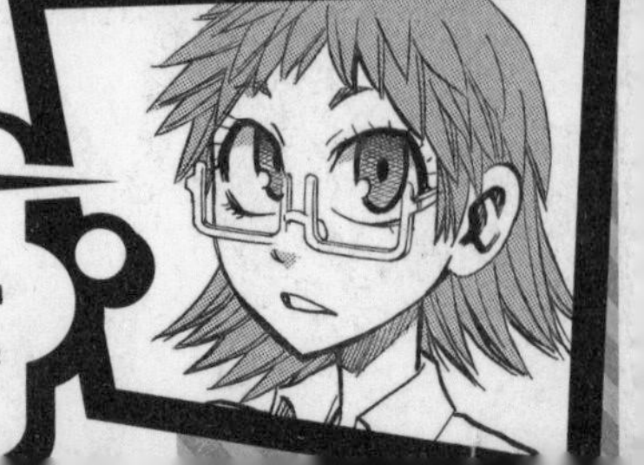

AKEMI MIKAN
THE QUEEN OF PURE EVIL

Editor-in-chief of the school newspaper and a childhood friend of Asahi's. Possibly straying from the path of villainy since her favorite pair of glasses became the **Goddess of Fortune, Fuku-chan.**

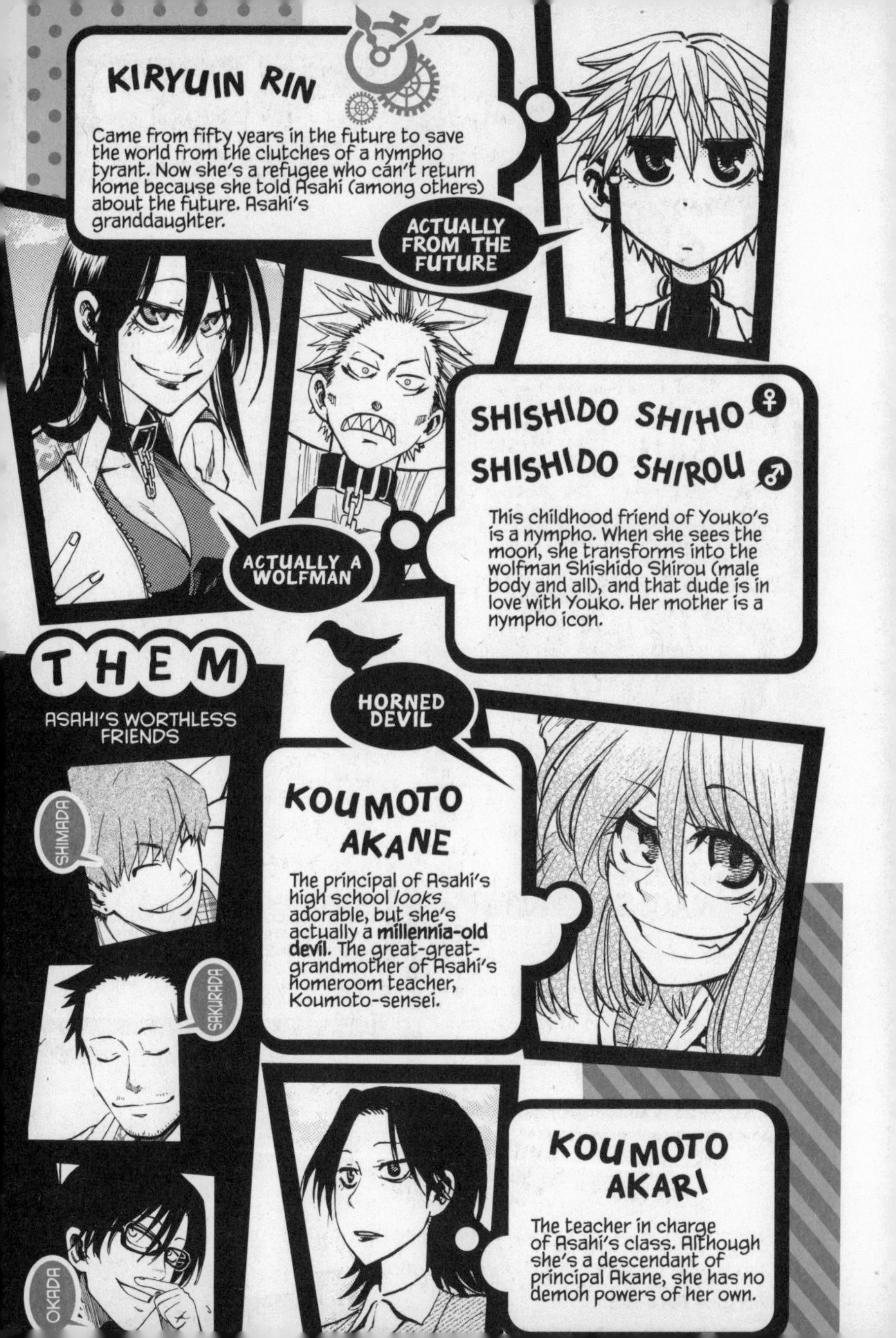

KIRYUIN RIN
Came from fifty years in the future to save the world from the clutches of a nympho tyrant. Now she's a refugee who can't return home because she told Asahi (among others) about the future. Asahi's granddaughter.
ACTUALLY FROM THE FUTURE
SHISHIDO SHIHO ♀
SHISHIDO SHIROU ♂
This childhood friend of Youko's is a nympho. When she sees the moon, she transforms into the wolfman Shishido Shirou (male body and all), and that dude is in love with Youko. Her mother is a nympho icon.
ACTUALLY A WOLFMAN
HORNED DEVIL
KOUMOTO AKANE
The principal of Asahi's high school *looks* adorable, but she's actually a **millennia-old devil.** The great-great-grandmother of Asahi's homeroom teacher, Koumoto-sensei.
THEM
ASAHI'S WORTHLESS FRIENDS
SHIMADA
SAKURADA
OKADA
KOUMOTO AKARI
The teacher in charge of Asahi's class. Although she's a descendant of principal Akane, she has no demon powers of her own.

SEVEN SEAS ENTERTAINMENT PRESENTS

My Monster Secret
"Actually, I am..."

story and art by Eiji Masuda

VOLUME 6

TRANSLATION
Alethea and Athena Nibley

ADAPTATION
Lianne Sentar

LETTERING AND LAYOUT
Annaliese Christman

LOGO DESIGN
Karis Page

COVER DESIGN
Nicky Lim

PROOFREADER
Shanti Whitesides

ASSISTANT EDITOR
Jenn Grunigen

PRODUCTION ASSISTANT
CK Russell

PRODUCTION MANAGER
Lissa Pattillo

EDITOR IN CHIEF
Adam Arnold

PUBLISHER
Jason DeAngelis

JITSUHA WATASHIHA Volume 6
© EIJI MASUDA 2014
Originally published in Japan in 2014 by Akita Publishing Co., Ltd.
English translation rights arranged with Akita Publishing Co., Ltd.
through TOHAN CORPORATION, Tokyo.

Seven Seas books may be purchased in bulk for promotional, educational, or
business use. Please contact your local bookseller or the Macmillan Corporate
and Premium Sales Department at 1-800-221-7945, extension 5442, or by
e-mail at MacmillanSpecialMarkets@macmillan.com.

Seven Seas and the Seven Seas logo are trademarks of
Seven Seas Entertainment, LLC. All rights reserved.

ISBN: 978-1-626924-55-0

Printed in Canada

First Printing: April 2017

10 9 8 7 6 5 4 3 2 1

FOLLOW US ONLINE: www.gomanga.com

READING DIRECTIONS

This book reads from *right to left*, Japanese style.
If this is your first time reading manga, you start
reading from the top right panel on each page and
take it from there. If you get lost, just follow the
numbered diagram here. It may seem backwards at
first, but you'll get the hang of it! Have fun!!

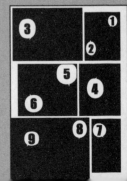

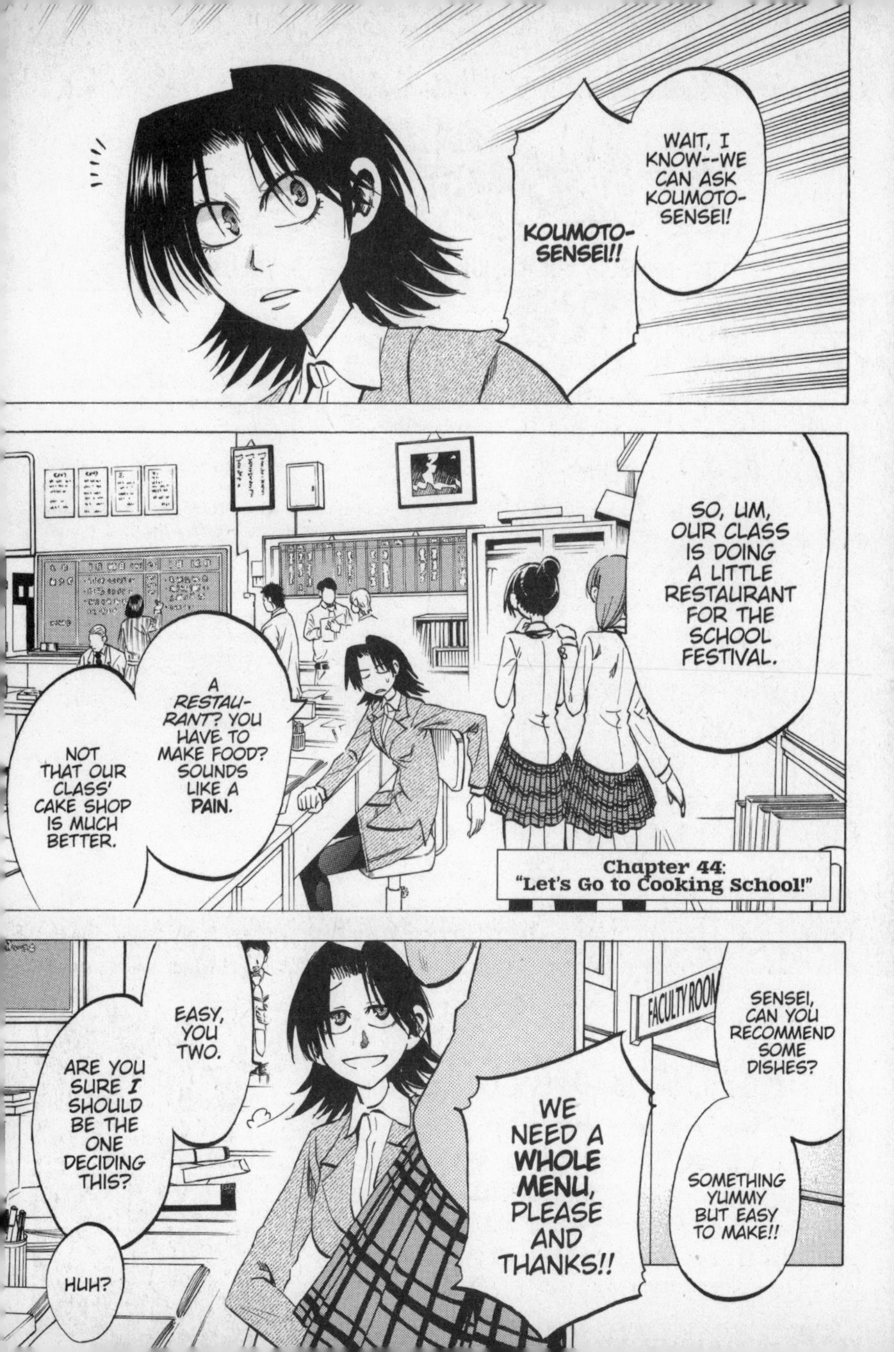
WAIT, I KNOW--WE CAN ASK KOUMOTO-SENSEI!
KOUMOTO-SENSEI!!
SO, UM, OUR CLASS IS DOING A LITTLE RESTAURANT FOR THE SCHOOL FESTIVAL.
A RESTAURANT? YOU HAVE TO MAKE FOOD? SOUNDS LIKE A PAIN.
NOT THAT OUR CLASS' CAKE SHOP IS MUCH BETTER.
Chapter 44: "Let's Go to Cooking School!"
FACULTY ROOM
SENSEI, CAN YOU RECOMMEND SOME DISHES?
SOMETHING YUMMY BUT EASY TO MAKE!!
WE NEED A WHOLE MENU, PLEASE AND THANKS!!
EASY, YOU TWO.
ARE YOU SURE I SHOULD BE THE ONE DECIDING THIS?
HUH?

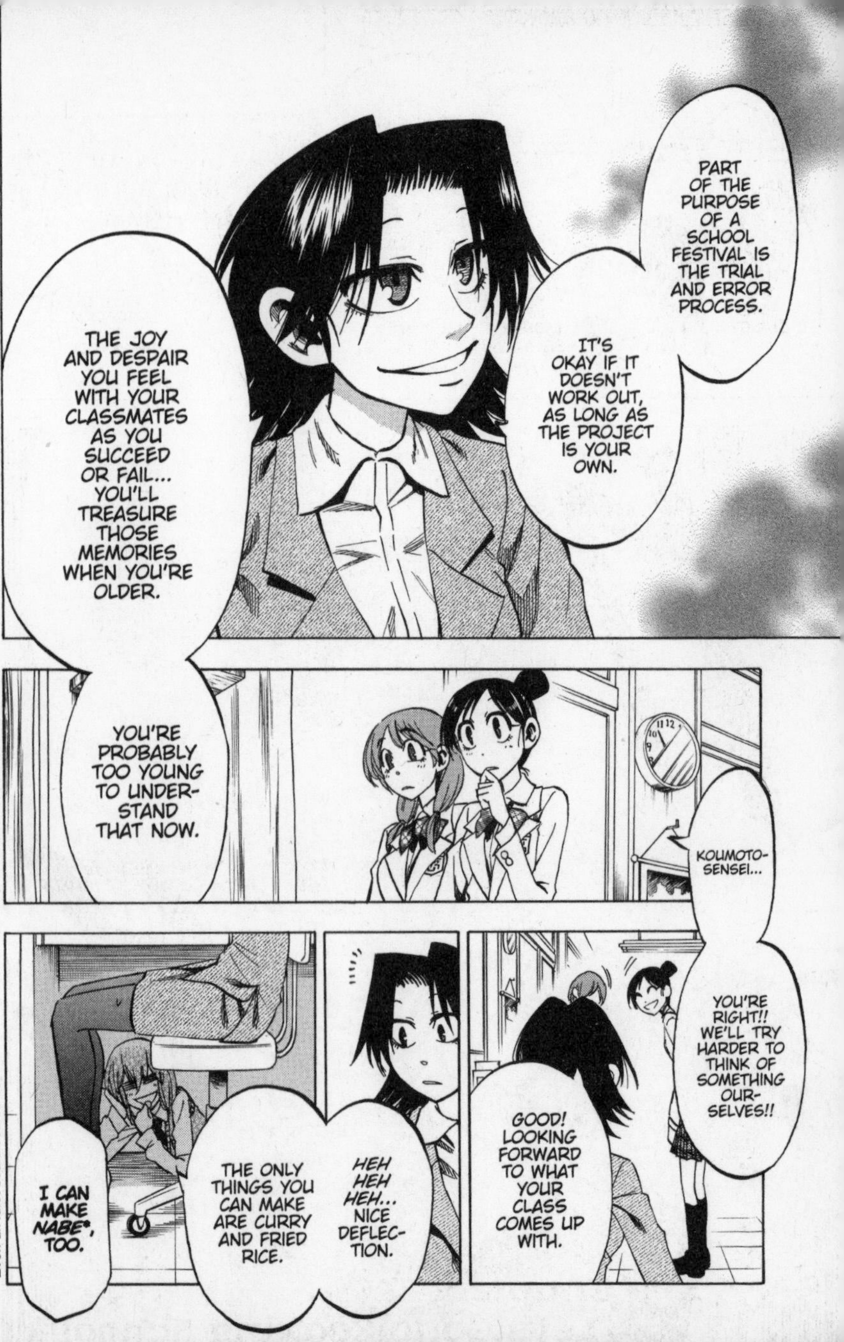
PART OF THE PURPOSE OF A SCHOOL FESTIVAL IS THE TRIAL AND ERROR PROCESS.
IT'S OKAY IF IT DOESN'T WORK OUT, AS LONG AS THE PROJECT IS YOUR OWN.
THE JOY AND DESPAIR YOU FEEL WITH YOUR CLASSMATES AS YOU SUCCEED OR FAIL... YOU'LL TREASURE THOSE MEMORIES WHEN YOU'RE OLDER.
YOU'RE PROBABLY TOO YOUNG TO UNDER-STAND THAT NOW.
KOUMOTO-SENSEI...
YOU'RE RIGHT!! WE'LL TRY HARDER TO THINK OF SOMETHING OUR-SELVES!!
GOOD! LOOKING FORWARD TO WHAT YOUR CLASS COMES UP WITH.
HEH HEH HEH... NICE DEFLEC-TION.
THE ONLY THINGS YOU CAN MAKE ARE CURRY AND FRIED RICE.
I CAN MAKE *NABE**, TOO.

*Even an idiot could cook these.

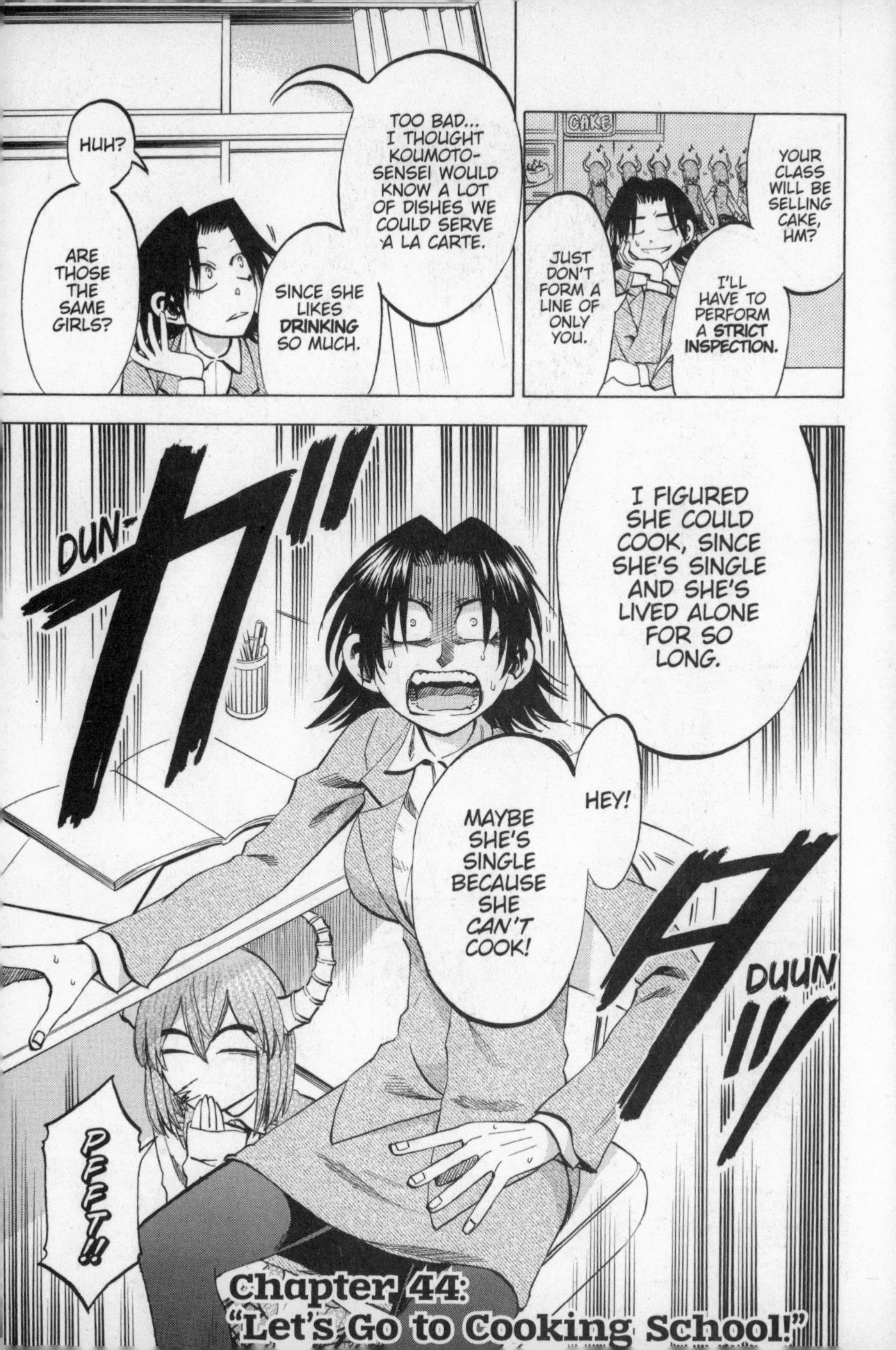
CAKE
YOUR CLASS WILL BE SELLING CAKE, HM?
I'LL HAVE TO PERFORM A **STRICT INSPECTION.**
JUST DON'T FORM A LINE OF ONLY YOU.
TOO BAD... I THOUGHT KOUMOTO-SENSEI WOULD KNOW A LOT OF DISHES WE COULD SERVE A LA CARTE.
SINCE SHE LIKES **DRINKING** SO MUCH.
HUH?
ARE THOSE THE SAME GIRLS?
DUN-
I FIGURED SHE COULD COOK, SINCE SHE'S SINGLE AND SHE'S LIVED ALONE FOR SO LONG.
HEY!
MAYBE SHE'S SINGLE BECAUSE SHE *CAN'T* COOK!
DUUN
PFFT!!

Chapter 44: "Let's Go to Cooking School!"

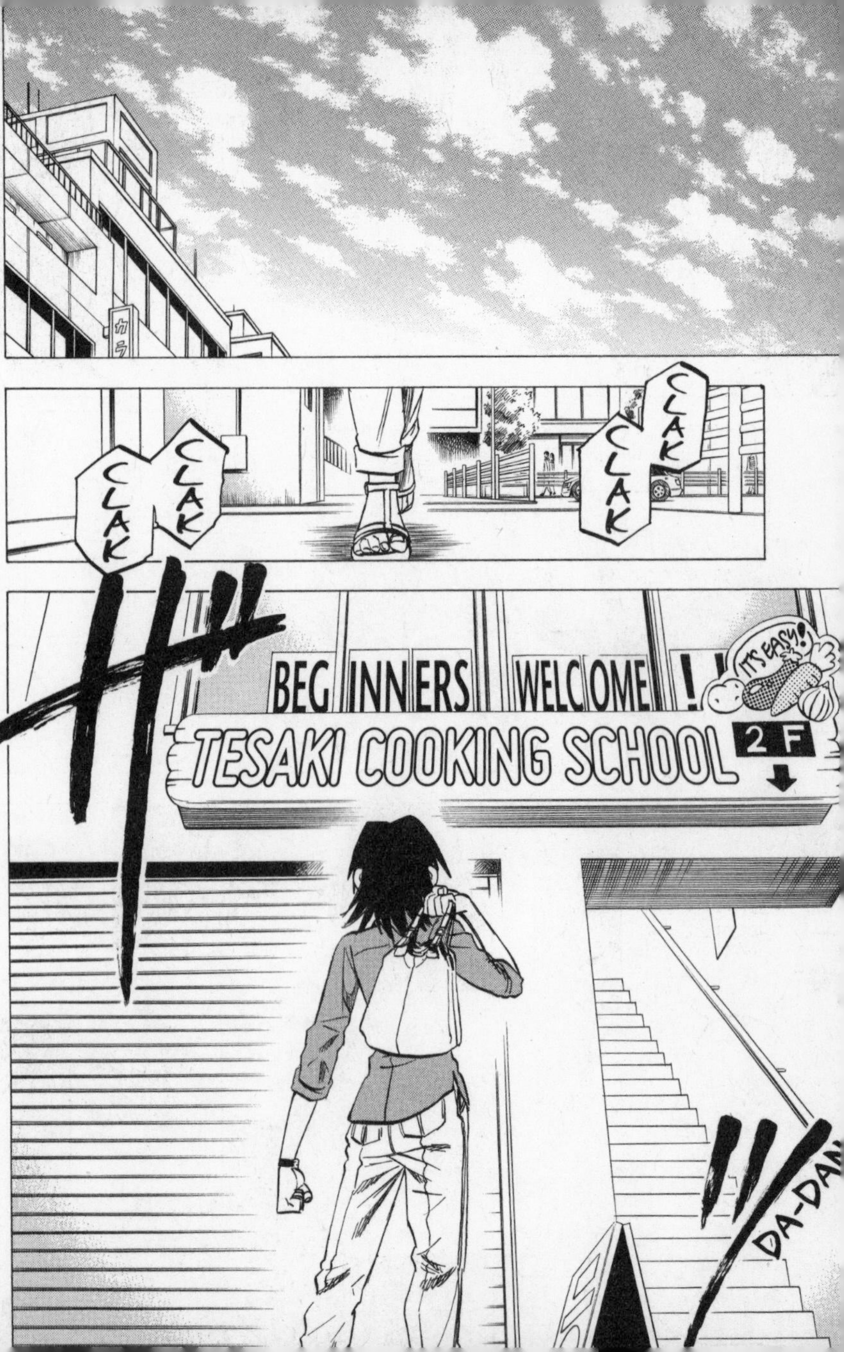
CLAK CLAK
CLAK CLAK
IT'S EASY!
BEGINNERS WELCOME!
TESAKI COOKING SCHOOL
2F
DA-DAN

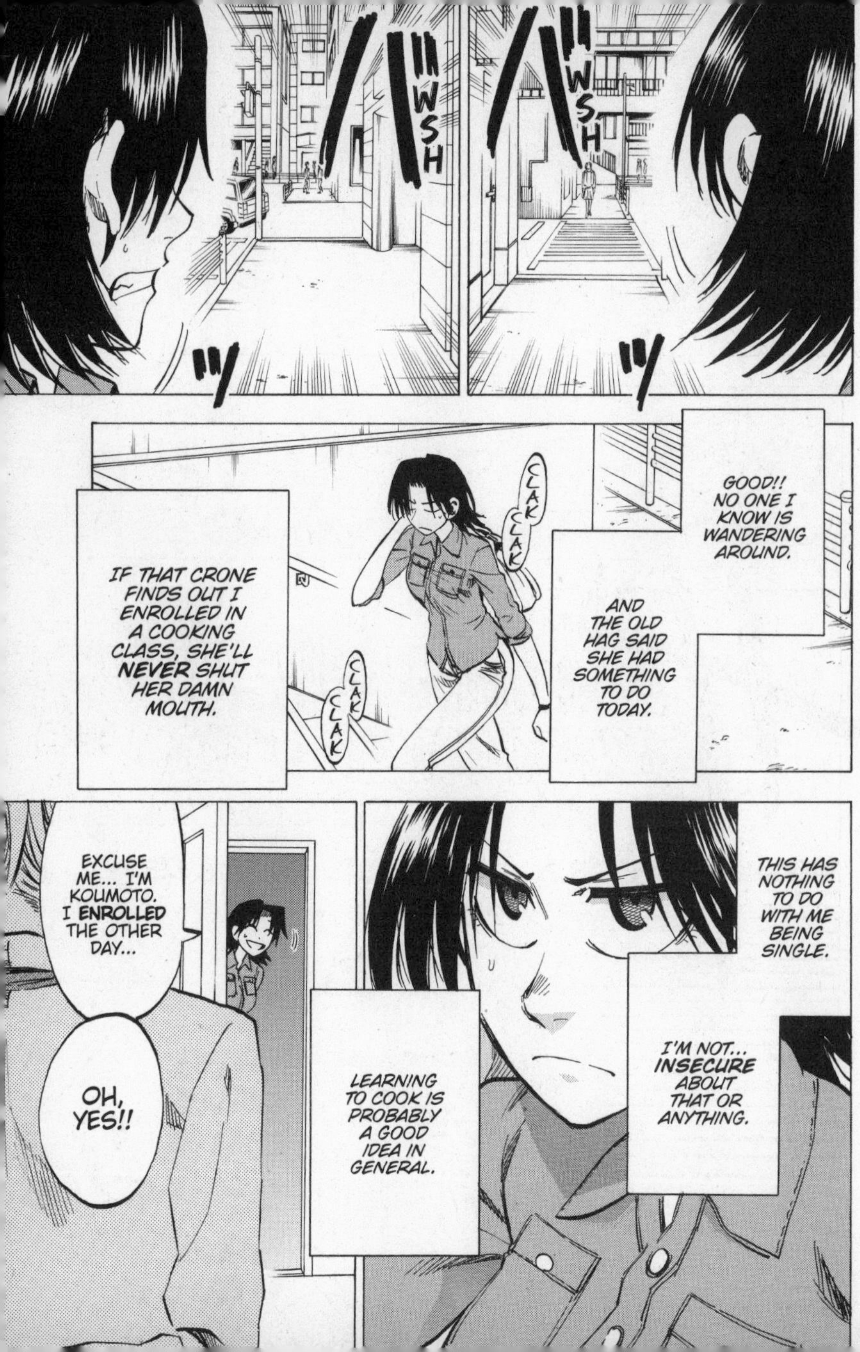
WSH
WSH
GOOD!! NO ONE I KNOW IS WANDERING AROUND.
AND THE OLD HAG SAID SHE HAD SOMETHING TO DO TODAY.
CLAK CLAK CLAK
IF THAT CRONE FINDS OUT I ENROLLED IN A COOKING CLASS, SHE'LL **NEVER** SHUT HER DAMN MOUTH.
CLAK CLAK CLAK
THIS HAS NOTHING TO DO WITH ME BEING SINGLE.
I'M NOT... **INSECURE** ABOUT THAT OR ANYTHING.
LEARNING TO COOK IS PROBABLY A GOOD IDEA IN GENERAL.
EXCUSE ME... I'M KOUMOTO. I **ENROLLED** THE OTHER DAY...
OH, YES!!

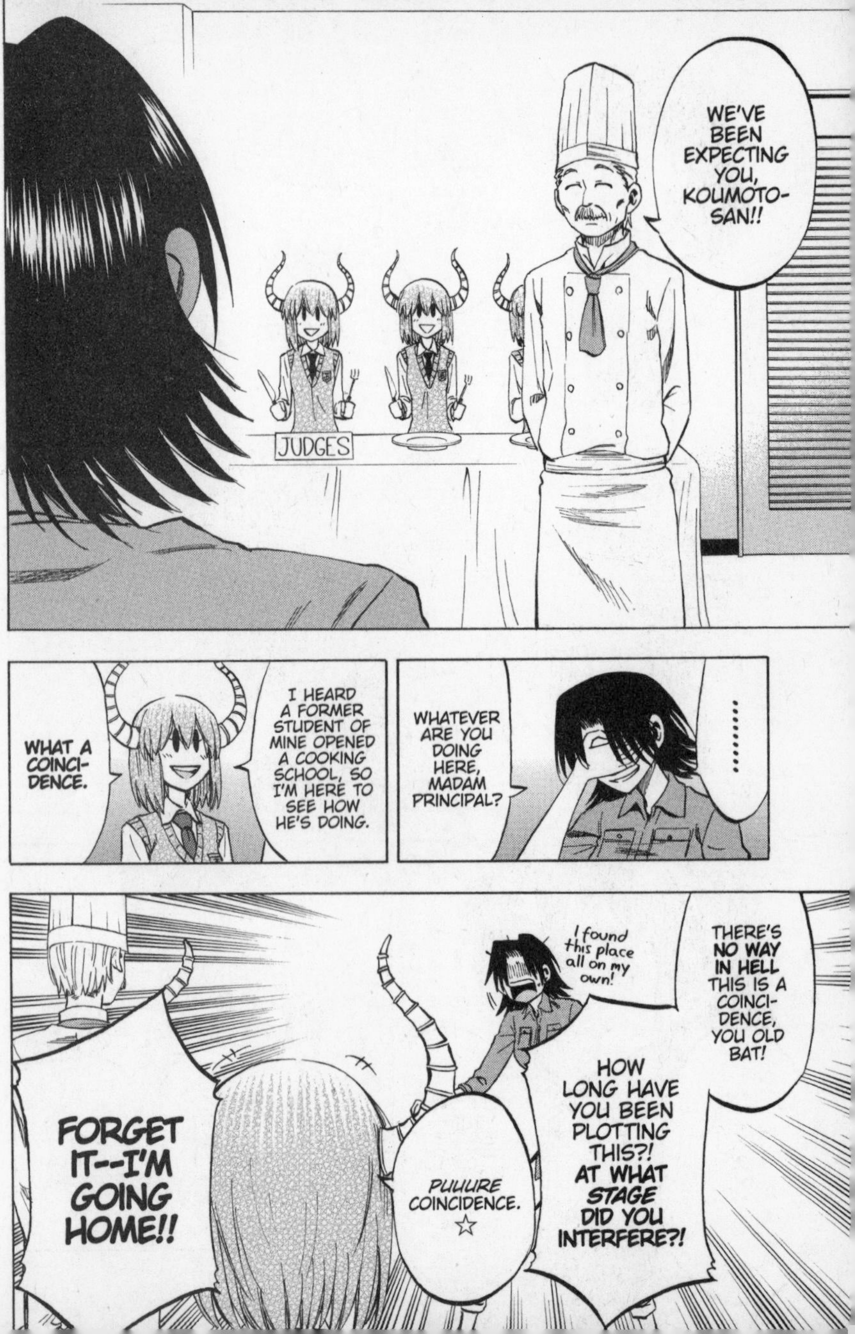
WE'VE BEEN EXPECTING YOU, KOUMOTO-SAN!!
JUDGES
....
WHATEVER ARE YOU DOING HERE, MADAM PRINCIPAL?
I HEARD A FORMER STUDENT OF MINE OPENED A COOKING SCHOOL, SO I'M HERE TO SEE HOW HE'S DOING.
WHAT A COINCIDENCE.
THERE'S NO WAY IN HELL THIS IS A COINCIDENCE, YOU OLD BAT!
I found this place all on my own!
HOW LONG HAVE YOU BEEN PLOTTING THIS?! AT WHAT STAGE DID YOU INTERFERE?!
PUUURE COINCIDENCE. ☆
FORGET IT--I'M GOING HOME!!

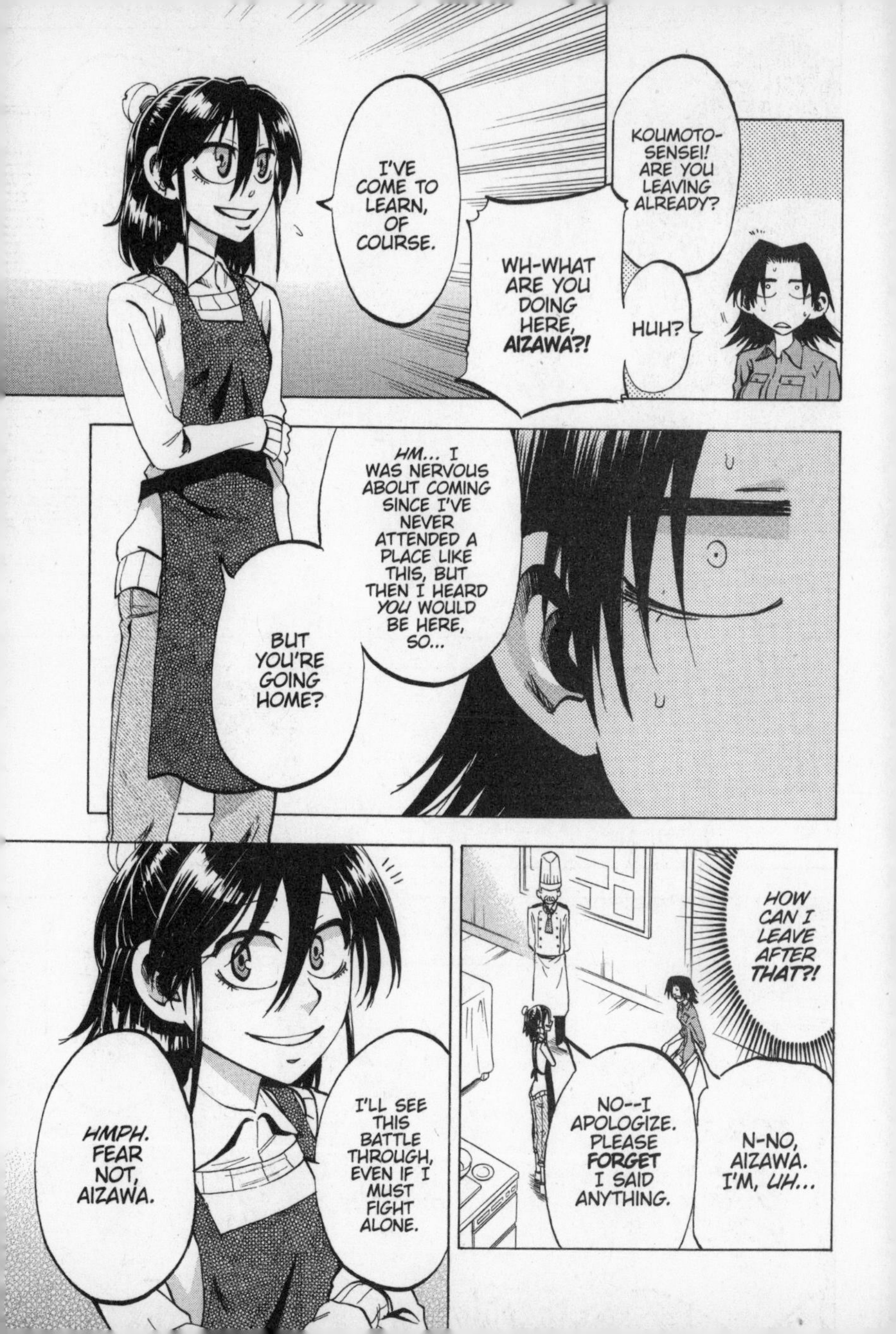
KOUMOTO-SENSEI! ARE YOU LEAVING ALREADY?
HUH?
WH-WHAT ARE YOU DOING HERE, AIZAWA?!
I'VE COME TO LEARN, OF COURSE.
HM... I WAS NERVOUS ABOUT COMING SINCE I'VE NEVER ATTENDED A PLACE LIKE THIS, BUT THEN I HEARD YOU WOULD BE HERE, SO...
BUT YOU'RE GOING HOME?
HOW CAN I LEAVE AFTER THAT?!
N-NO, AIZAWA. I'M, UH...
NO--I APOLOGIZE. PLEASE FORGET I SAID ANYTHING.
I'LL SEE THIS BATTLE THROUGH, EVEN IF I MUST FIGHT ALONE.
HMPH. FEAR NOT, AIZAWA.

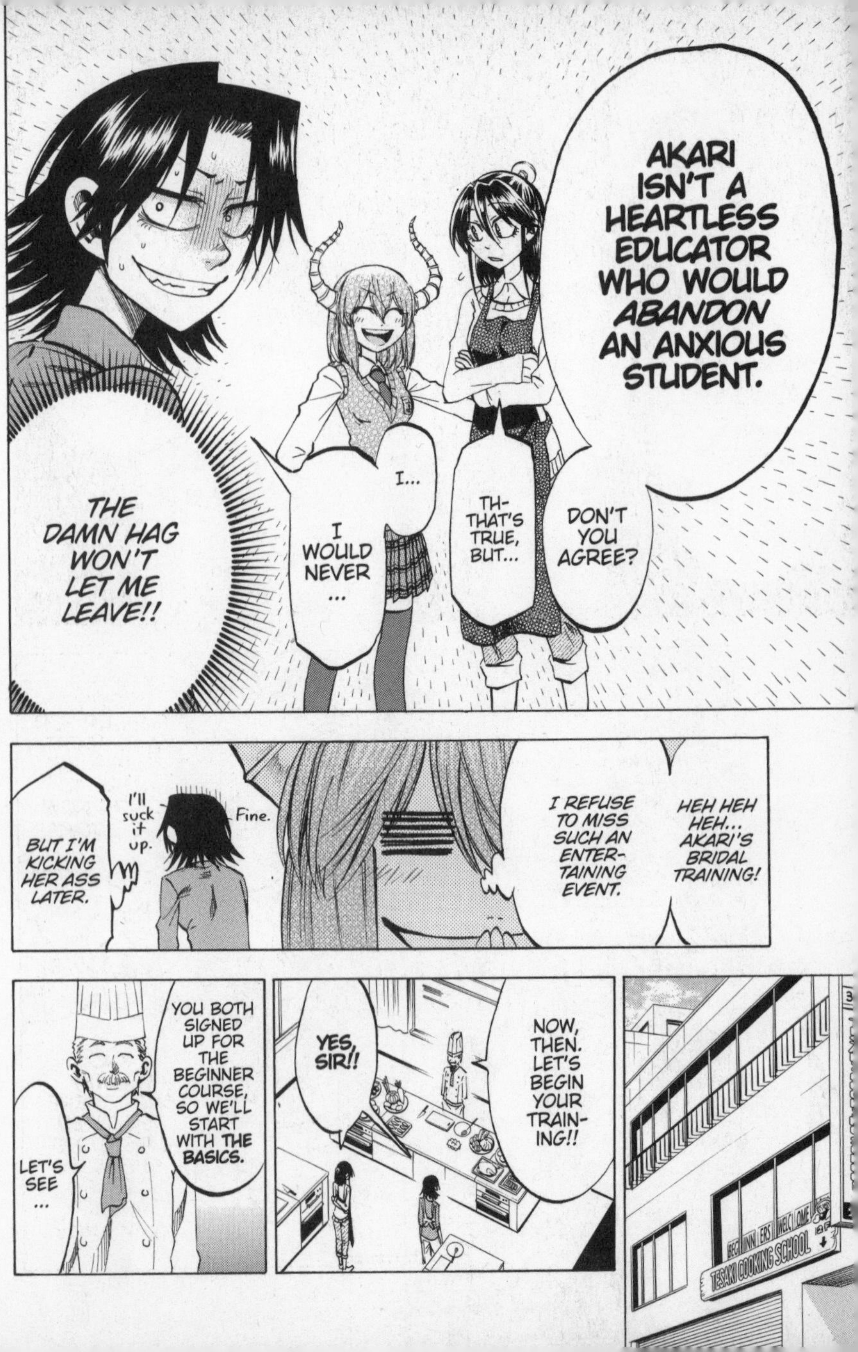
AKARI ISN'T A HEARTLESS EDUCATOR WHO WOULD ABANDON AN ANXIOUS STUDENT.
DON'T YOU AGREE?
TH-THAT'S TRUE, BUT...
I...
I WOULD NEVER ...
THE DAMN HAG WON'T LET ME LEAVE!!
HEH HEH HEH... AKARI'S BRIDAL TRAINING!
I REFUSE TO MISS SUCH AN ENTER-TAINING EVENT.
Fine.
I'll suck it up.
BUT I'M KICKING HER ASS LATER.
BEGINNERS WELCOME
TESAKI COOKING SCHOOL
NOW, THEN. LET'S BEGIN YOUR TRAIN-ING!!
YES, SIR!!
YOU BOTH SIGNED UP FOR THE BEGINNER COURSE, SO WE'LL START WITH THE BASICS.
LET'S SEE ...

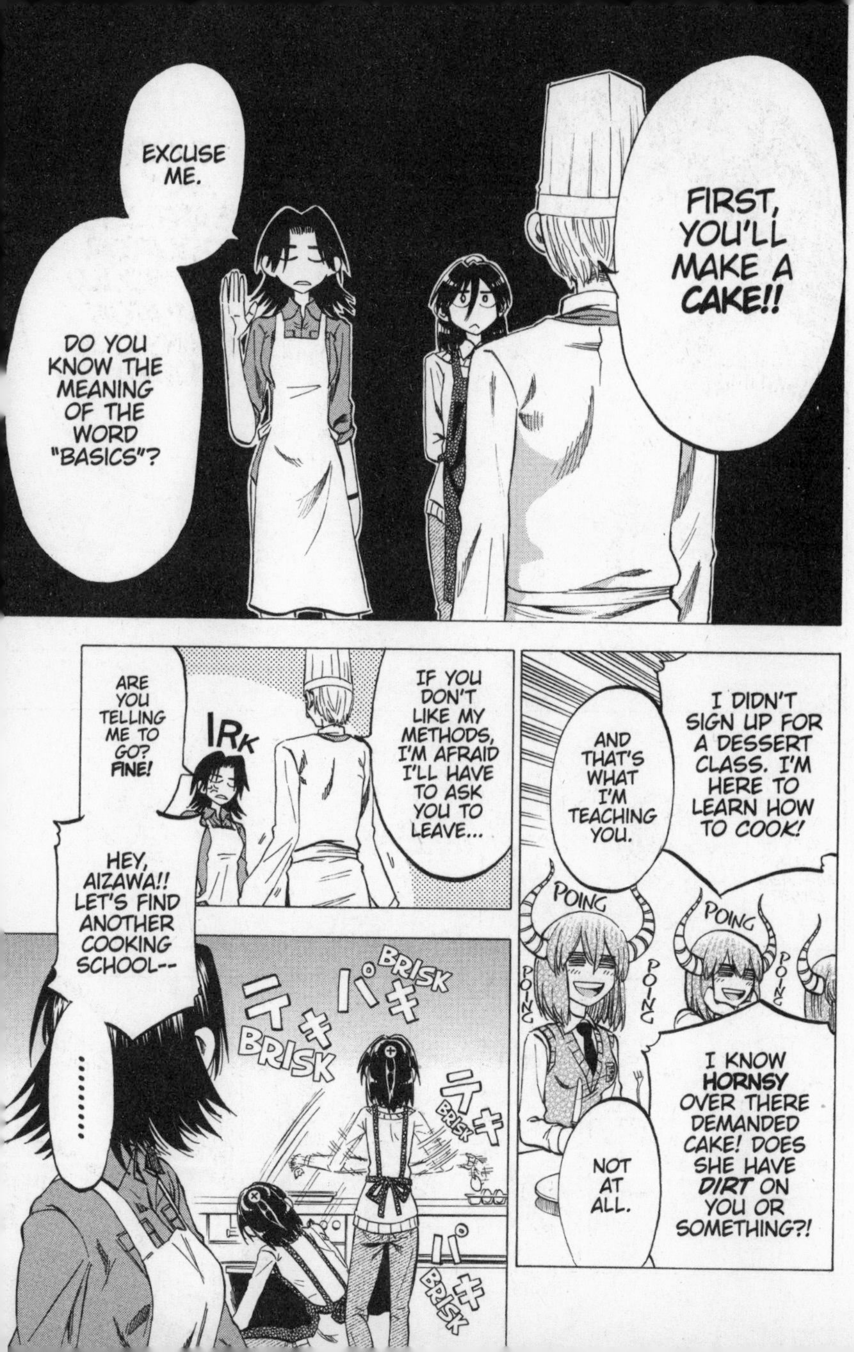
FIRST, YOU'LL MAKE A CAKE!!
EXCUSE ME.
DO YOU KNOW THE MEANING OF THE WORD "BASICS"?
I DIDN'T SIGN UP FOR A DESSERT CLASS. I'M HERE TO LEARN HOW TO COOK!
AND THAT'S WHAT I'M TEACHING YOU.
POING
POING
POING
POING
POING
I KNOW HORNSY OVER THERE DEMANDED CAKE! DOES SHE HAVE DIRT ON YOU OR SOMETHING?!
NOT AT ALL.
IF YOU DON'T LIKE MY METHODS, I'M AFRAID I'LL HAVE TO ASK YOU TO LEAVE...
IRK
ARE YOU TELLING ME TO GO? FINE!
HEY, AIZAWA!! LET'S FIND ANOTHER COOKING SCHOOL--
パキ BRISK
テキ BRISK
テキ BRISK
パキ BRISK
......

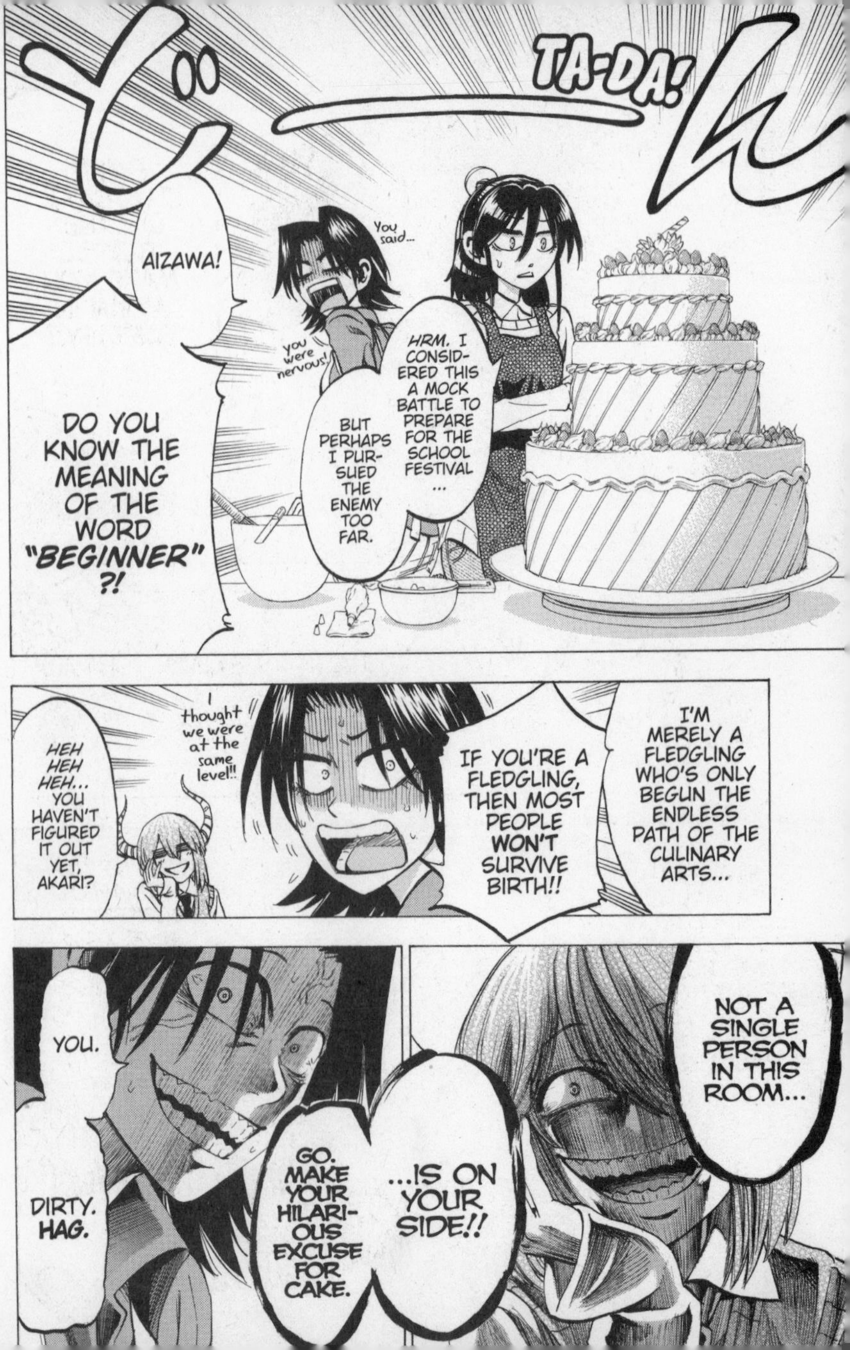
TA-DA!
HRM. I CONSIDERED THIS A MOCK BATTLE TO PREPARE FOR THE SCHOOL FESTIVAL...
BUT PERHAPS I PURSUED THE ENEMY TOO FAR.
You said... you were nervous!
AIZAWA!
DO YOU KNOW THE MEANING OF THE WORD "BEGINNER"?!
I'M MERELY A FLEDGLING WHO'S ONLY BEGUN THE ENDLESS PATH OF THE CULINARY ARTS...
IF YOU'RE A FLEDGLING, THEN MOST PEOPLE WON'T SURVIVE BIRTH!!
I thought we were at the same level!!
HEH HEH HEH... YOU HAVEN'T FIGURED IT OUT YET, AKARI?
NOT A SINGLE PERSON IN THIS ROOM...
...IS ON YOUR SIDE!!
GO. MAKE YOUR HILARIOUS EXCUSE FOR CAKE.
YOU.
DIRTY. HAG.

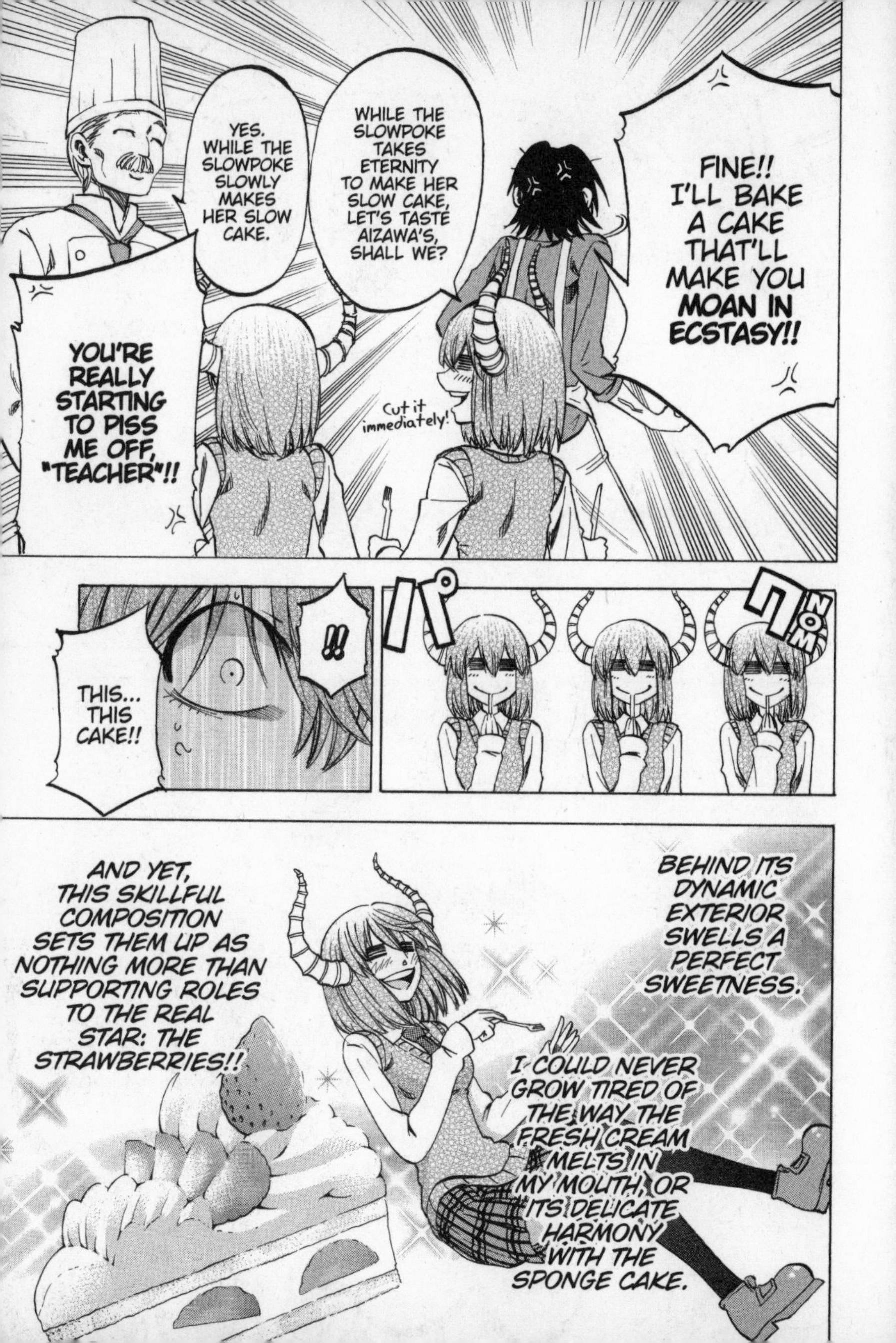
FINE!! I'LL BAKE A CAKE THAT'LL MAKE YOU MOAN IN ECSTASY!!
WHILE THE SLOWPOKE TAKES ETERNITY TO MAKE HER SLOW CAKE, LET'S TASTE AIZAWA'S, SHALL WE?
YES. WHILE THE SLOWPOKE SLOWLY MAKES HER SLOW CAKE.
Cut it immediately!
YOU'RE REALLY STARTING TO PISS ME OFF, "TEACHER"!!
NOM
パ
!!
THIS... THIS CAKE!!
BEHIND ITS DYNAMIC EXTERIOR SWELLS A PERFECT SWEETNESS.
AND YET, THIS SKILLFUL COMPOSITION SETS THEM UP AS NOTHING MORE THAN SUPPORTING ROLES TO THE REAL STAR: THE STRAWBERRIES!!
I COULD NEVER GROW TIRED OF THE WAY THE FRESH CREAM MELTS IN MY MOUTH, OR ITS DELICATE HARMONY WITH THE SPONGE CAKE.

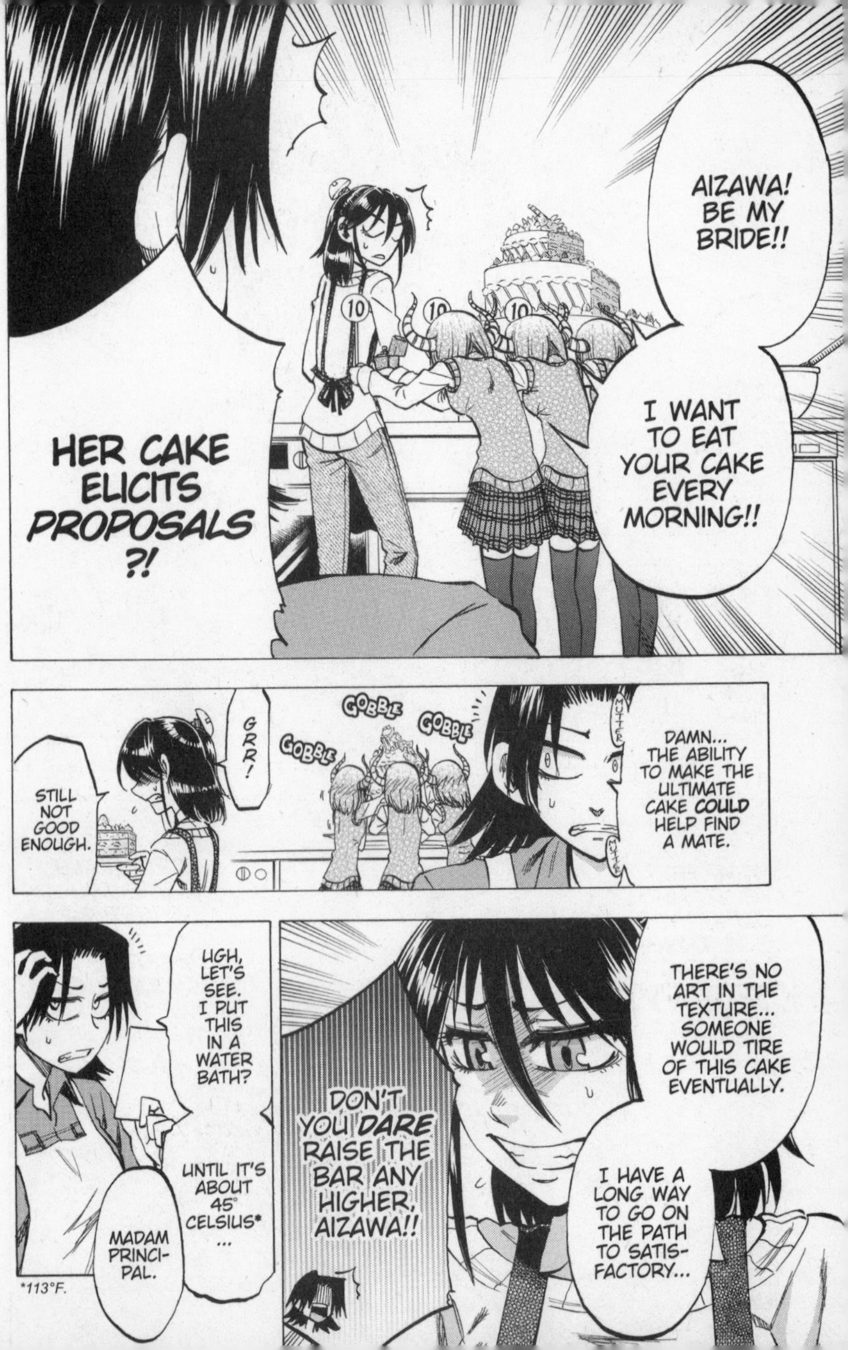
AIZAWA! BE MY BRIDE!!
I WANT TO EAT YOUR CAKE EVERY MORNING!!
HER CAKE ELICITS PROPOSALS ?!
MUTTER
DAMN... THE ABILITY TO MAKE THE ULTIMATE CAKE COULD HELP FIND A MATE.
MUTTER
GOBBLE
GOBBLE
GOBBLE
GRR!
STILL NOT GOOD ENOUGH.
THERE'S NO ART IN THE TEXTURE... SOMEONE WOULD TIRE OF THIS CAKE EVENTUALLY.
I HAVE A LONG WAY TO GO ON THE PATH TO SATIS-FACTORY...
DON'T YOU DARE RAISE THE BAR ANY HIGHER, AIZAWA!!
UGH, LET'S SEE. I PUT THIS IN A WATER BATH?
UNTIL IT'S ABOUT 45° CELSIUS* ...
MADAM PRINCI-PAL.

*113°F.

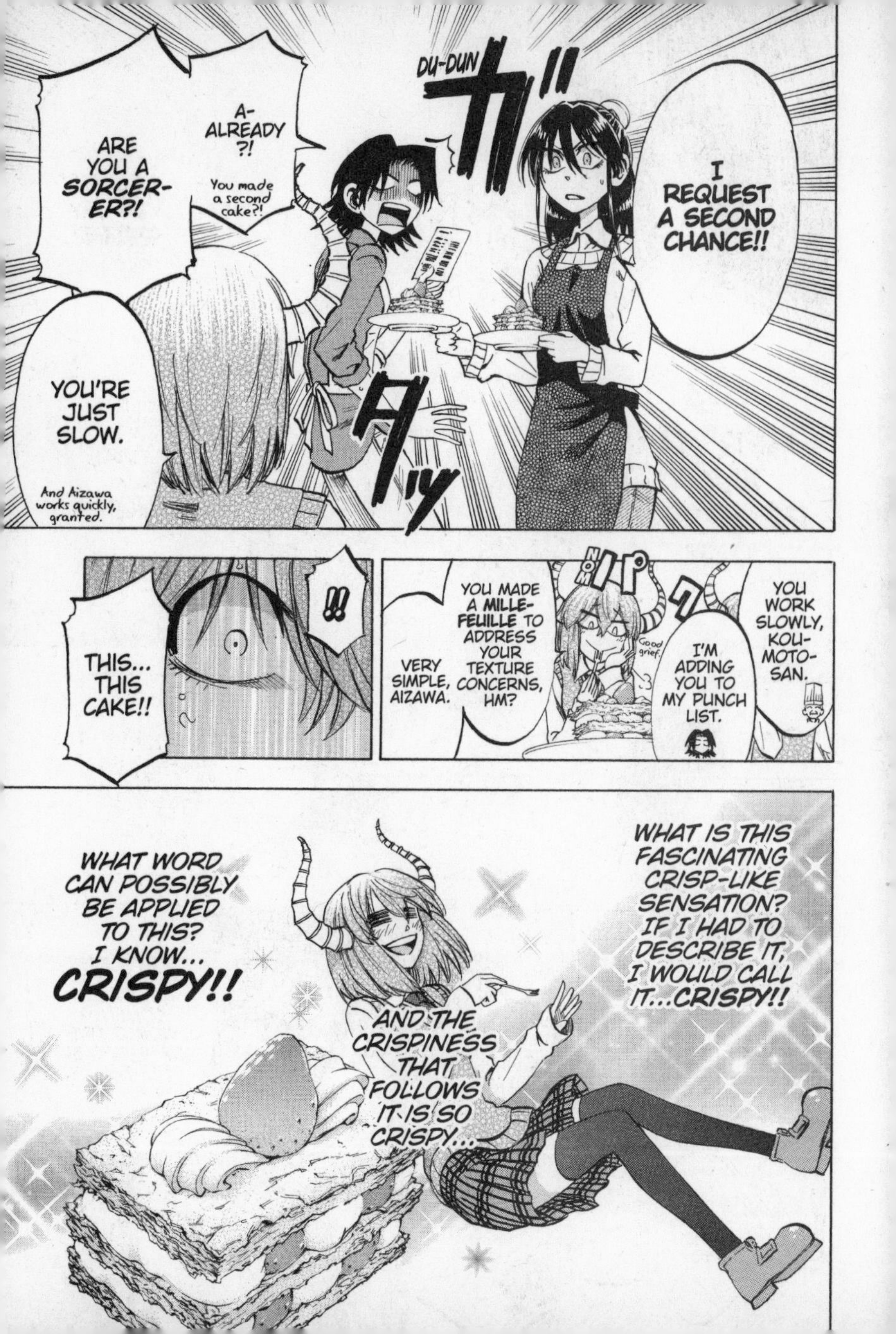
DU-DUN
I REQUEST A SECOND CHANCE!!
A-ALREADY?!
You made a second cake?!
ARE YOU A SORCERER?!
YOU'RE JUST SLOW.
And Aizawa works quickly, granted.
YOU WORK SLOWLY, KOUMOTO-SAN.
NOM
I'M ADDING YOU TO MY PUNCH LIST.
Good grief.
YOU MADE A MILLE-FEUILLE TO ADDRESS YOUR TEXTURE CONCERNS, HM?
VERY SIMPLE, AIZAWA.
!!
THIS... THIS CAKE!!
WHAT IS THIS FASCINATING CRISP-LIKE SENSATION? IF I HAD TO DESCRIBE IT, I WOULD CALL IT...CRISPY!!
AND THE CRISPINESS THAT FOLLOWS IT IS SO CRISPY...
WHAT WORD CAN POSSIBLY BE APPLIED TO THIS? I KNOW... CRISPY!!

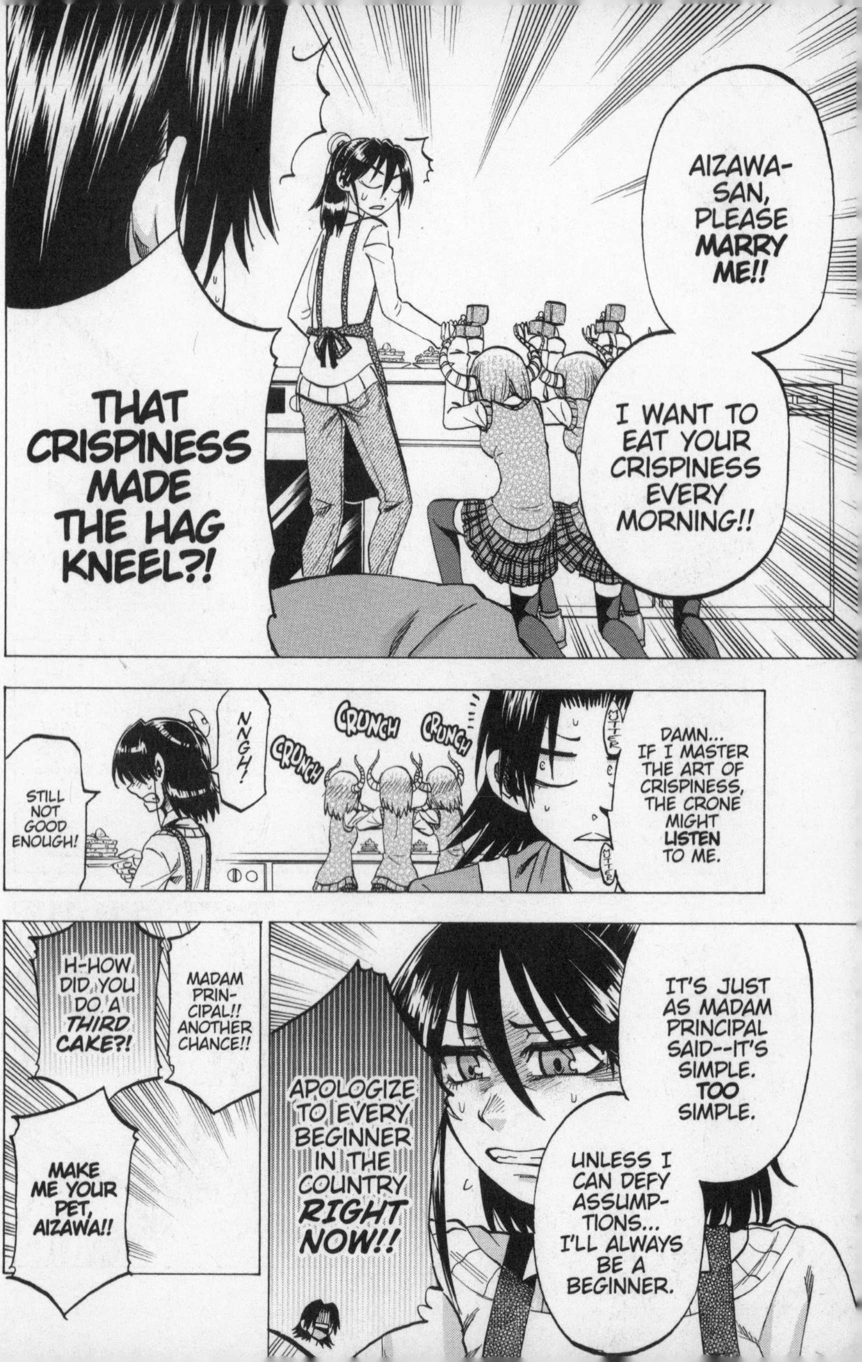
AIZAWA-SAN, PLEASE MARRY ME!!
I WANT TO EAT YOUR CRISPINESS EVERY MORNING!!
THAT CRISPINESS MADE THE HAG KNEEL?!
DAMN... IF I MASTER THE ART OF CRISPINESS, THE CRONE MIGHT LISTEN TO ME.
MUTTER
MUTTER
CRUNCH
CRUNCH
CRUNCH
NNGH!
STILL NOT GOOD ENOUGH!
IT'S JUST AS MADAM PRINCIPAL SAID--IT'S SIMPLE. TOO SIMPLE.
UNLESS I CAN DEFY ASSUMPTIONS... I'LL ALWAYS BE A BEGINNER.
APOLOGIZE TO EVERY BEGINNER IN THE COUNTRY RIGHT NOW!!
MADAM PRINCIPAL!! ANOTHER CHANCE!!
H-HOW DID YOU DO A THIRD CAKE?!
MAKE ME YOUR PET, AIZAWA!!

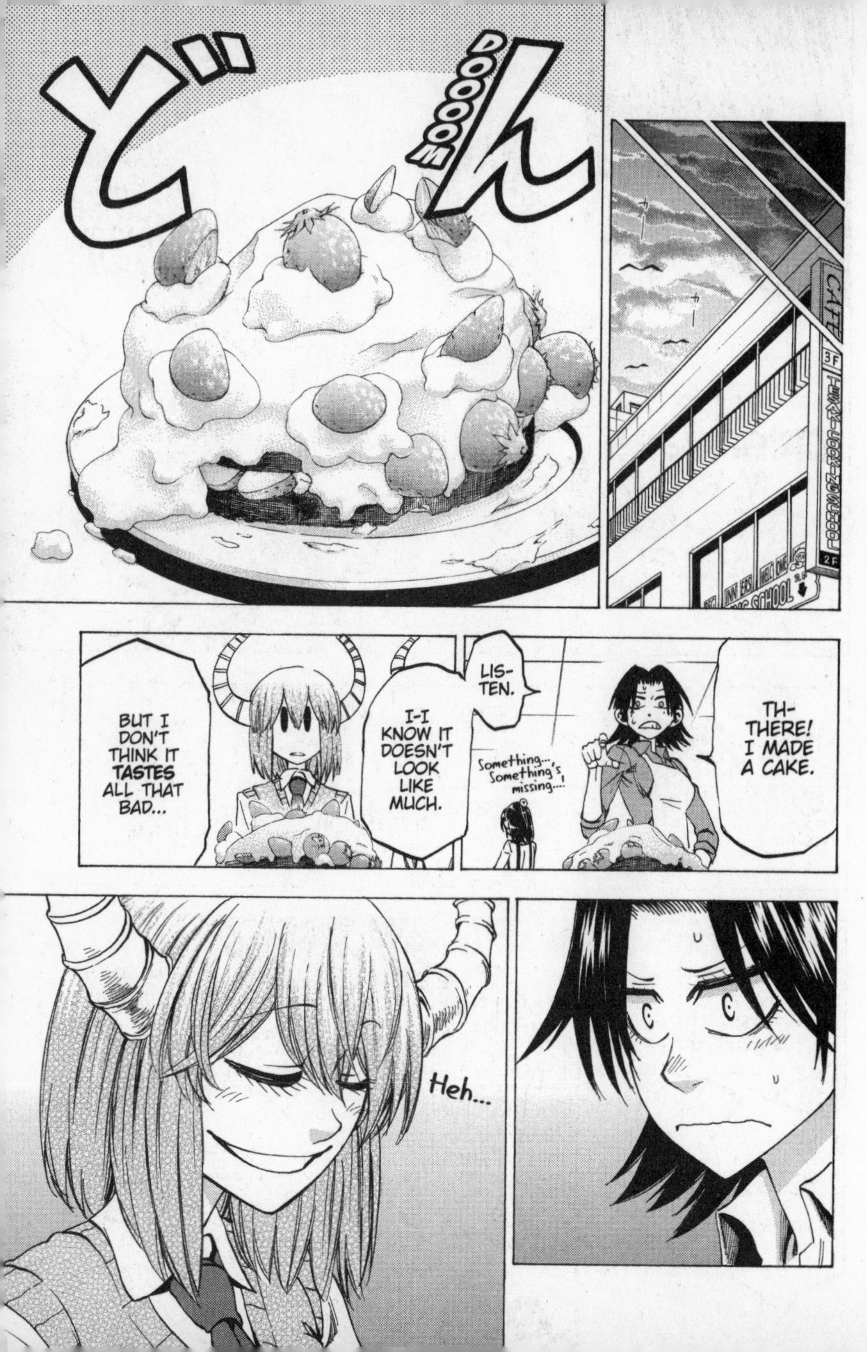
3F
2F
どん
DOOOOOM
TH-THERE! I MADE A CAKE.
LIS-TEN.
Something... Something's missing...!
I-I KNOW IT DOESN'T LOOK LIKE MUCH.
BUT I DON'T THINK IT TASTES ALL THAT BAD...
Heh...

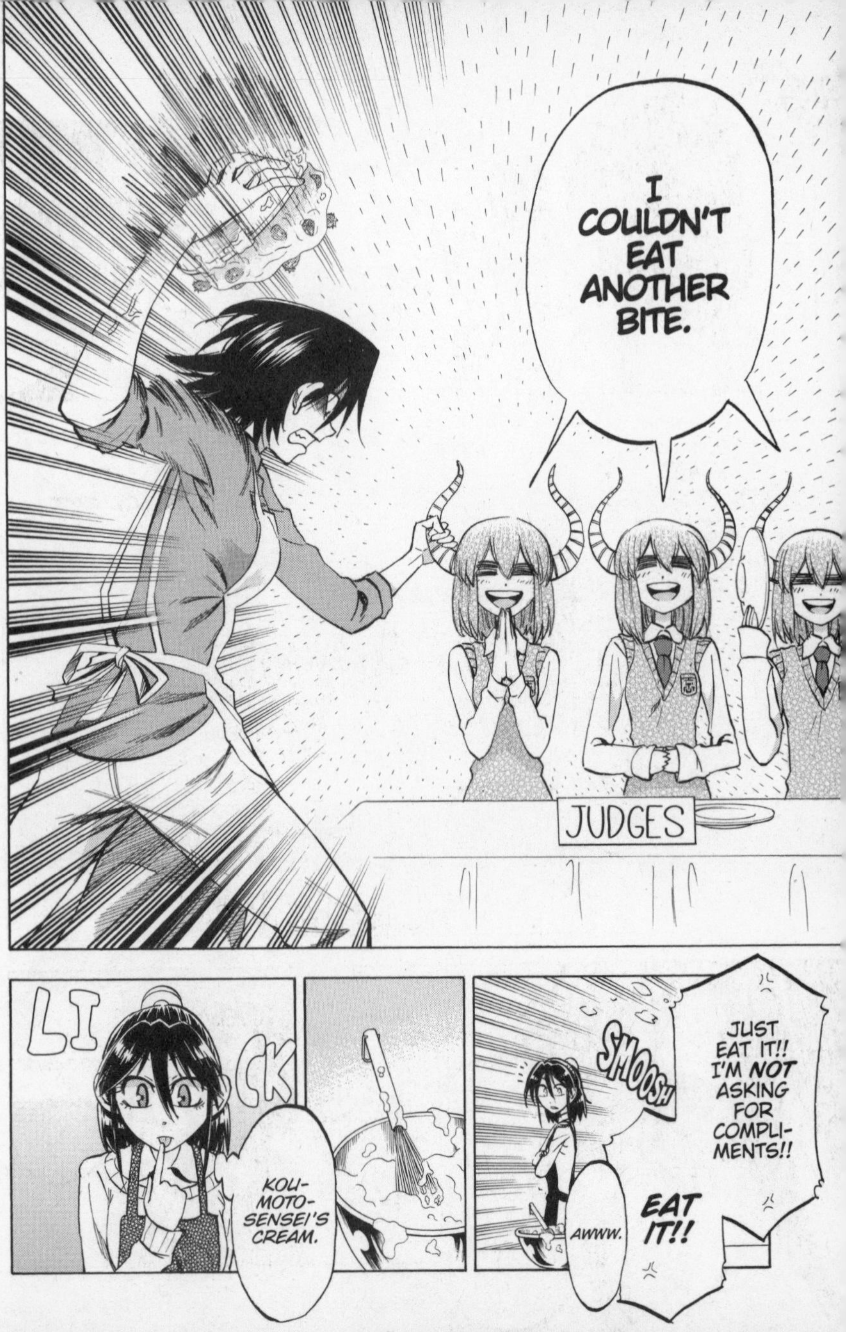
I COULDN'T EAT ANOTHER BITE.
JUDGES
JUST EAT IT!! I'M *NOT* ASKING FOR COMPLIMENTS!!
SMOOSH
EAT IT!!
AWWW.
LICK
KOU-MOTO-SENSEI'S CREAM.

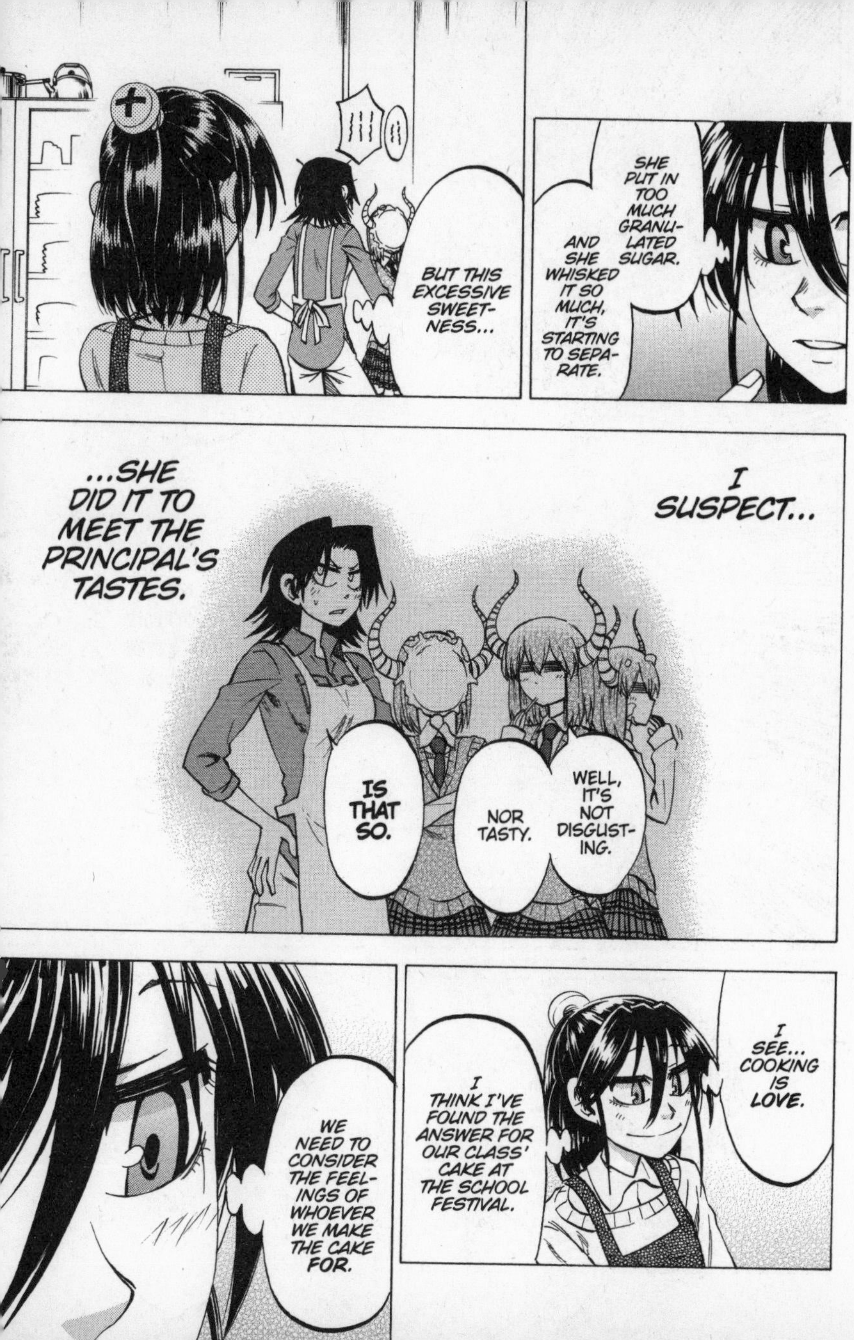
SHE PUT IN TOO MUCH GRANULATED SUGAR.
AND SHE WHISKED IT SO MUCH, IT'S STARTING TO SEPARATE.
BUT THIS EXCESSIVE SWEETNESS...
I SUSPECT...
...SHE DID IT TO MEET THE PRINCIPAL'S TASTES.
WELL, IT'S NOT DISGUSTING.
NOR TASTY.
IS THAT SO.
I SEE... COOKING IS LOVE.
I THINK I'VE FOUND THE ANSWER FOR OUR CLASS' CAKE AT THE SCHOOL FESTIVAL.
WE NEED TO CONSIDER THE FEELINGS OF WHOEVER WE MAKE THE CAKE FOR.

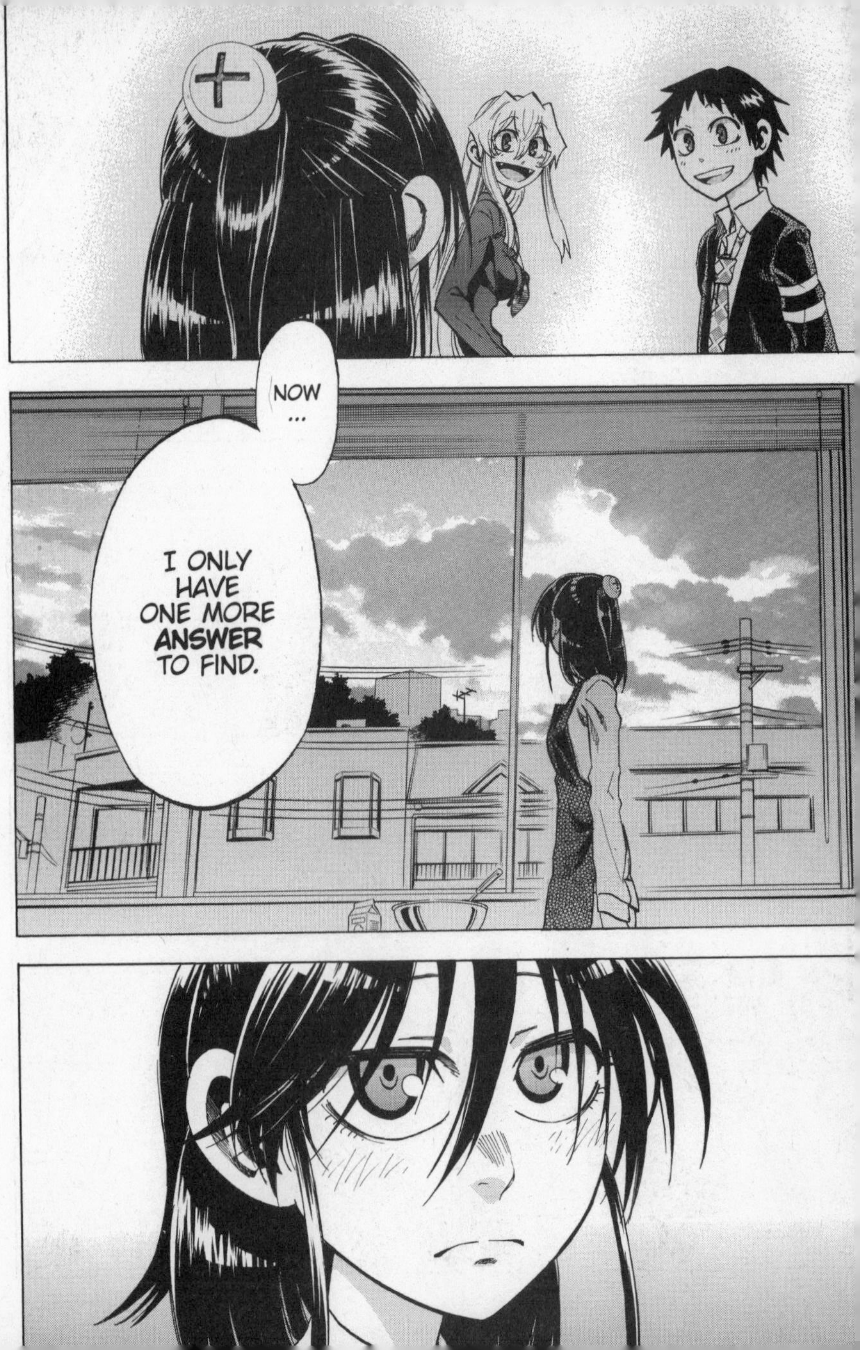
NOW ...
I ONLY HAVE ONE MORE ANSWER TO FIND.

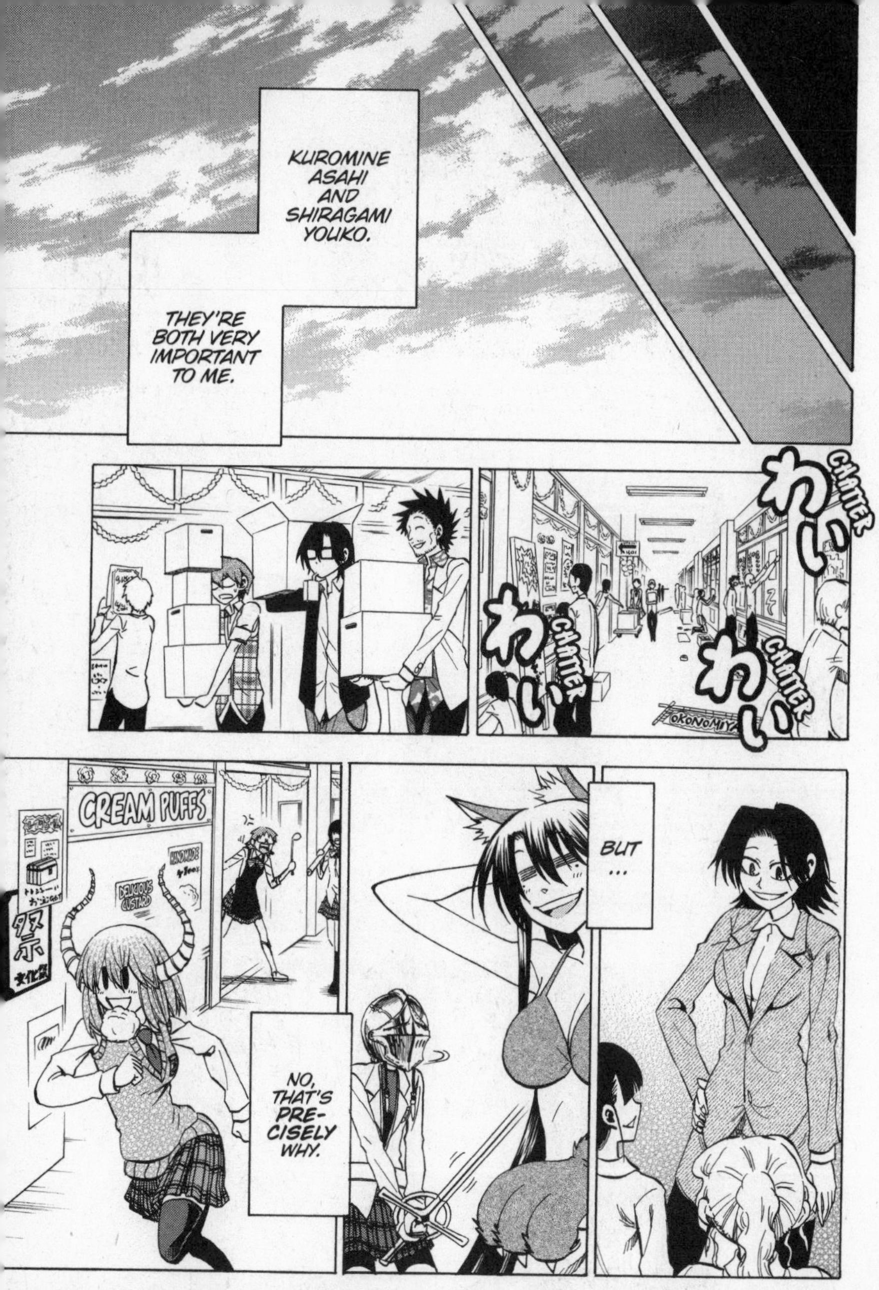
KUROMINE ASAHI AND SHIRAGAMI YOUKO.
THEY'RE BOTH VERY IMPORTANT TO ME.
わい CHATTER
わい CHATTER
わい CHATTER
OKONOMIYA
BUT ...
NO, THAT'S PRE-CISELY WHY.
CREAM PUFFS
HANDMADE
DELICIOUS CUSTARD

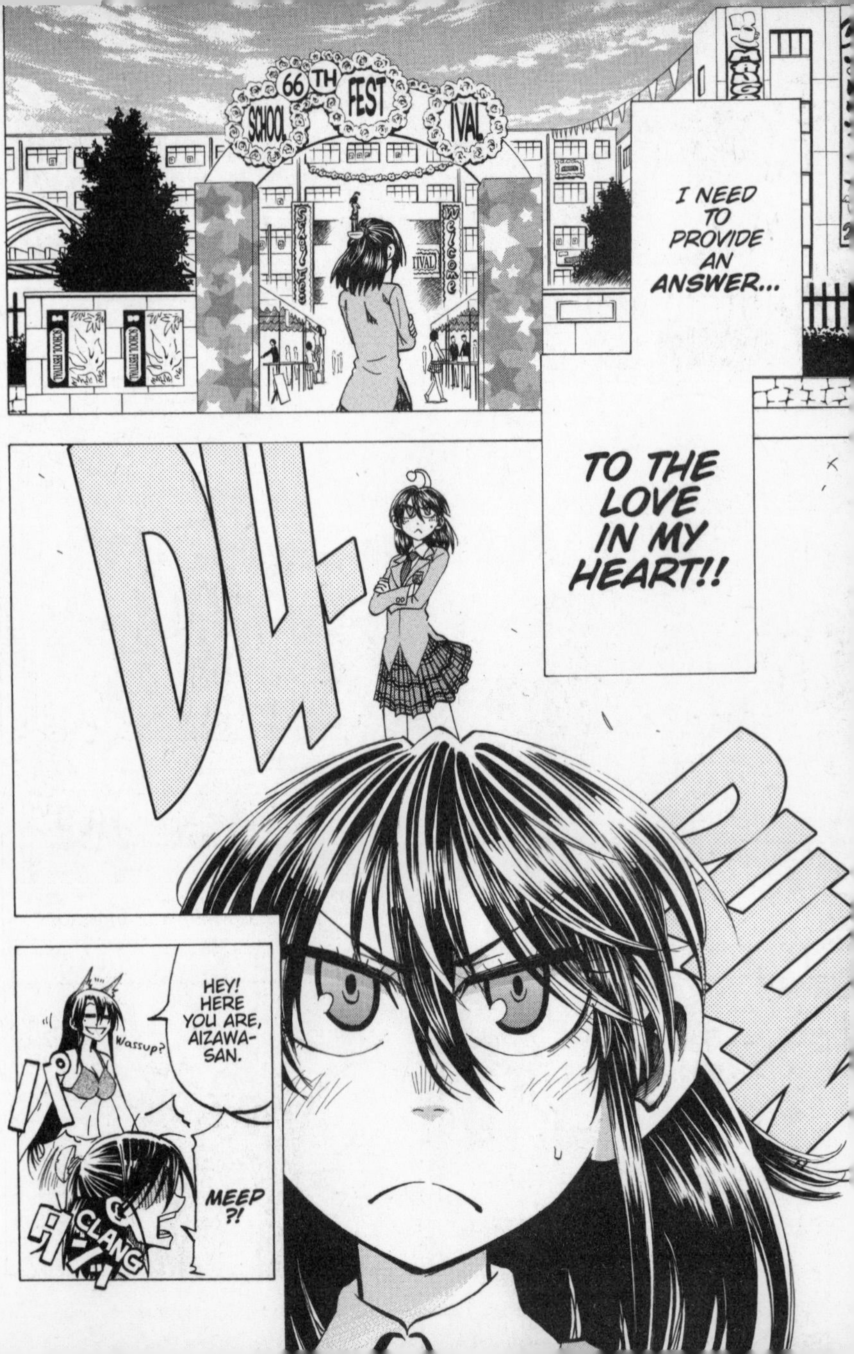
66 TH
SCHOOL
FEST
IVAL
I NEED TO PROVIDE AN ANSWER...
TO THE LOVE IN MY HEART!!
DUH-
DUH
HEY! HERE YOU ARE, AIZAWA-SAN.
Wassup?
MEEP ?!
CLANG

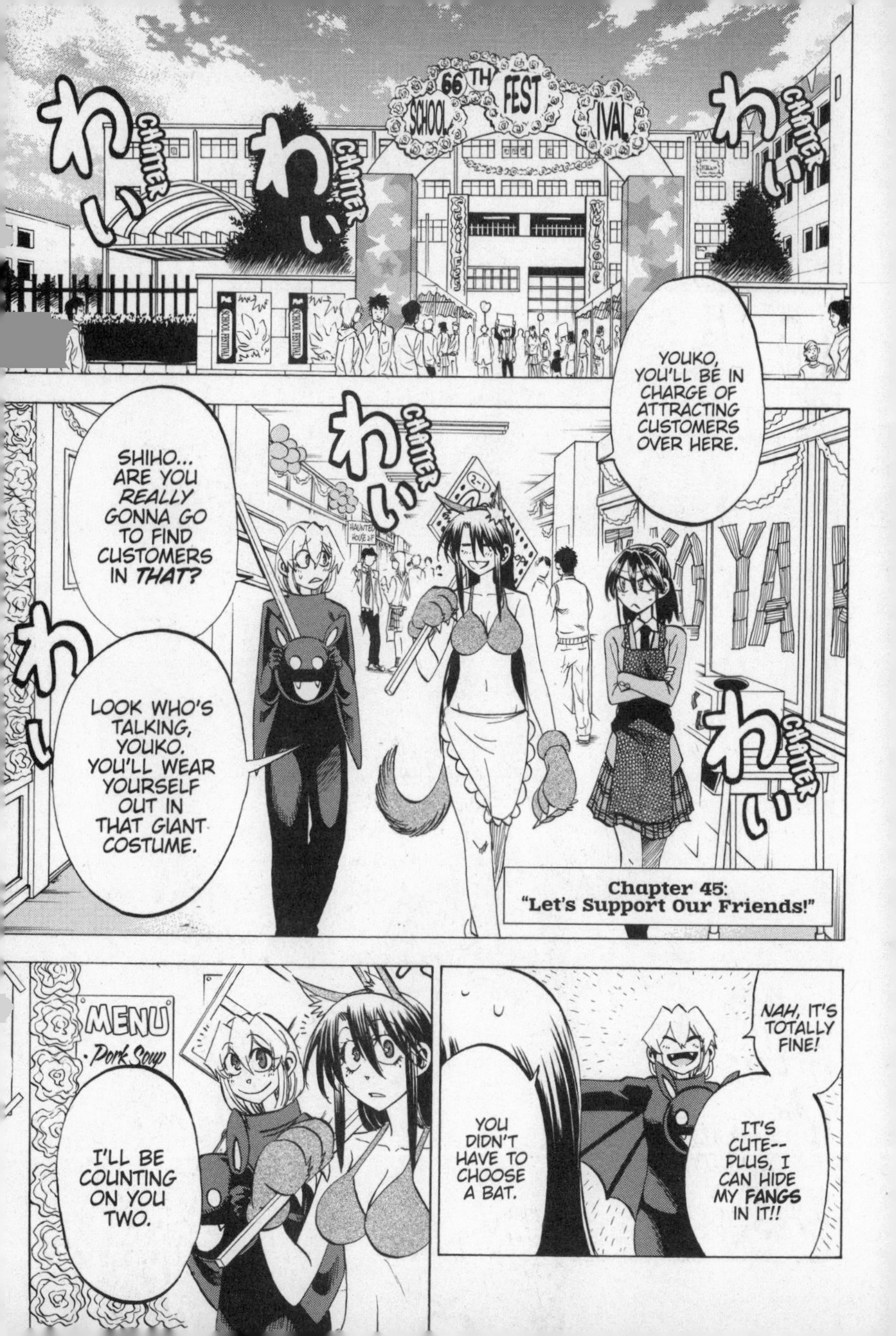

わい CHATTER
66TH SCHOOL FEST IVAL
わい CHATTER
わい CHATTER
SCHOOL FESTIVAL
SCHOOL FESTIVAL
YOUKO, YOU'LL BE IN CHARGE OF ATTRACTING CUSTOMERS OVER HERE.
わい CHATTER
SHIHO... ARE YOU *REALLY* GONNA GO TO FIND CUSTOMERS IN *THAT?*
HAUNTED HOUSE 2F
わい CHATTER
わい
LOOK WHO'S TALKING, YOUKO. YOU'LL WEAR YOURSELF OUT IN THAT GIANT COSTUME.
Chapter 45: "Let's Support Our Friends!"
NAH, IT'S TOTALLY FINE!
IT'S CUTE-- PLUS, I CAN HIDE MY **FANGS** IN IT!!
YOU DIDN'T HAVE TO CHOOSE A BAT.
MENU
· Pork Soup
I'LL BE COUNTING ON YOU TWO.

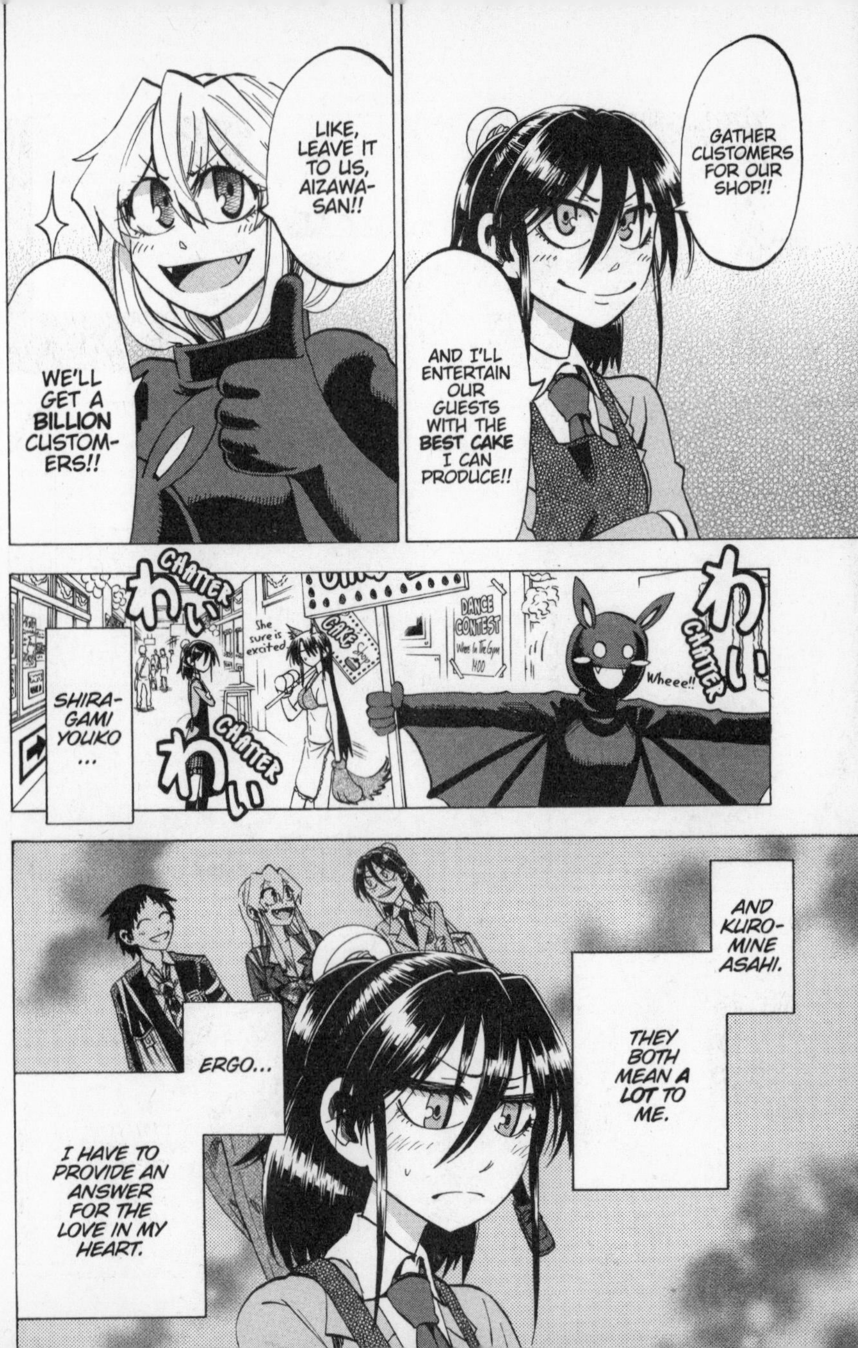
GATHER CUSTOMERS FOR OUR SHOP!!
AND I'LL ENTERTAIN OUR GUESTS WITH THE BEST CAKE I CAN PRODUCE!!
LIKE, LEAVE IT TO US, AIZAWA-SAN!!
WE'LL GET A BILLION CUSTOM-ERS!!
わい
CHATTER
Wheee!!
DANCE CONTEST
CAKE
She sure is excited
わい
CHATTER
わい
CHATTER
SHIRA-GAMI YOUKO ...
AND KURO-MINE ASAHI.
THEY BOTH MEAN A LOT TO ME.
ERGO...
I HAVE TO PROVIDE AN ANSWER FOR THE LOVE IN MY HEART.

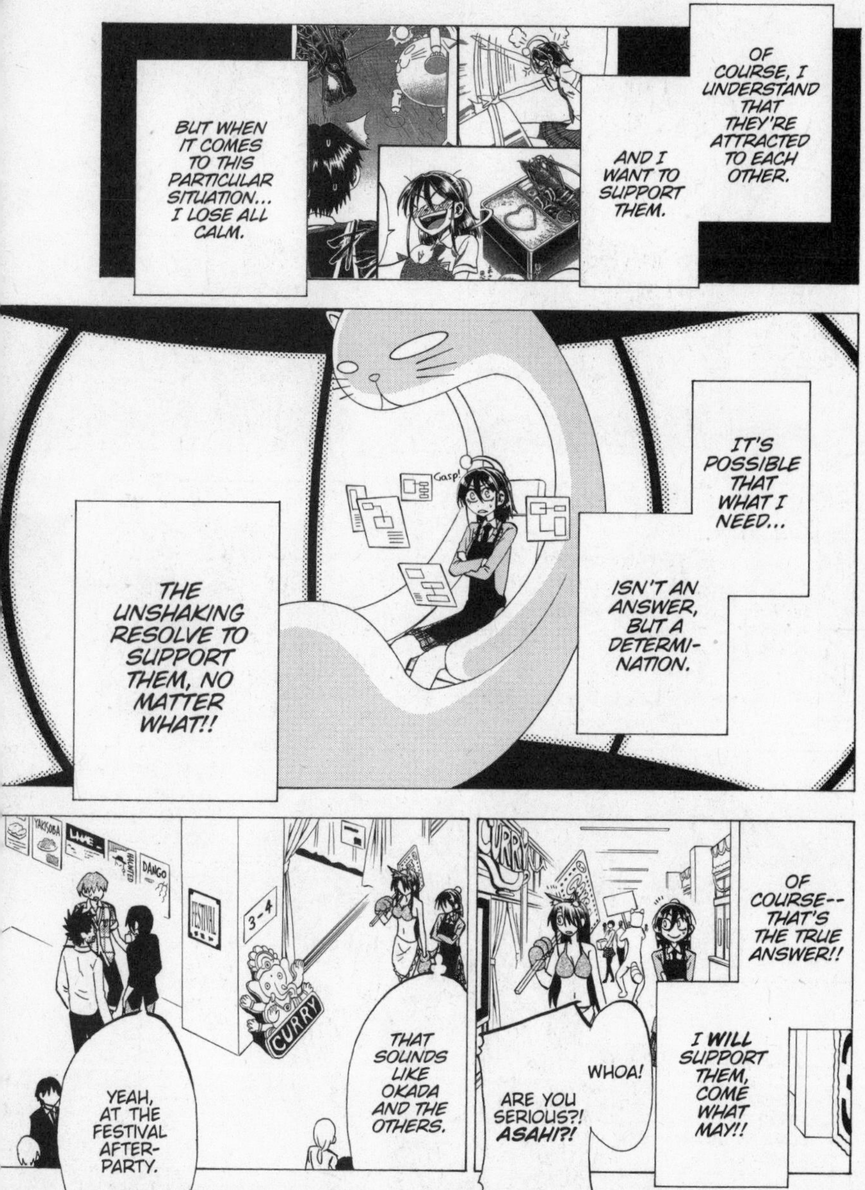
OF COURSE, I UNDERSTAND THAT THEY'RE ATTRACTED TO EACH OTHER.
AND I WANT TO SUPPORT THEM.
BUT WHEN IT COMES TO THIS PARTICULAR SITUATION... I LOSE ALL CALM.
IT'S POSSIBLE THAT WHAT I NEED...
ISN'T AN ANSWER, BUT A DETERMINATION.
Gasp!
THE UNSHAKING RESOLVE TO SUPPORT THEM, NO MATTER WHAT!!
OF COURSE--THAT'S THE TRUE ANSWER!!
I WILL SUPPORT THEM, COME WHAT MAY!!
WHOA!
ARE YOU SERIOUS?! ASAHI?!
CURRY
THAT SOUNDS LIKE OKADA AND THE OTHERS.
CURRY
3-4
FESTIVAL
YAKISOBA
HAUNTED
DANGO
YEAH, AT THE FESTIVAL AFTER-PARTY.

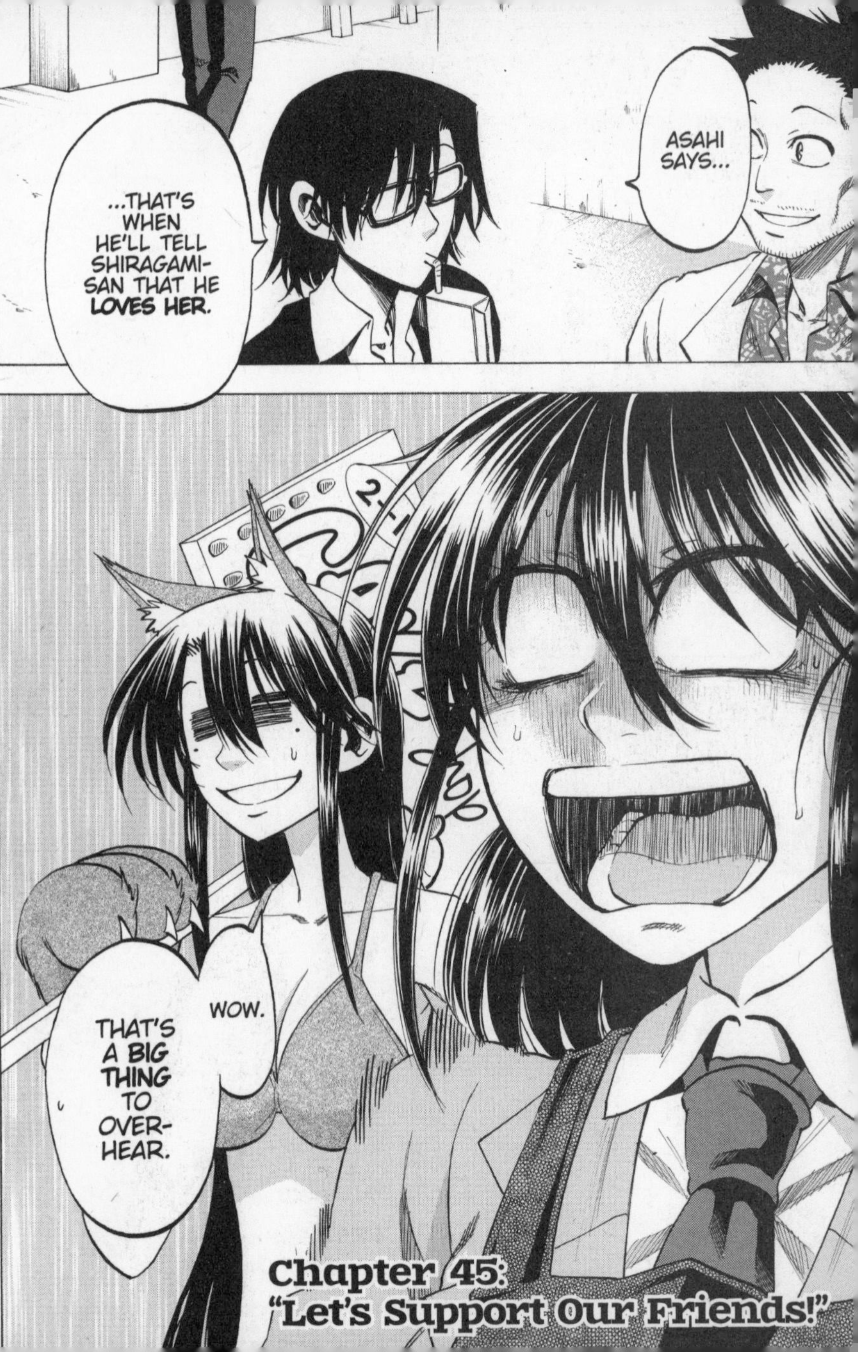
ASAHI SAYS...
...THAT'S WHEN HE'LL TELL SHIRAGAMI-SAN THAT HE LOVES HER.
WOW.
THAT'S A BIG THING TO OVER-HEAR.
Chapter 45: "Let's Support Our Friends!"

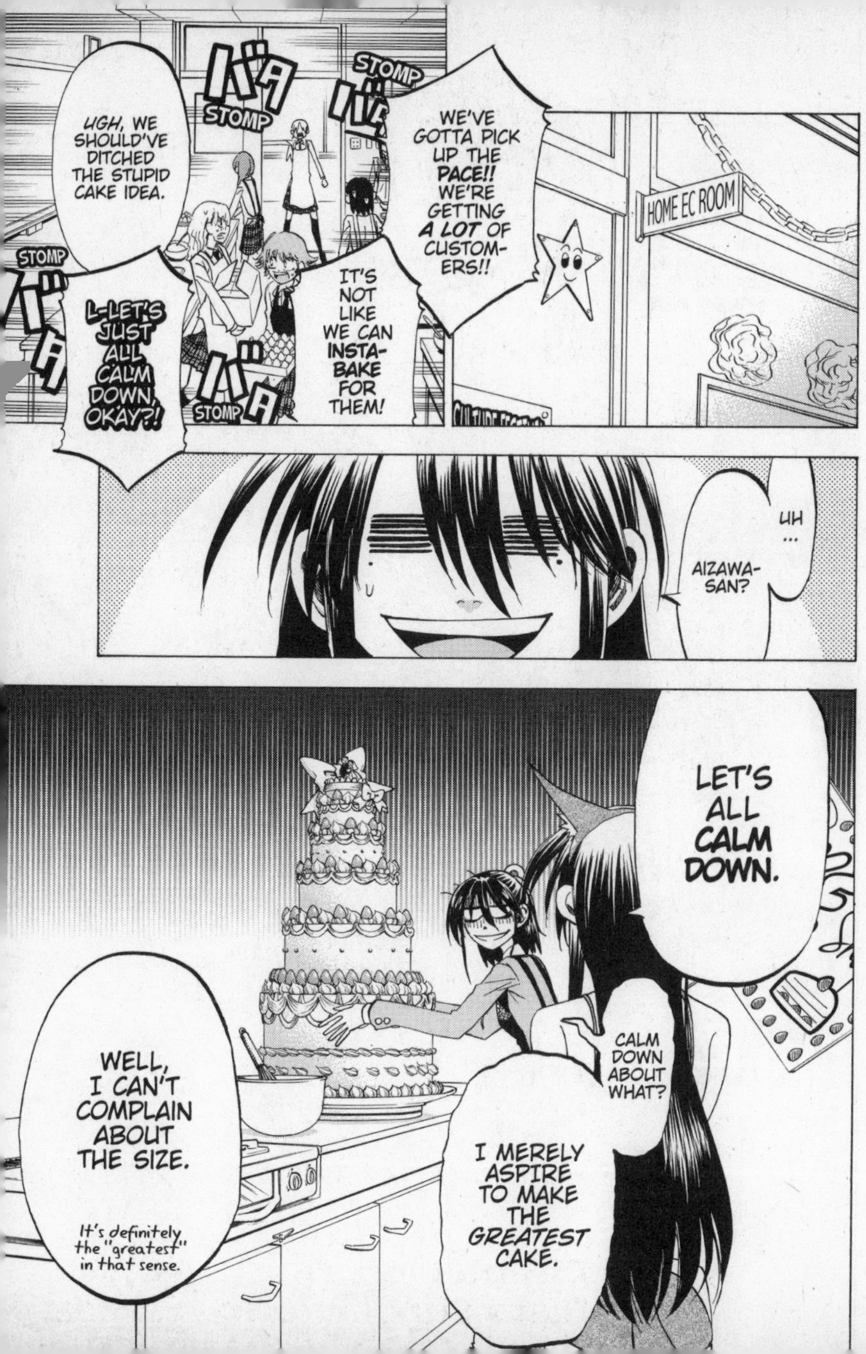
HOME EC ROOM
WE'VE GOTTA PICK UP THE PACE!! WE'RE GETTING A LOT OF CUSTOMERS!!
STOMP
STOMP
UGH, WE SHOULD'VE DITCHED THE STUPID CAKE IDEA.
IT'S NOT LIKE WE CAN INSTA-BAKE FOR THEM!
STOMP
STOMP
L-LET'S JUST ALL CALM DOWN, OKAY?!
UH ... AIZAWA-SAN?
LET'S ALL CALM DOWN.
CALM DOWN ABOUT WHAT?
I MERELY ASPIRE TO MAKE THE GREATEST CAKE.
WELL, I CAN'T COMPLAIN ABOUT THE SIZE.
It's definitely the "greatest" in that sense.

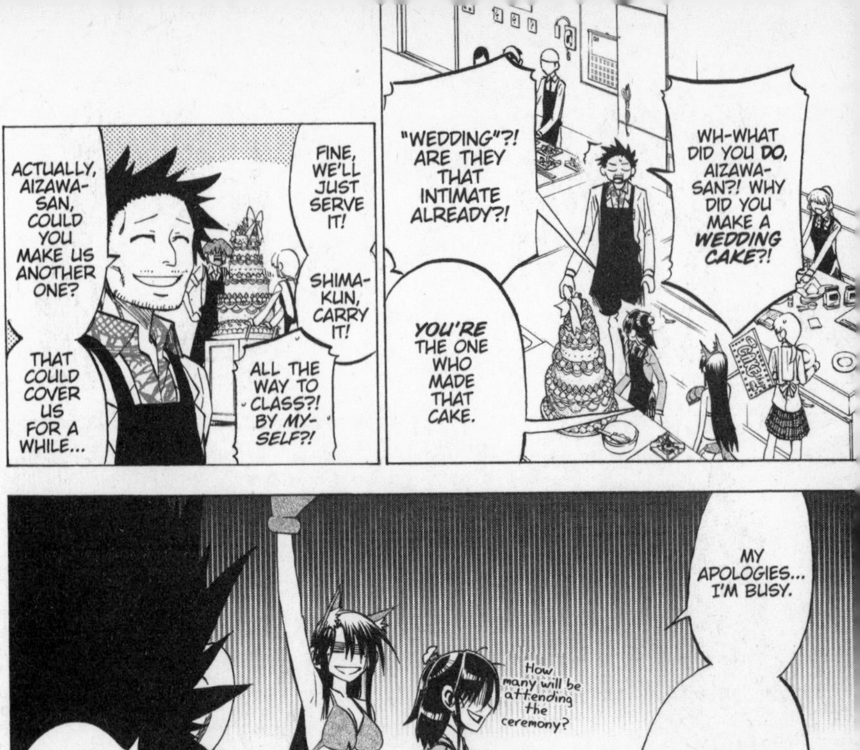
WH-WHAT DID YOU DO, AIZAWA-SAN?! WHY DID YOU MAKE A WEDDING CAKE?!
"WEDDING"?! ARE THEY THAT INTIMATE ALREADY?!
YOU'RE THE ONE WHO MADE THAT CAKE.
FINE, WE'LL JUST SERVE IT!
SHIMA-KUN, CARRY IT!
ALL THE WAY TO CLASS?! BY MYSELF?!
ACTUALLY, AIZAWA-SAN, COULD YOU MAKE US ANOTHER ONE?
THAT COULD COVER US FOR A WHILE...
MY APOLOGIES... I'M BUSY.
I HAVE MY HANDS FULL MAKING KOUHAKU MANJU*.
How many will be attending the ceremony?
I KNOW IT'S EARLY, BUT CAN I TAKE AIZAWA-SAN ON BREAK?
OR SHE MIGHT START COOKING FOR THE RECEPTION.
YES, DO THAT.

*Red and white sticky rice cakes with sweet red bean filling, served at auspicious events like weddings.

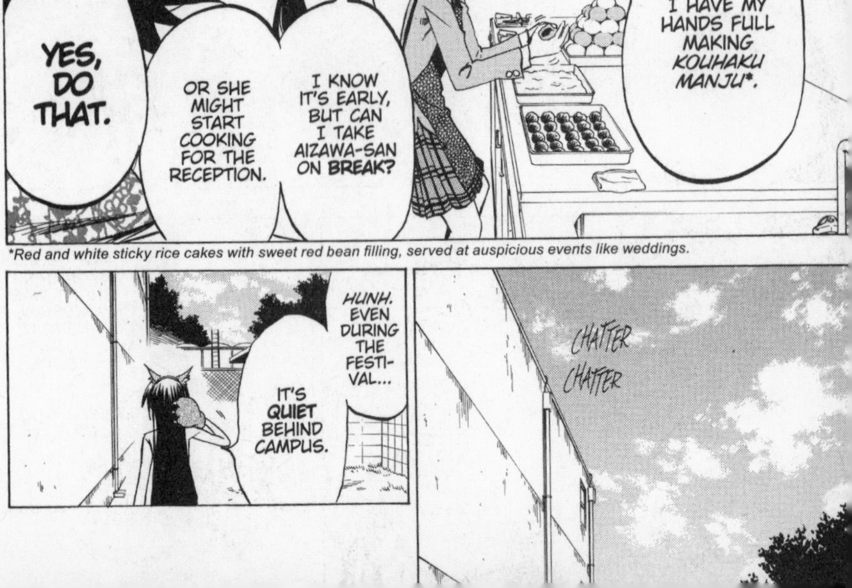
CHATTER
CHATTER
HUNH. EVEN DURING THE FESTIVAL...
IT'S QUIET BEHIND CAMPUS.

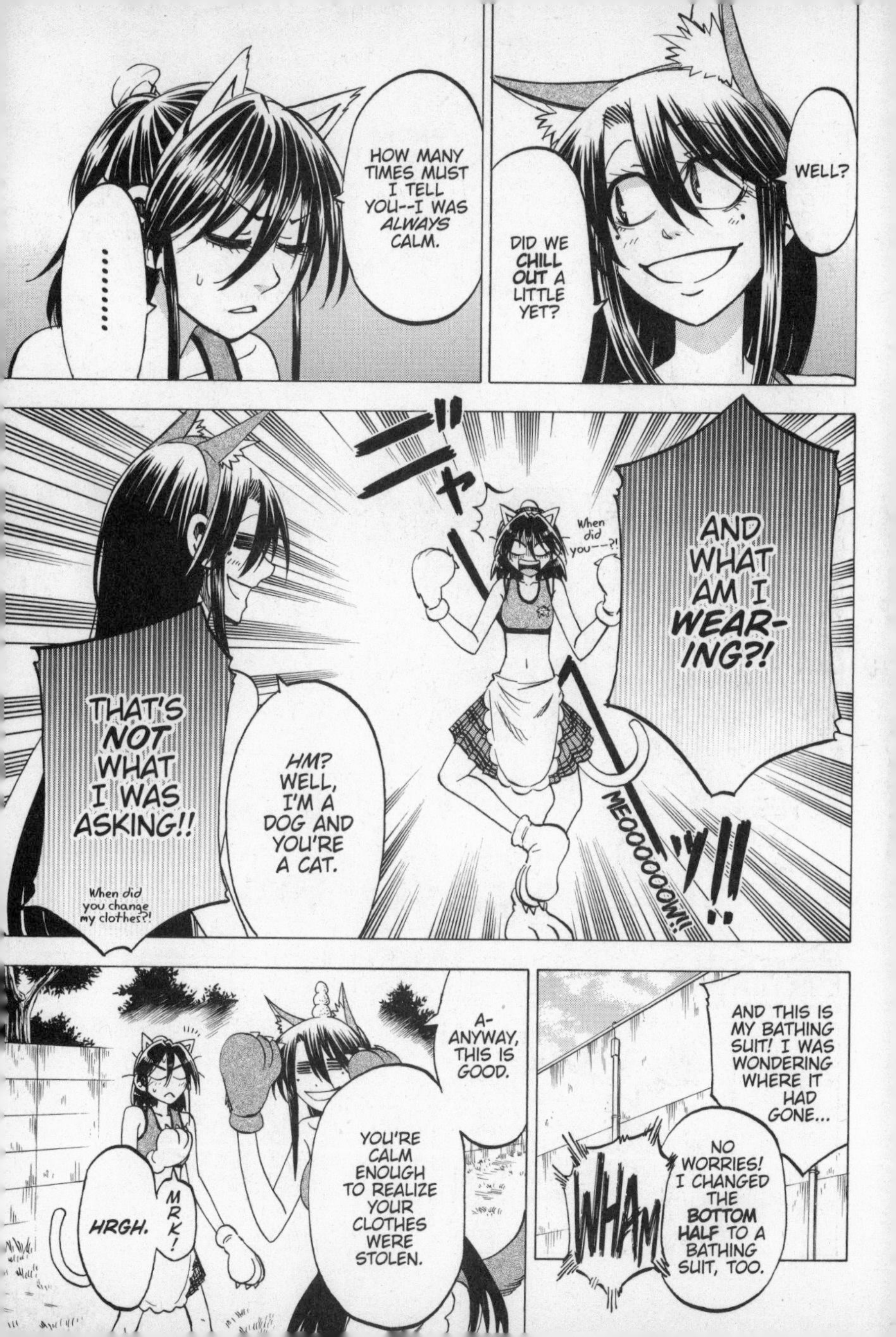

WELL?
DID WE CHILL OUT A LITTLE YET?
HOW MANY TIMES MUST I TELL YOU--I WAS ALWAYS CALM.
......
AND WHAT AM I WEARING?!
When did you--?!
MEOOOOOOOW!!!
HM? WELL, I'M A DOG AND YOU'RE A CAT.
THAT'S NOT WHAT I WAS ASKING!!
When did you change my clothes?!
AND THIS IS MY BATHING SUIT! I WAS WONDERING WHERE IT HAD GONE...
NO WORRIES! I CHANGED THE BOTTOM HALF TO A BATHING SUIT, TOO.
WHAM
A- ANYWAY, THIS IS GOOD.
YOU'RE CALM ENOUGH TO REALIZE YOUR CLOTHES WERE STOLEN.
MRK!
HRGH.

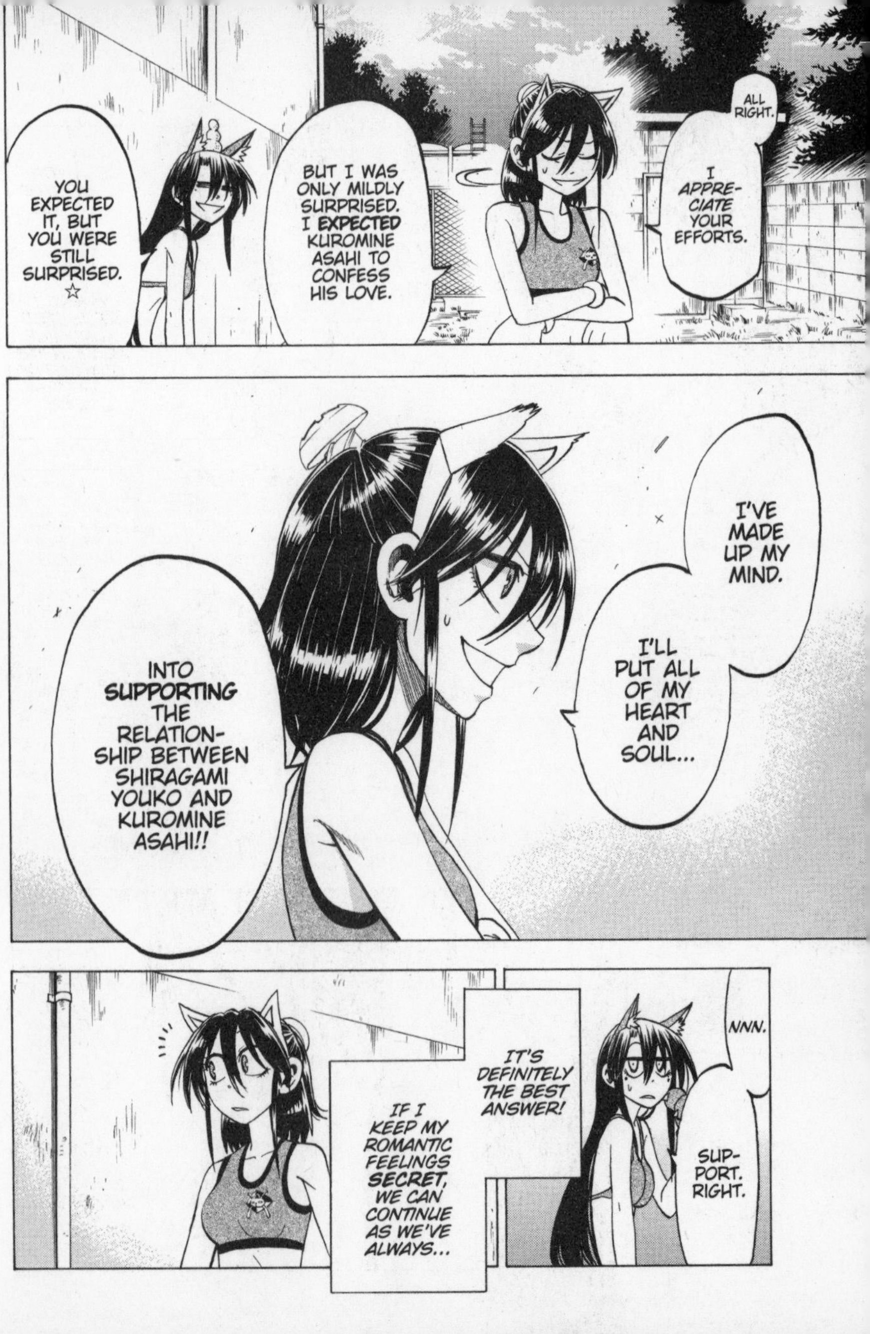
ALL RIGHT.
I APPRECIATE YOUR EFFORTS.
BUT I WAS ONLY MILDLY SURPRISED. I EXPECTED KUROMINE ASAHI TO CONFESS HIS LOVE.
YOU EXPECTED IT, BUT YOU WERE STILL SURPRISED. ☆
I'VE MADE UP MY MIND.
I'LL PUT ALL OF MY HEART AND SOUL...
INTO SUPPORTING THE RELATIONSHIP BETWEEN SHIRAGAMI YOUKO AND KUROMINE ASAHI!!
NNN.
SUPPORT. RIGHT.
IT'S DEFINITELY THE BEST ANSWER!
IF I KEEP MY ROMANTIC FEELINGS SECRET, WE CAN CONTINUE AS WE'VE ALWAYS...

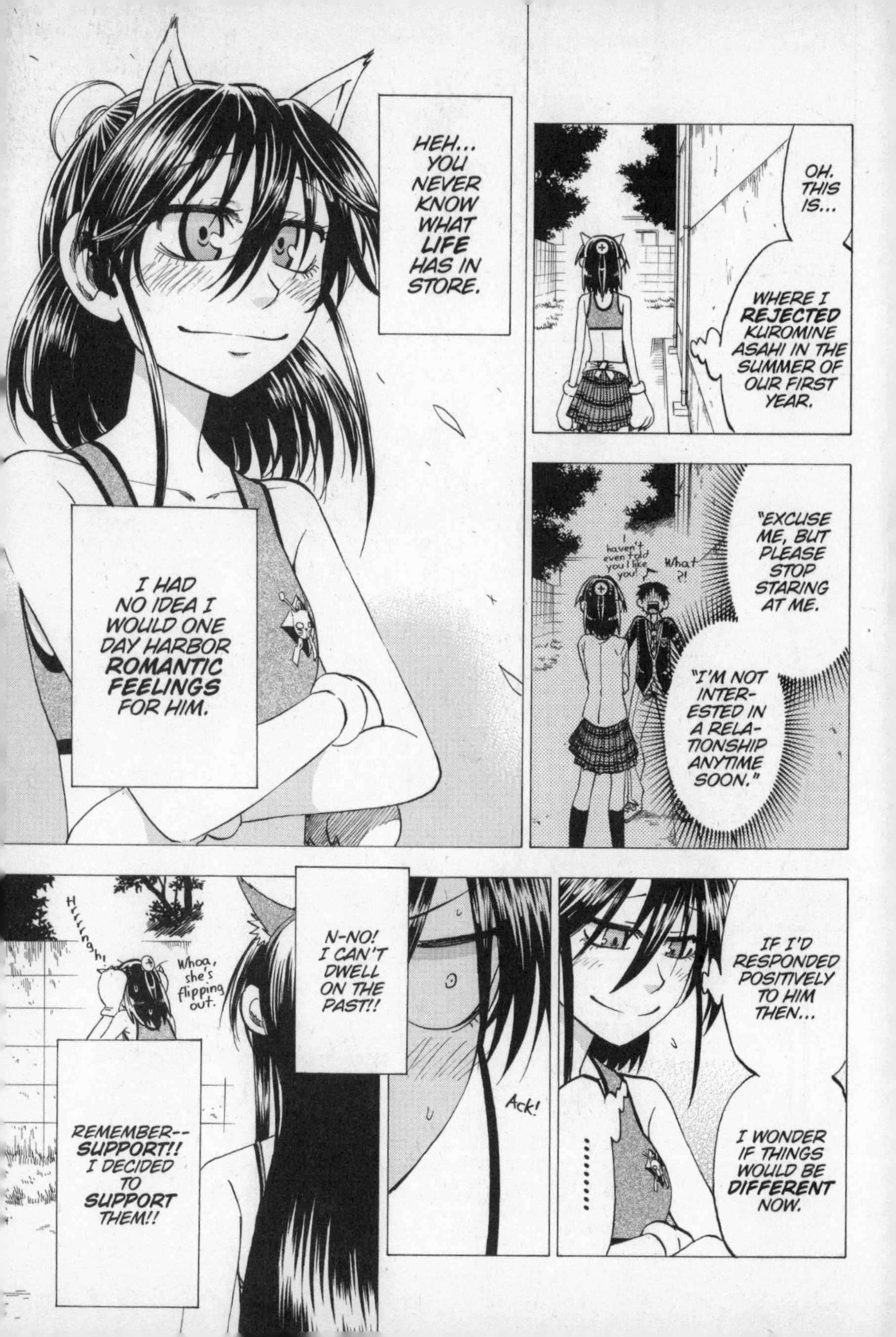
OH. THIS IS...
WHERE I **REJECTED** KUROMINE ASAHI IN THE SUMMER OF OUR FIRST YEAR.
"EXCUSE ME, BUT PLEASE STOP STARING AT ME.
I haven't even told you I like you!
What ?!
"I'M NOT INTERESTED IN A RELATIONSHIP ANYTIME SOON."
HEH... YOU NEVER KNOW WHAT **LIFE** HAS IN STORE.
I HAD NO IDEA I WOULD ONE DAY HARBOR **ROMANTIC FEELINGS** FOR HIM.
IF I'D RESPONDED POSITIVELY TO HIM THEN...
I WONDER IF THINGS WOULD BE **DIFFERENT** NOW.
N-NO! I CAN'T DWELL ON THE PAST!!
Ack!
......
Hrrrngh!
Whoa, she's flipping out.
REMEMBER-- **SUPPORT!!** I DECIDED TO **SUPPORT** THEM!!

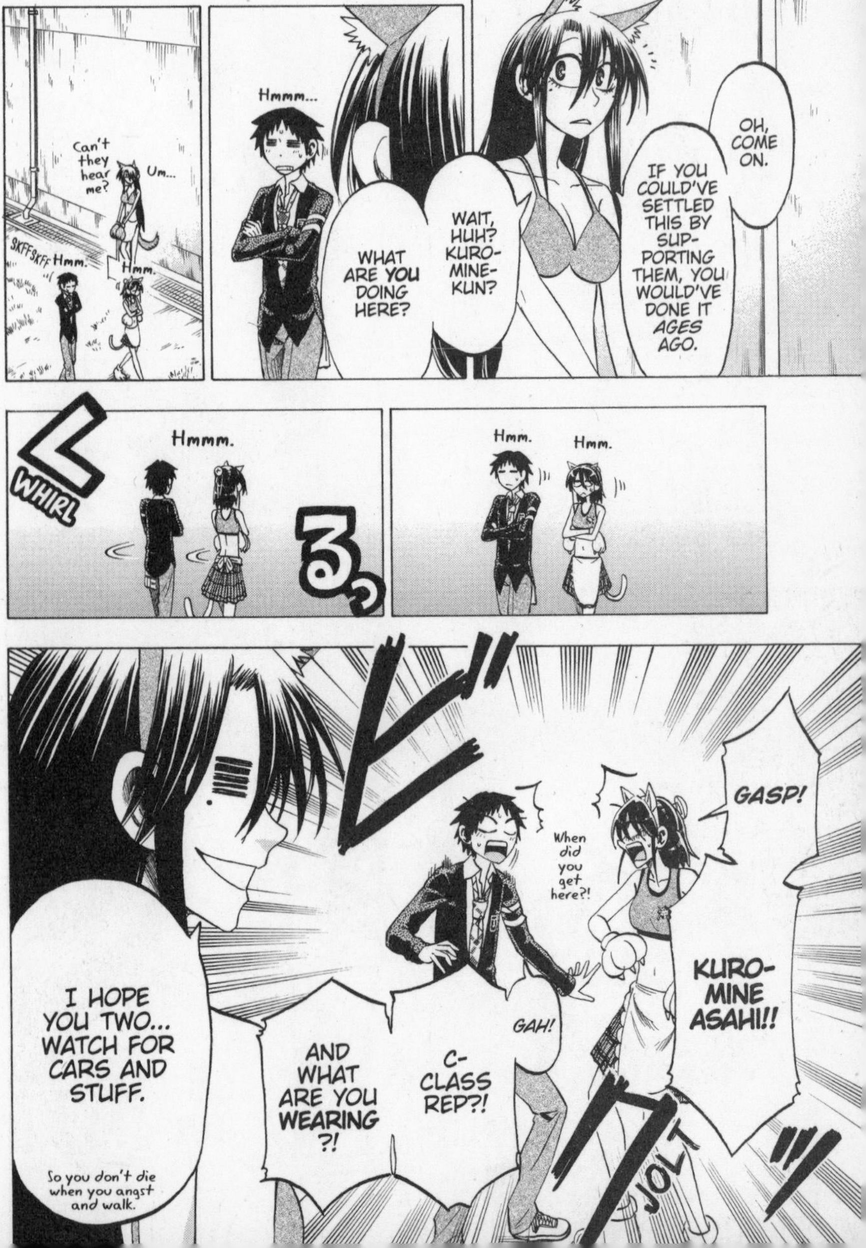
OH, COME ON.
IF YOU COULD'VE SETTLED THIS BY SUP-PORTING THEM, YOU WOULD'VE DONE IT AGES AGO.
WAIT, HUH? KURO-MINE-KUN?
WHAT ARE YOU DOING HERE?
Hmmm...
Um...
Can't they hear me?
SKFFSKFF
Hmm.
Hmm.
Hmm.
Hmm.
るっ
Hmmm.
WHIRL
GASP!
KURO-MINE ASAHI!!
When did you get here?!
JOLT
GAH!
C-CLASS REP?!
AND WHAT ARE YOU WEARING?!
I HOPE YOU TWO... WATCH FOR CARS AND STUFF.
So you don't die when you angst and walk.

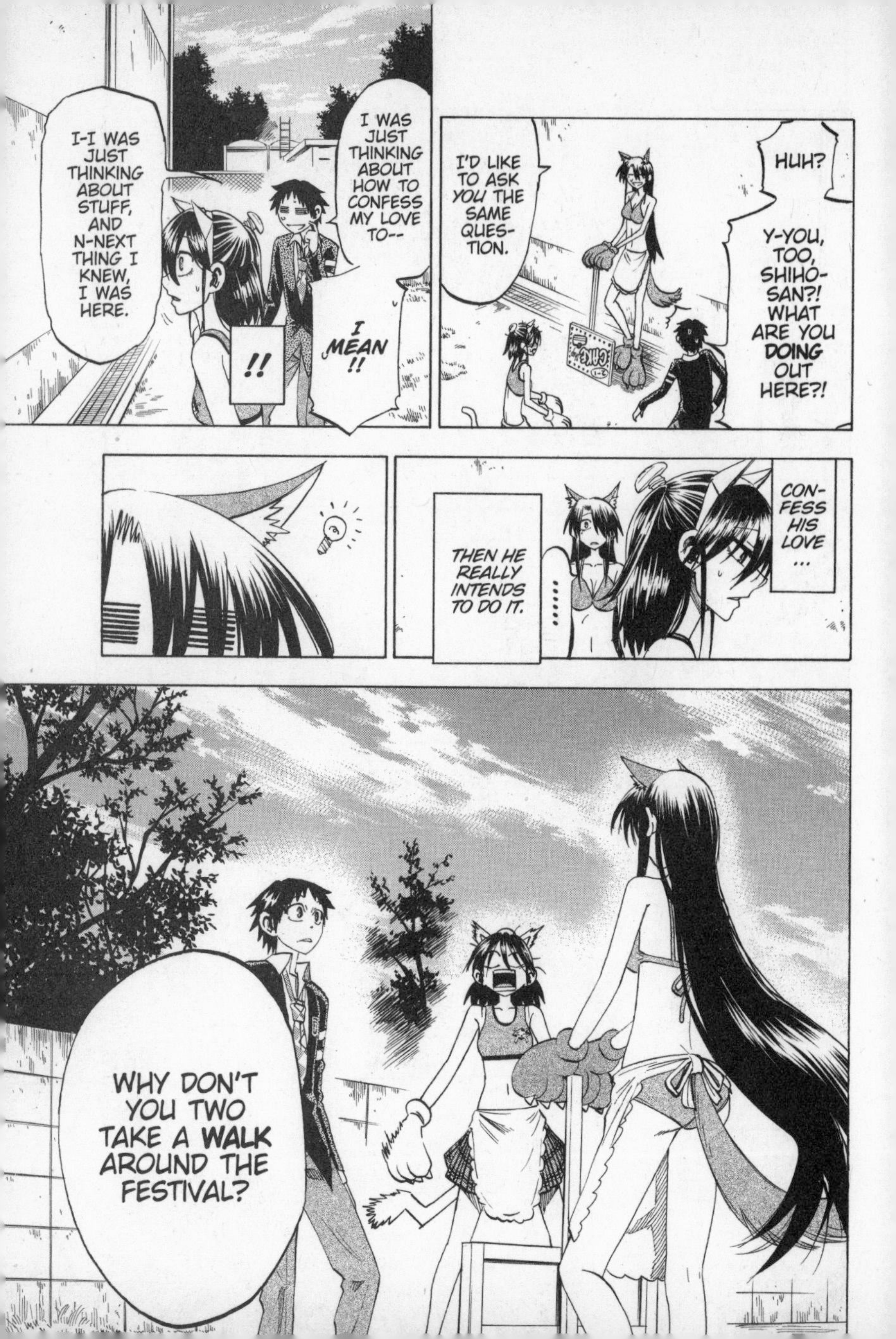
HUH?
Y-YOU, TOO, SHIHO-SAN?! WHAT ARE YOU **DOING** OUT HERE?!
I'D LIKE TO ASK *YOU* THE SAME QUES-TION.
I WAS JUST THINKING ABOUT HOW TO CONFESS MY LOVE TO--
I MEAN!!
!!
I-I WAS JUST THINKING ABOUT STUFF, AND N-NEXT THING I KNEW, I WAS HERE.
CON-FESS HIS LOVE...
......
THEN HE REALLY INTENDS TO DO IT.
WHY DON'T YOU TWO TAKE A **WALK** AROUND THE FESTIVAL?

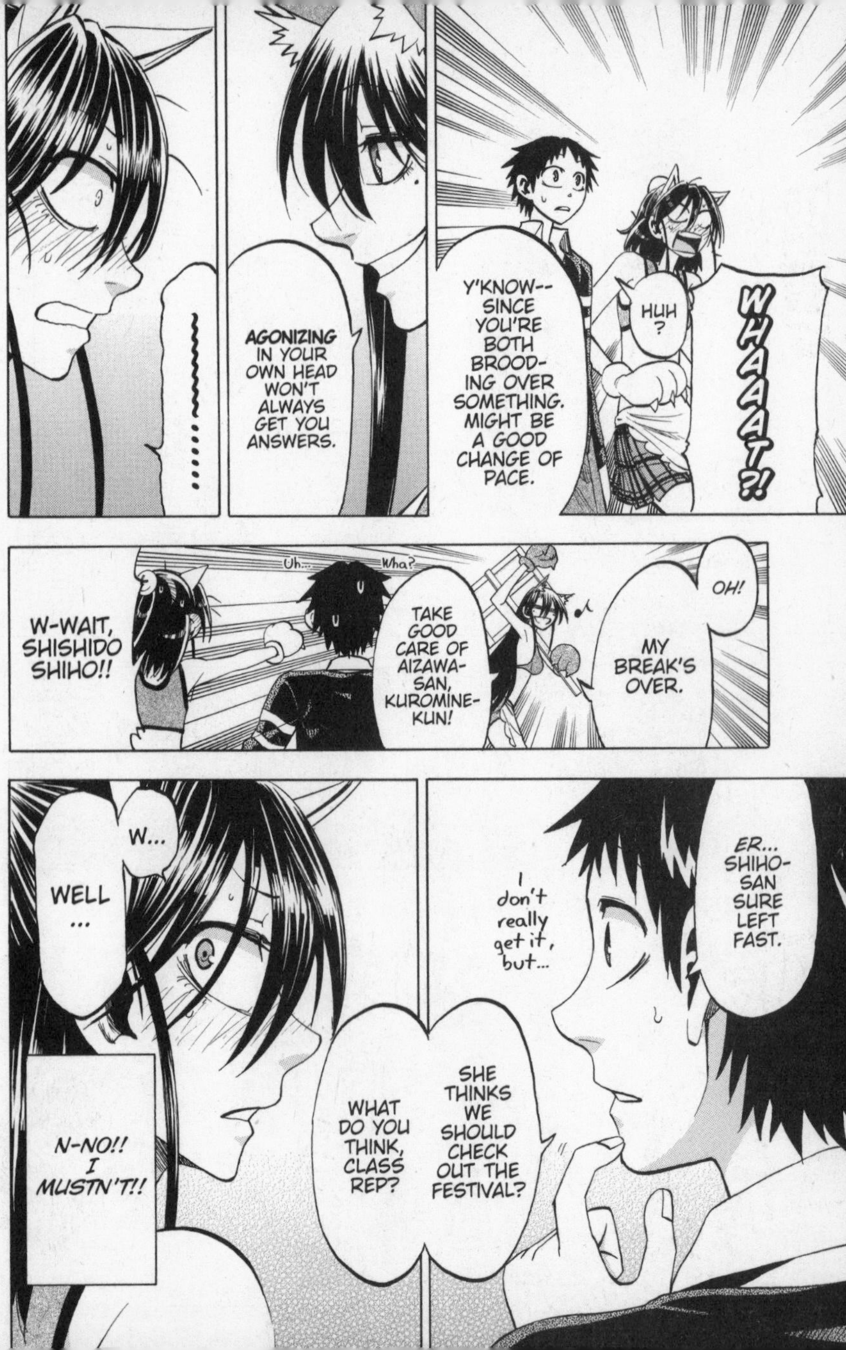
WHAAAAT?!
HUH ?
Y'KNOW-- SINCE YOU'RE BOTH BROODING OVER SOMETHING. MIGHT BE A GOOD CHANGE OF PACE.
AGONIZING IN YOUR OWN HEAD WON'T ALWAYS GET YOU ANSWERS.
~~~~~~......
OH!
MY BREAK'S OVER.
TAKE GOOD CARE OF AIZAWA-SAN, KUROMINE-KUN!
Wha?
Uh...
W-WAIT, SHISHIDO SHIHO!!
ER... SHIHO-SAN SURE LEFT FAST.
I don't really get it, but...
SHE THINKS WE SHOULD CHECK OUT THE FESTIVAL?
WHAT DO YOU THINK, CLASS REP?
W...
WELL ...
N-NO!! I MUSTN'T!!
~~~~~~

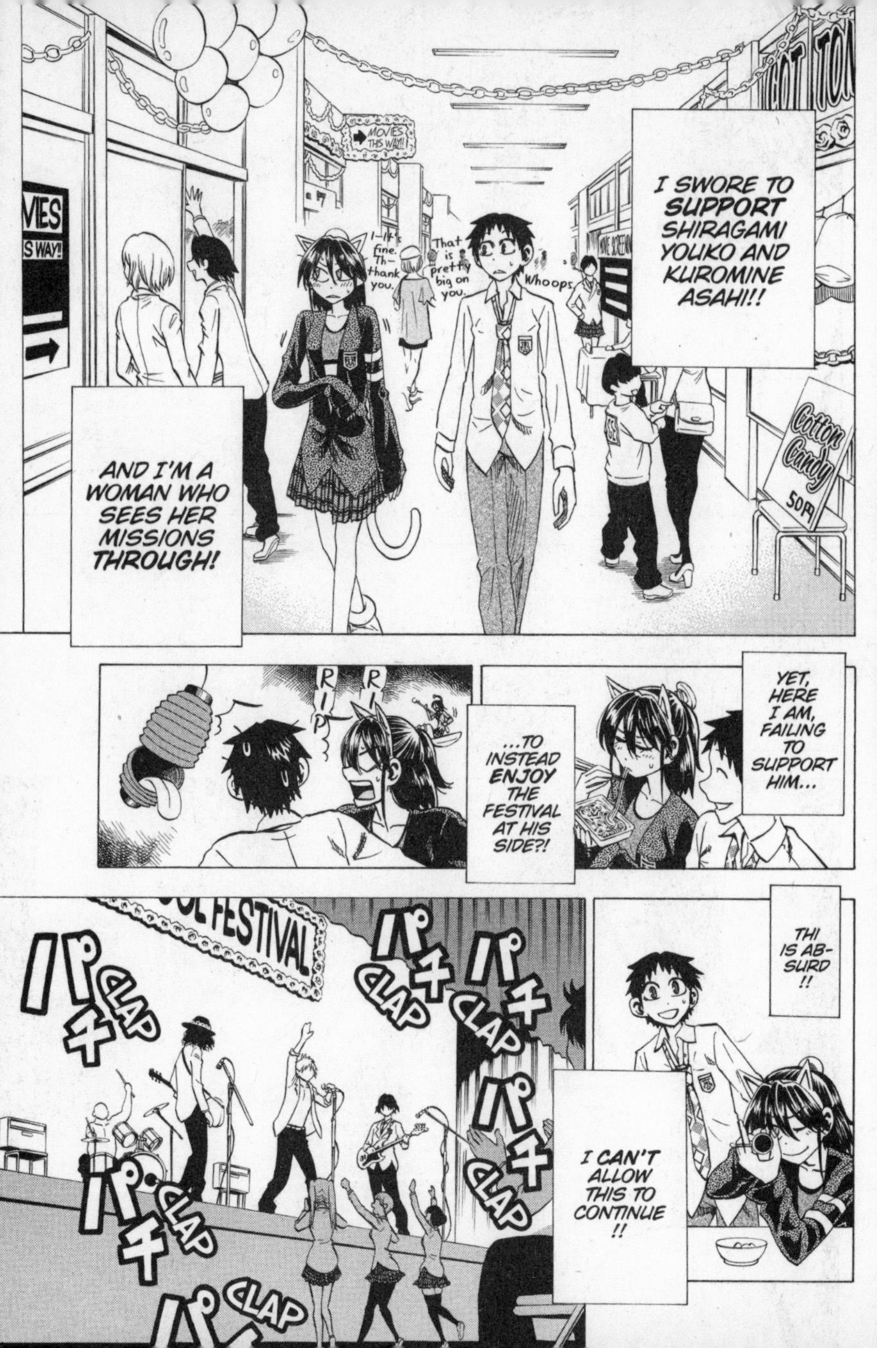
I SWORE TO SUPPORT SHIRAGAMI YOUKO AND KUROMINE ASAHI!!
Whoops.
That is pretty big on you.
I-It's fine. Th-thank you.
MOVIES THIS WAY!!
Cotton Candy
AND I'M A WOMAN WHO SEES HER MISSIONS THROUGH!
YET, HERE I AM, FAILING TO SUPPORT HIM...
...TO INSTEAD ENJOY THE FESTIVAL AT HIS SIDE?!
RIP
RIP
THI IS AB-SURD !!
I CAN'T ALLOW THIS TO CONTINUE !!
FESTIVAL
パチ CLAP
パチ CLAP
パチ CLAP
パチ CLAP
パチ CLAP
パ CLAP

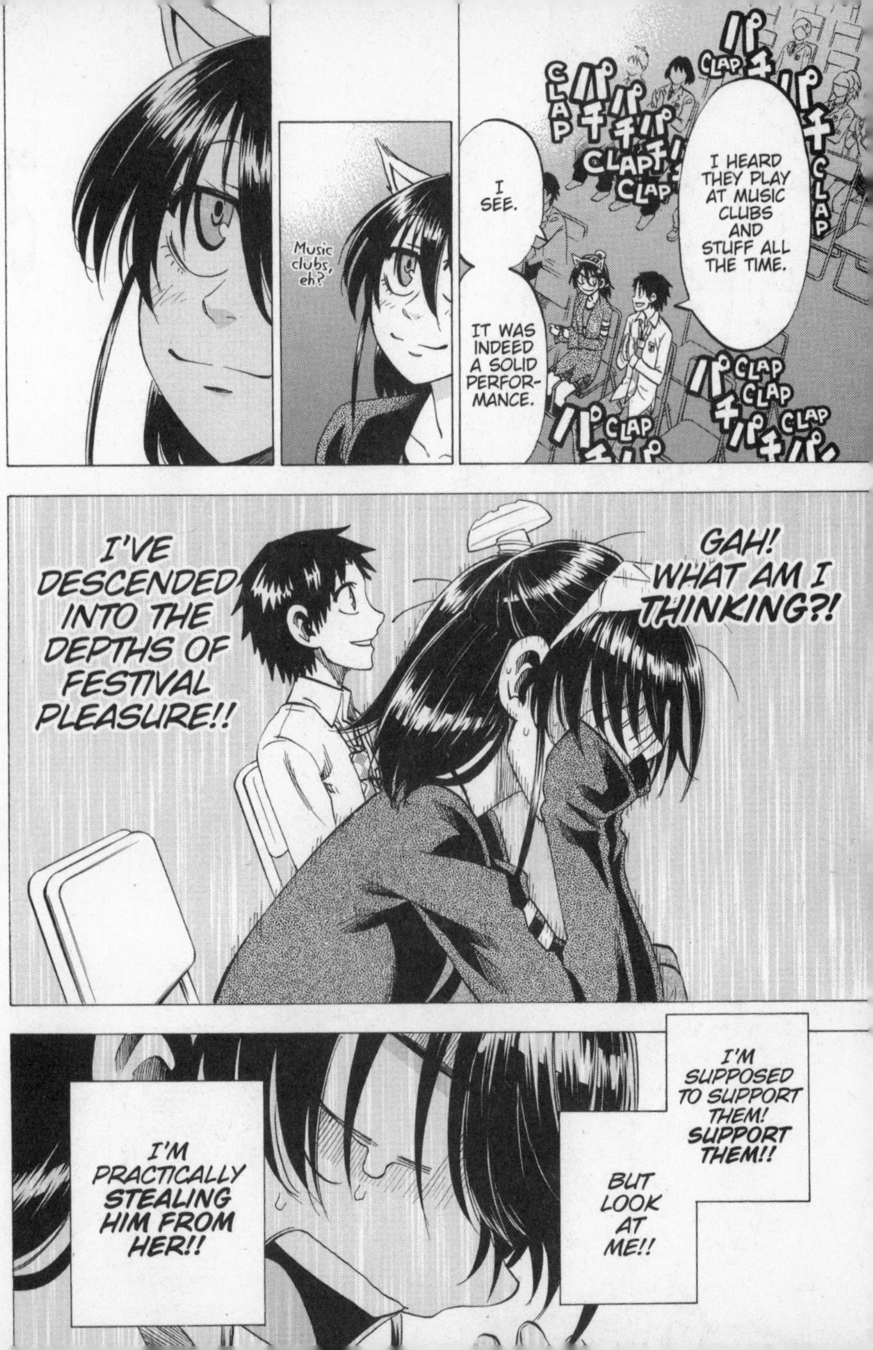

パチパチ CLAP CLAP
I HEARD THEY PLAY AT MUSIC CLUBS AND STUFF ALL THE TIME.
I SEE.
IT WAS INDEED A SOLID PERFORMANCE.
パチパチ CLAP CLAP
Music clubs, eh?
GAH! WHAT AM I THINKING?!
I'VE DESCENDED INTO THE DEPTHS OF FESTIVAL PLEASURE!!
I'M SUPPOSED TO SUPPORT THEM! SUPPORT THEM!!
BUT LOOK AT ME!!
I'M PRACTICALLY STEALING HIM FROM HER!!

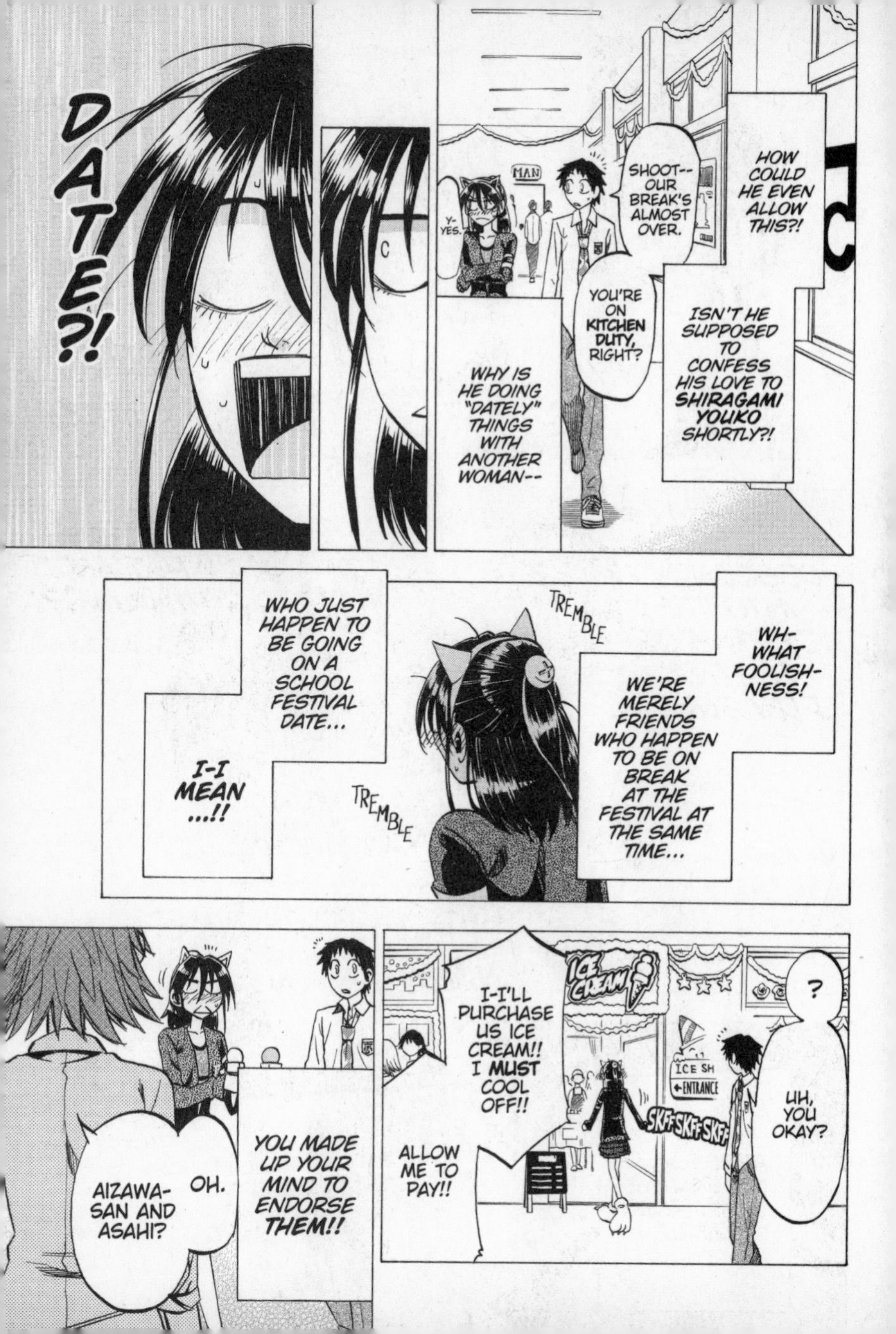
HOW COULD HE EVEN ALLOW THIS?!
ISN'T HE SUPPOSED TO CONFESS HIS LOVE TO SHIRAGAMI YOUKO SHORTLY?!
MAN
SHOOT-- OUR BREAK'S ALMOST OVER.
Y-YES.
YOU'RE ON KITCHEN DUTY, RIGHT?
WHY IS HE DOING "DATELY" THINGS WITH ANOTHER WOMAN--
DATE?!
WH-WHAT FOOLISHNESS!
WE'RE MERELY FRIENDS WHO HAPPEN TO BE ON BREAK AT THE FESTIVAL AT THE SAME TIME...
TREMBLE
WHO JUST HAPPEN TO BE GOING ON A SCHOOL FESTIVAL DATE...
I-I MEAN ...!!
TREMBLE
?
I-I'LL PURCHASE US ICE CREAM!! I MUST COOL OFF!!
ICE CREAM
ICE SH
←ENTRANCE
SKFF SKFF SKFF
UH, YOU OKAY?
ALLOW ME TO PAY!!
YOU MADE UP YOUR MIND TO ENDORSE THEM!!
OH.
AIZAWA-SAN AND ASAHI?

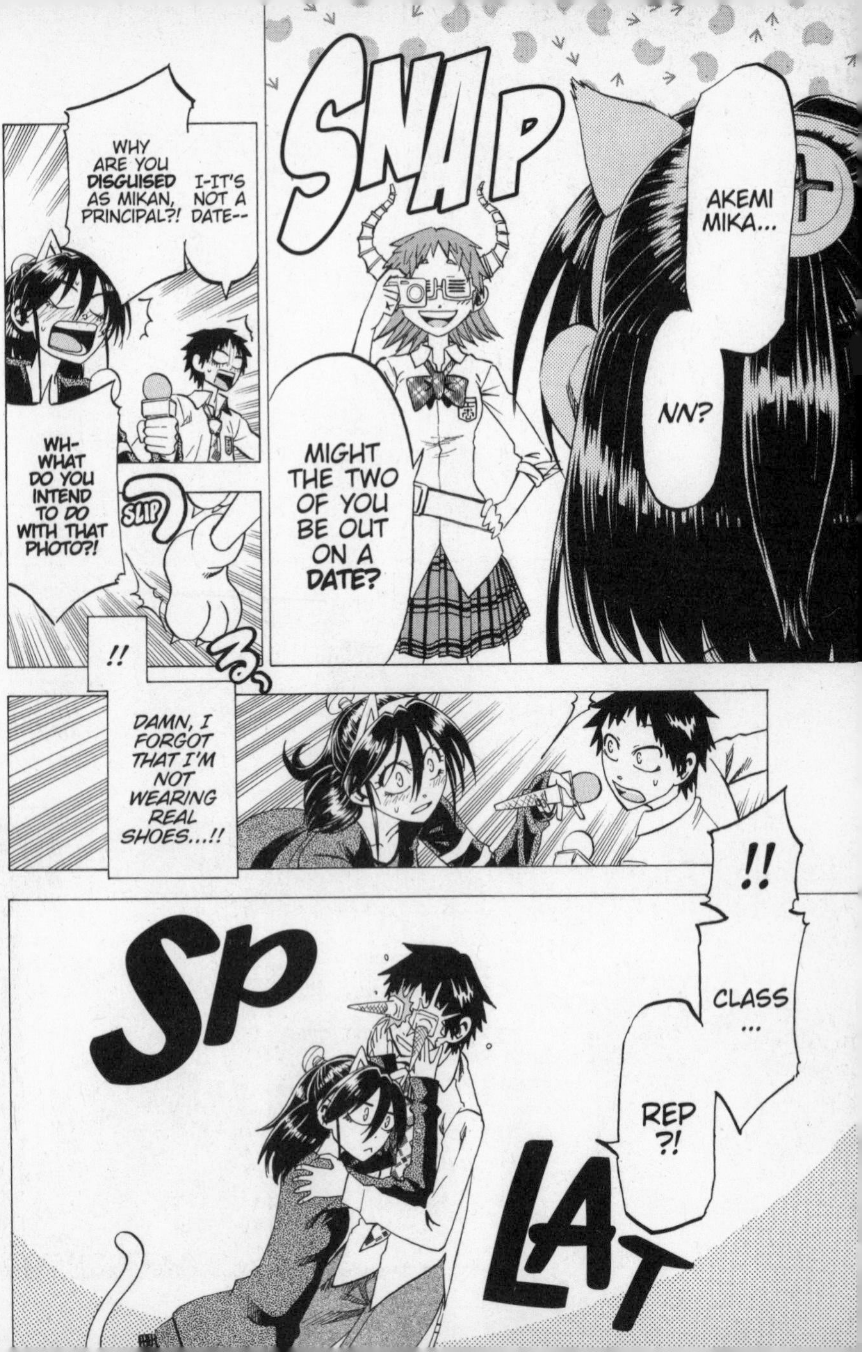
AKEMI MIKA...
NN?
SNAP
MIGHT THE TWO OF YOU BE OUT ON A DATE?
I-IT'S NOT A DATE--
WHY ARE YOU DISGUISED AS MIKAN, PRINCIPAL?!
WH-WHAT DO YOU INTEND TO DO WITH THAT PHOTO?!
SLIP
!!
DAMN, I FORGOT THAT I'M NOT WEARING REAL SHOES...!!
!!
CLASS ... REP ?!
SPLAT

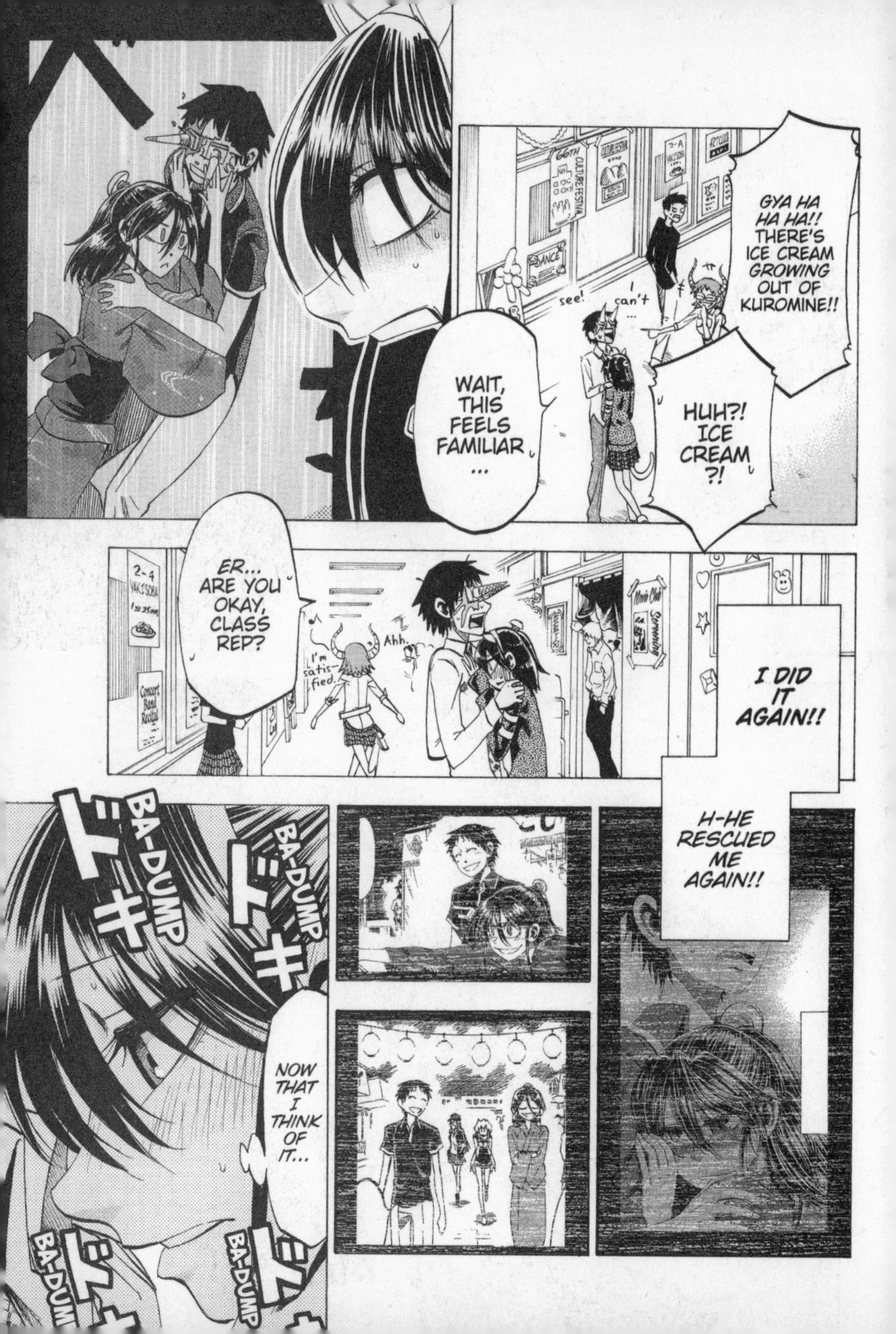
GYA HA HA HA!! THERE'S ICE CREAM GROWING OUT OF KUROMINE!!
I can't ...
see!
HUH?! ICE CREAM ?!
66TH CULTURE FESTIVAL
DANCE
ART CLUB
WAIT, THIS FEELS FAMILIAR ...
I DID IT AGAIN!!
Movie Club Screening
Ahh.
I'm satis-fied.
ER... ARE YOU OKAY, CLASS REP?
2-4 YAKISOBA
Concert Band Recital
H-HE RESCUED ME AGAIN!!
NOW THAT I THINK OF IT...
BA-DUMP
BA-DUMP
BA-DUMP
BA-DUM

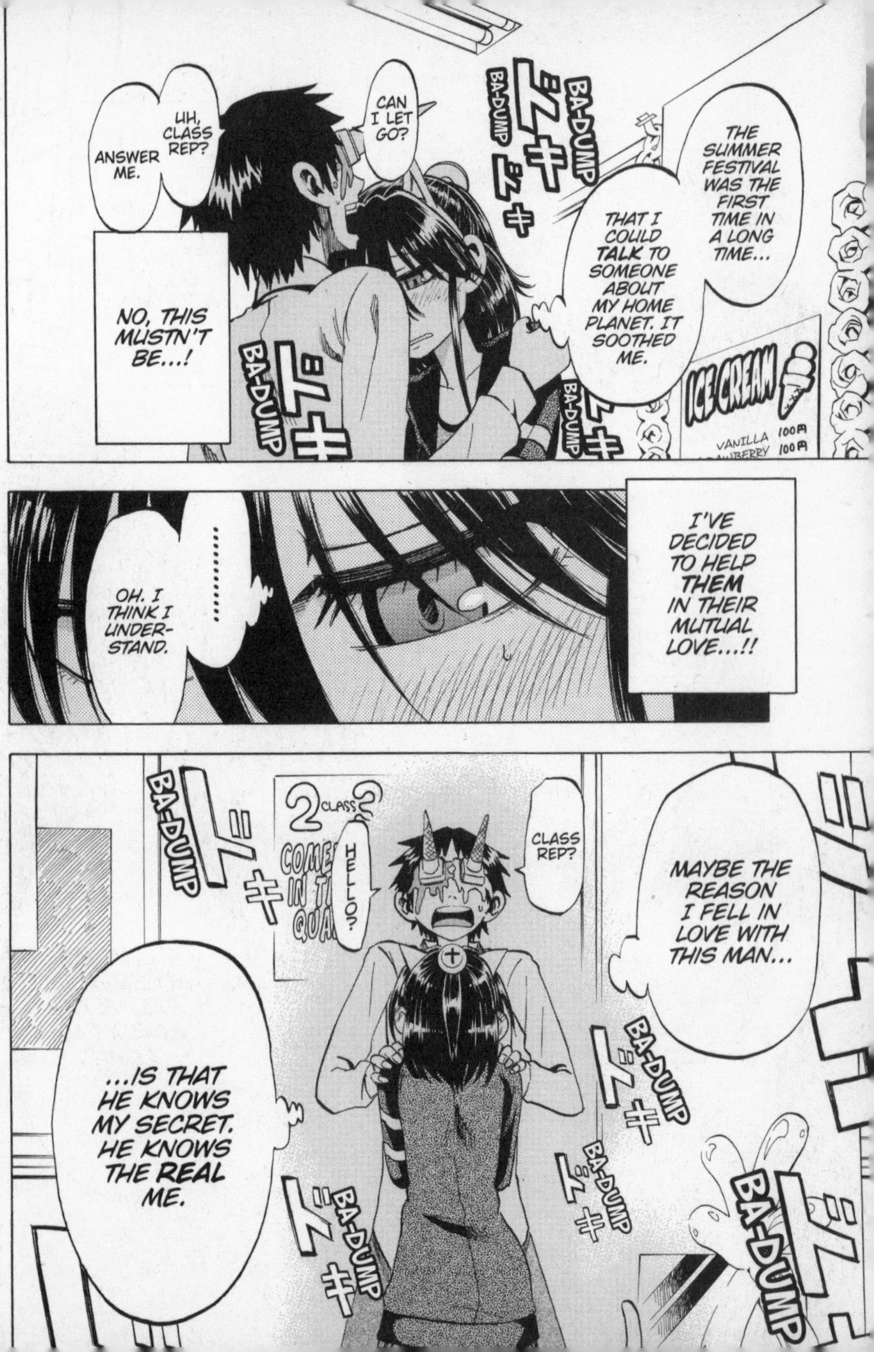
THE SUMMER FESTIVAL WAS THE FIRST TIME IN A LONG TIME...
THAT I COULD TALK TO SOMEONE ABOUT MY HOME PLANET. IT SOOTHED ME.
BA-DUMP
BA-DUMP
CAN I LET GO?
UH, CLASS REP?
ANSWER ME.
NO, THIS MUSTN'T BE...!
BA-DUMP
ICE CREAM
VANILLA 100円
I'VE DECIDED TO HELP THEM IN THEIR MUTUAL LOVE...!!
......
OH. I THINK I UNDERSTAND.
BA-DUMP
MAYBE THE REASON I FELL IN LOVE WITH THIS MAN...
CLASS REP?
HELLO?
BA-DUMP
BA-DUMP
BA-DUMP
BA-DUMP
...IS THAT HE KNOWS MY SECRET. HE KNOWS THE REAL ME.

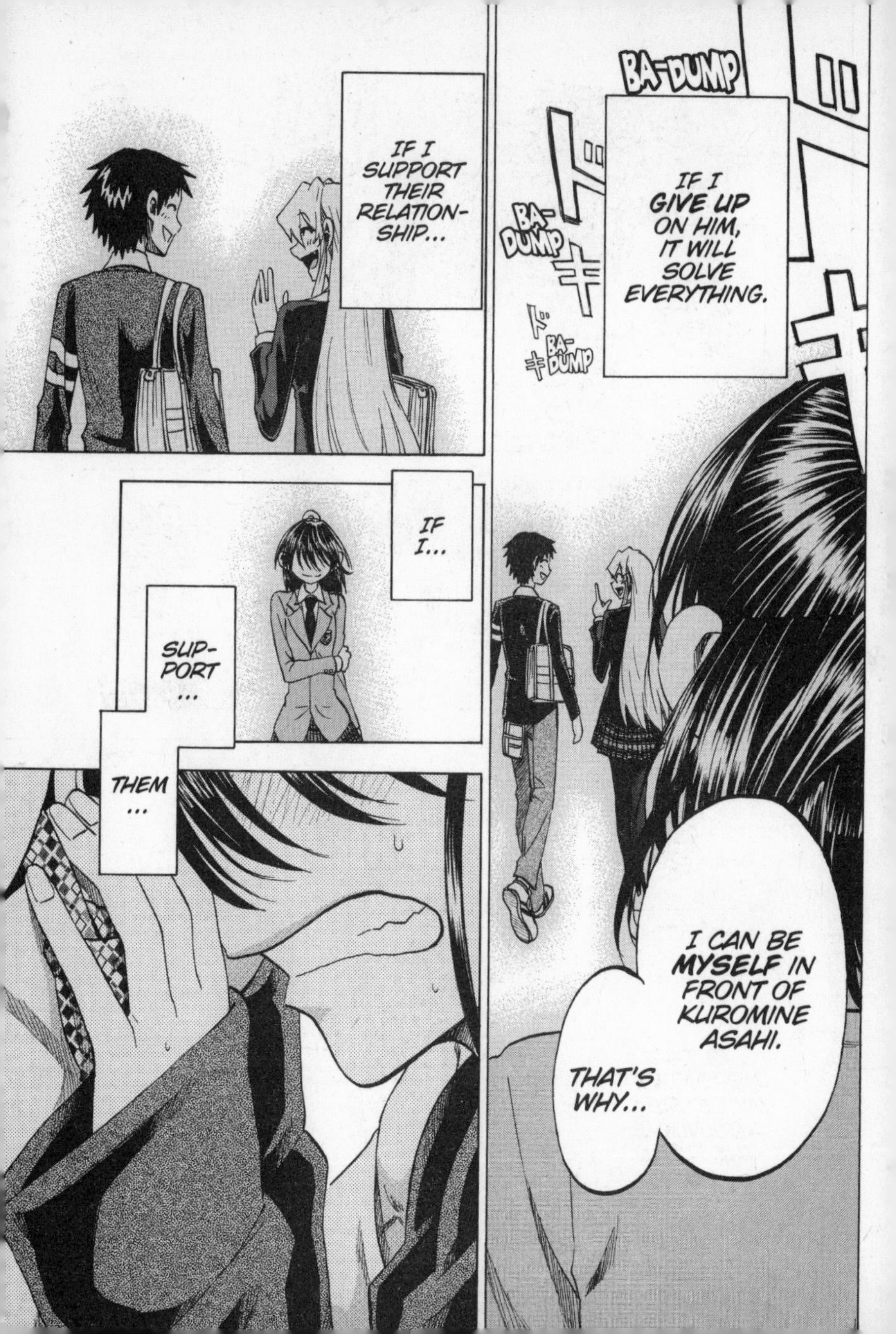
BA-DUMP
BA-DUMP
IF I GIVE UP ON HIM, IT WILL SOLVE EVERYTHING.
BA-DUMP
I CAN BE **MYSELF** IN FRONT OF KUROMINE ASAHI.
THAT'S WHY...
IF I SUPPORT THEIR RELATIONSHIP...
IF I...
SUPPORT...
THEM...

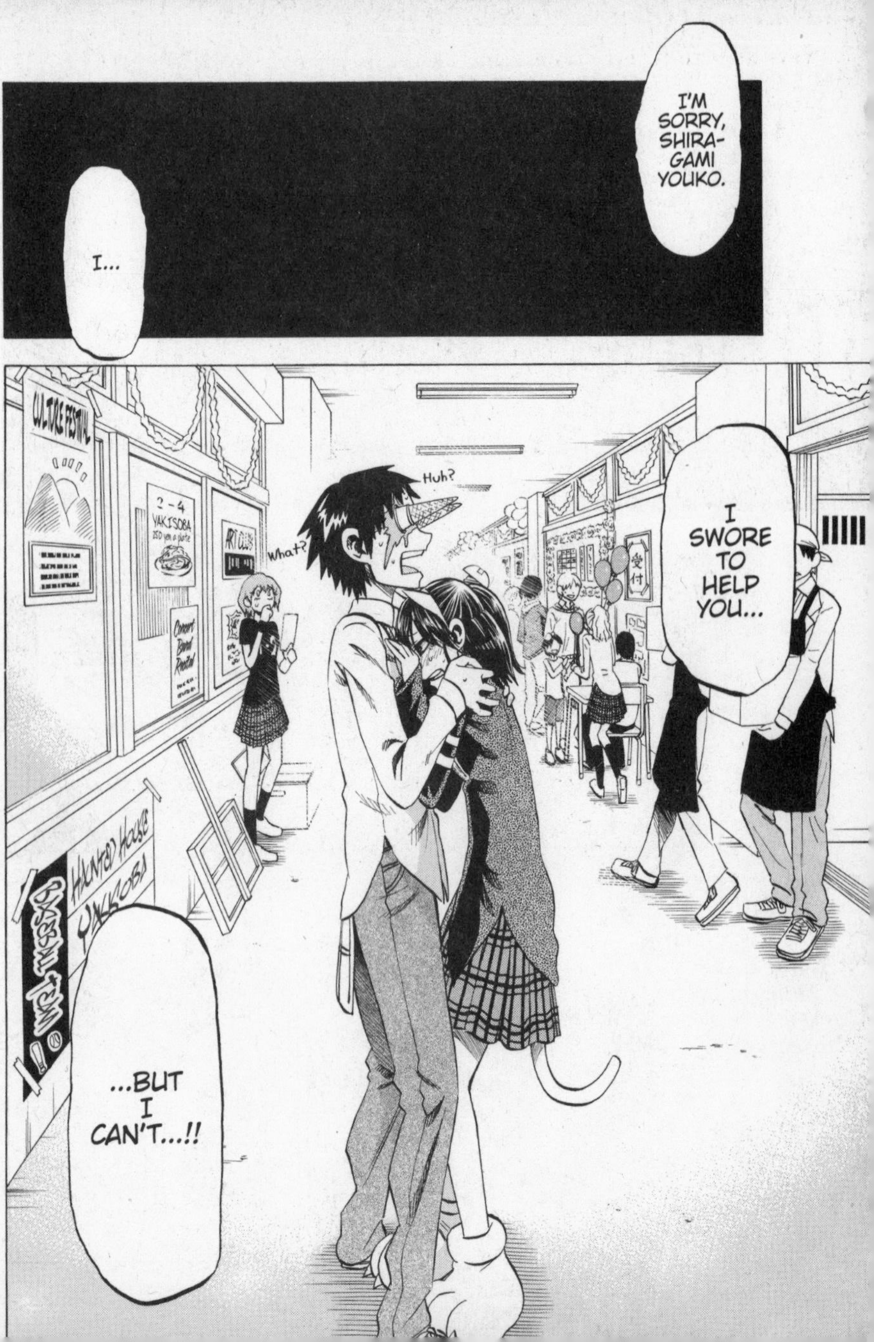
I'M SORRY, SHIRAGAMI YOUKO.
I...
I SWORE TO HELP YOU...
Huh?
What?
...BUT I CAN'T...!!
CULTURE FESTIVAL
2-4 YAKISOBA 150 yen a plate
ART CLUB
Concert Band Recital
受付
HAUNTED HOUSE
YAKISOBA

Chapter 46: "Let's Stop That Love Confession!"

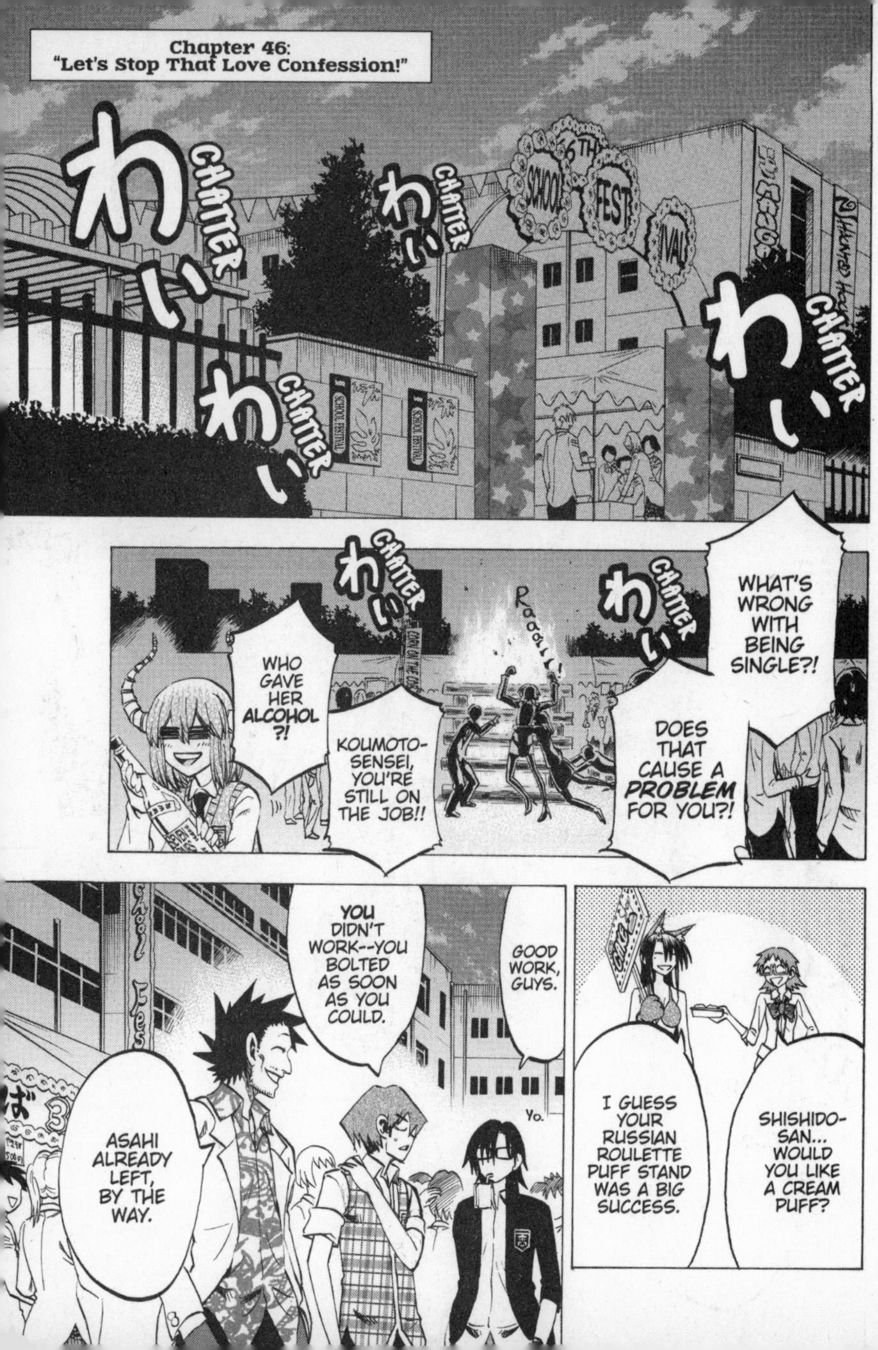
わい
CHATTER
わい
CHATTER
わい
CHATTER
わい
CHATTER
SCHOOL 6TH FEST IVAL
SCHOOL FESTIVAL
わい
CHATTER
わい
CHATTER
WHAT'S WRONG WITH BEING SINGLE?!
DOES THAT CAUSE A PROBLEM FOR YOU?!
KOUMOTO-SENSEI, YOU'RE STILL ON THE JOB!!
WHO GAVE HER ALCOHOL?!
SHISHIDO-SAN... WOULD YOU LIKE A CREAM PUFF?
I GUESS YOUR RUSSIAN ROULETTE PUFF STAND WAS A BIG SUCCESS.
GOOD WORK, GUYS.
YOU DIDN'T WORK--YOU BOLTED AS SOON AS YOU COULD.
Yo.
ASAHI ALREADY LEFT, BY THE WAY.

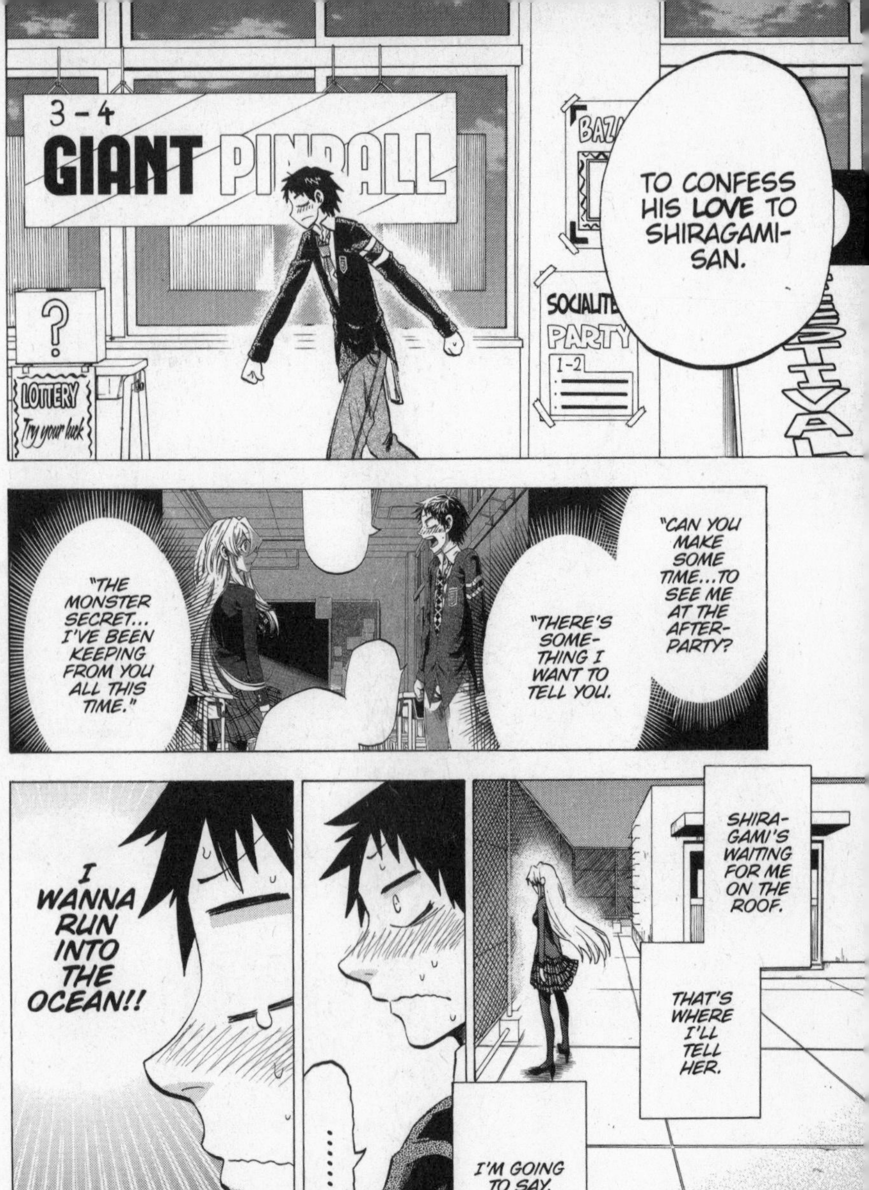
TO CONFESS HIS LOVE TO SHIRAGAMI-SAN.
SOCIALITE PARTY
1-2
3-4
GIANT PINBALL
?
LOTTERY
Try your luck
"CAN YOU MAKE SOME TIME...TO SEE ME AT THE AFTER-PARTY?
"THERE'S SOME-THING I WANT TO TELL YOU.
"THE MONSTER SECRET... I'VE BEEN KEEPING FROM YOU ALL THIS TIME."
SHIRA-GAMI'S WAITING FOR ME ON THE ROOF.
THAT'S WHERE I'LL TELL HER.
I'M GOING TO SAY, "SHIRAGAMI, I LOVE YOU."
......
I WANNA RUN INTO THE OCEAN!!

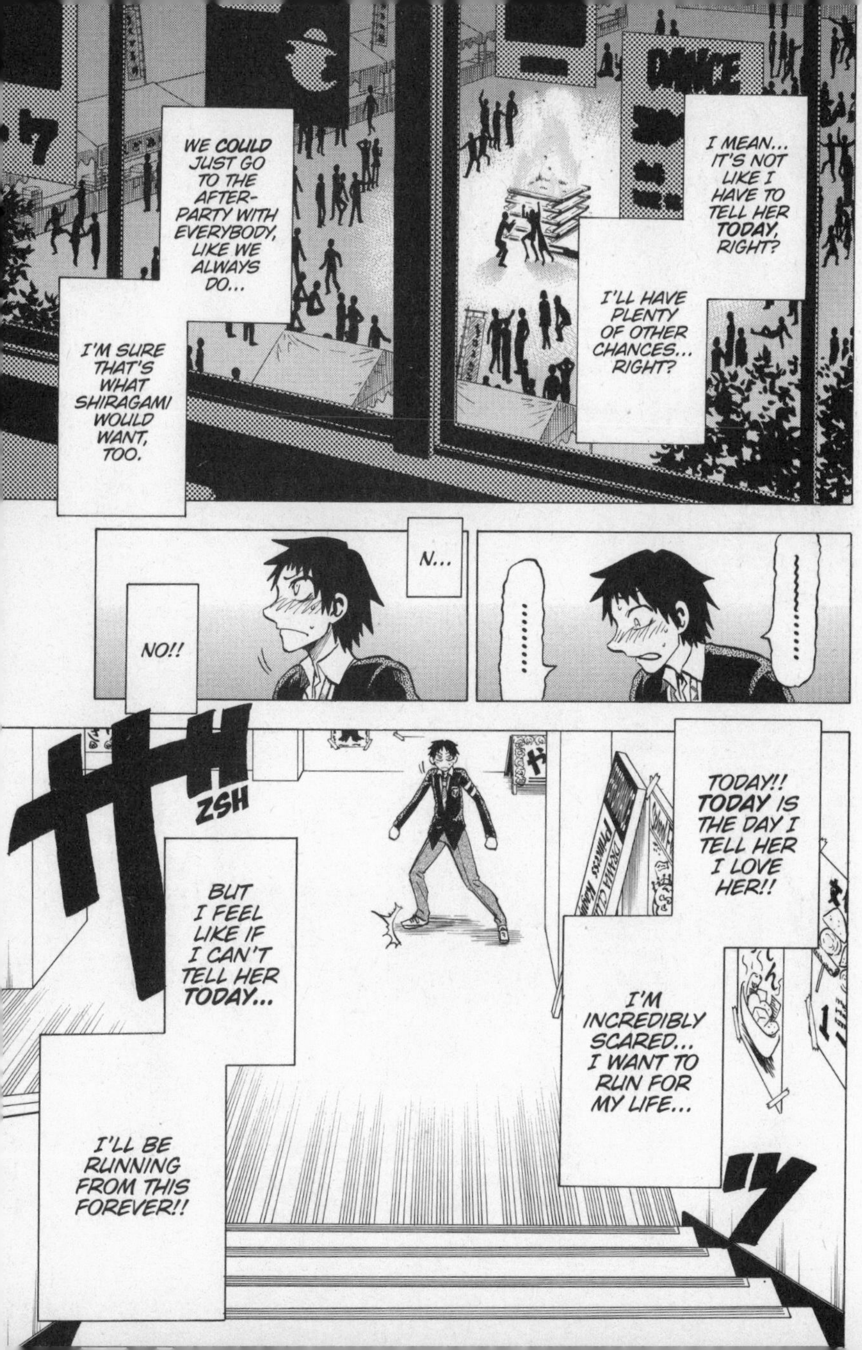
I MEAN... IT'S NOT LIKE I HAVE TO TELL HER TODAY, RIGHT?
I'LL HAVE PLENTY OF OTHER CHANCES... RIGHT?
WE COULD JUST GO TO THE AFTER-PARTY WITH EVERYBODY, LIKE WE ALWAYS DO...
I'M SURE THAT'S WHAT SHIRAGAMI WOULD WANT, TOO.
......
......
N...
NO!!
TODAY!! TODAY IS THE DAY I TELL HER I LOVE HER!!
I'M INCREDIBLY SCARED... I WANT TO RUN FOR MY LIFE...
ZSH
BUT I FEEL LIKE IF I CAN'T TELL HER TODAY...
I'LL BE RUNNING FROM THIS FOREVER!!

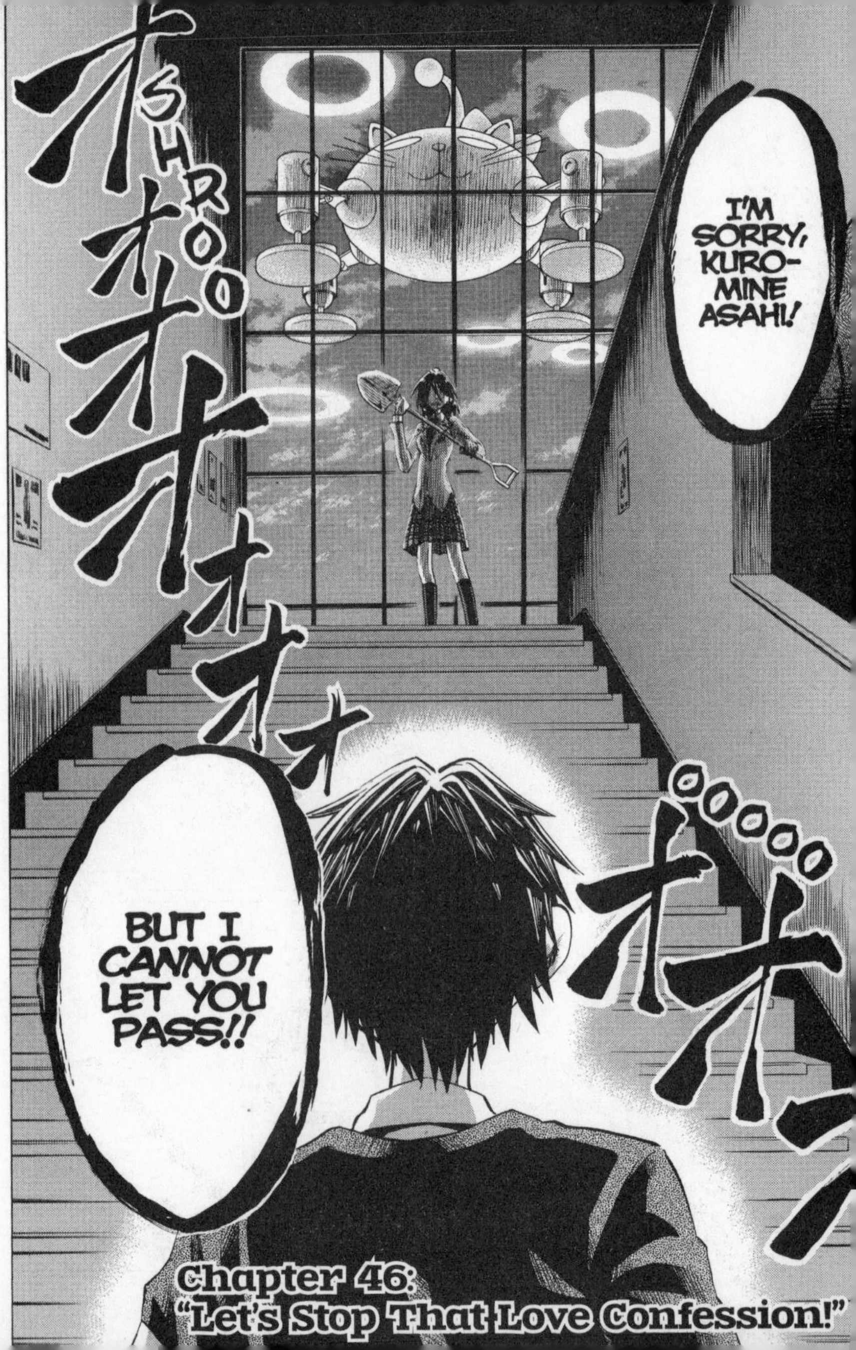
I'M SORRY, KURO-MINE ASAHI!
BUT I CANNOT LET YOU PASS!!

Chapter 46: "Let's Stop That Love Confession!"

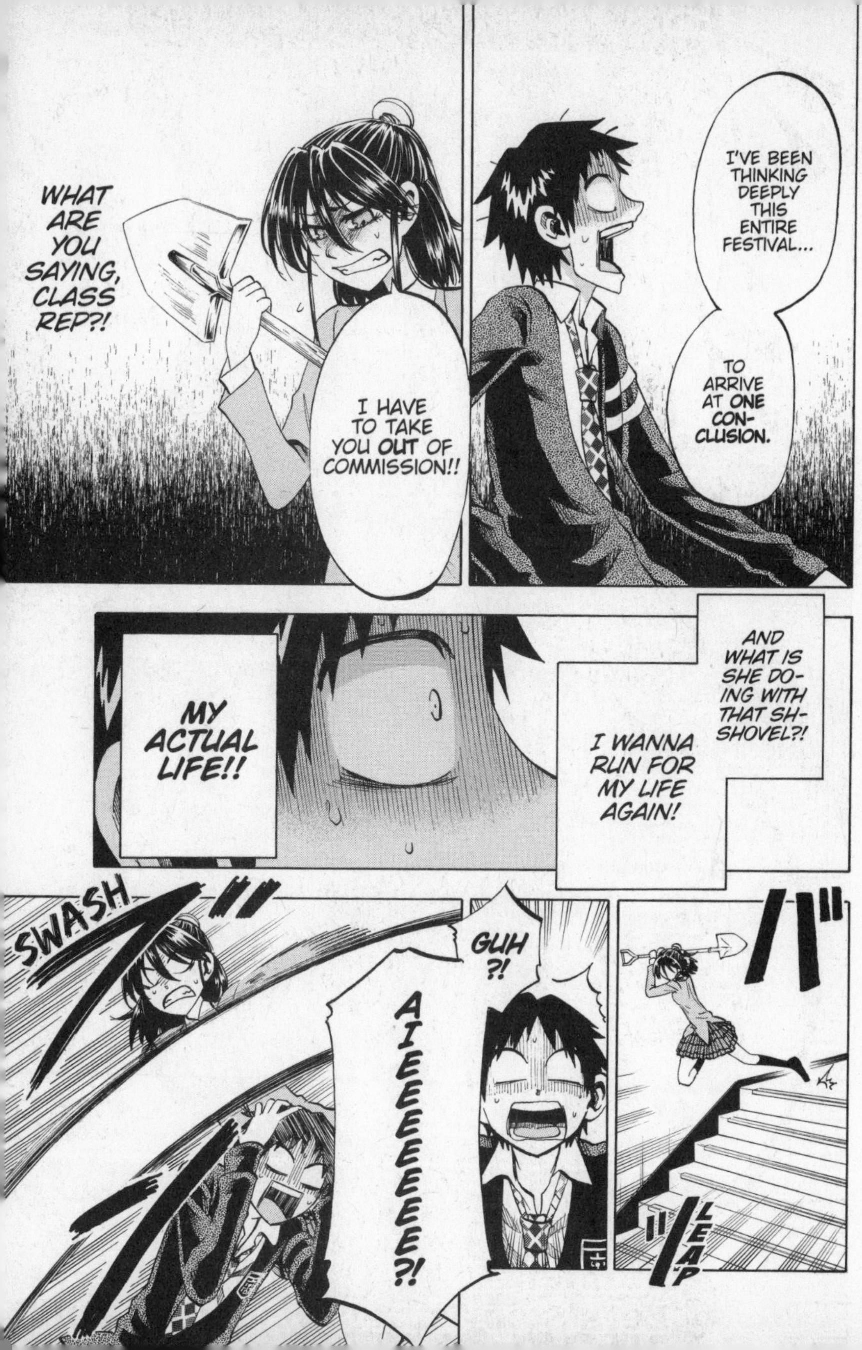
I'VE BEEN THINKING DEEPLY THIS ENTIRE FESTIVAL...
TO ARRIVE AT ONE CON-CLUSION.
I HAVE TO TAKE YOU OUT OF COMMISSION!!
WHAT ARE YOU SAYING, CLASS REP?!
AND WHAT IS SHE DO-ING WITH THAT SH-SHOVEL?!
I WANNA RUN FOR MY LIFE AGAIN!
MY ACTUAL LIFE!!
LEAP
GUH ?!
AIEEEEEEEE?!
SWASH

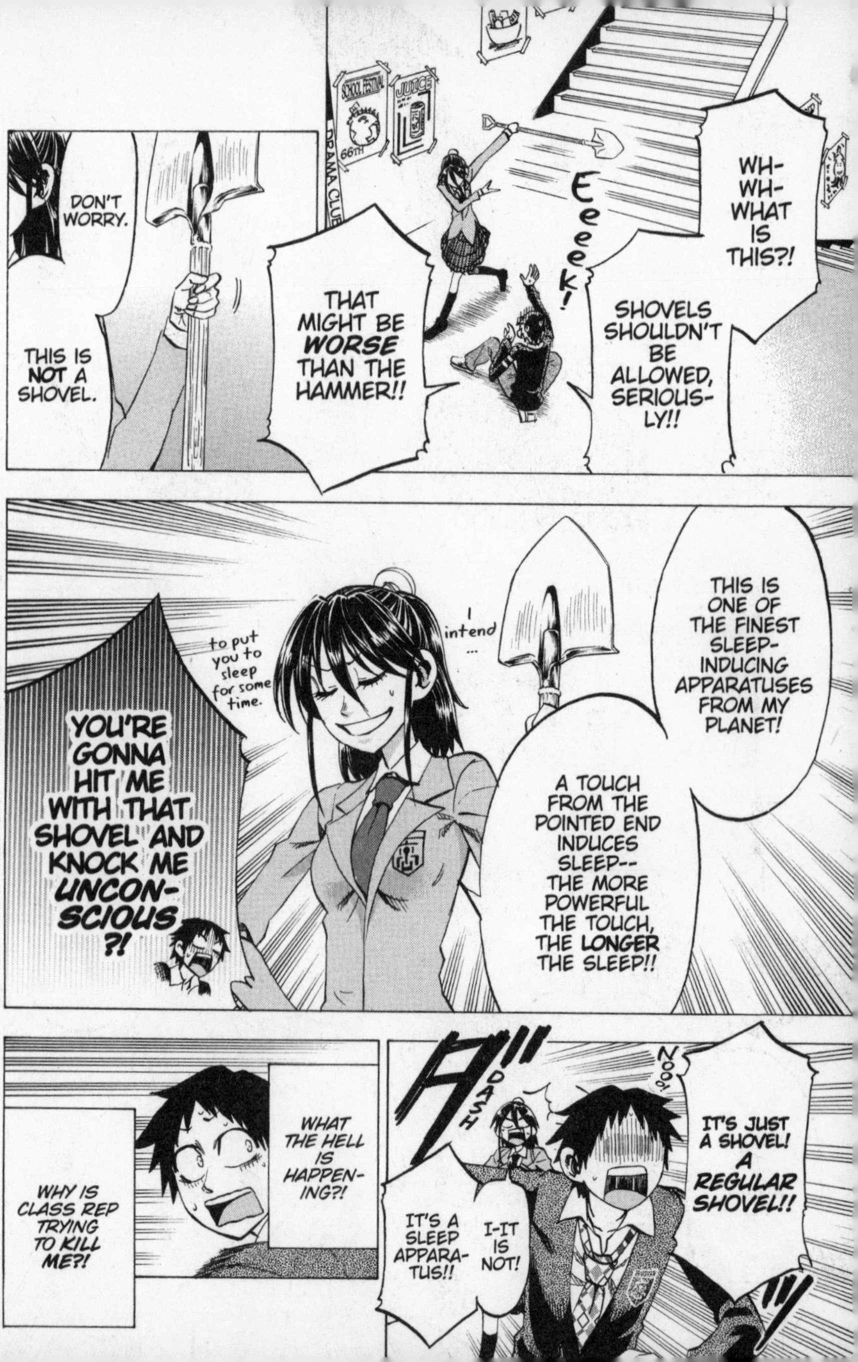
SCHOOL FESTIVAL
66TH
JUICE
DRAMA CLUB
WH-WH-WHAT IS THIS?!
SHOVELS SHOULDN'T BE ALLOWED, SERIOUSLY!!
Eeeek!
THAT MIGHT BE WORSE THAN THE HAMMER!!
DON'T WORRY.
THIS IS NOT A SHOVEL.
THIS IS ONE OF THE FINEST SLEEP-INDUCING APPARATUSES FROM MY PLANET!
A TOUCH FROM THE POINTED END INDUCES SLEEP-- THE MORE POWERFUL THE TOUCH, THE LONGER THE SLEEP!!
I intend ...
to put you to sleep for some time.
YOU'RE GONNA HIT ME WITH THAT SHOVEL AND KNOCK ME UNCONSCIOUS?!
NOOO!
DASH
IT'S JUST A SHOVEL! A REGULAR SHOVEL!!
I-IT IS NOT!
IT'S A SLEEP APPARATUS!!
WHAT THE HELL IS HAPPENING?!
WHY IS CLASS REP TRYING TO KILL ME?!

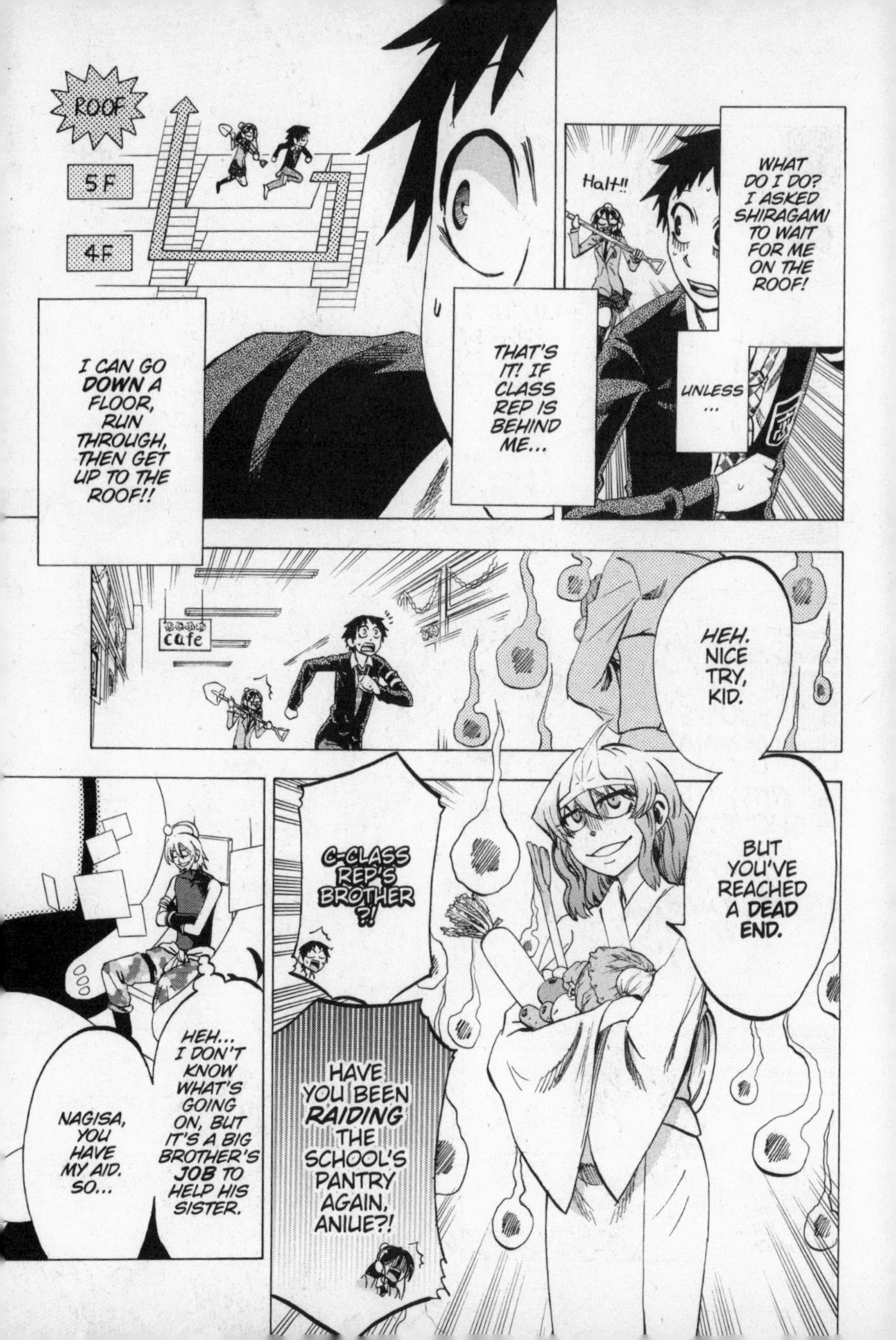
WHAT DO I DO? I ASKED SHIRAGAMI TO WAIT FOR ME ON THE ROOF!
Halt!!
UNLESS...
THAT'S IT! IF CLASS REP IS BEHIND ME...
ROOF
5F
4F
I CAN GO DOWN A FLOOR, RUN THROUGH, THEN GET UP TO THE ROOF!!
cafe
HEH. NICE TRY, KID.
BUT YOU'VE REACHED A DEAD END.
C-CLASS REP'S BROTHER?!
HAVE YOU BEEN RAIDING THE SCHOOL'S PANTRY AGAIN, ANIUE?!
HEH... I DON'T KNOW WHAT'S GOING ON, BUT IT'S A BIG BROTHER'S JOB TO HELP HIS SISTER.
NAGISA, YOU HAVE MY AID. SO...

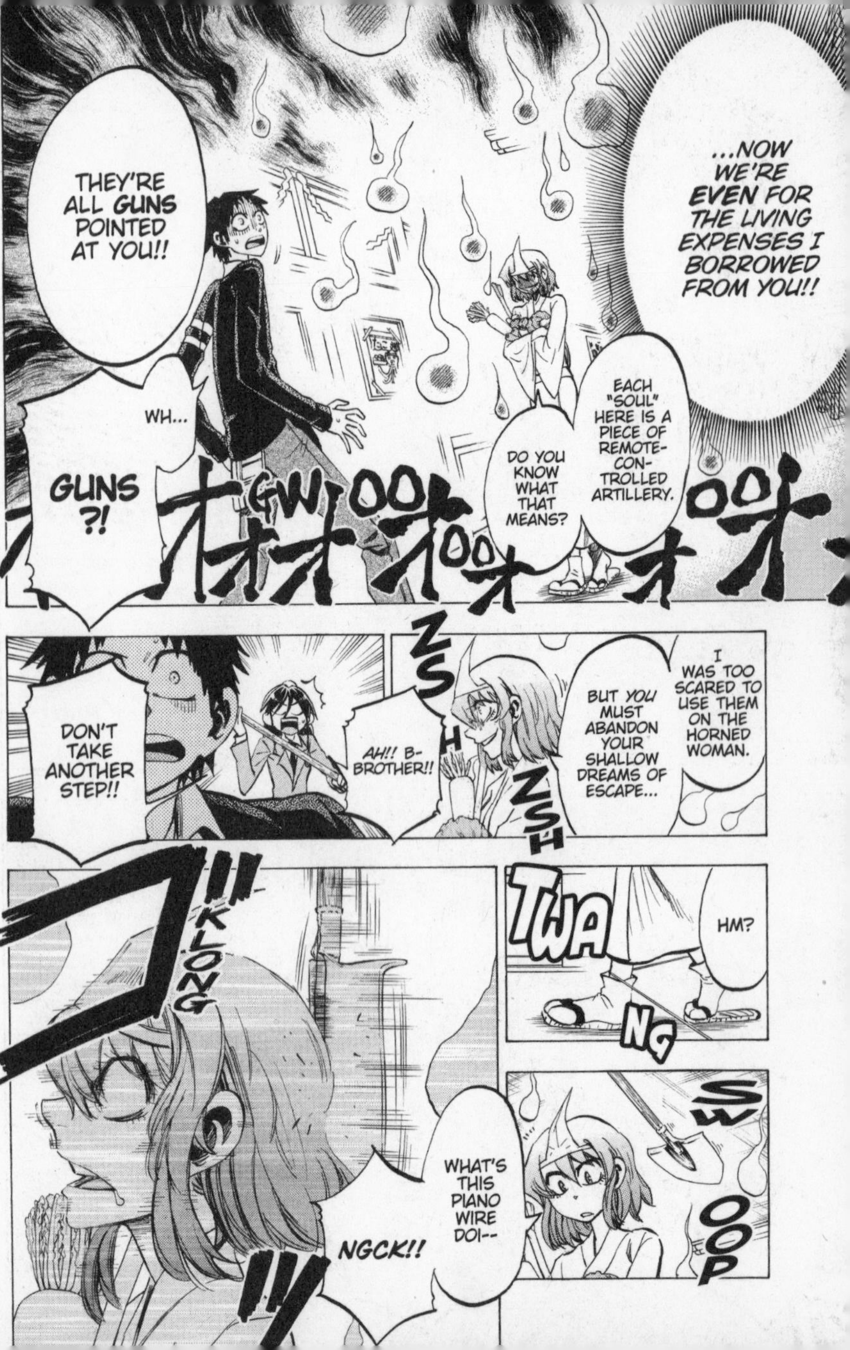
...NOW WE'RE EVEN FOR THE LIVING EXPENSES I BORROWED FROM YOU!!
EACH "SOUL" HERE IS A PIECE OF REMOTE-CONTROLLED ARTILLERY.
DO YOU KNOW WHAT THAT MEANS?
THEY'RE ALL GUNS POINTED AT YOU!!
WH...
GUNS ?!
GWOOOOOO
I WAS TOO SCARED TO USE THEM ON THE HORNED WOMAN.
BUT YOU MUST ABANDON YOUR SHALLOW DREAMS OF ESCAPE...
ZSH ZSH
AH!! B-BROTHER!!
DON'T TAKE ANOTHER STEP!!
HM?
TWANG
SWOOP
WHAT'S THIS PIANO WIRE DOI--
KLONG
NGCK!!

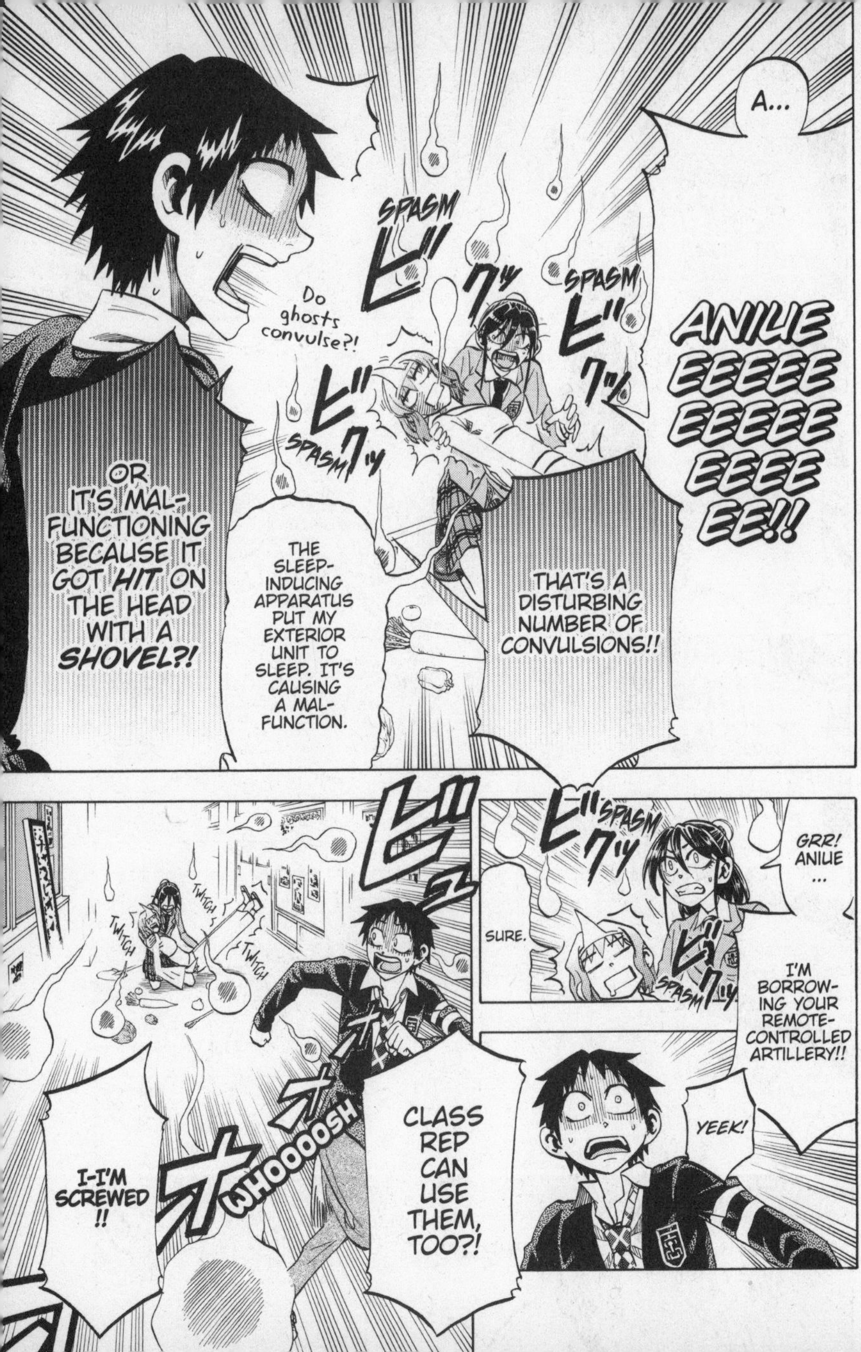
A...
ANIUE EEEEE EEEEE EEEE EE!!
SPASM
THAT'S A DISTURBING NUMBER OF CONVULSIONS!!
SPASM
Do ghosts convulse?!
SPASM
THE SLEEP-INDUCING APPARATUS PUT MY EXTERIOR UNIT TO SLEEP. IT'S CAUSING A MAL-FUNCTION.
OR IT'S MAL-FUNCTIONING BECAUSE IT GOT HIT ON THE HEAD WITH A SHOVEL?!
GRR! ANIUE ...
SPASM
SURE.
SPASM
I'M BORROW-ING YOUR REMOTE-CONTROLLED ARTILLERY!!
YEEK!
CLASS REP CAN USE THEM, TOO?!
WHOOOOSH
TWITCH
TWITCH
TWITCH
I-I'M SCREWED !!

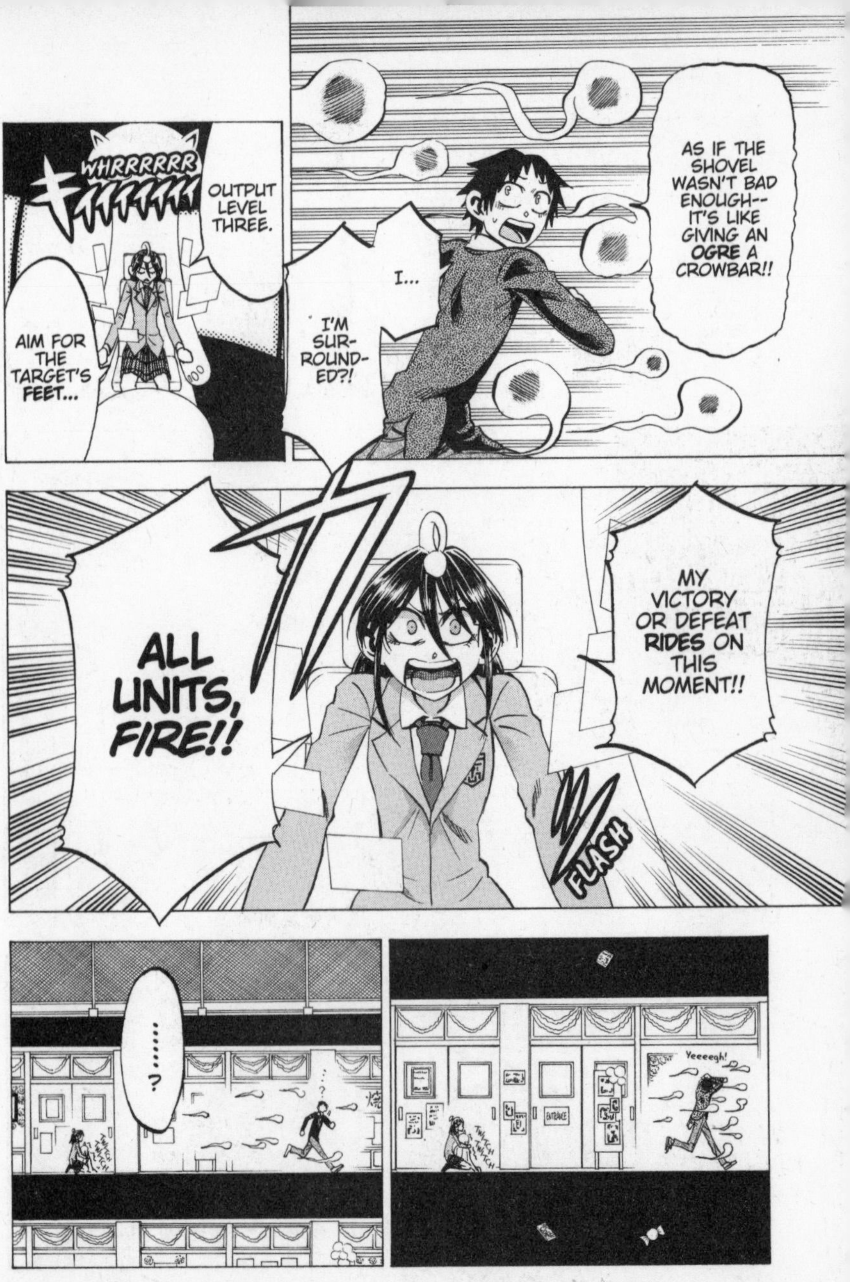
AS IF THE SHOVEL WASN'T BAD ENOUGH-- IT'S LIKE GIVING AN OGRE A CROWBAR!!
I...
I'M SUR-ROUND-ED?!
WHRRRRRR
キイイイイイ
OUTPUT LEVEL THREE.
AIM FOR THE TARGET'S FEET...
MY VICTORY OR DEFEAT RIDES ON THIS MOMENT!!
ALL UNITS, FIRE!!
FLASH
Yeeeegh!
ENTRANCE
TWITCH TWITCH
......?
...?
TWITCH TWITCH

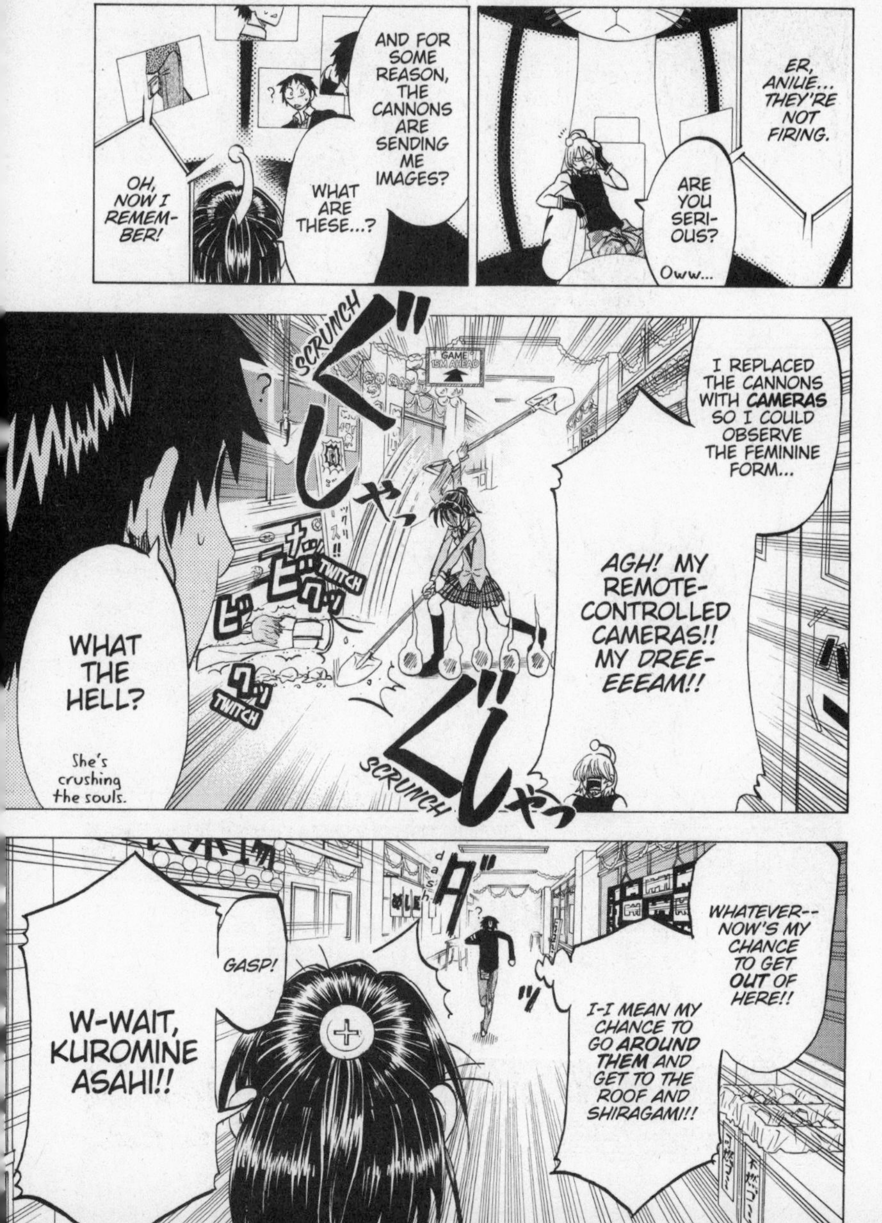
ER, ANIUE... THEY'RE NOT FIRING.
ARE YOU SERIOUS?
Oww...
AND FOR SOME REASON, THE CANNONS ARE SENDING ME IMAGES?
WHAT ARE THESE...?
OH, NOW I REMEMBER!
I REPLACED THE CANNONS WITH CAMERAS SO I COULD OBSERVE THE FEMININE FORM...
AGH! MY REMOTE-CONTROLLED CAMERAS!! MY DREE-EEEAM!!
SCRUNCH
GAME 15M AHEAD
TWITCH
TWITCH
SCRUNCH
WHAT THE HELL?
She's crushing the souls.
WHATEVER--NOW'S MY CHANCE TO GET OUT OF HERE!!
I-I MEAN MY CHANCE TO GO AROUND THEM AND GET TO THE ROOF AND SHIRAGAMI!!
dash
GASP!
W-WAIT, KUROMINE ASAHI!!

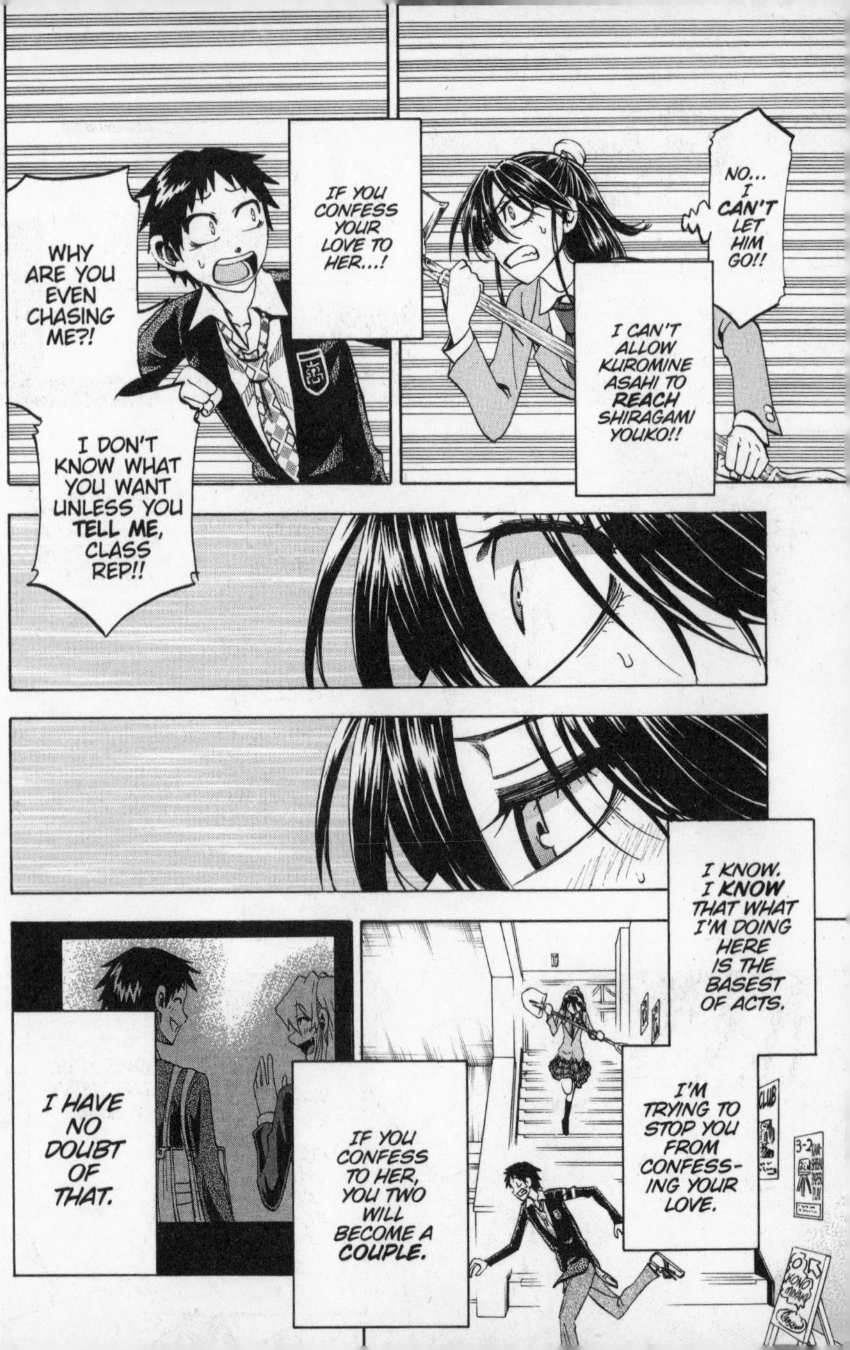
NO... I CAN'T LET HIM GO!!
I CAN'T ALLOW KUROMINE ASAHI TO REACH SHIRAGAMI YOUKO!!
IF YOU CONFESS YOUR LOVE TO HER...!
WHY ARE YOU EVEN CHASING ME?!
I DON'T KNOW WHAT YOU WANT UNLESS YOU TELL ME, CLASS REP!!
I KNOW. I KNOW THAT WHAT I'M DOING HERE IS THE BASEST OF ACTS.
I'M TRYING TO STOP YOU FROM CONFESS-ING YOUR LOVE.
CLUB
3-2
IF YOU CONFESS TO HER, YOU TWO WILL BECOME A COUPLE.
I HAVE NO DOUBT OF THAT.

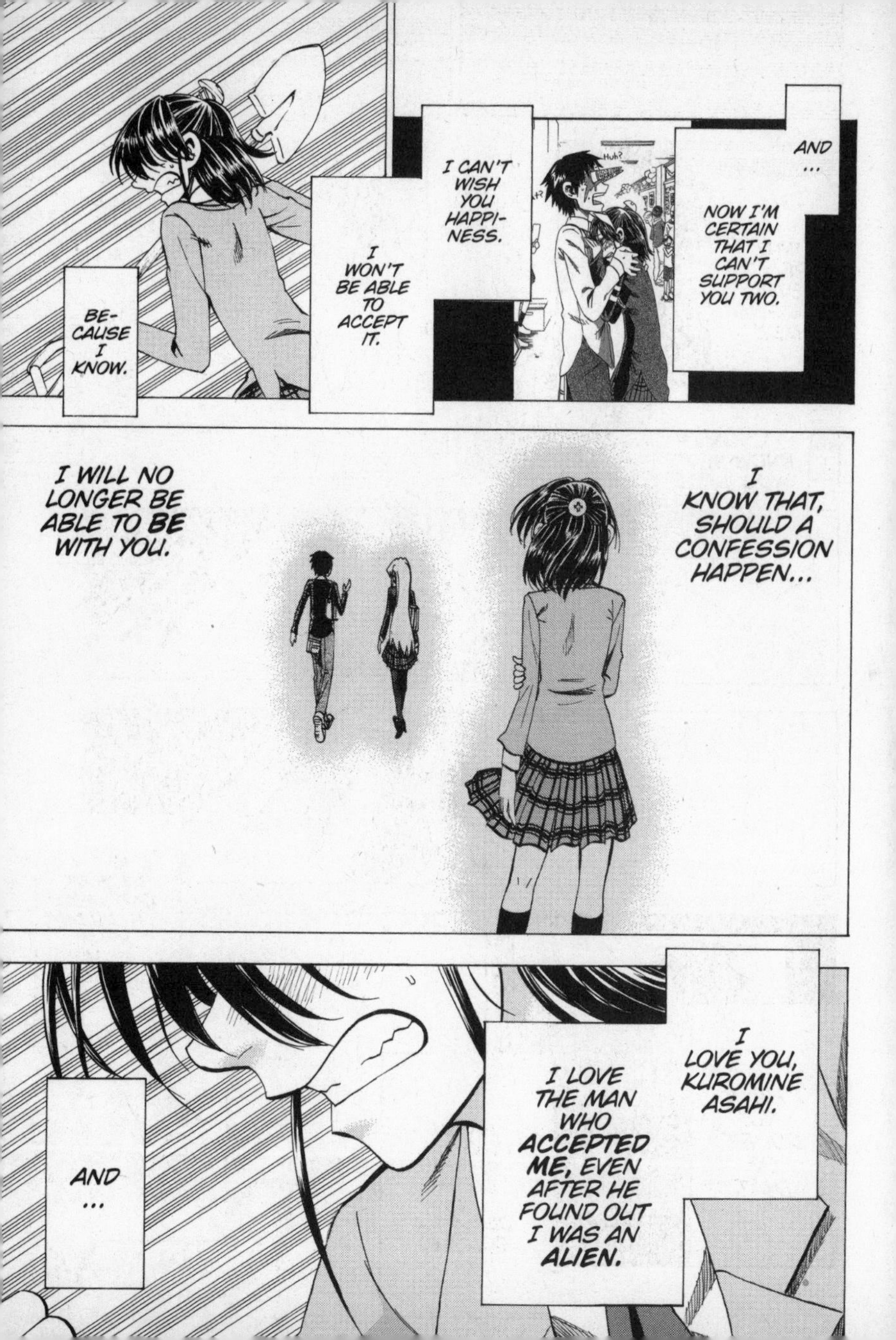
AND ...
NOW I'M CERTAIN THAT I CAN'T SUPPORT YOU TWO.
Huh?
I CAN'T WISH YOU HAPPI-NESS.
I WON'T BE ABLE TO ACCEPT IT.
BE-CAUSE I KNOW.
I KNOW THAT, SHOULD A CONFESSION HAPPEN...
I WILL NO LONGER BE ABLE TO BE WITH YOU.
I LOVE YOU, KUROMINE ASAHI.
I LOVE THE MAN WHO ACCEPTED ME, EVEN AFTER HE FOUND OUT I WAS AN ALIEN.
AND ...

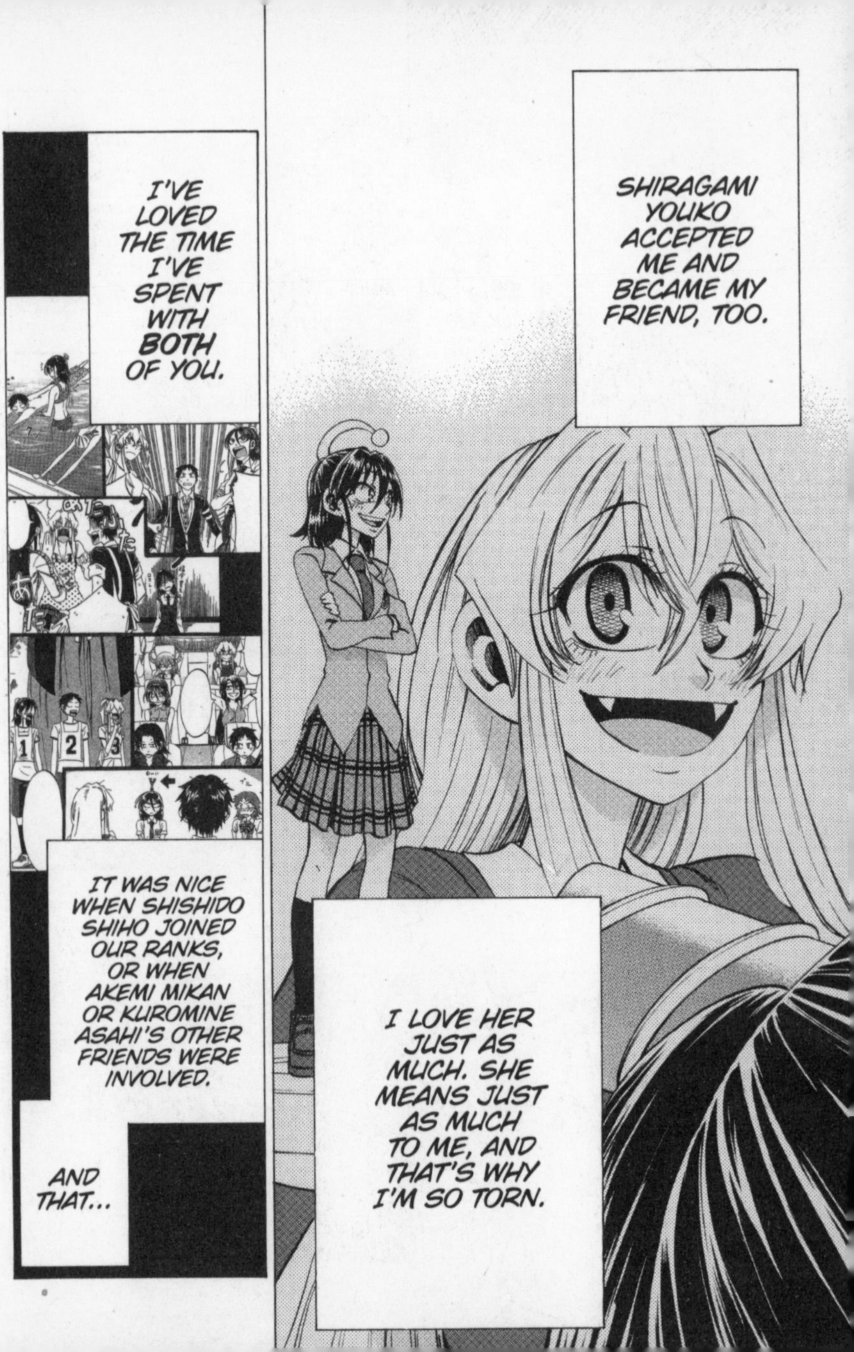
SHIRAGAMI YOUKO ACCEPTED ME AND BECAME MY FRIEND, TOO.
I LOVE HER JUST AS MUCH. SHE MEANS JUST AS MUCH TO ME, AND THAT'S WHY I'M SO TORN.
I'VE LOVED THE TIME I'VE SPENT WITH BOTH OF YOU.
1
2
3
IT WAS NICE WHEN SHISHIDO SHIHO JOINED OUR RANKS, OR WHEN AKEMI MIKAN OR KUROMINE ASAHI'S OTHER FRIENDS WERE INVOLVED.
AND THAT...

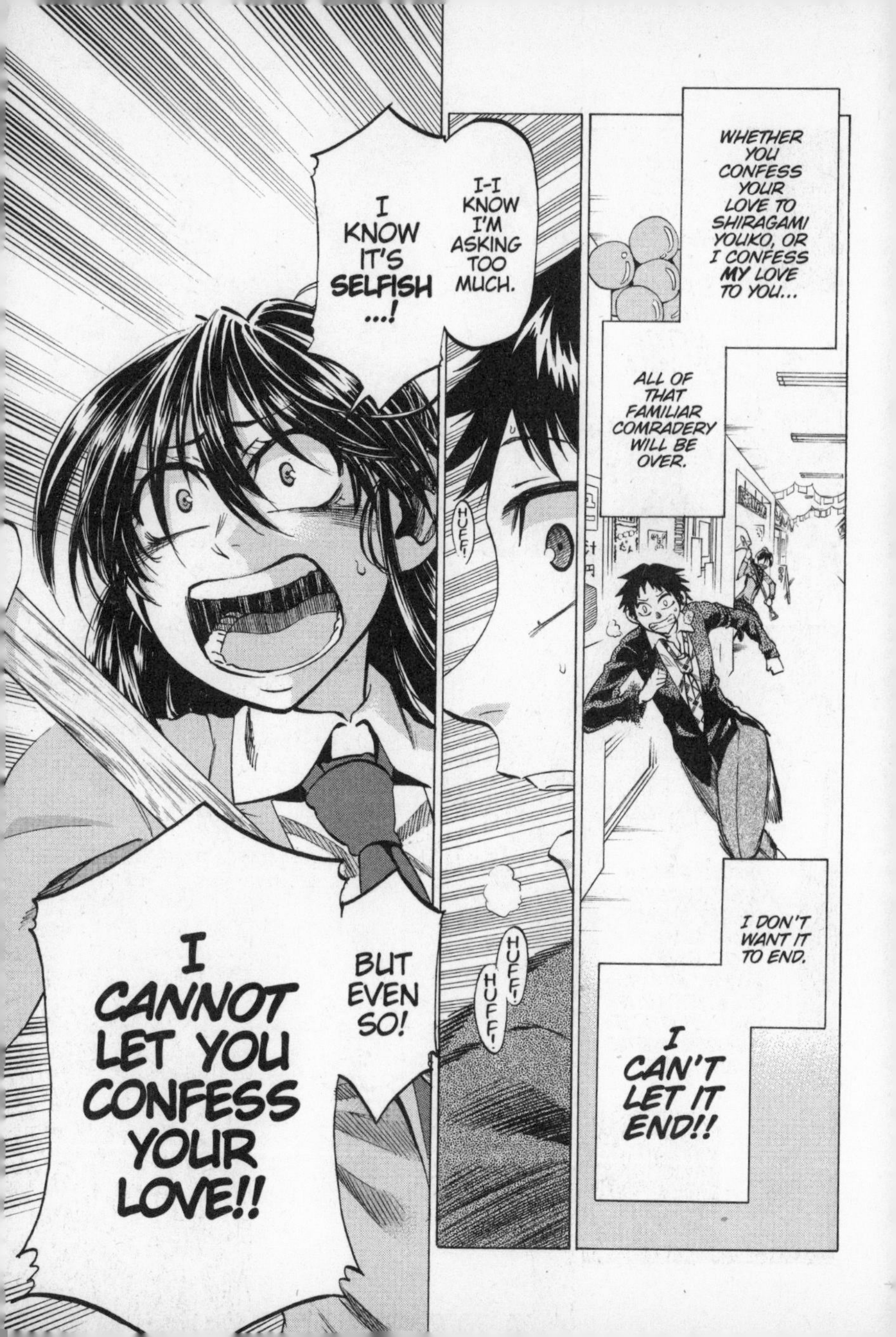
WHETHER YOU CONFESS YOUR LOVE TO SHIRAGAMI YOUKO, OR I CONFESS MY LOVE TO YOU...
ALL OF THAT FAMILIAR COMRADERY WILL BE OVER.
I DON'T WANT IT TO END.
I CAN'T LET IT END!!
I-I KNOW I'M ASKING TOO MUCH.
I KNOW IT'S SELFISH...!
HUFF!
HUFF! HUFF!
BUT EVEN SO!
I CANNOT LET YOU CONFESS YOUR LOVE!!

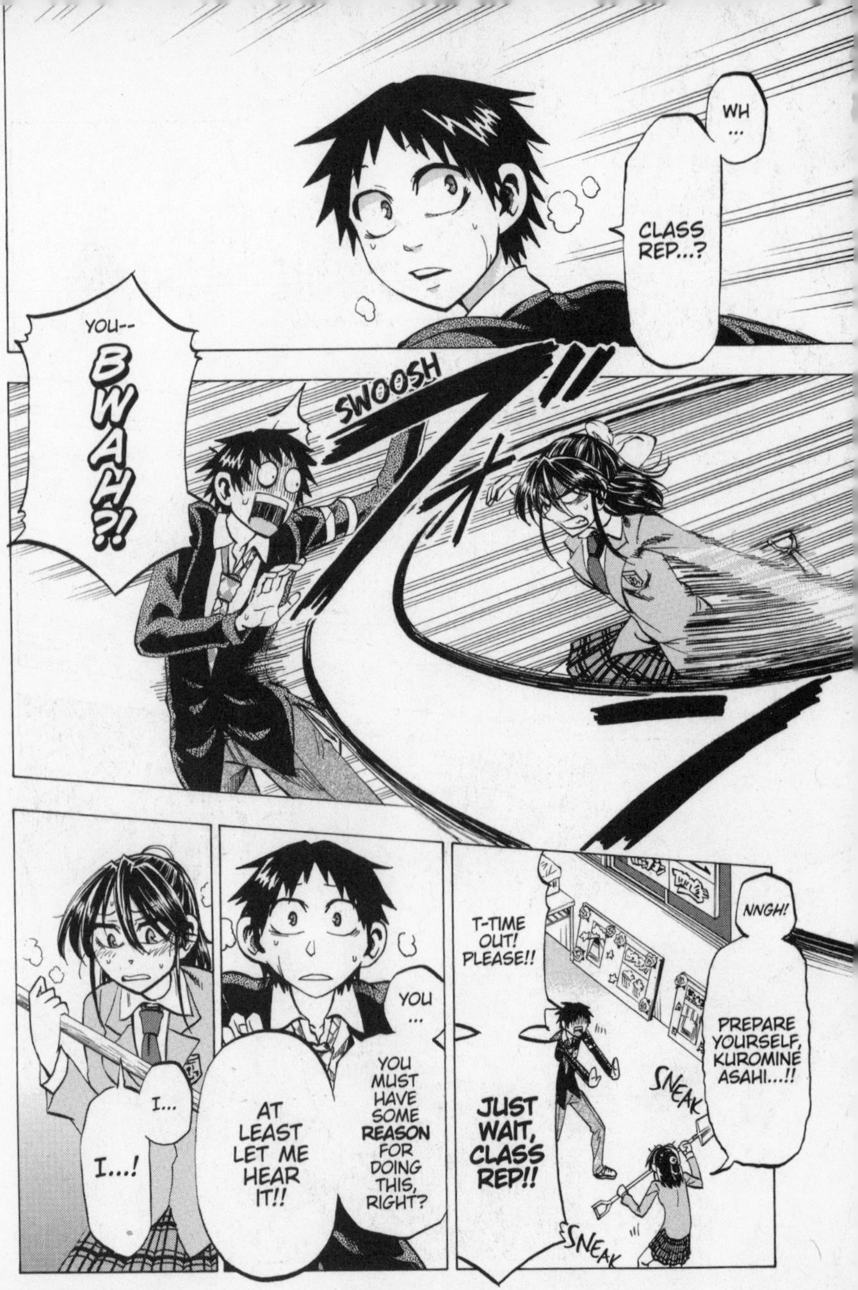
WH ...
CLASS REP...?
SWOOSH
YOU-- BWAH?!
NNGH!
PREPARE YOURSELF, KUROMINE ASAHI...!!
SNEAK
T-TIME OUT! PLEASE!!
JUST WAIT, CLASS REP!!
SNEAK
YOU ...
YOU MUST HAVE SOME REASON FOR DOING THIS, RIGHT?
AT LEAST LET ME HEAR IT!!
I...
I...!

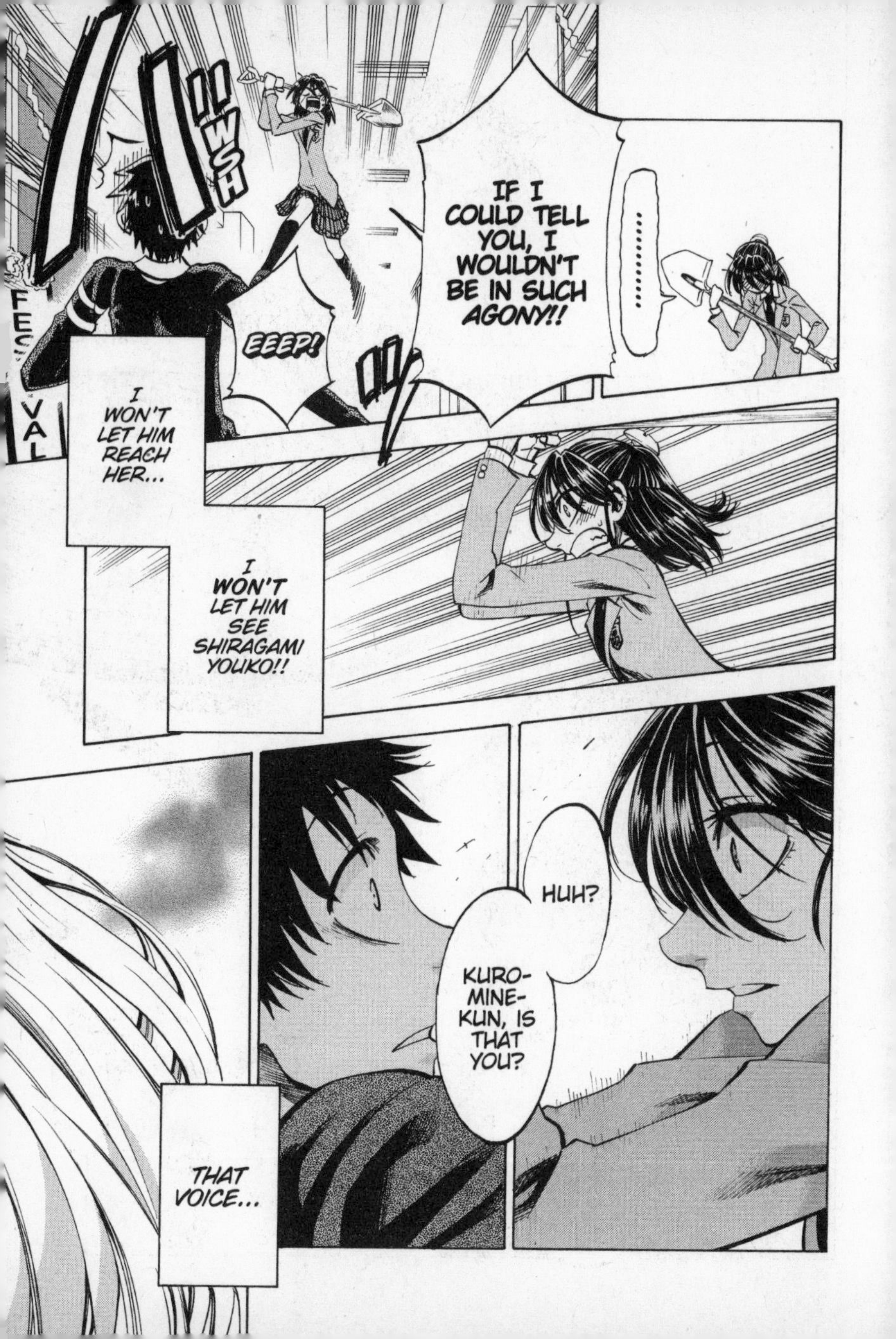
......
IF I COULD TELL YOU, I WOULDN'T BE IN SUCH AGONY!!
WSH
EEEP!
I WON'T LET HIM REACH HER...
I WON'T LET HIM SEE SHIRAGAMI YOUKO!!
HUH?
KURO-MINE-KUN, IS THAT YOU?
THAT VOICE...

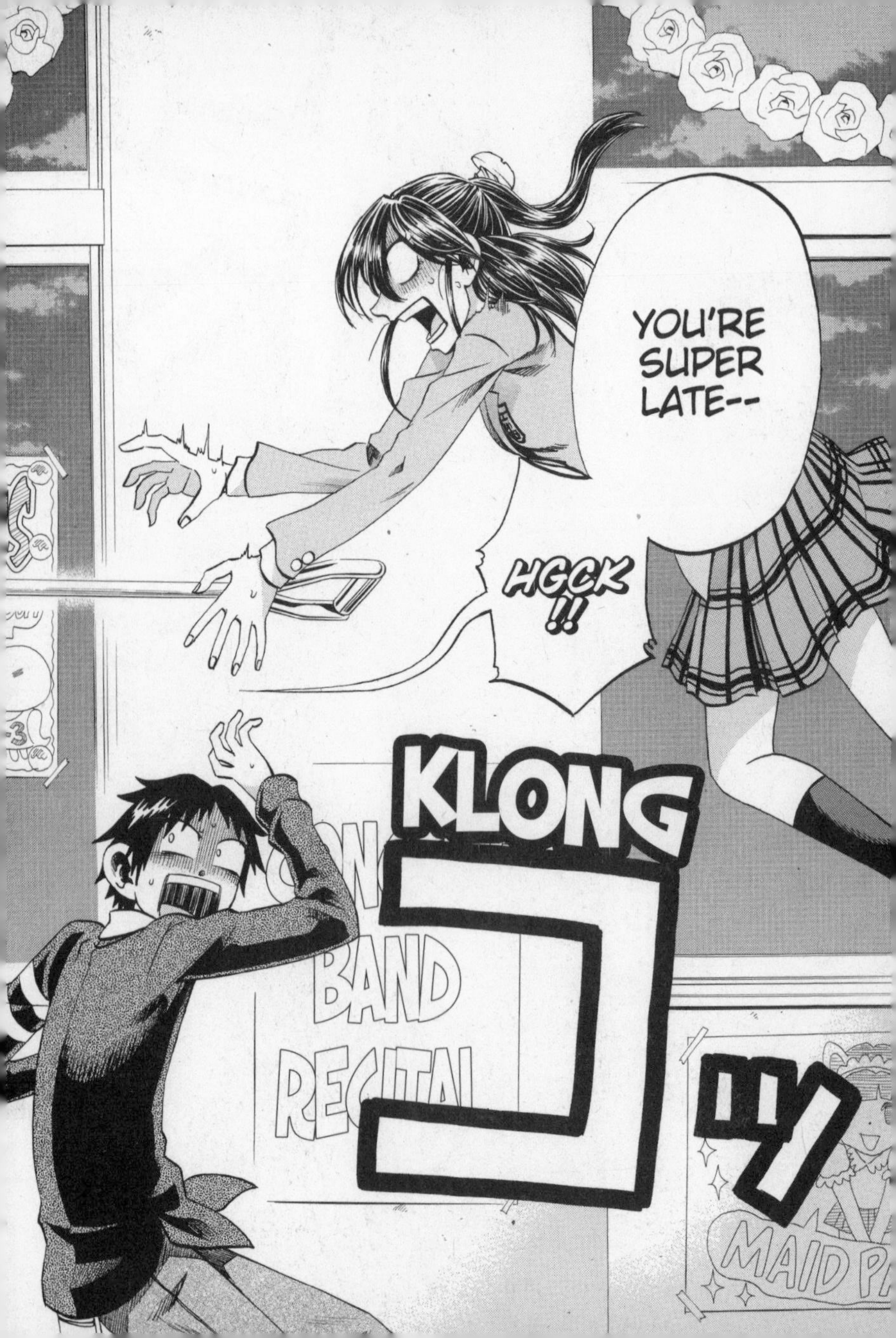
YOU'RE SUPER LATE--
HGCK !!
KLONG
BAND RECITAL
MAID PA

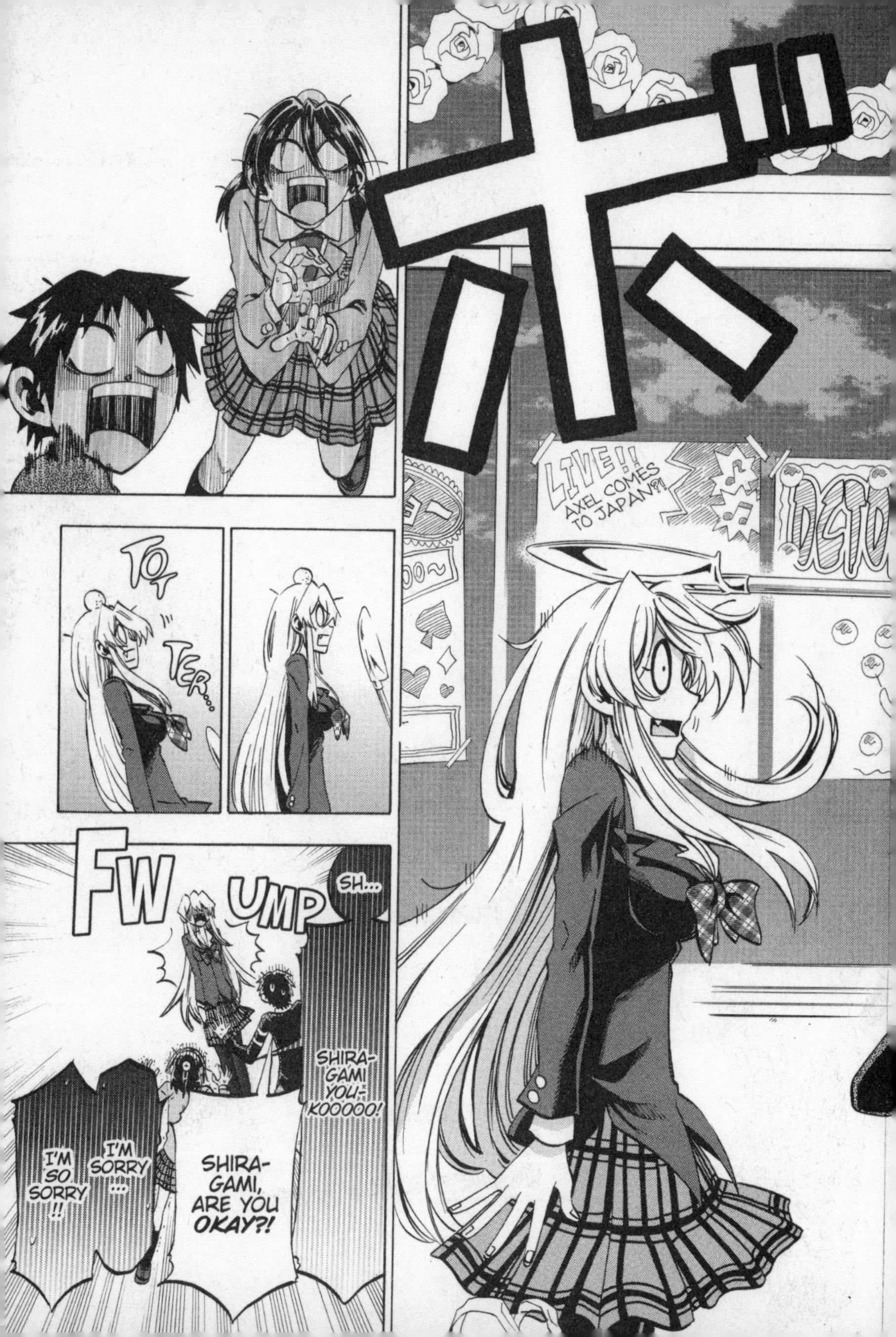
LIVE!!
AXEL COMES TO JAPAN?!
TOT
TER...
FW
UMP
SH...
SHIRA-GAMI YOU-KOOOOO!
SHIRA-GAMI, ARE YOU OKAY?!
I'M SORRY...
I'M SO SORRY!!

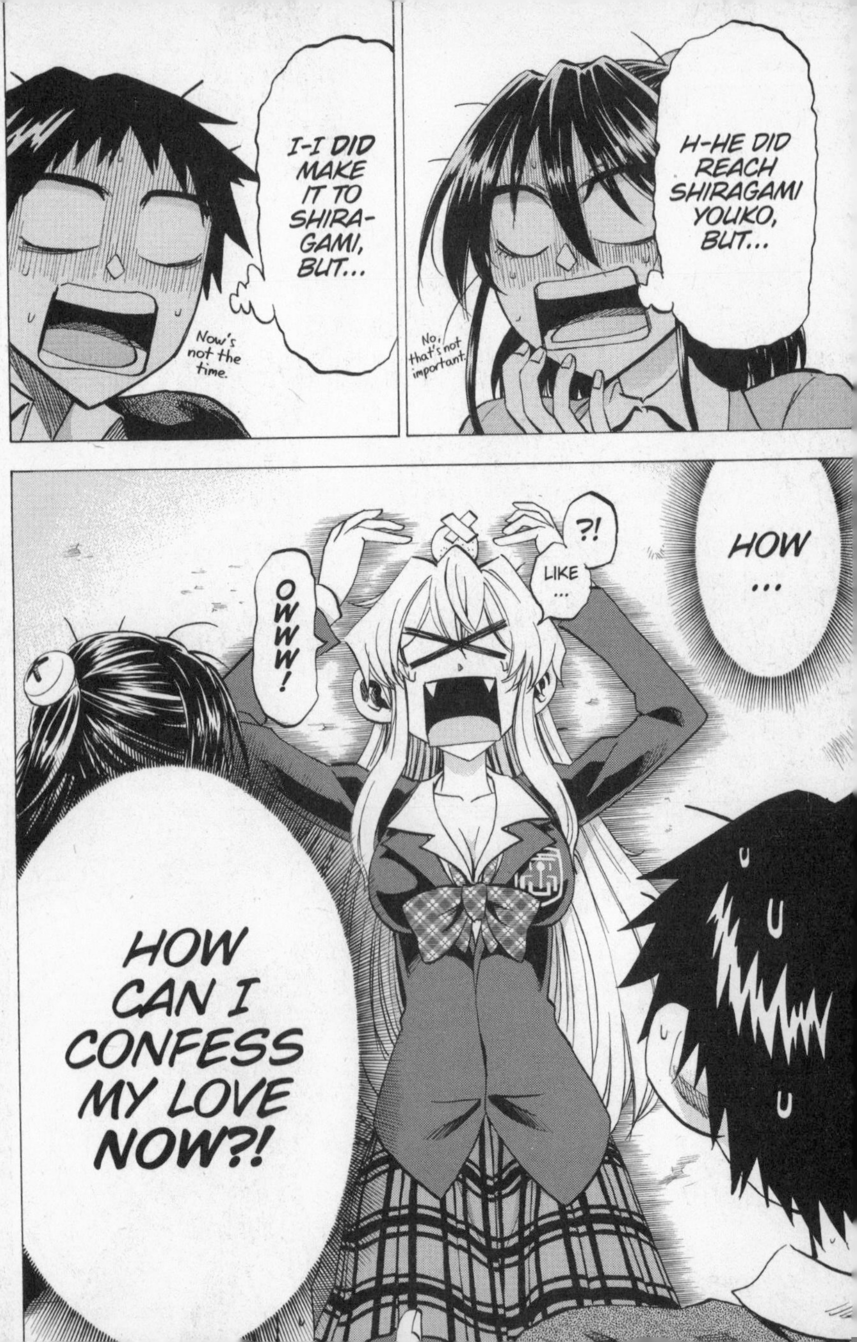
H-HE DID REACH SHIRAGAMI YOUKO, BUT...
No, that's not important.
I-I DID MAKE IT TO SHIRA-GAMI, BUT...
Now's not the time.
HOW ...
?!
LIKE ...
OWWW!
HOW CAN I CONFESS MY LOVE NOW?!

Chapter 47: "Let's Confess Our Love!!"

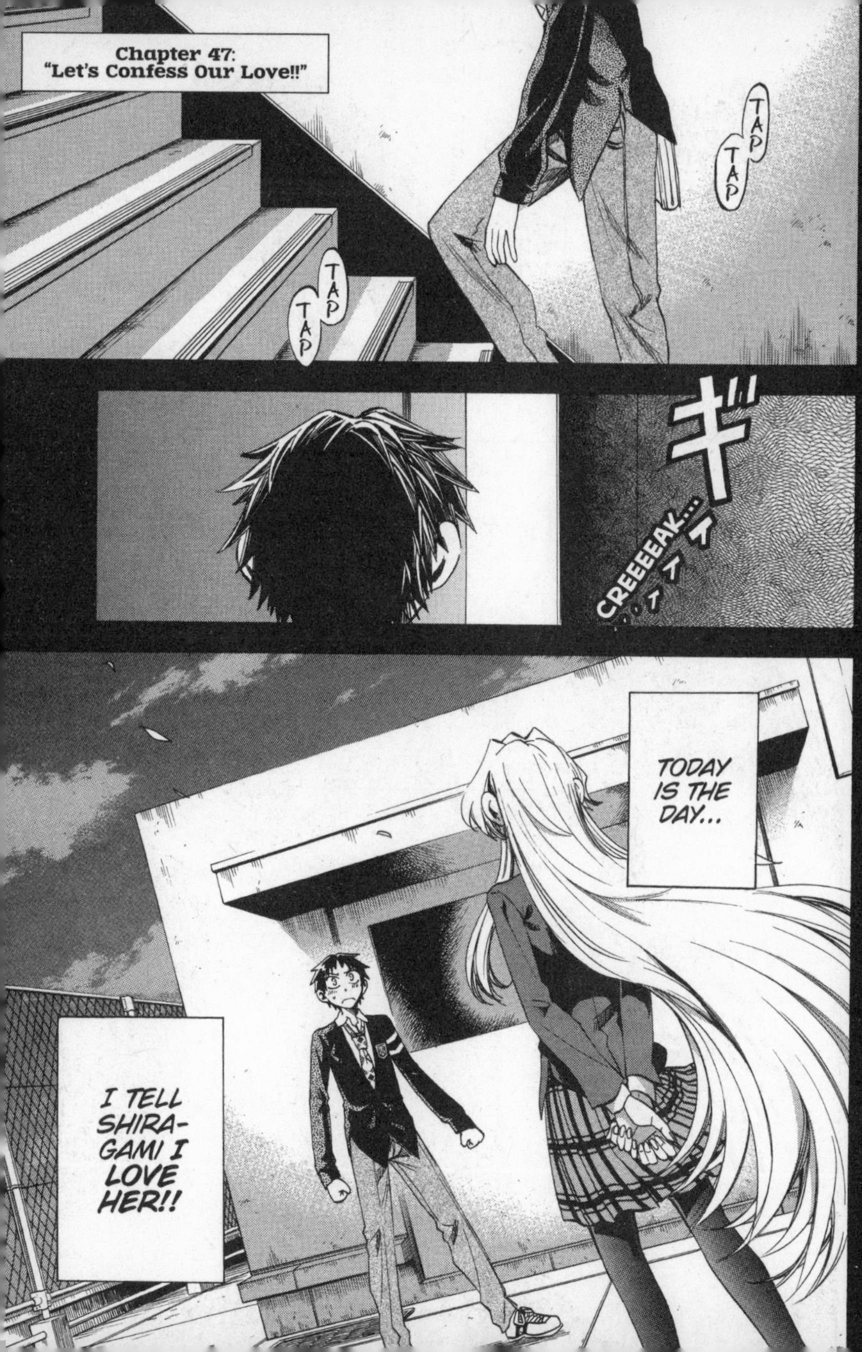
TAP TAP
TAP TAP
ギィィィ…
CREEEEAK…
TODAY IS THE DAY...
I TELL SHIRAGAMI I LOVE HER!!

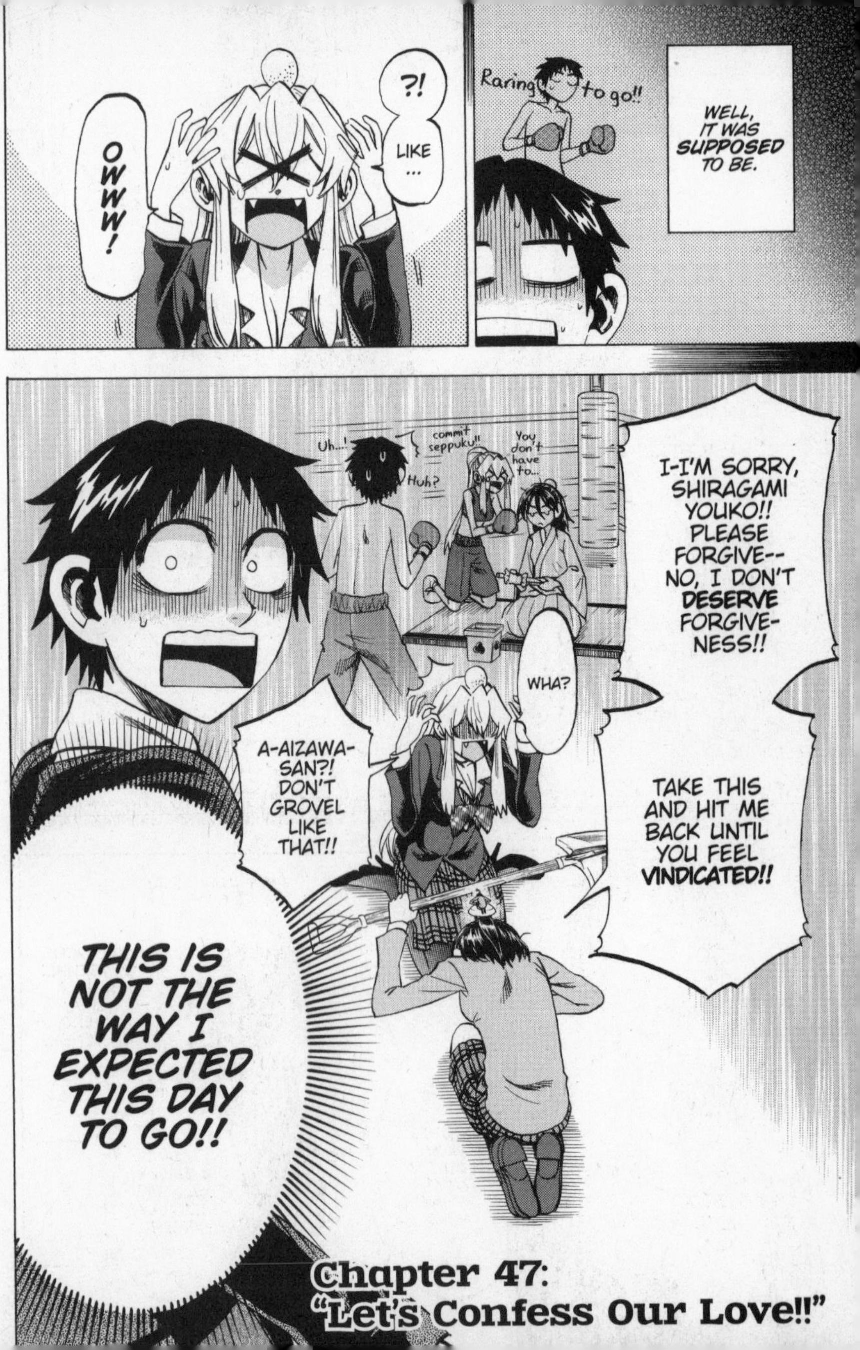
WELL, IT WAS SUPPOSED TO BE.
Raring to go!!
?!
LIKE ...
OWWW!
I-I'M SORRY, SHIRAGAMI YOUKO!! PLEASE FORGIVE-- NO, I DON'T DESERVE FORGIVENESS!!
TAKE THIS AND HIT ME BACK UNTIL YOU FEEL VINDICATED!!
You don't have to...
commit seppuku!!
Uh...!
Huh?
WHA?
A-AIZAWA-SAN?! DON'T GROVEL LIKE THAT!!
THIS IS NOT THE WAY I EXPECTED THIS DAY TO GO!!
Chapter 47: "Let's Confess Our Love!!"

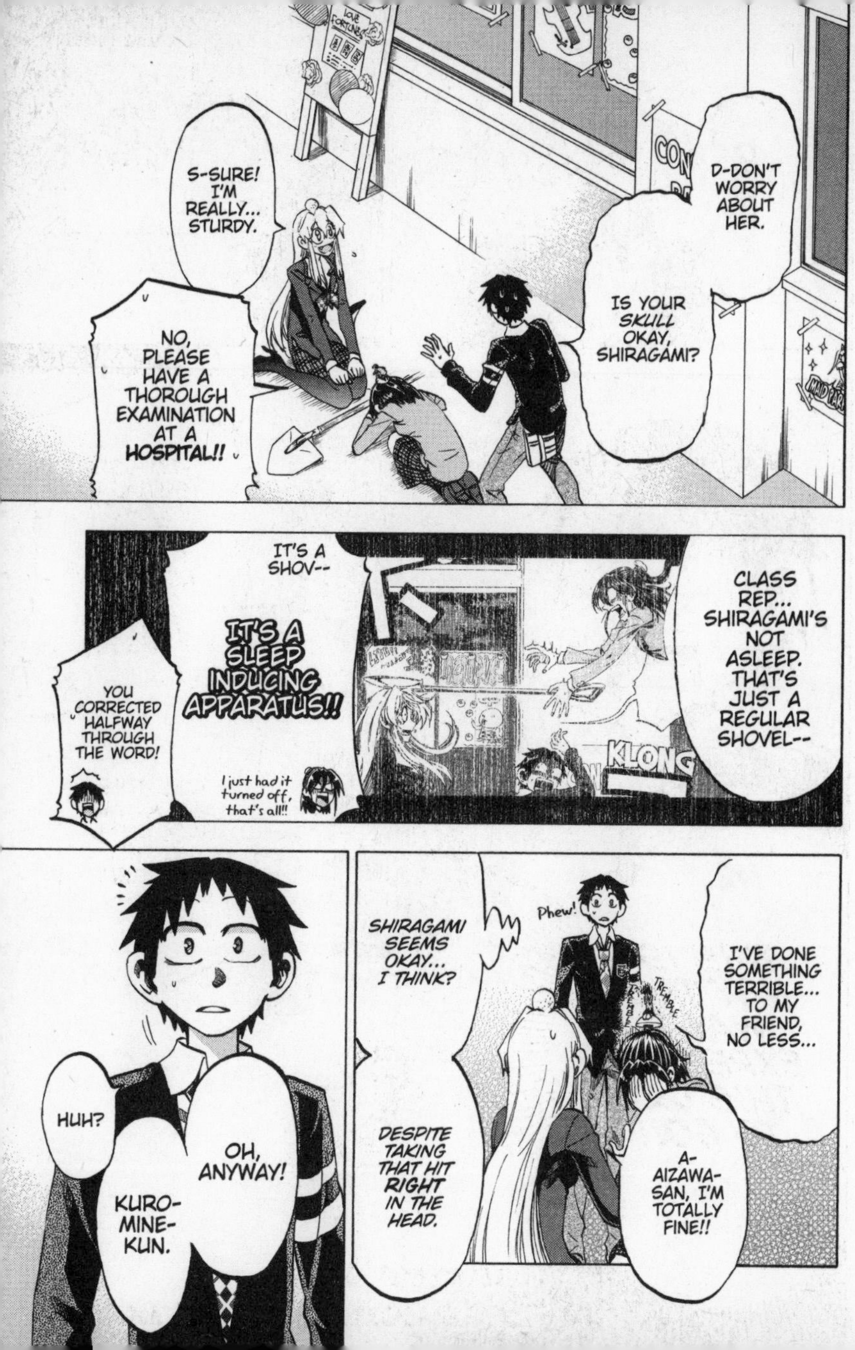
D-DON'T WORRY ABOUT HER.
IS YOUR SKULL OKAY, SHIRAGAMI?
S-SURE! I'M REALLY... STURDY.
NO, PLEASE HAVE A THOROUGH EXAMINATION AT A HOSPITAL!!
CLASS REP... SHIRAGAMI'S NOT ASLEEP. THAT'S JUST A REGULAR SHOVEL--
KLONG
IT'S A SHOV--
IT'S A SLEEP INDUCING APPARATUS!!
I just had it turned off, that's all!!
YOU CORRECTED HALFWAY THROUGH THE WORD!
I'VE DONE SOMETHING TERRIBLE... TO MY FRIEND, NO LESS...
TREMBLE
TREMBLE
Phew!
SHIRAGAMI SEEMS OKAY... I THINK?
A-AIZAWA-SAN, I'M TOTALLY FINE!!
DESPITE TAKING THAT HIT RIGHT IN THE HEAD.
OH, ANYWAY!
KURO-MINE-KUN.
HUH?

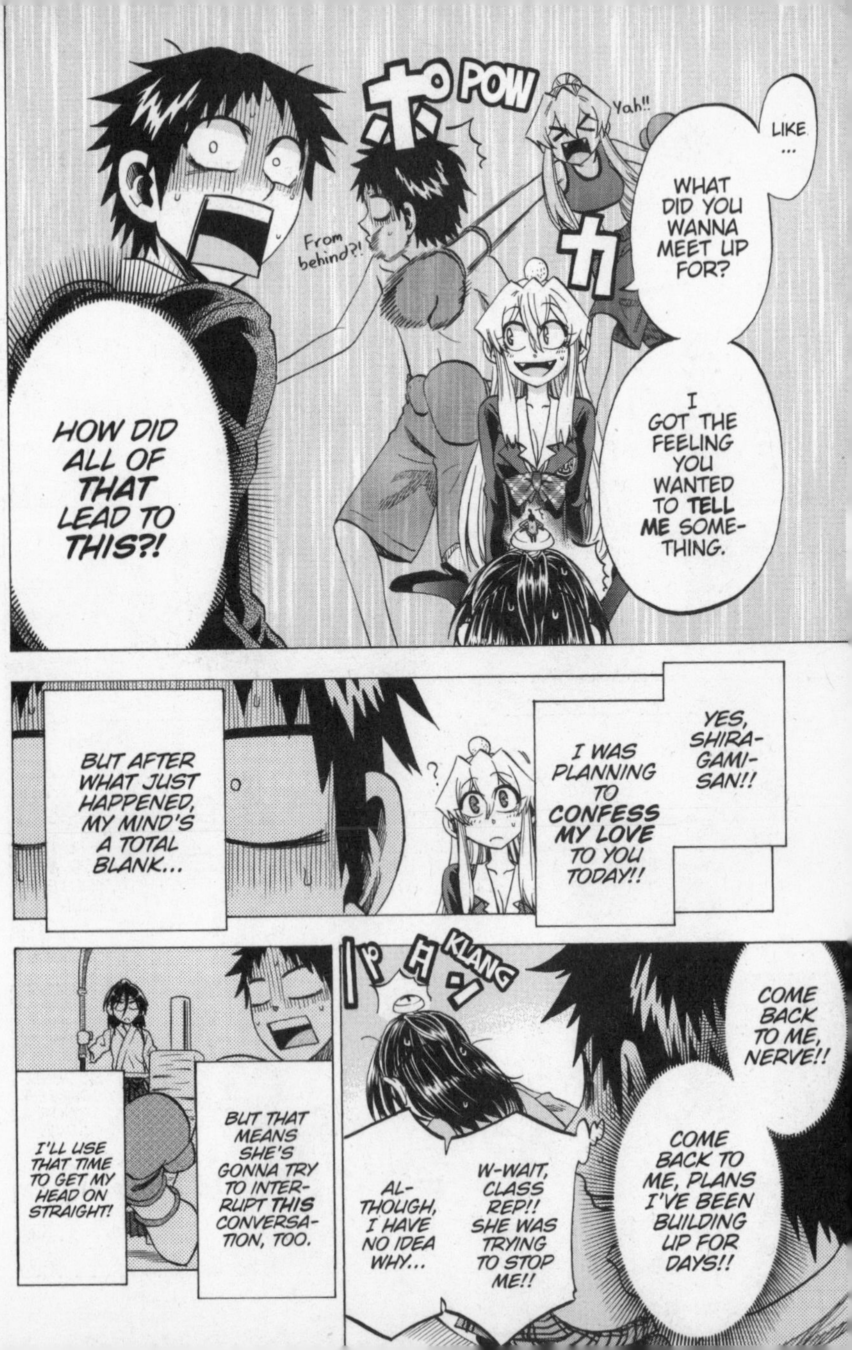
LIKE...
WHAT DID YOU WANNA MEET UP FOR?
Yah!!
POW
From behind?!
I GOT THE FEELING YOU WANTED TO TELL ME SOMETHING.
HOW DID ALL OF THAT LEAD TO THIS?!
YES, SHIRAGAMI-SAN!!
I WAS PLANNING TO CONFESS MY LOVE TO YOU TODAY!!
BUT AFTER WHAT JUST HAPPENED, MY MIND'S A TOTAL BLANK...
COME BACK TO ME, NERVE!!
COME BACK TO ME, PLANS I'VE BEEN BUILDING UP FOR DAYS!!
KLANG
W-WAIT, CLASS REP!! SHE WAS TRYING TO STOP ME!!
ALTHOUGH, I HAVE NO IDEA WHY...
BUT THAT MEANS SHE'S GONNA TRY TO INTERRUPT THIS CONVERSATION, TOO.
I'LL USE THAT TIME TO GET MY HEAD ON STRAIGHT!

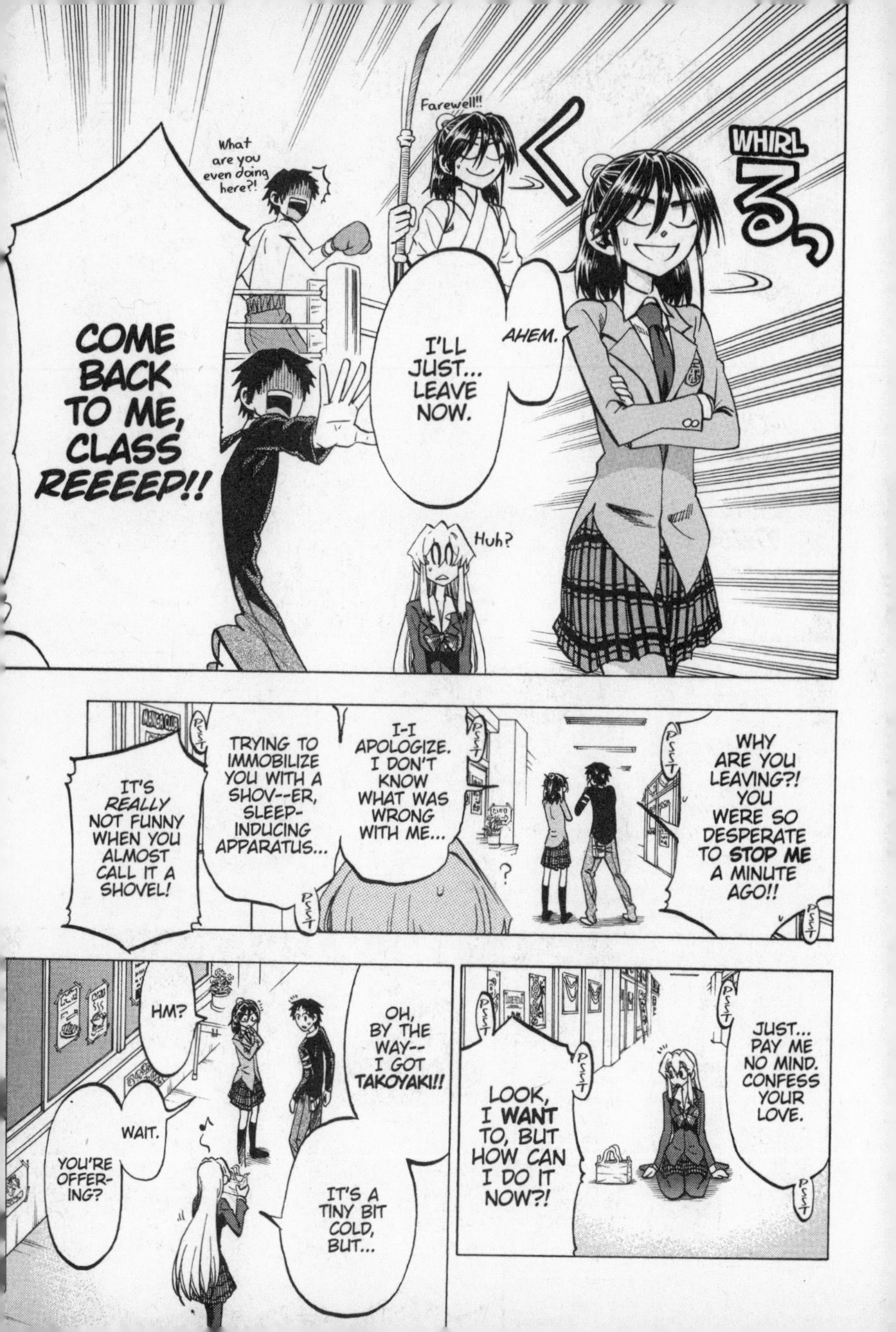
WHIRL
AHEM.
I'LL JUST... LEAVE NOW.
Farewell!!
What are you even doing here?!
Huh?
COME BACK TO ME, CLASS REEEEP!!
PSST
WHY ARE YOU LEAVING?! YOU WERE SO DESPERATE TO STOP ME A MINUTE AGO!!
PSST
I-I APOLOGIZE. I DON'T KNOW WHAT WAS WRONG WITH ME...
PSST
TRYING TO IMMOBILIZE YOU WITH A SHOV--ER, SLEEP-INDUCING APPARATUS...
PSST
IT'S REALLY NOT FUNNY WHEN YOU ALMOST CALL IT A SHOVEL!
PSST
JUST... PAY ME NO MIND. CONFESS YOUR LOVE.
PSST
LOOK, I WANT TO, BUT HOW CAN I DO IT NOW?!
PSST
OH, BY THE WAY-- I GOT TAKOYAKI!!
HM?
IT'S A TINY BIT COLD, BUT...
WAIT.
YOU'RE OFFERING?

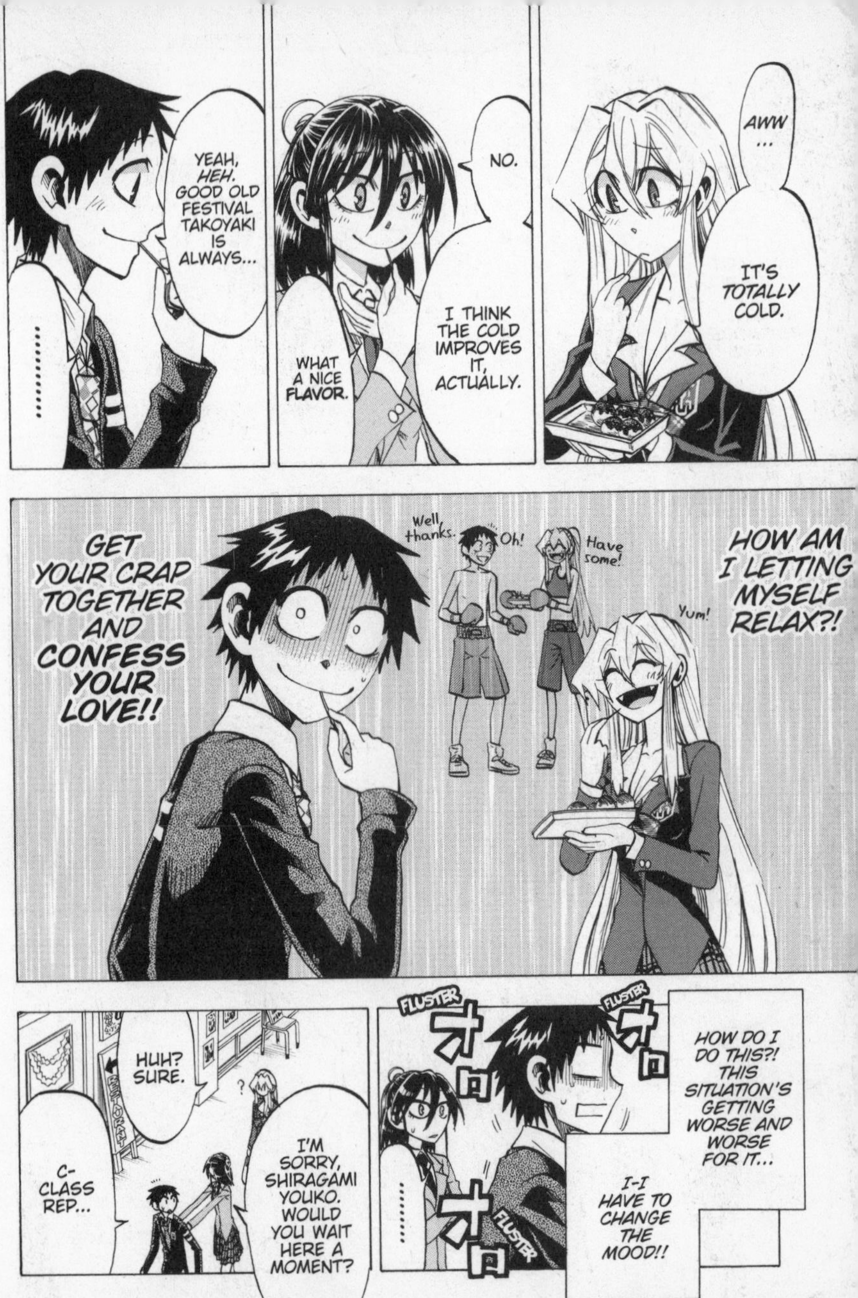
AWW...
IT'S TOTALLY COLD.
NO.
I THINK THE COLD IMPROVES IT, ACTUALLY.
WHAT A NICE FLAVOR.
YEAH, HEH. GOOD OLD FESTIVAL TAKOYAKI IS ALWAYS...
......
HOW AM I LETTING MYSELF RELAX?!
Have some!
Oh!
Well thanks.
Yum!
GET YOUR CRAP TOGETHER AND CONFESS YOUR LOVE!!
FLUSTER
FLUSTER
HOW DO I DO THIS?! THIS SITUATION'S GETTING WORSE AND WORSE FOR IT...
I-I HAVE TO CHANGE THE MOOD!!
FLUSTER
......
I'M SORRY, SHIRAGAMI YOUKO. WOULD YOU WAIT HERE A MOMENT?
HUH? SURE.
?
C-CLASS REP...

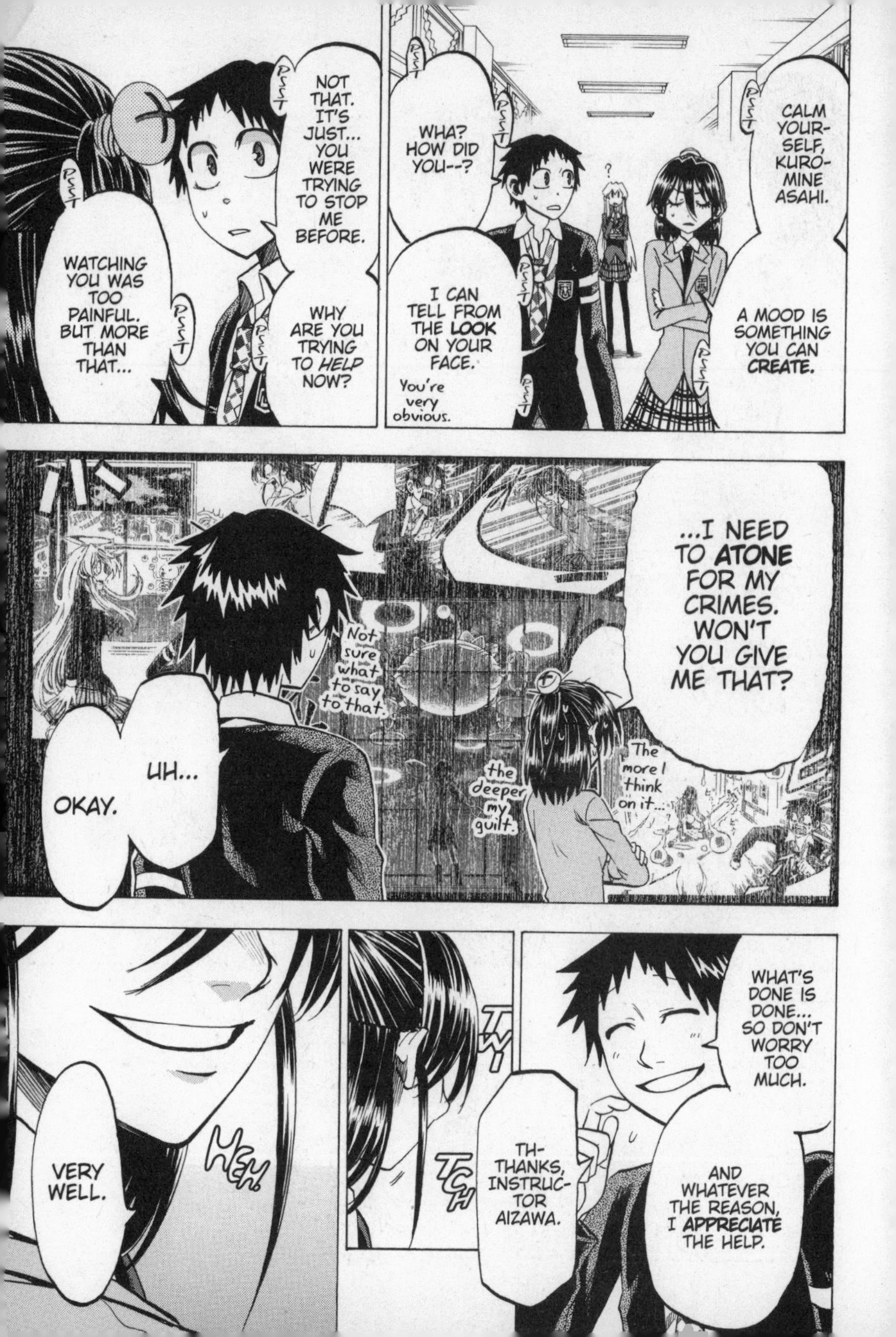

PSST
CALM YOURSELF, KUROMINE ASAHI.
PSST
A MOOD IS SOMETHING YOU CAN CREATE.
PSST
WHA? HOW DID YOU--?
PSST
I CAN TELL FROM THE LOOK ON YOUR FACE.
You're very obvious.
PSST
NOT THAT. IT'S JUST... YOU WERE TRYING TO STOP ME BEFORE.
PSST
WHY ARE YOU TRYING TO HELP NOW?
PSST
WATCHING YOU WAS TOO PAINFUL. BUT MORE THAN THAT...
...I NEED TO ATONE FOR MY CRIMES. WON'T YOU GIVE ME THAT?
The more I think on it...
the deeper my guilt.
Not sure what to say to that.
UH...
OKAY.
WHAT'S DONE IS DONE... SO DON'T WORRY TOO MUCH.
AND WHATEVER THE REASON, I APPRECIATE THE HELP.
TWI
TCH
TH-THANKS, INSTRUCTOR AIZAWA.
HEH
VERY WELL.

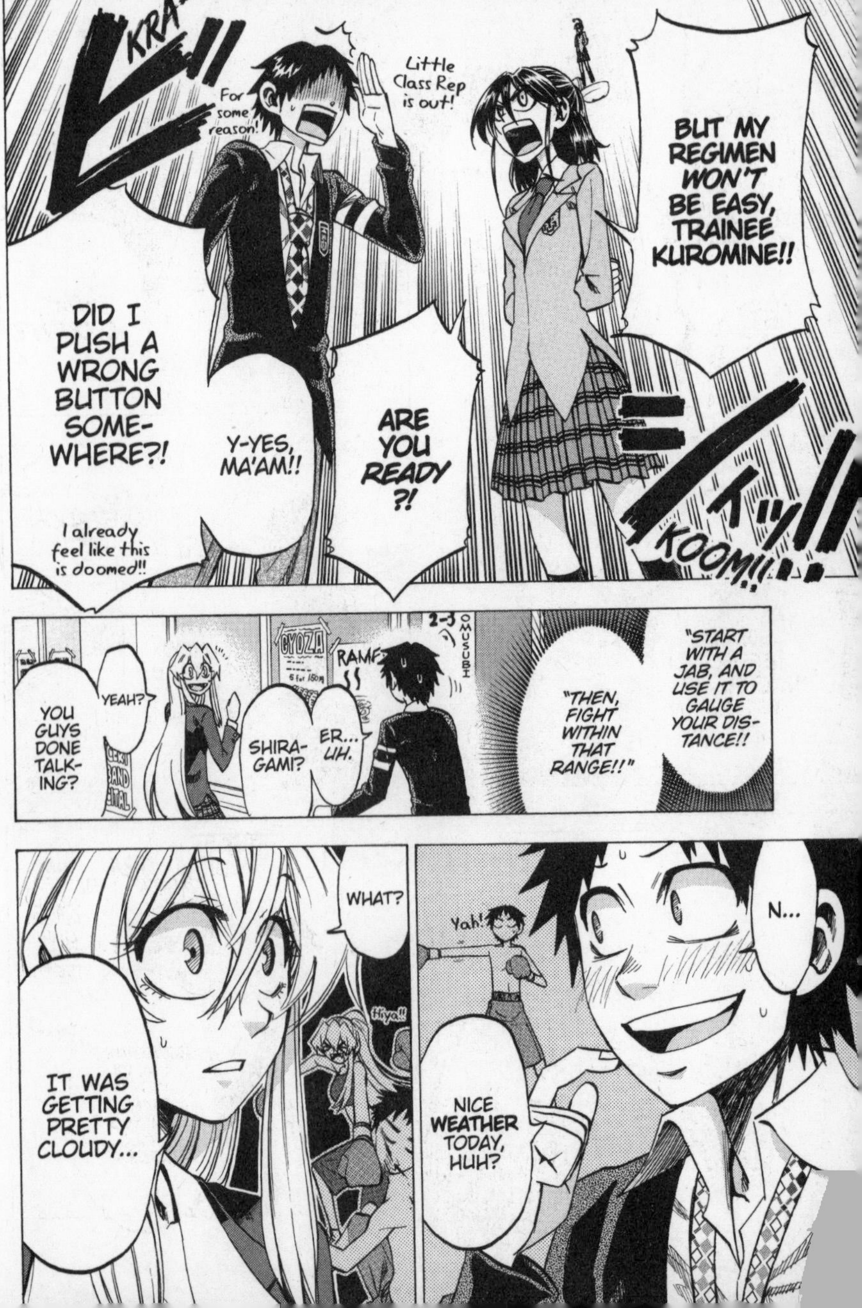
BUT MY REGIMEN WON'T BE EASY, TRAINEE KUROMINE!!
KOOM!!
Little Class Rep is out!
For some reason!
KRA-
ARE YOU READY?!
Y-YES, MA'AM!!
DID I PUSH A WRONG BUTTON SOME-WHERE?!
I already feel like this is doomed!!
"START WITH A JAB, AND USE IT TO GAUGE YOUR DIS-TANCE!!
"THEN, FIGHT WITHIN THAT RANGE!!"
2-3
OMUSUBI
GYOZA
ER... UH.
SHIRAGAMI?
YEAH?
YOU GUYS DONE TALK-ING?
N...
Yah!
NICE WEATHER TODAY, HUH?
WHAT?
Hiya!!
IT WAS GETTING PRETTY CLOUDY...

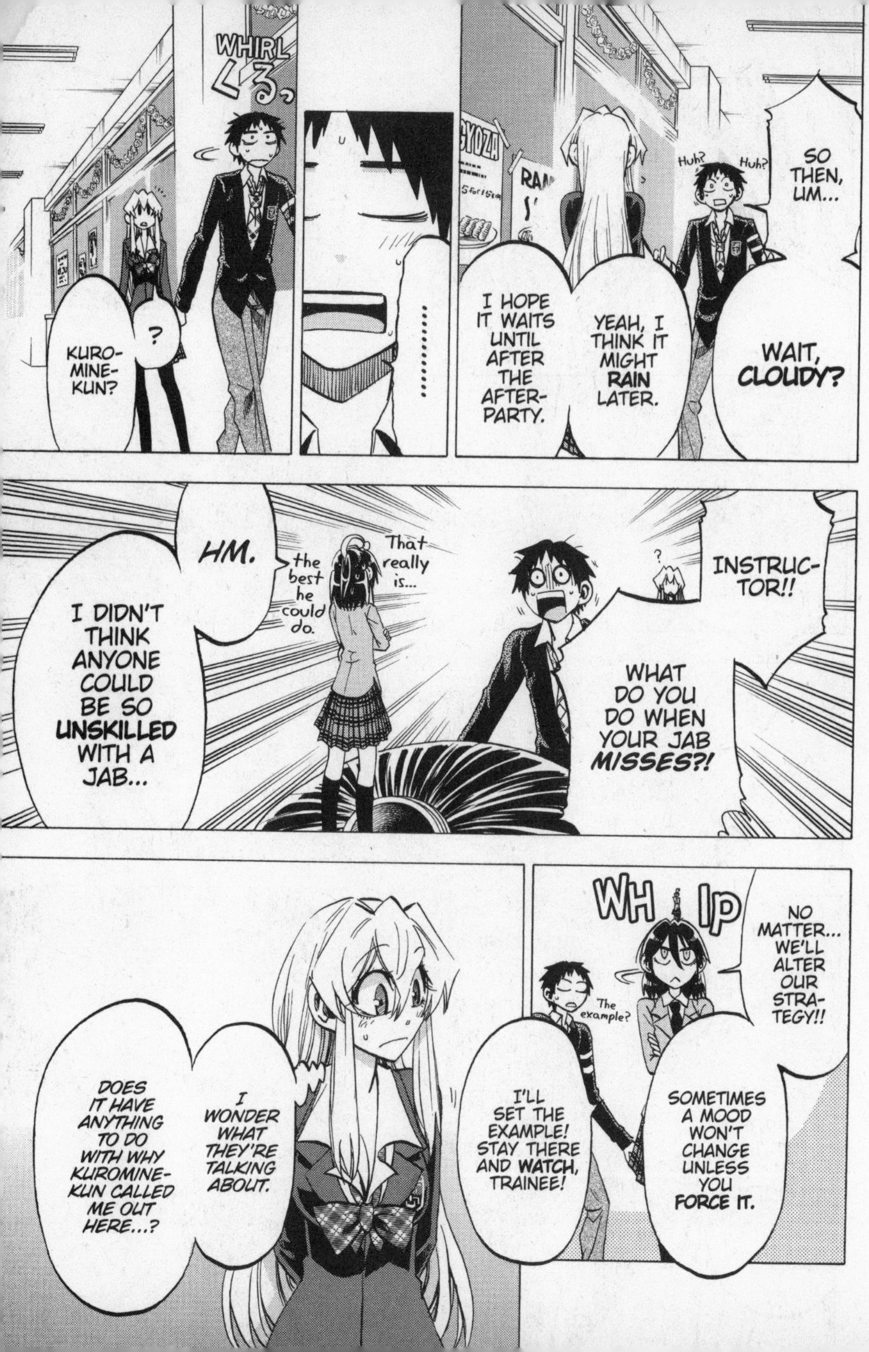
SO THEN, UM...
Huh?
Huh?
WAIT, CLOUDY?
YEAH, I THINK IT MIGHT RAIN LATER.
I HOPE IT WAITS UNTIL AFTER THE AFTER-PARTY.
GYOZA
......
WHIRL くるっ
?
KURO-MINE-KUN?
INSTRUCTOR!!
?
WHAT DO YOU DO WHEN YOUR JAB MISSES?!
That really is... the best he could do.
HM.
I DIDN'T THINK ANYONE COULD BE SO UNSKILLED WITH A JAB...
WHIP
NO MATTER... WE'LL ALTER OUR STRATEGY!!
SOMETIMES A MOOD WON'T CHANGE UNLESS YOU FORCE IT.
The example?
I'LL SET THE EXAMPLE! STAY THERE AND WATCH, TRAINEE!
I WONDER WHAT THEY'RE TALKING ABOUT.
DOES IT HAVE ANYTHING TO DO WITH WHY KUROMINE-KUN CALLED ME OUT HERE...?

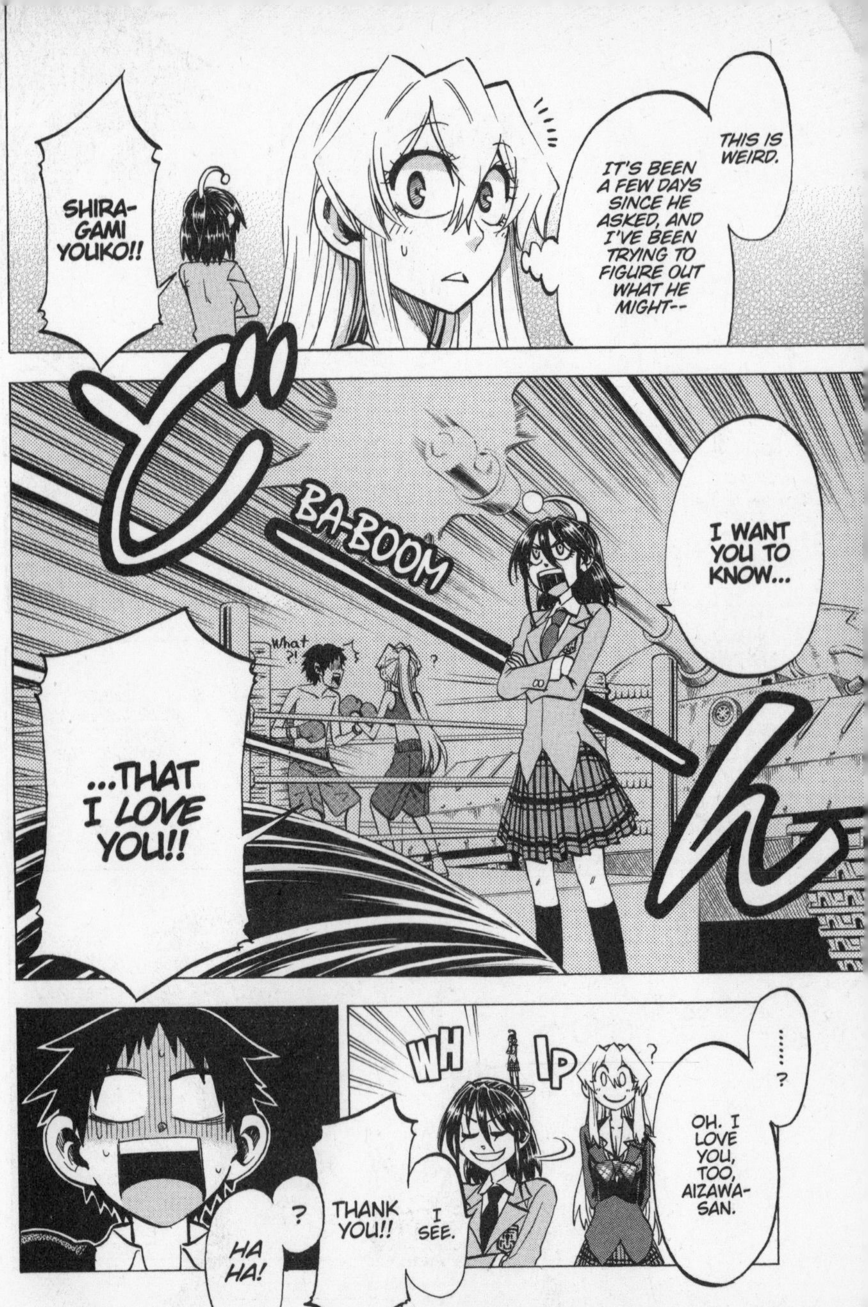
THIS IS WEIRD.
IT'S BEEN A FEW DAYS SINCE HE ASKED, AND I'VE BEEN TRYING TO FIGURE OUT WHAT HE MIGHT--
SHIRA-GAMI YOUKO!!
I WANT YOU TO KNOW...
どん
BA-BOOM
What ?!
?
...THAT I LOVE YOU!!
......?
OH. I LOVE YOU, TOO, AIZAWA-SAN.
?
WHIP
I SEE.
THANK YOU!!
?
HA HA!

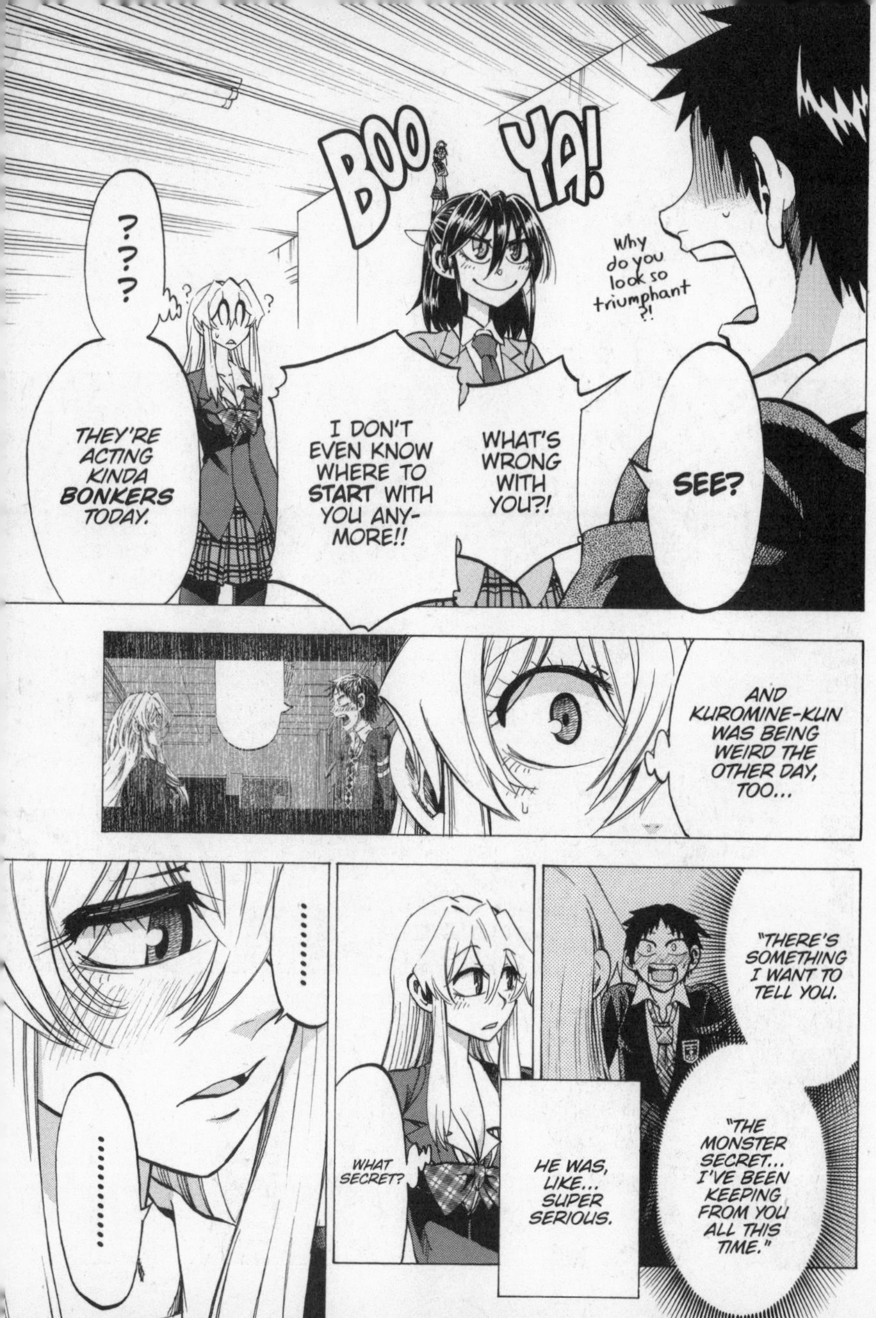
SEE?
BOO YA!
Why do you look so triumphant?!
WHAT'S WRONG WITH YOU?! I DON'T EVEN KNOW WHERE TO START WITH YOU ANY-MORE!!
???
THEY'RE ACTING KINDA BONKERS TODAY.
AND KUROMINE-KUN WAS BEING WEIRD THE OTHER DAY, TOO...
"THERE'S SOMETHING I WANT TO TELL YOU.
"THE MONSTER SECRET... I'VE BEEN KEEPING FROM YOU ALL THIS TIME."
HE WAS, LIKE... SUPER SERIOUS.
WHAT SECRET?
......
......

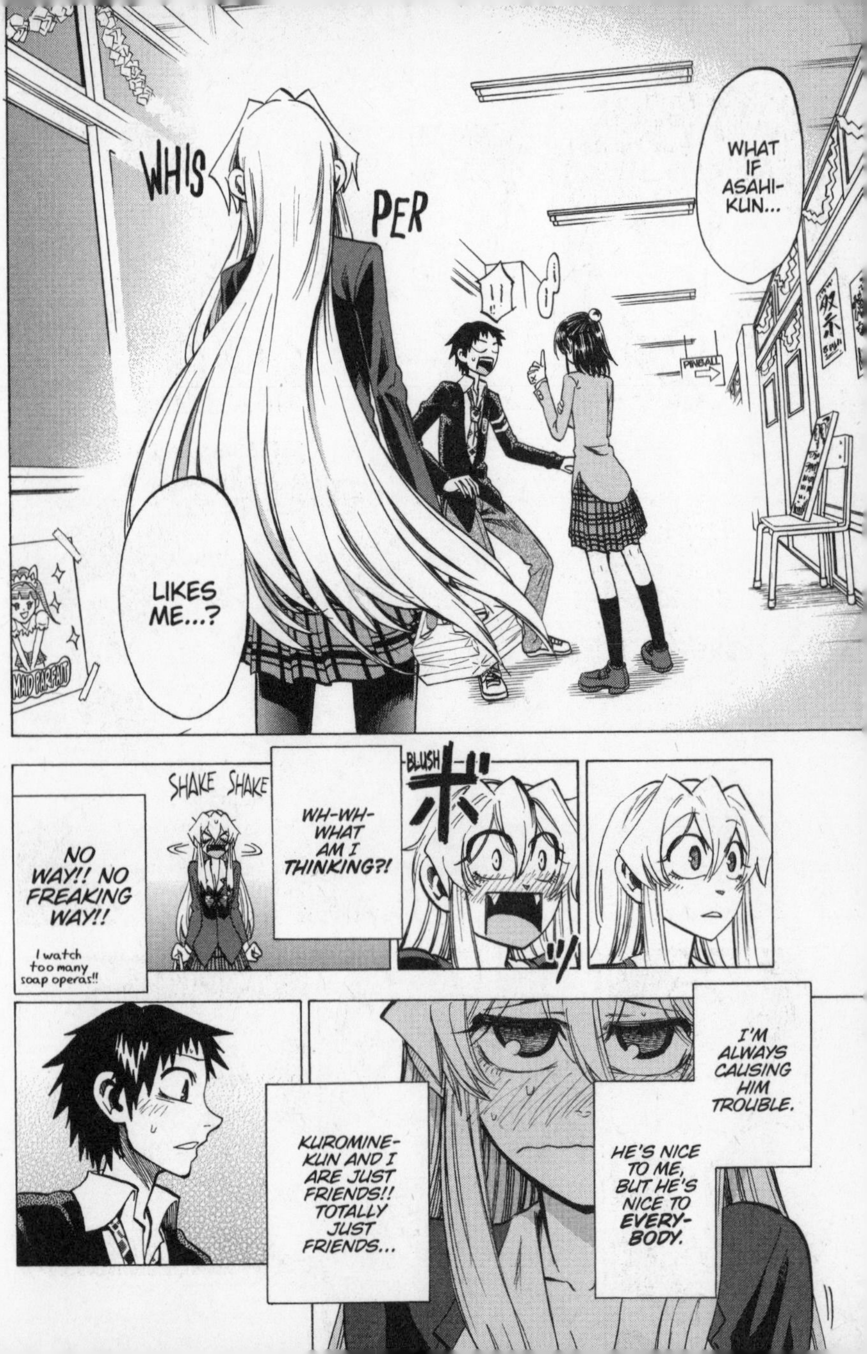
WHAT IF ASAHI-KUN...
PINBALL
WHIS PER
LIKES ME...?
MAID PARFAIT
BLUSH
WH-WH-WHAT AM I THINKING?!
SHAKE SHAKE
NO WAY!! NO FREAKING WAY!!
I watch too many soap operas!!
I'M ALWAYS CAUSING HIM TROUBLE.
HE'S NICE TO ME, BUT HE'S NICE TO EVERYBODY.
KUROMINE-KUN AND I ARE JUST FRIENDS!! TOTALLY JUST FRIENDS...

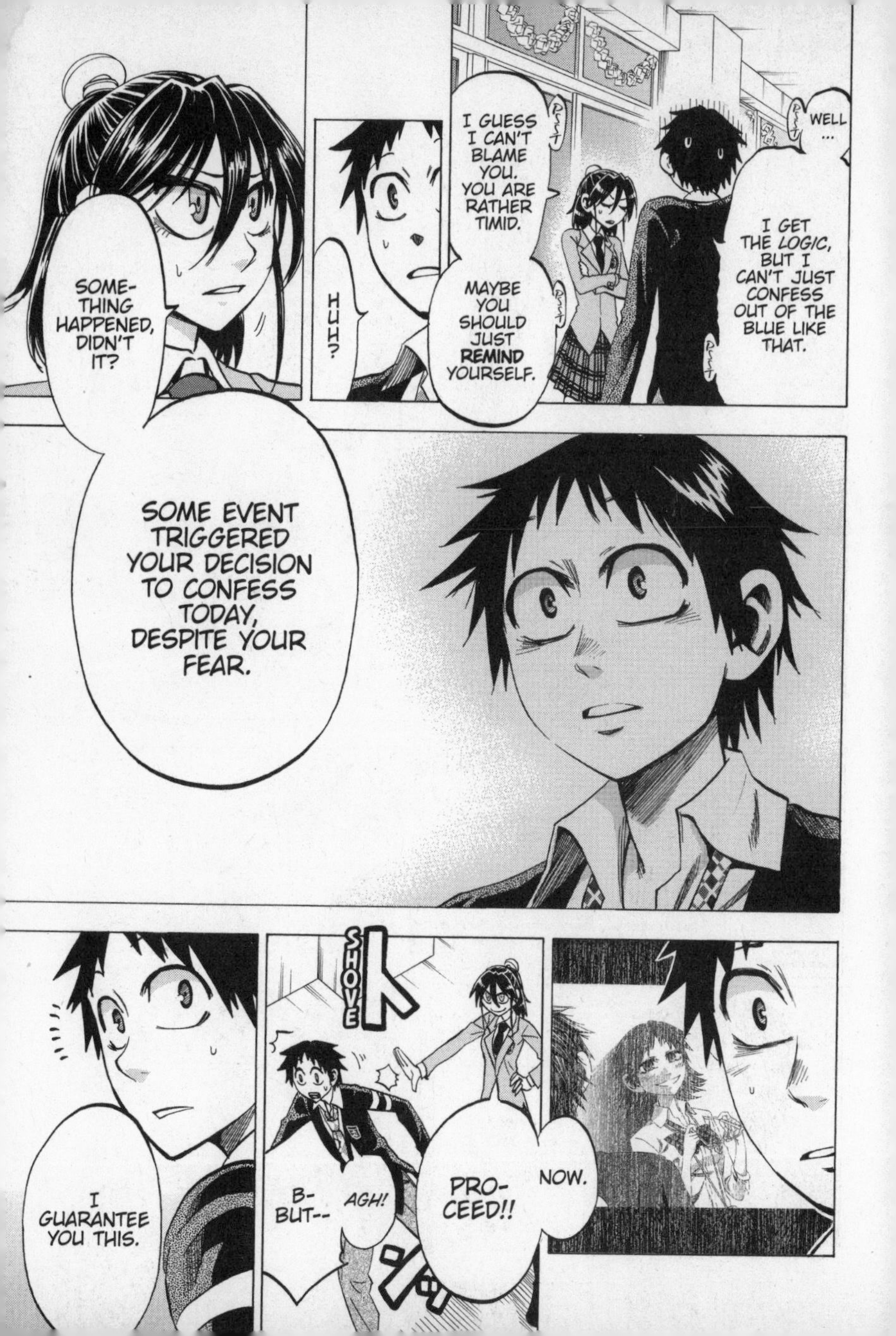
PSST
WELL ...
I GET THE *LOGIC*, BUT I CAN'T JUST CONFESS OUT OF THE BLUE LIKE THAT.
PSST
I GUESS I CAN'T BLAME YOU. YOU ARE RATHER TIMID.
PSST
MAYBE YOU SHOULD JUST **REMIND** YOURSELF.
HUH?
SOMETHING HAPPENED, DIDN'T IT?
SOME EVENT TRIGGERED YOUR DECISION TO CONFESS TODAY, DESPITE YOUR FEAR.
NOW.
SHOVE
PRO-CEED!!
AGH!
B-BUT--
I GUARANTEE YOU THIS.

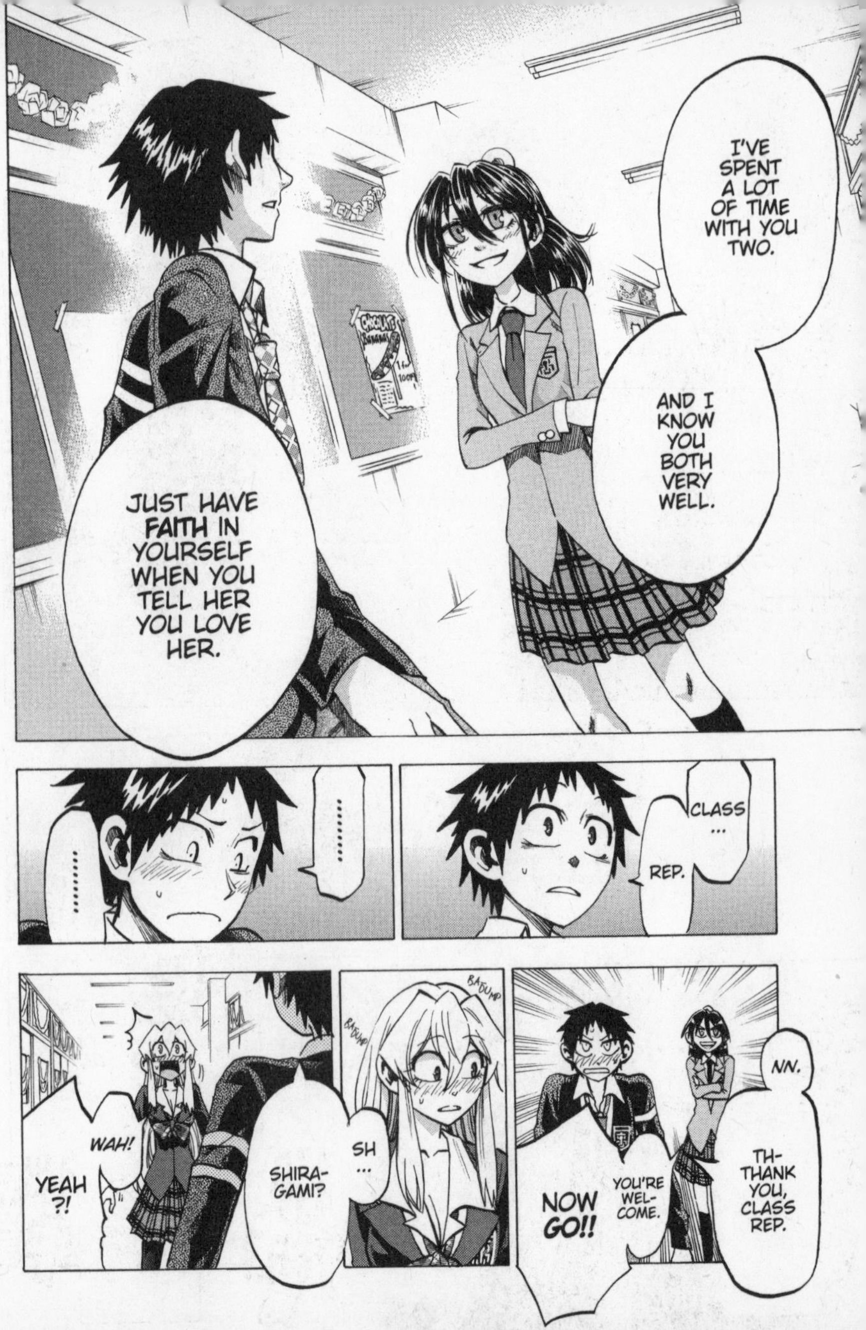
I'VE SPENT A LOT OF TIME WITH YOU TWO.
AND I KNOW YOU BOTH VERY WELL.
JUST HAVE FAITH IN YOURSELF WHEN YOU TELL HER YOU LOVE HER.
CLASS ... REP.
......
......
NN.
TH-THANK YOU, CLASS REP.
YOU'RE WEL-COME.
NOW GO!!
BADUMP
BADUMP
SH ...
SHIRA-GAMI?
WAH!
YEAH ?!

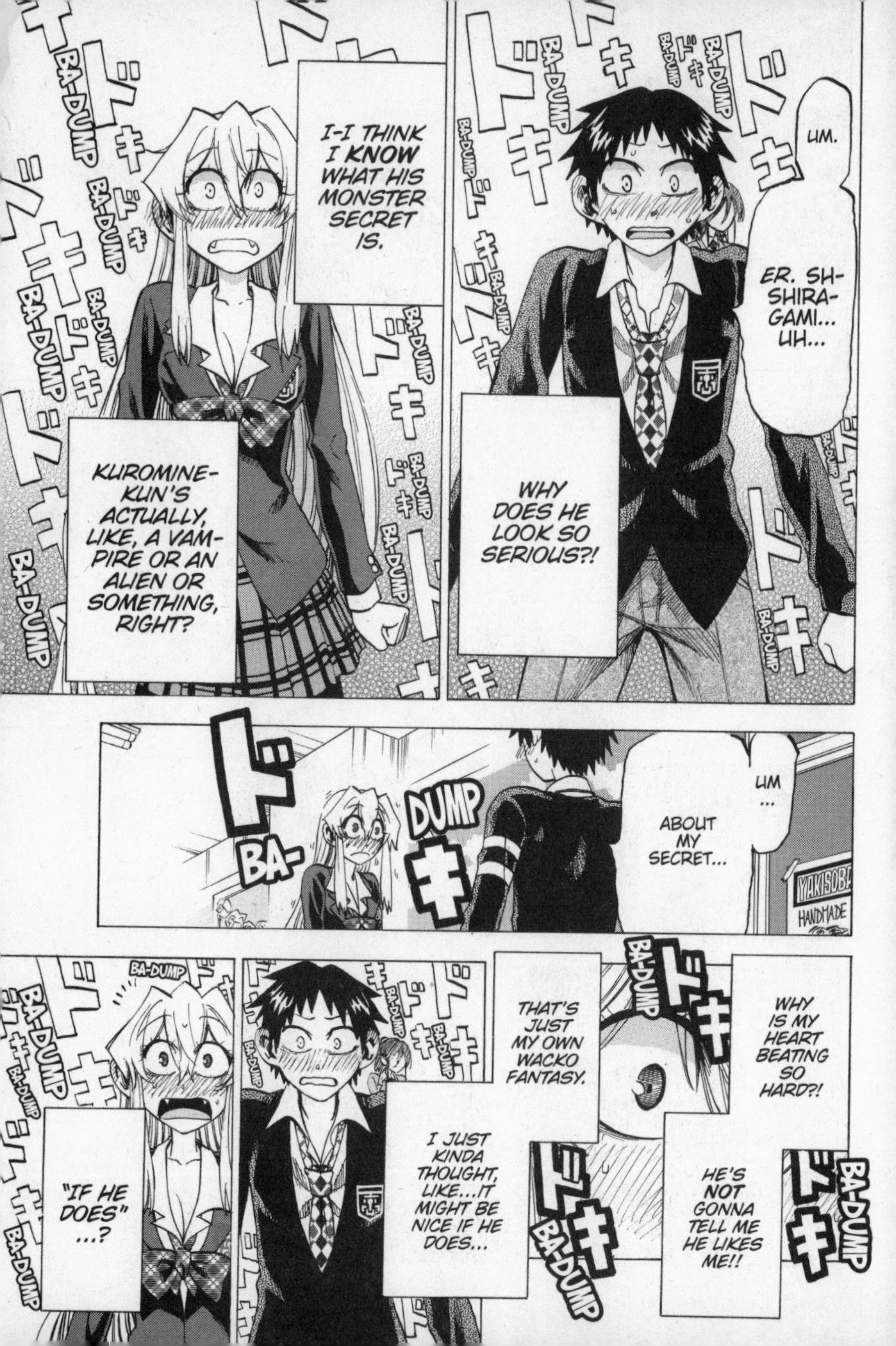
BA-DUMP
UM.
ER. SH-SHIRAGAMI... UH...
WHY DOES HE LOOK SO SERIOUS?!
BA-DUMP
I-I THINK I KNOW WHAT HIS MONSTER SECRET IS.
KUROMINE-KUN'S ACTUALLY, LIKE, A VAM-PIRE OR AN ALIEN OR SOMETHING, RIGHT?
UM ...
ABOUT MY SECRET...
YAKISOBA
HANDMADE
BA-DUMP
WHY IS MY HEART BEATING SO HARD?!
HE'S NOT GONNA TELL ME HE LIKES ME!!
THAT'S JUST MY OWN WACKO FANTASY.
I JUST KINDA THOUGHT, LIKE...IT MIGHT BE NICE IF HE DOES...
BA-DUMP
"IF HE DOES" ...?

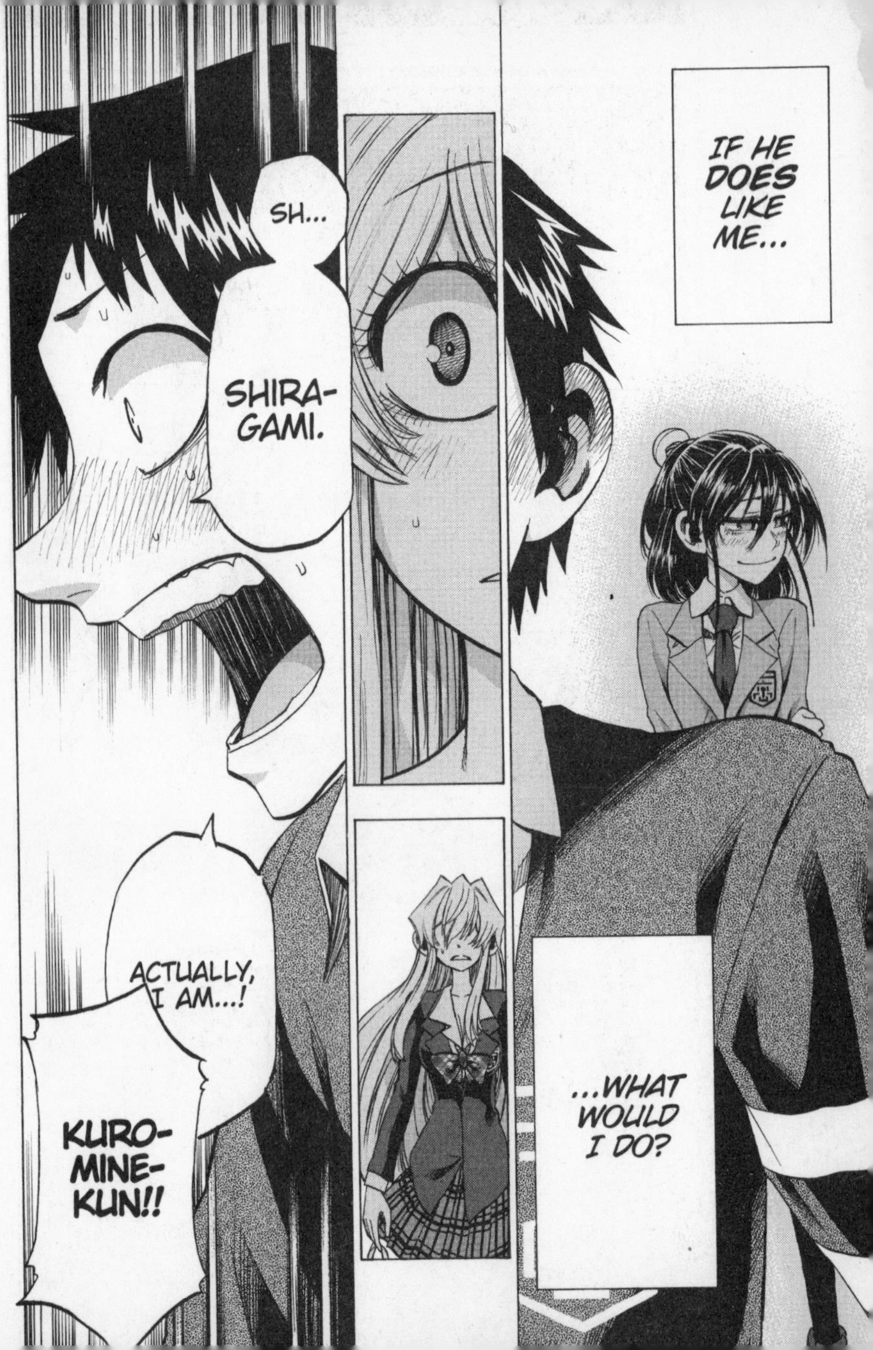
IF HE DOES LIKE ME...
...WHAT WOULD I DO?
SH...
SHIRA-GAMI.
ACTUALLY, I AM...!
KURO-MINE-KUN!!

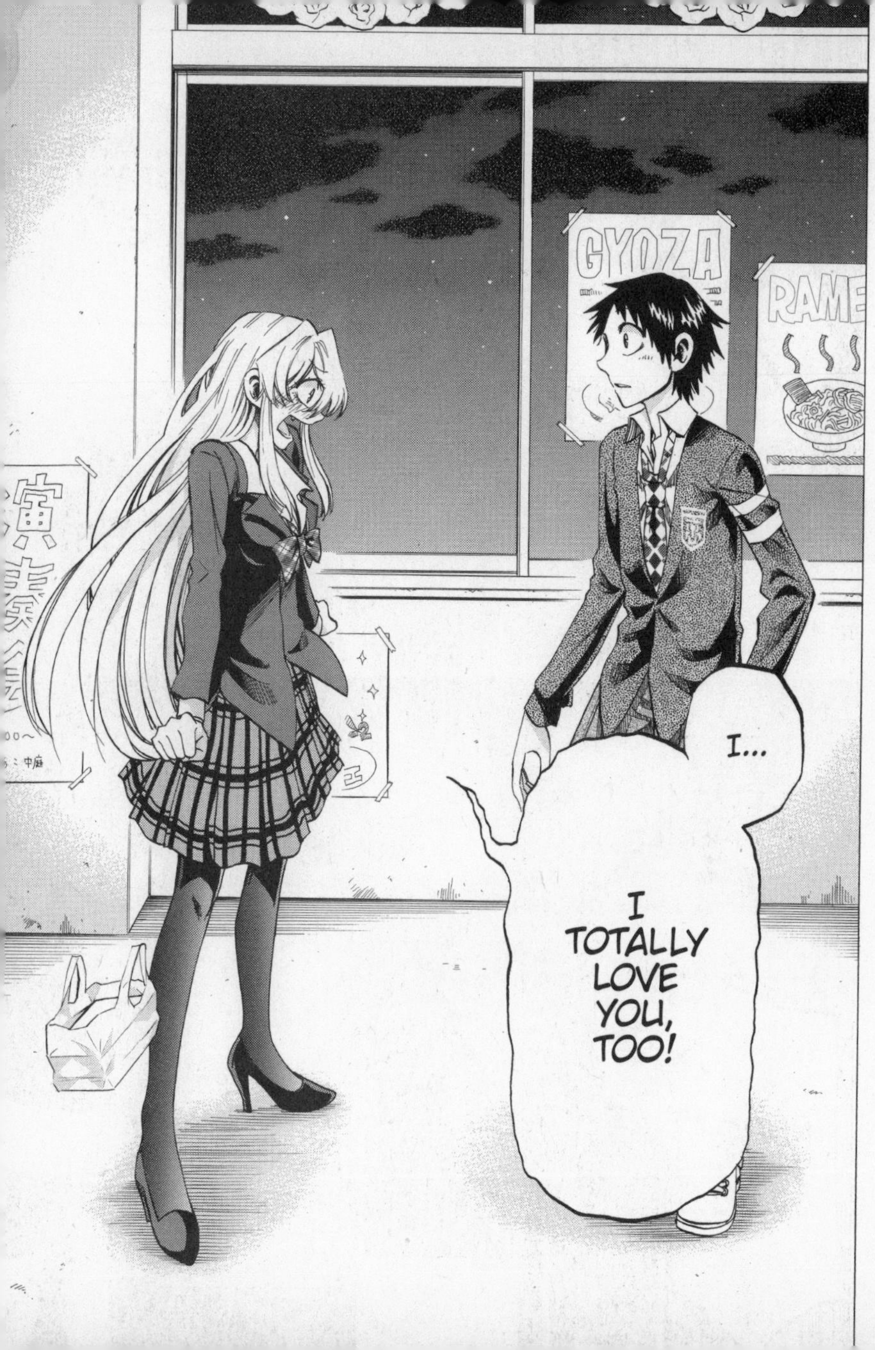
GYOZA
I...
I TOTALLY LOVE YOU, TOO!

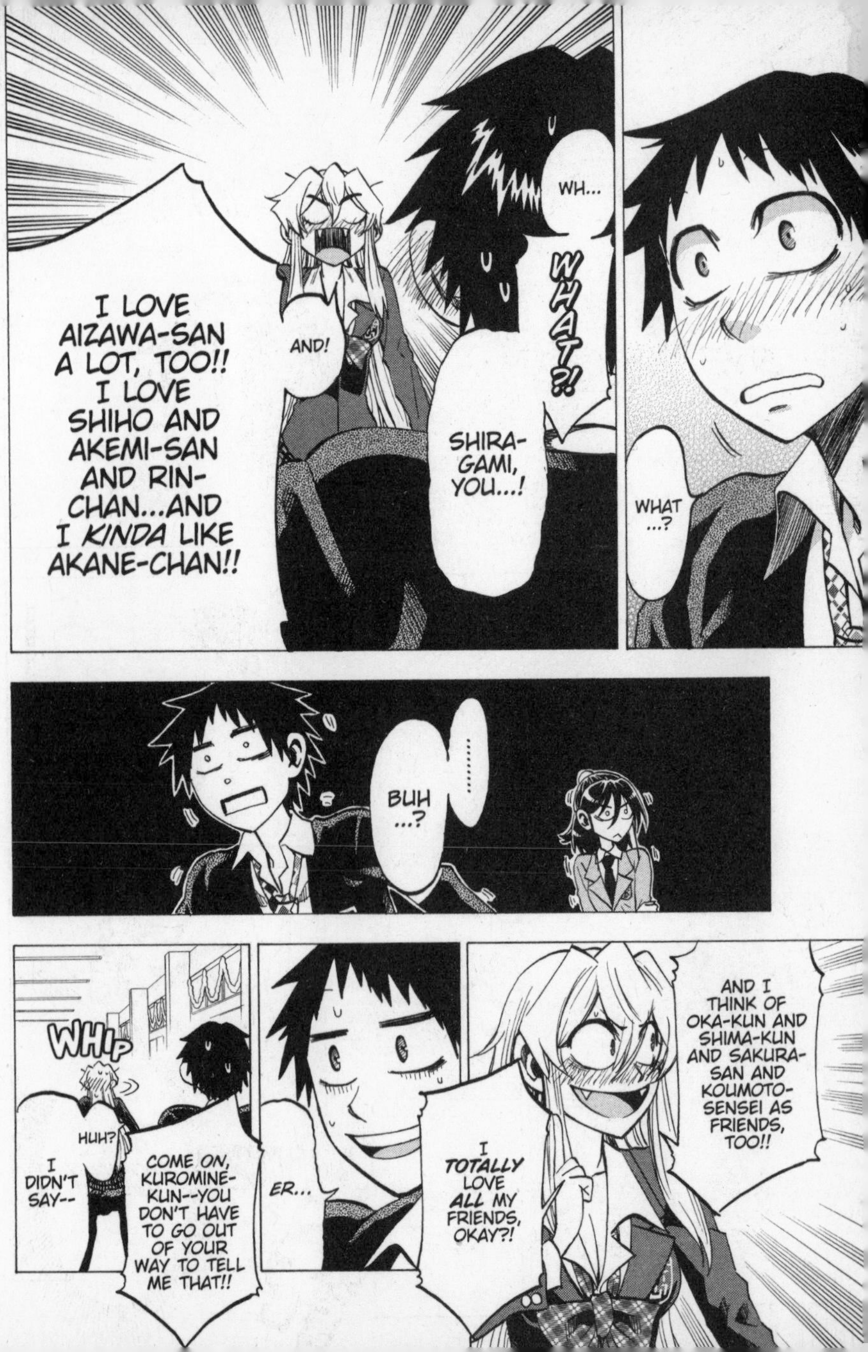
WHAT
...?
WH...
WHAT?!
AND!
SHIRA-GAMI, YOU...!
I LOVE AIZAWA-SAN A LOT, TOO!! I LOVE SHIHO AND AKEMI-SAN AND RIN-CHAN...AND I *KINDA* LIKE AKANE-CHAN!!
......
BUH ...?
AND I THINK OF OKA-KUN AND SHIMA-KUN AND SAKURA-SAN AND KOUMOTO-SENSEI AS FRIENDS, TOO!!
I ***TOTALLY*** LOVE ***ALL*** MY FRIENDS, OKAY?!
ER...
WHIP
COME ON, KUROMINE-KUN--YOU DON'T HAVE TO GO OUT OF YOUR WAY TO TELL ME THAT!!
HUH?
I DIDN'T SAY--

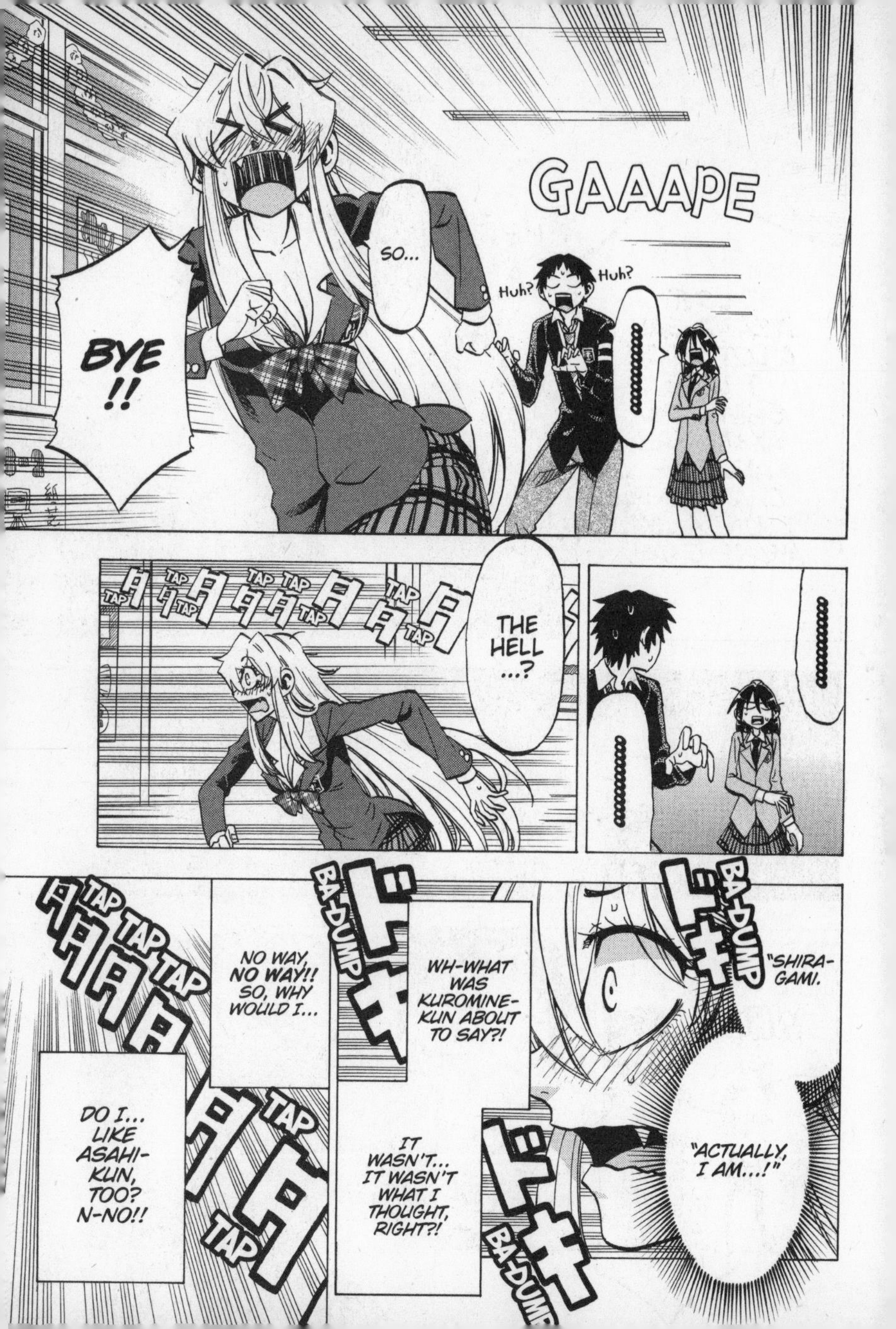
GAAAPE
Huh?
Huh?
......
SO...
BYE !!
......
......
THE HELL ...?
TAP TAP TAP TAP TAP TAP TAP TAP
ドキ BA-DUMP
"SHIRA-GAMI.
"ACTUALLY, I AM...!"
ドキ BA-DUMP
ドキ BA-DUMP
WH-WHAT WAS KUROMINE-KUN ABOUT TO SAY?!
IT WASN'T... IT WASN'T WHAT I THOUGHT, RIGHT?!
NO WAY, NO WAY!! SO, WHY WOULD I...
DO I... LIKE ASAHI-KUN, TOO? N-NO!!
TAP TAP TAP
TAP
TAP

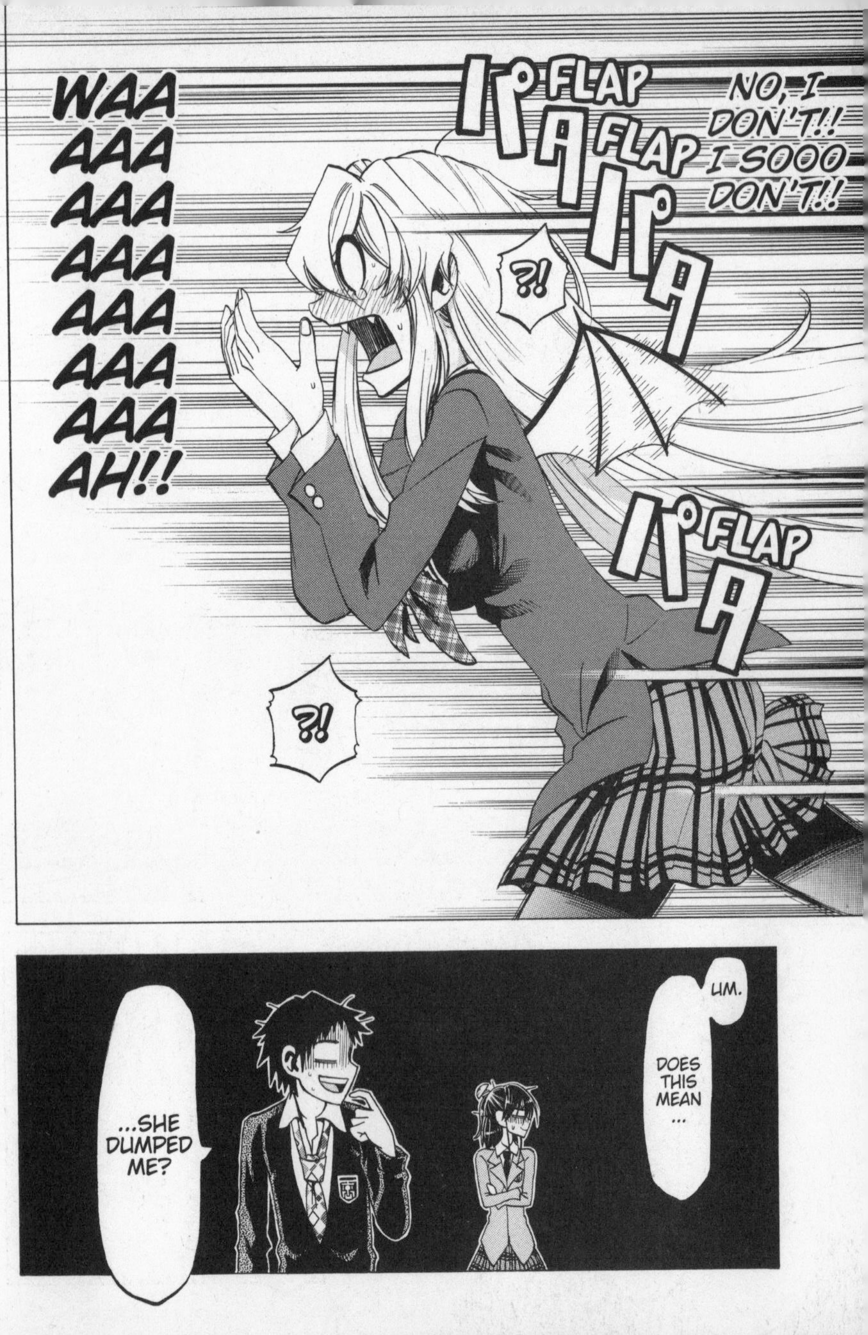
NO, I DON'T!! I SOOO DON'T!!
パタパタ
FLAP FLAP
?!
WAAAAAAAAAAAAAAAAAAAAAH!!
?!
パタ
FLAP
UM.
DOES THIS MEAN...
...SHE DUMPED ME?

Chapter 48:
"Let's Seduce Him!"

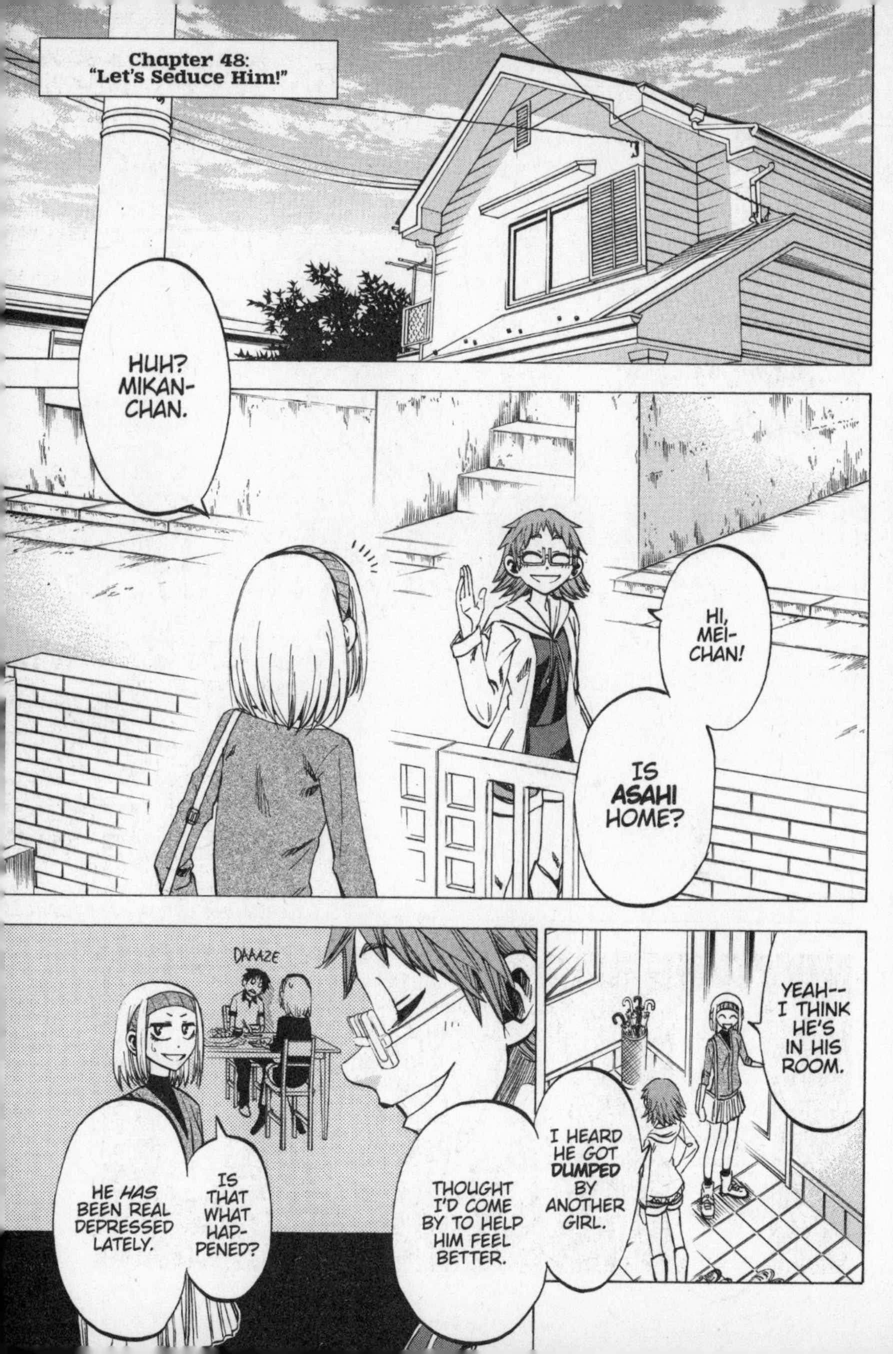
HUH? MIKAN-CHAN.
HI, MEI-CHAN!
IS ASAHI HOME?
YEAH-- I THINK HE'S IN HIS ROOM.
I HEARD HE GOT DUMPED BY ANOTHER GIRL.
THOUGHT I'D COME BY TO HELP HIM FEEL BETTER.
DAAAZE
IS THAT WHAT HAP-PENED?
HE *HAS* BEEN REAL DEPRESSED LATELY.

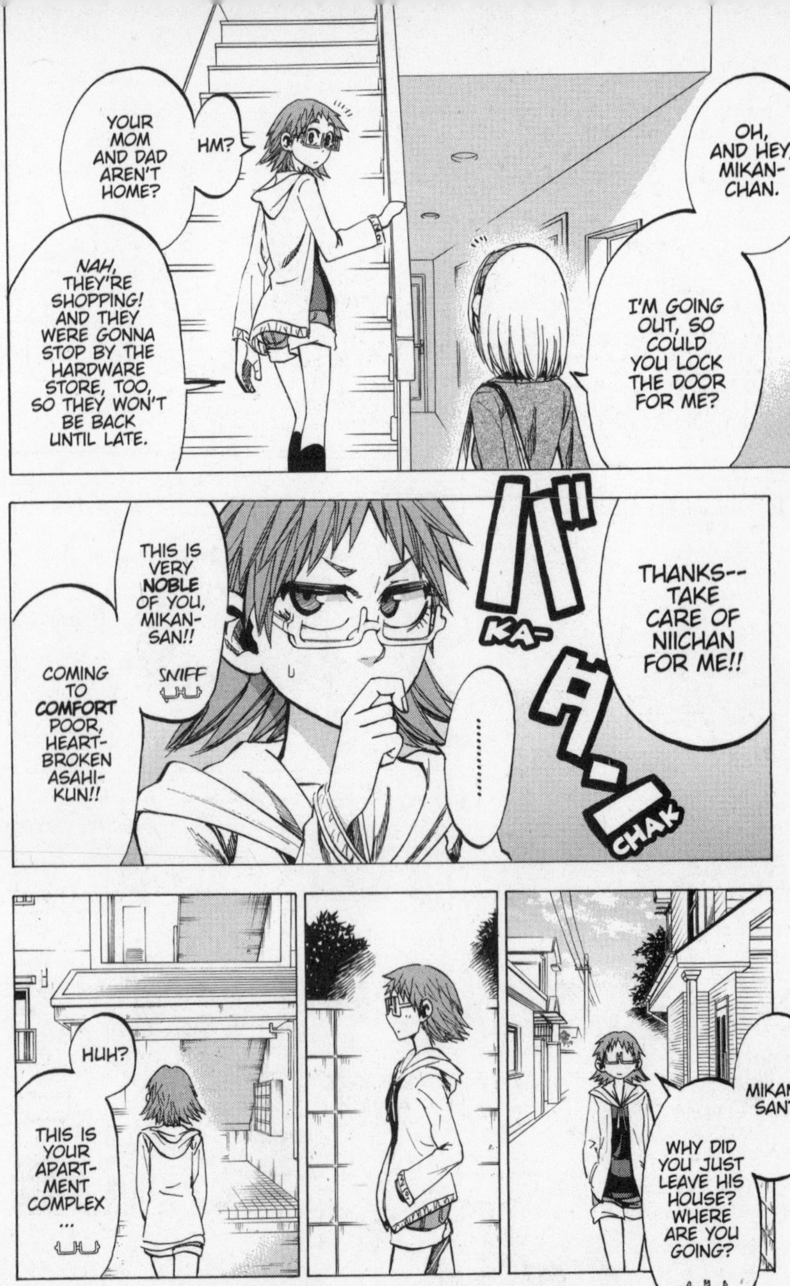
OH, AND HEY, MIKAN-CHAN.
I'M GOING OUT, SO COULD YOU LOCK THE DOOR FOR ME?
HM?
YOUR MOM AND DAD AREN'T HOME?
NAH, THEY'RE SHOPPING! AND THEY WERE GONNA STOP BY THE HARDWARE STORE, TOO, SO THEY WON'T BE BACK UNTIL LATE.
KA-
CHAK
THANKS--TAKE CARE OF NIICHAN FOR ME!!
......
THIS IS VERY NOBLE OF YOU, MIKAN-SAN!!
SNIFF
COMING TO COMFORT POOR, HEART-BROKEN ASAHI-KUN!!
MIKAN-SAN?
WHY DID YOU JUST LEAVE HIS HOUSE? WHERE ARE YOU GOING?
HUH?
THIS IS YOUR APARTMENT COMPLEX ...

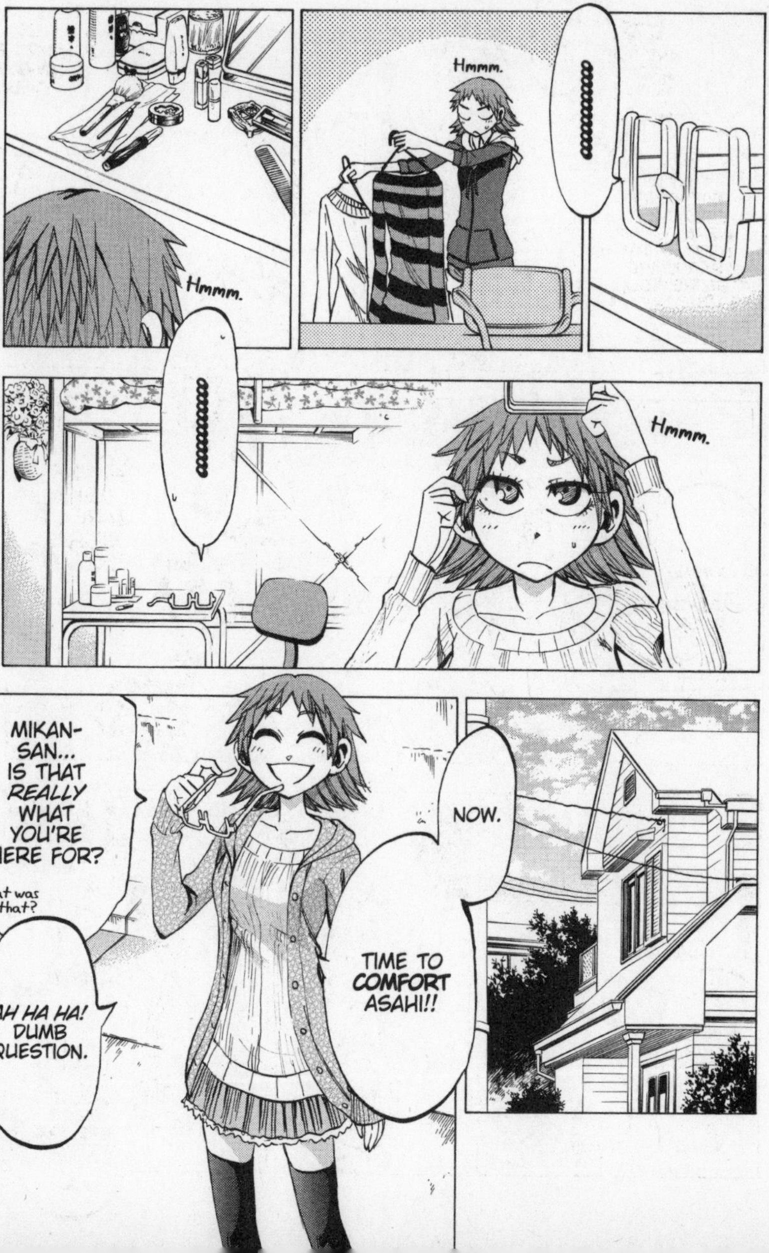

....
Hmmm.
Hmmm.
....
Hmmm.
....
NOW.
TIME TO COMFORT ASAHI!!
MIKAN-SAN... IS THAT *REALLY* WHAT YOU'RE HERE FOR?
What was all that?
AH HA HA! DUMB QUESTION.

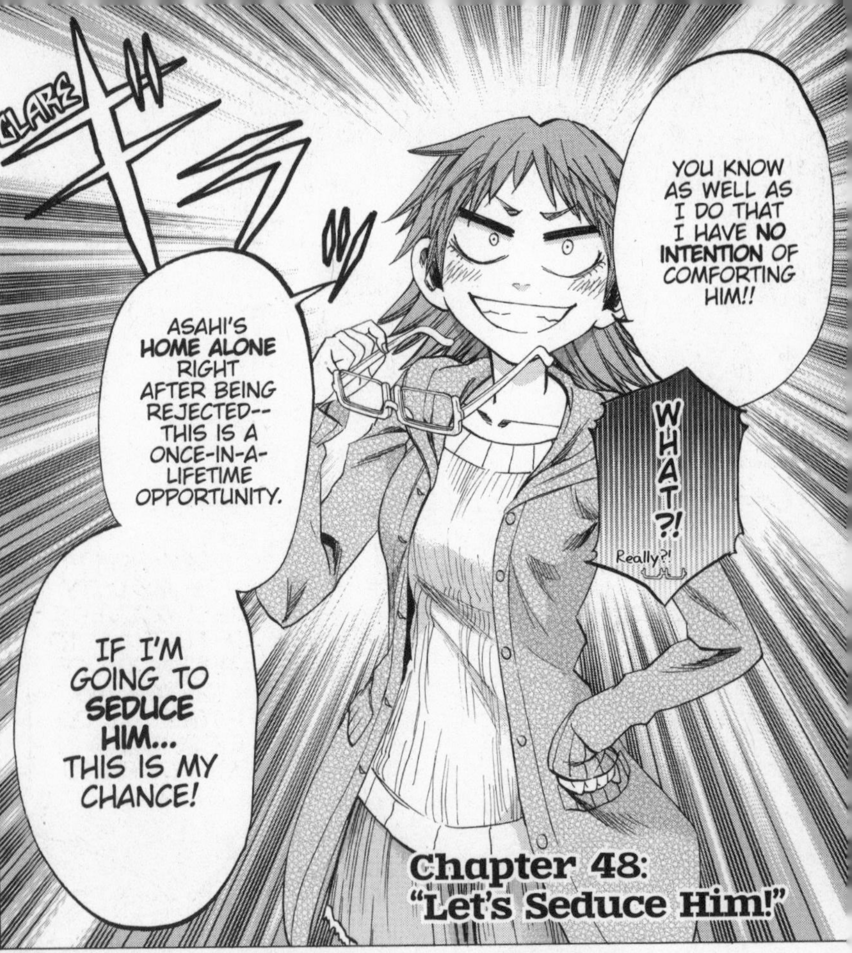
YOU KNOW AS WELL AS I DO THAT I HAVE **NO INTENTION** OF COMFORTING HIM!!
WHAT?!
Really?!
GLARE
ASAHI'S **HOME ALONE** RIGHT AFTER BEING REJECTED-- THIS IS A ONCE-IN-A-LIFETIME OPPORTUNITY.
IF I'M GOING TO **SEDUCE HIM...** THIS IS MY CHANCE!
Chapter 48: "Let's Seduce Him!"

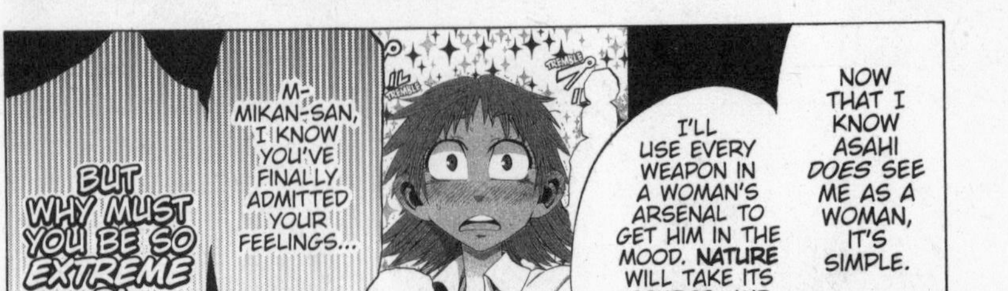
NOW THAT I KNOW ASAHI *DOES* SEE ME AS A WOMAN, IT'S SIMPLE.
I'LL USE EVERY WEAPON IN A WOMAN'S ARSENAL TO GET HIM IN THE MOOD. **NATURE** WILL TAKE ITS COURSE, AND THE REST WILL WORK ITSELF OUT.
TREMBLE
TREMBLE
M-MIKAN-SAN, I KNOW YOU'VE FINALLY ADMITTED YOUR FEELINGS...
BUT WHY MUST YOU BE SO *EXTREME* ?!

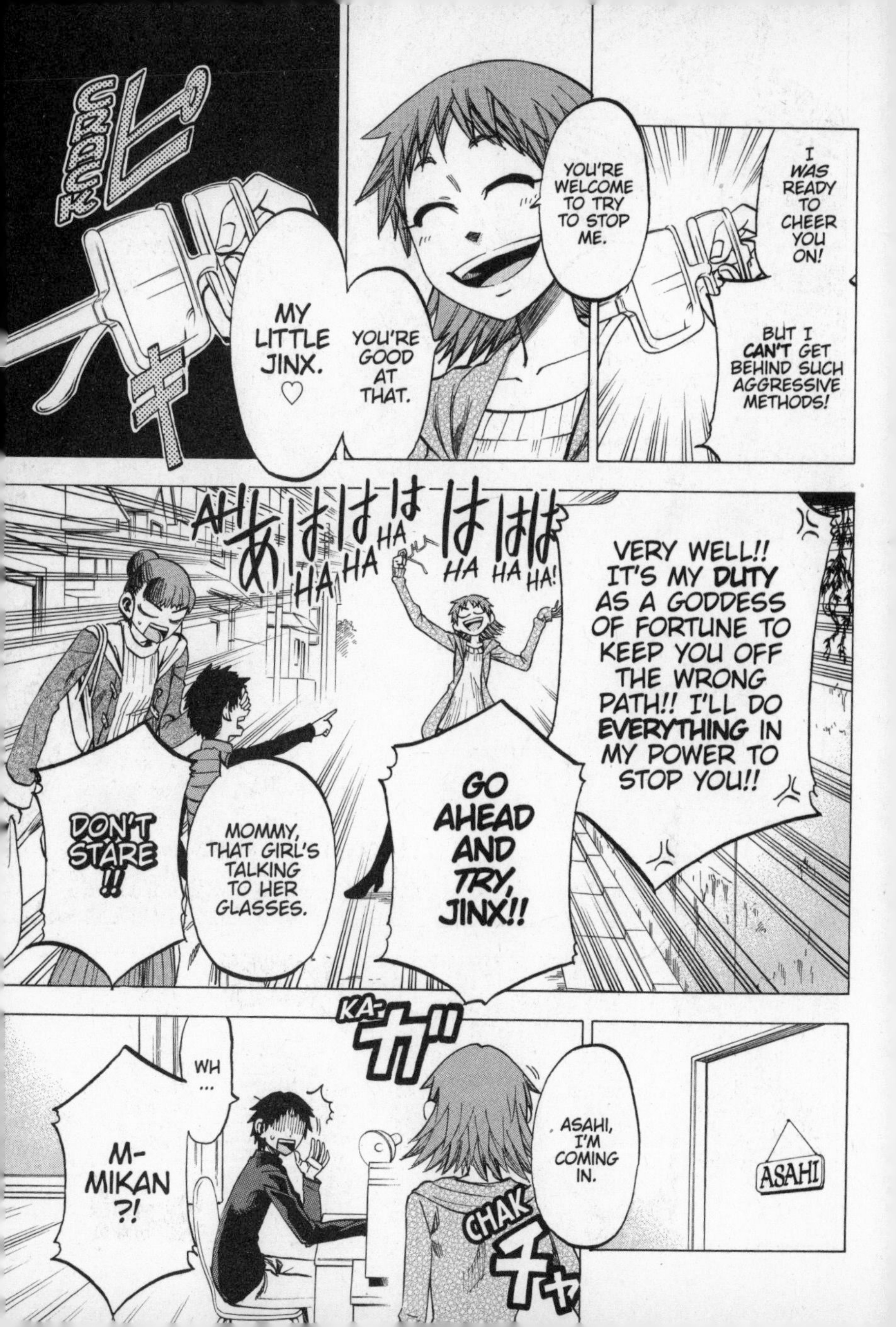
I WAS READY TO CHEER YOU ON!
BUT I CAN'T GET BEHIND SUCH AGGRESSIVE METHODS!
YOU'RE WELCOME TO TRY TO STOP ME.
YOU'RE GOOD AT THAT.
MY LITTLE JINX. ♡
CRACK
ピキ
VERY WELL!! IT'S MY DUTY AS A GODDESS OF FORTUNE TO KEEP YOU OFF THE WRONG PATH!! I'LL DO EVERYTHING IN MY POWER TO STOP YOU!!
AH HA HA HA HA HA HA HA!
あはははははは
GO AHEAD AND TRY, JINX!!
MOMMY, THAT GIRL'S TALKING TO HER GLASSES.
DON'T STARE!!
ASAHI
ASAHI, I'M COMING IN.
CHAK
チャ
KA-
ガ
WH...
M-MIKAN?!

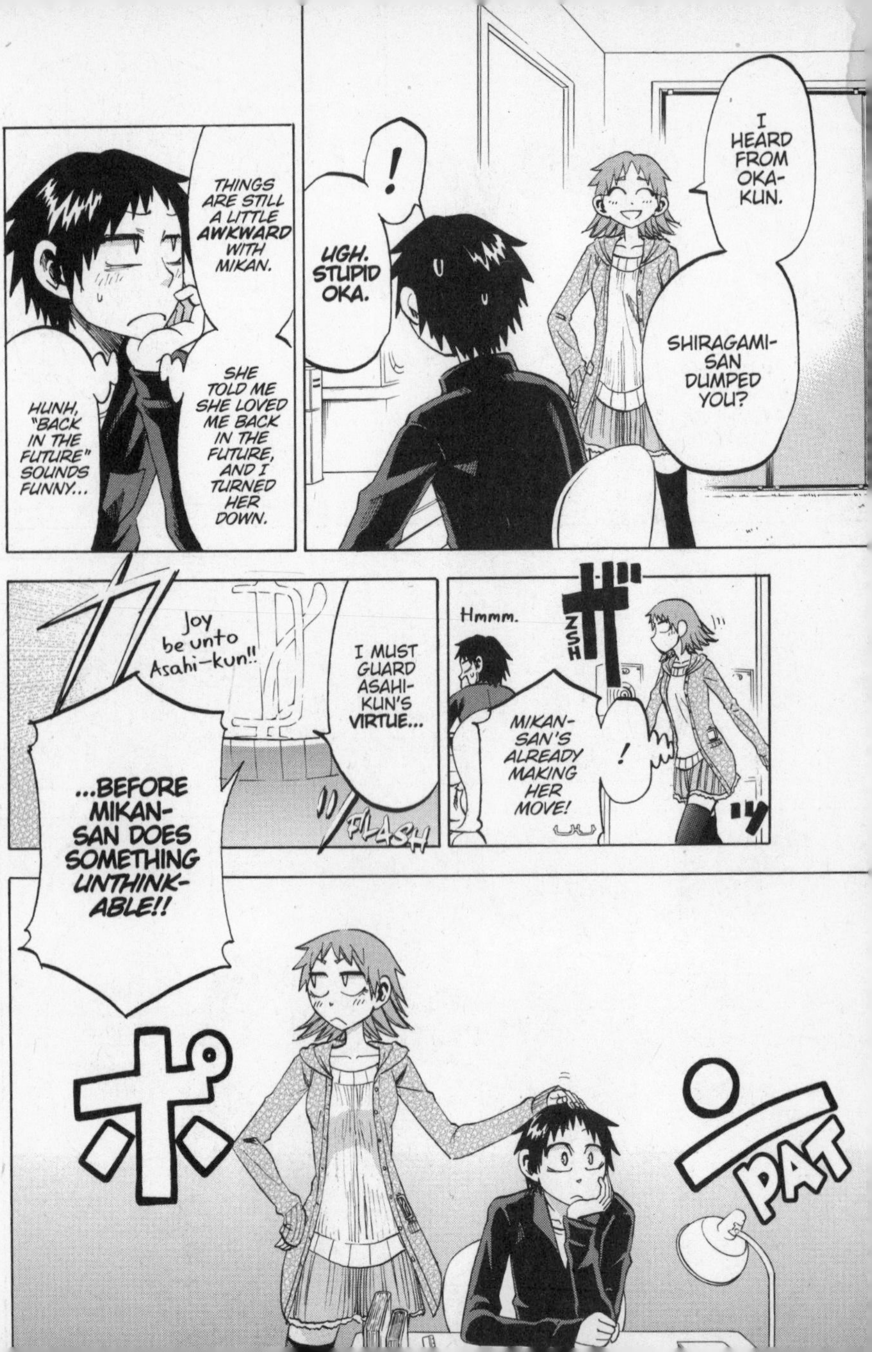
I HEARD FROM OKA-KUN.
SHIRAGAMI-SAN DUMPED YOU?
!
UGH. STUPID OKA.
THINGS ARE STILL A LITTLE AWKWARD WITH MIKAN.
SHE TOLD ME SHE LOVED ME BACK IN THE FUTURE, AND I TURNED HER DOWN.
HUNH, "BACK IN THE FUTURE" SOUNDS FUNNY...
Hmmm.
ZSH
MIKAN-SAN'S ALREADY MAKING HER MOVE!
!
I MUST GUARD ASAHI-KUN'S VIRTUE...
Joy be unto Asahi-kun!!
FLASH
...BEFORE MIKAN-SAN DOES SOMETHING UNTHINKABLE!!
PAT

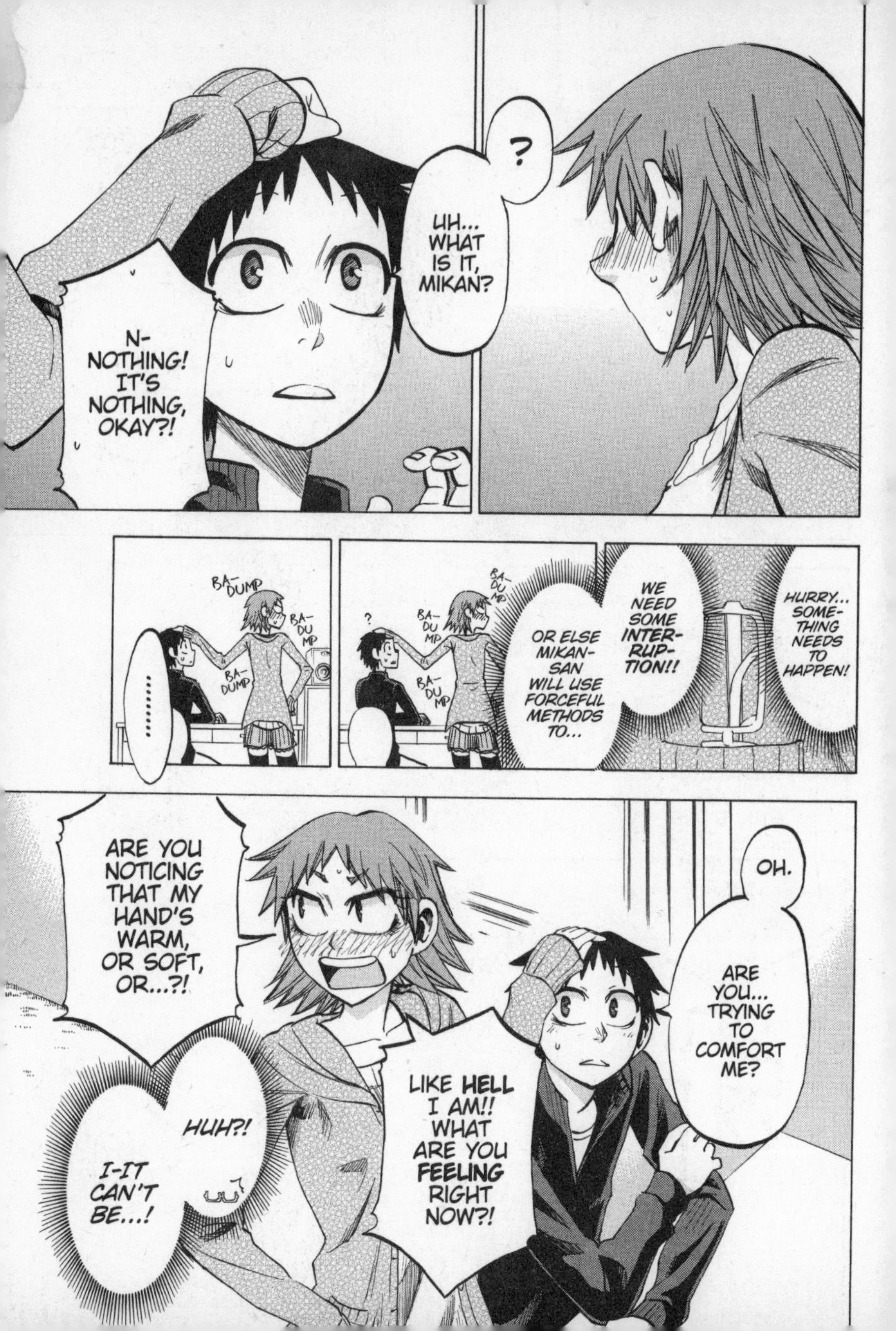
?
UH... WHAT IS IT, MIKAN?
N-NOTHING! IT'S NOTHING, OKAY?!
HURRY... SOMETHING NEEDS TO HAPPEN!
WE NEED SOME INTERRUPTION!!
OR ELSE MIKAN-SAN WILL USE FORCEFUL METHODS TO...
BA-DUMP
?
BA-DUMP
BA-DUMP
BA-DUMP
BA-DUMP
BA-DUMP
......
OH.
ARE YOU... TRYING TO COMFORT ME?
ARE YOU NOTICING THAT MY HAND'S WARM, OR SOFT, OR...?!
LIKE HELL I AM!! WHAT ARE YOU FEELING RIGHT NOW?!
HUH?!
I-IT CAN'T BE...!

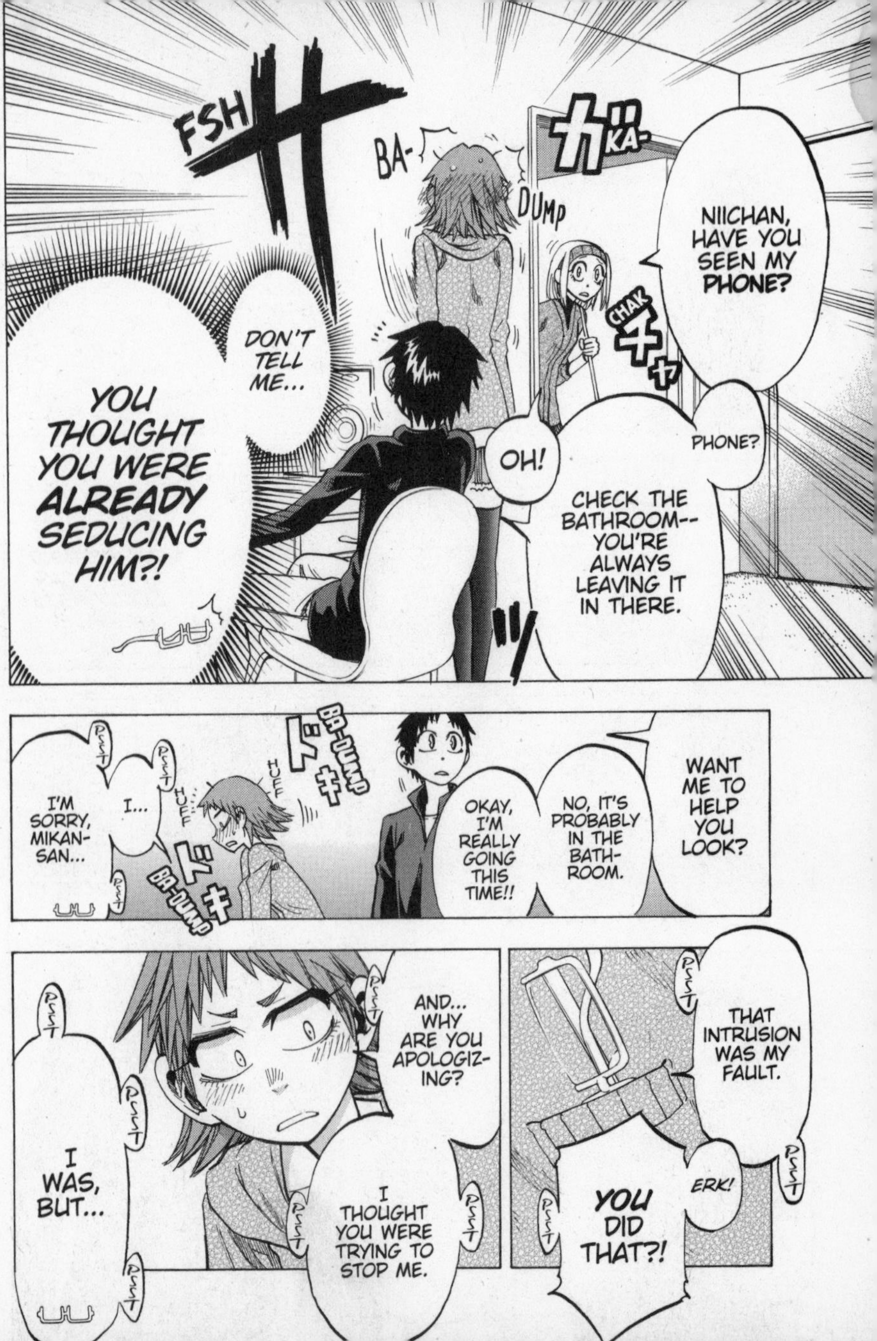
KA-
NIICHAN, HAVE YOU SEEN MY PHONE?
BA-
DUMP
CHAK
FSH
PHONE?
OH!
CHECK THE BATHROOM-- YOU'RE ALWAYS LEAVING IT IN THERE.
DON'T TELL ME...
YOU THOUGHT YOU WERE **ALREADY** SEDUCING HIM?!
WANT ME TO HELP YOU LOOK?
NO, IT'S PROBABLY IN THE BATH-ROOM.
OKAY, I'M REALLY GOING THIS TIME!!
BA-DUMP
HUFF
HUFF
BA-DUMP
PSST
I...
PSST
I'M SORRY, MIKAN-SAN...
PSST
PSST
THAT INTRUSION WAS MY FAULT.
PSST
ERK!
PSST
YOU DID THAT?!
PSST
AND... WHY ARE YOU APOLOGIZ-ING?
PSST
I THOUGHT YOU WERE TRYING TO STOP ME.
PSST
PSST
I WAS, BUT...
PSST

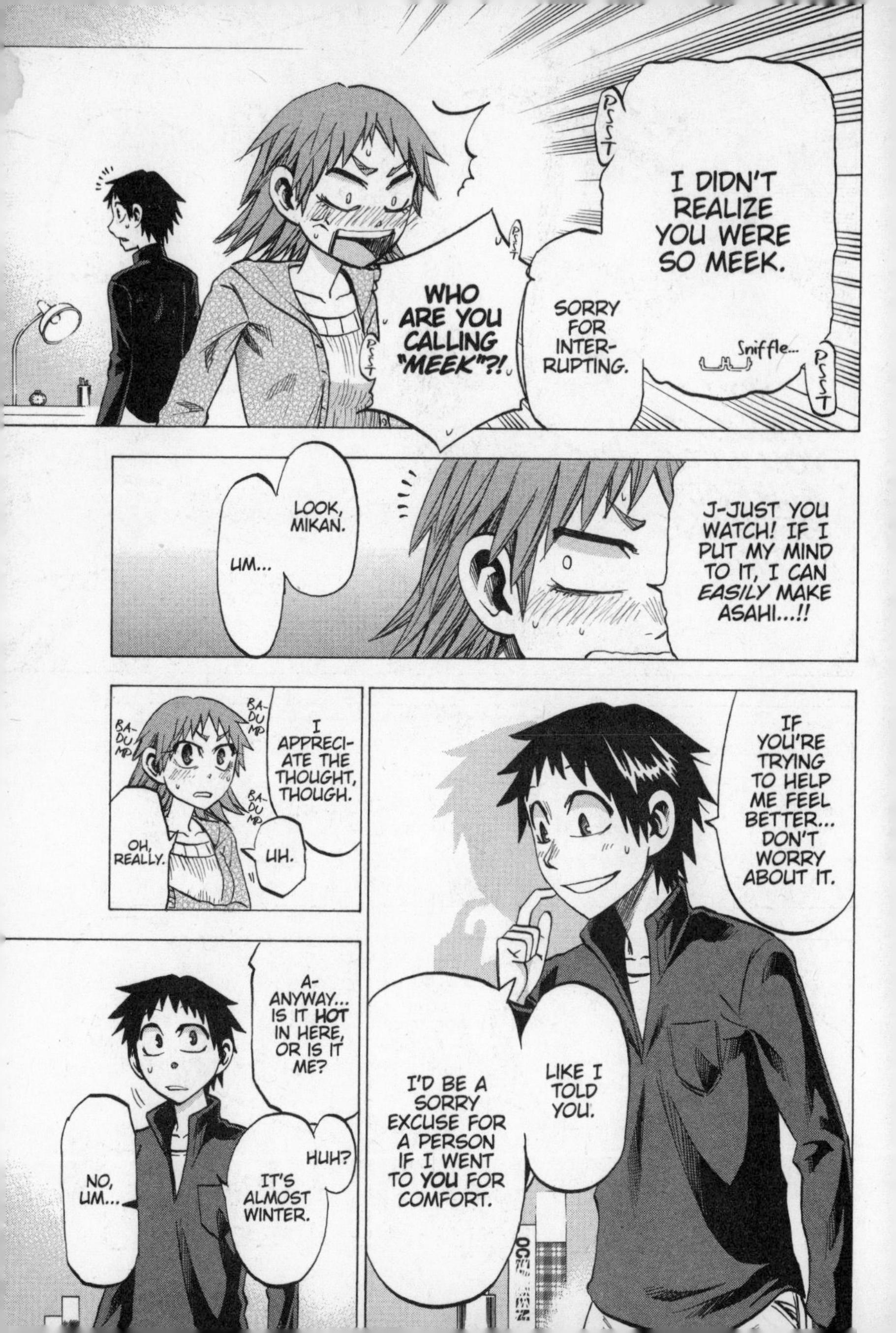
PSST
I DIDN'T REALIZE YOU WERE SO MEEK.
Sniffle...
PSST
SORRY FOR INTER-RUPTING.
PSST
WHO ARE YOU CALLING "MEEK"?!
PSST
J-JUST YOU WATCH! IF I PUT MY MIND TO IT, I CAN EASILY MAKE ASAHI...!!
LOOK, MIKAN.
UM...
IF YOU'RE TRYING TO HELP ME FEEL BETTER... DON'T WORRY ABOUT IT.
LIKE I TOLD YOU.
I'D BE A SORRY EXCUSE FOR A PERSON IF I WENT TO YOU FOR COMFORT.
BA-DUMP
I APPRECIATE THE THOUGHT, THOUGH.
BA-DUMP
BA-DUMP
UH.
OH, REALLY.
A-ANYWAY... IS IT HOT IN HERE, OR IS IT ME?
HUH?
IT'S ALMOST WINTER.
NO, UM...

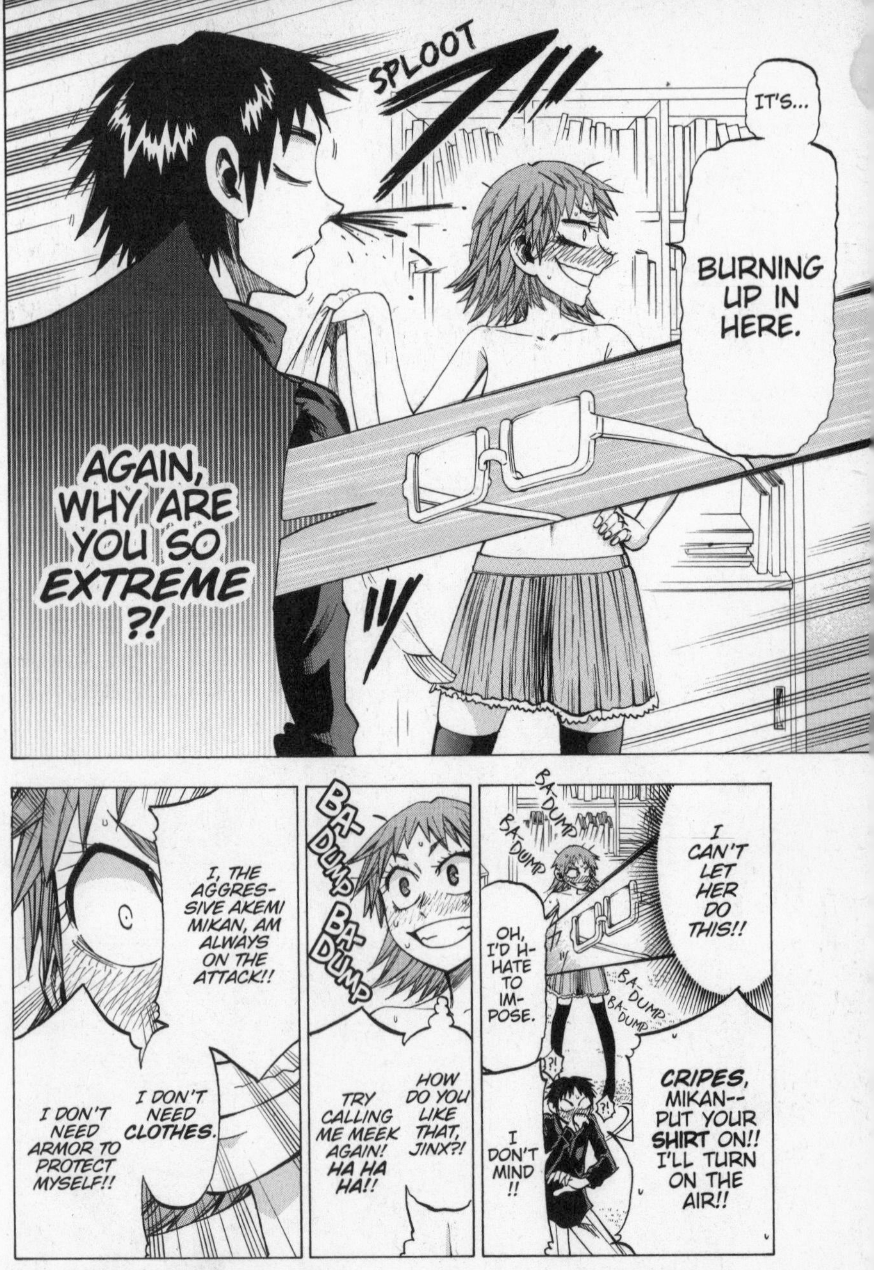
IT'S...
BURNING UP IN HERE.
SPLOOT
AGAIN, WHY ARE YOU SO EXTREME ?!
I CAN'T LET HER DO THIS!!
BA-DUMP BA-DUMP
BA-DUMP BA-DUMP
OH, I'D H-HATE TO IMPOSE.
I DON'T MIND !!
CRIPES, MIKAN-- PUT YOUR SHIRT ON!! I'LL TURN ON THE AIR!!
BA-DUMP BA-DUMP
HOW DO YOU LIKE THAT, JINX?!
TRY CALLING ME MEEK AGAIN! HA HA HA!!
I, THE AGGRES-SIVE AKEMI MIKAN, AM ALWAYS ON THE ATTACK!!
I DON'T NEED CLOTHES.
I DON'T NEED ARMOR TO PROTECT MYSELF!!

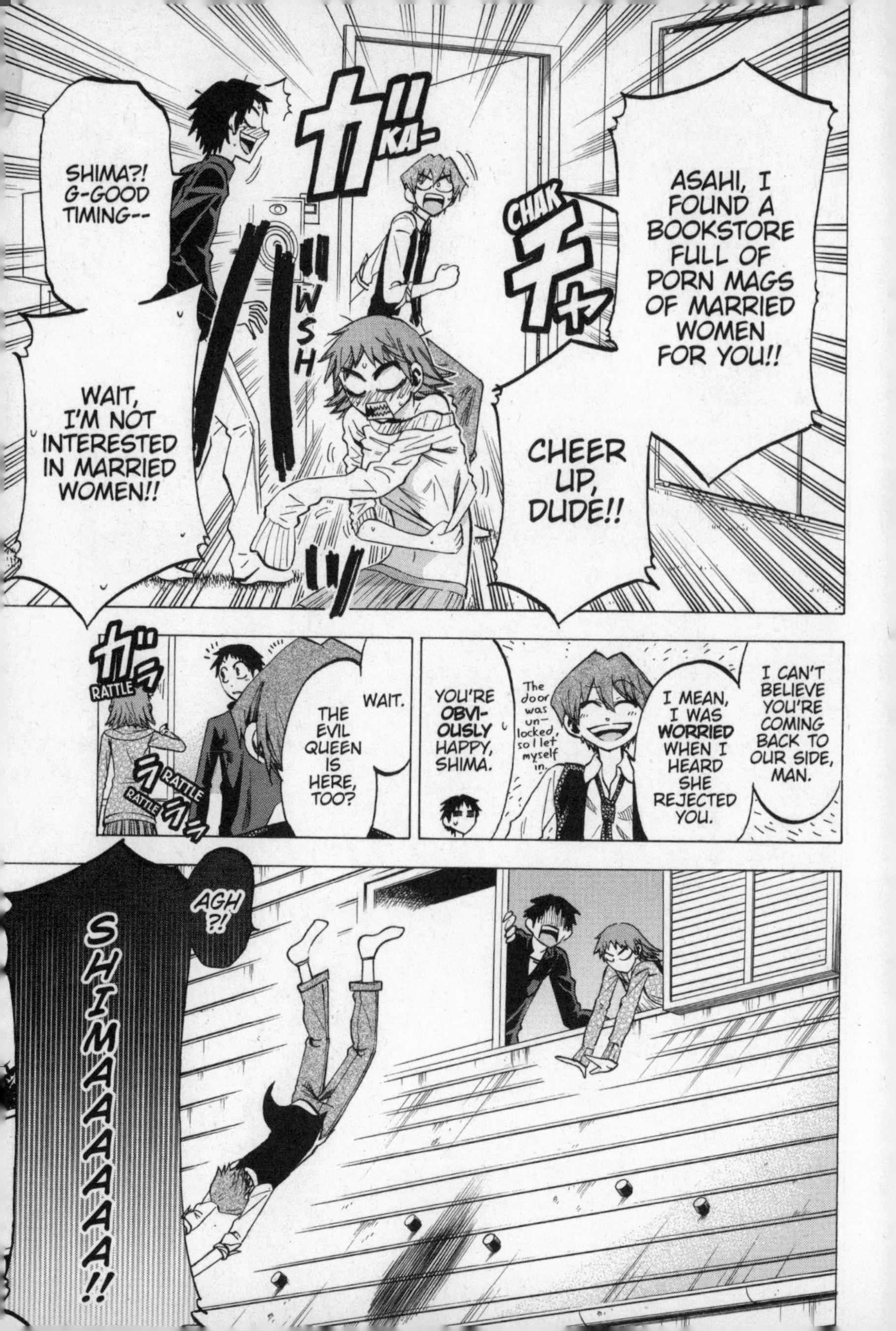
ASAHI, I FOUND A BOOKSTORE FULL OF PORN MAGS OF MARRIED WOMEN FOR YOU!!
CHAK
CHEER UP, DUDE!!
KA-
SHIMA?! G-GOOD TIMING--
WSH
WAIT, I'M NOT INTERESTED IN MARRIED WOMEN!!
I CAN'T BELIEVE YOU'RE COMING BACK TO OUR SIDE, MAN.
I MEAN, I WAS WORRIED WHEN I HEARD SHE REJECTED YOU.
The door was unlocked, so I let myself in.
YOU'RE OBVIOUSLY HAPPY, SHIMA.
WAIT. THE EVIL QUEEN IS HERE, TOO?
RATTLE
RATTLE
RATTLE
AGH?!
SHIMAAAAAAAA!!

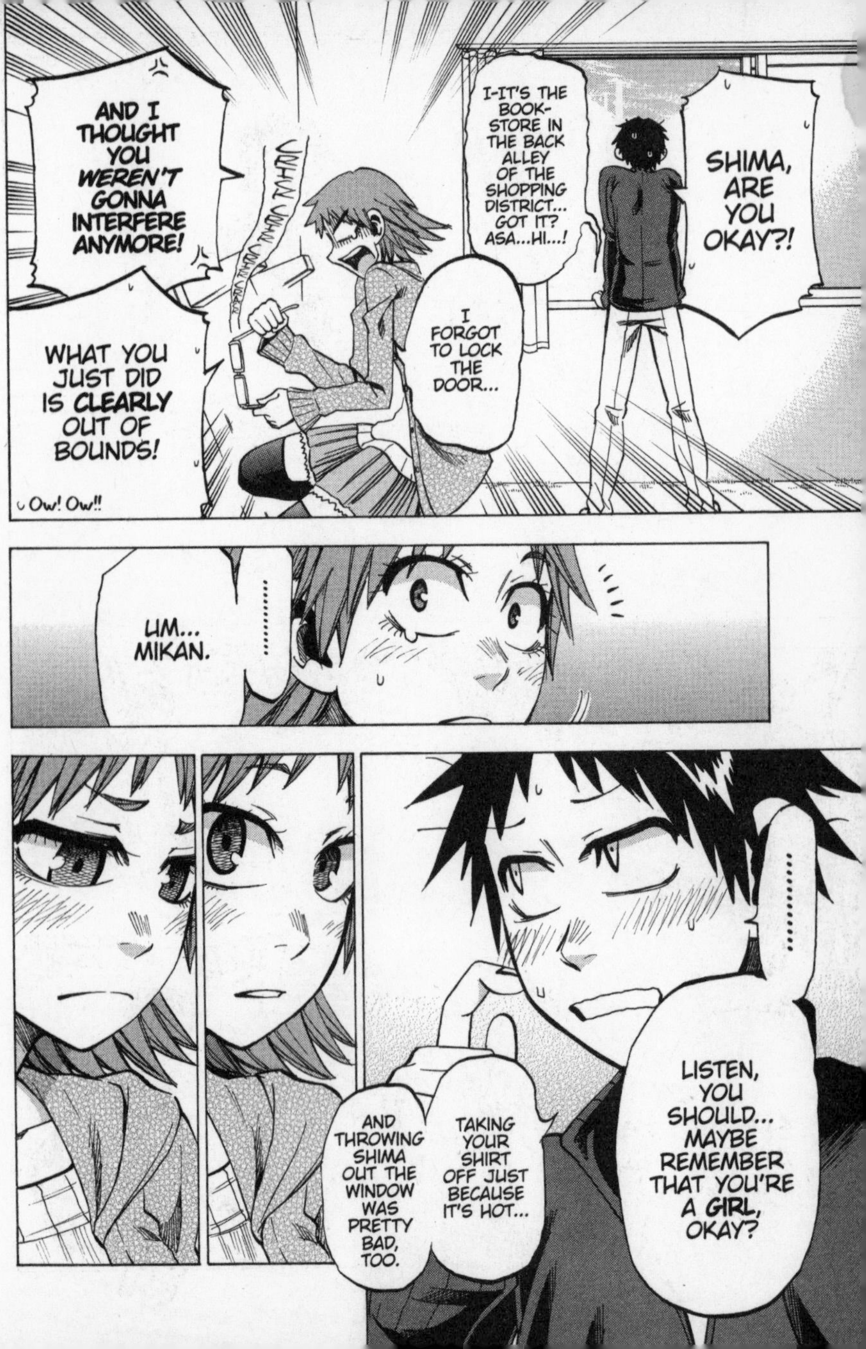
SHIMA, ARE YOU OKAY?!
I-IT'S THE BOOK-STORE IN THE BACK ALLEY OF THE SHOPPING DISTRICT... GOT IT? ASA...HI...!
I FORGOT TO LOCK THE DOOR...
AND I THOUGHT YOU WEREN'T GONNA INTERFERE ANYMORE!
WHAT YOU JUST DID IS CLEARLY OUT OF BOUNDS!
Ow! Ow!!
....
UM... MIKAN.
....
LISTEN, YOU SHOULD... MAYBE REMEMBER THAT YOU'RE A GIRL, OKAY?
TAKING YOUR SHIRT OFF JUST BECAUSE IT'S HOT...
AND THROWING SHIMA OUT THE WINDOW WAS PRETTY BAD, TOO.

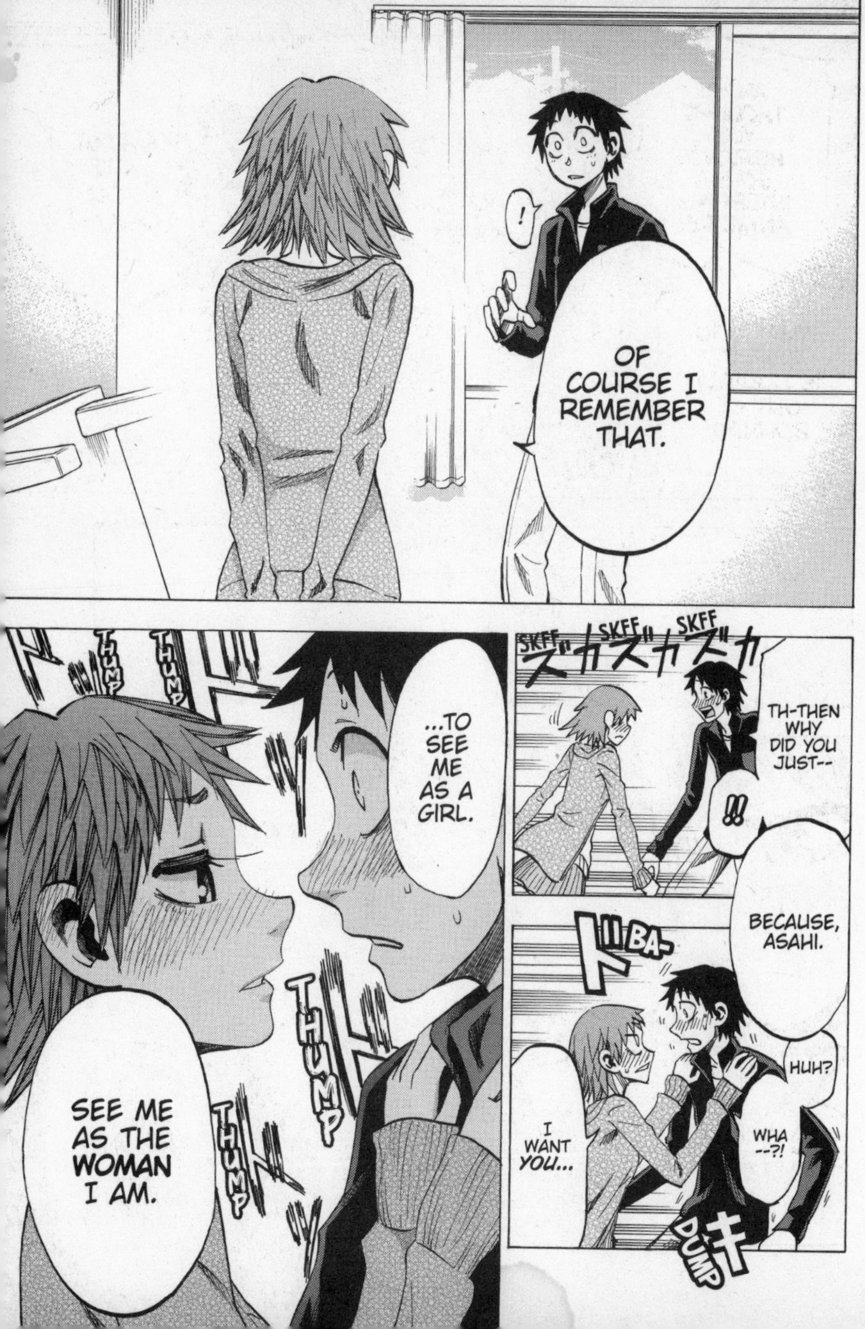
!
OF COURSE I REMEMBER THAT.
SKFF SKFF SKFF
ズカズカズカ
TH-THEN WHY DID YOU JUST--
!!
BA-
BECAUSE, ASAHI.
HUH?
WHA--?!
I WANT YOU...
DUMP
...TO SEE ME AS A GIRL.
THUMP
THUMP
SEE ME AS THE WOMAN I AM.
THUMP
THUMP

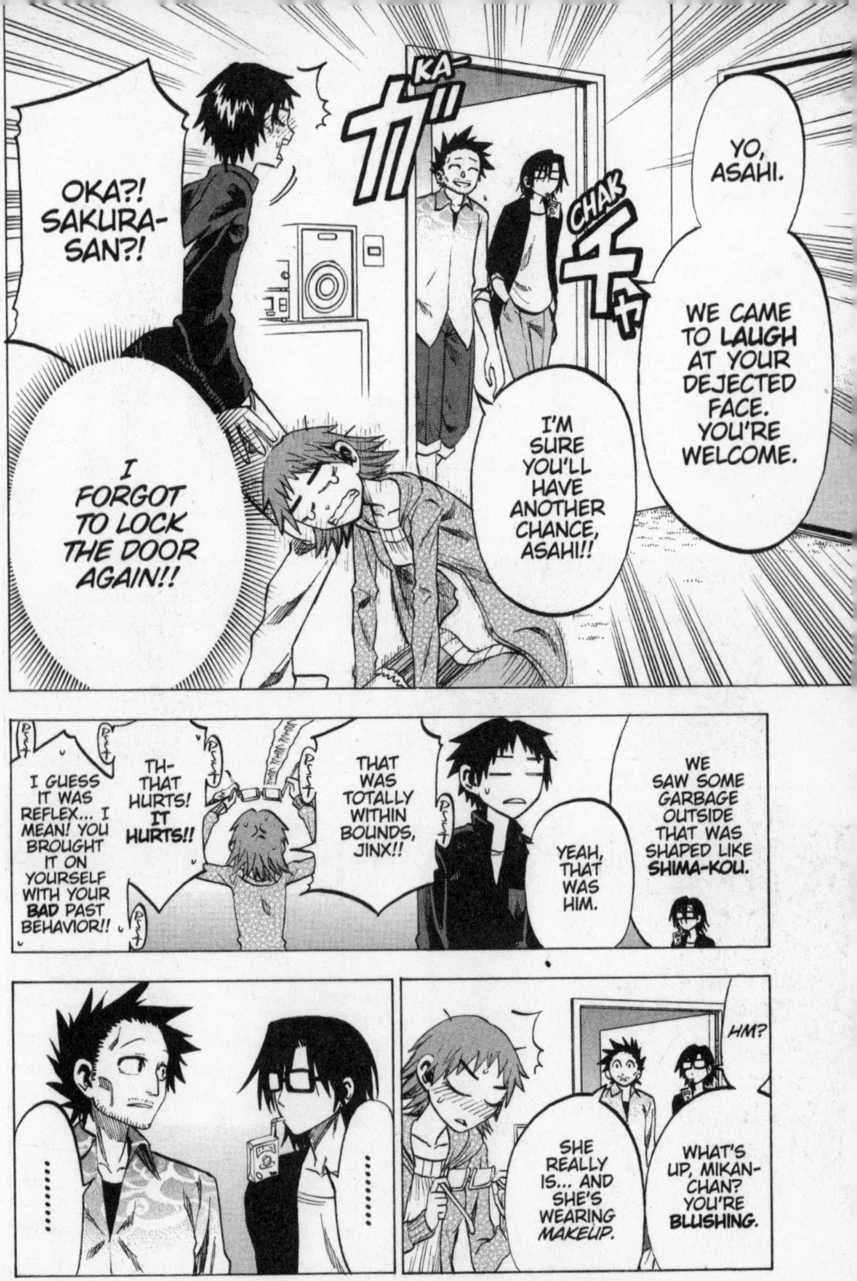
YO, ASAHI.
WE CAME TO LAUGH AT YOUR DEJECTED FACE. YOU'RE WELCOME.
CHAK
I'M SURE YOU'LL HAVE ANOTHER CHANCE, ASAHI!!
KA-
OKA?! SAKURA-SAN?!
I FORGOT TO LOCK THE DOOR AGAIN!!
WE SAW SOME GARBAGE OUTSIDE THAT WAS SHAPED LIKE SHIMA-KOU.
YEAH, THAT WAS HIM.
THAT WAS TOTALLY WITHIN BOUNDS, JINX!!
TH-THAT HURTS! IT HURTS!!
I GUESS IT WAS REFLEX... I MEAN! YOU BROUGHT IT ON YOURSELF WITH YOUR BAD PAST BEHAVIOR!!
HM?
WHAT'S UP, MIKAN-CHAN? YOU'RE BLUSHING.
SHE REALLY IS... AND SHE'S WEARING MAKEUP.
......
......

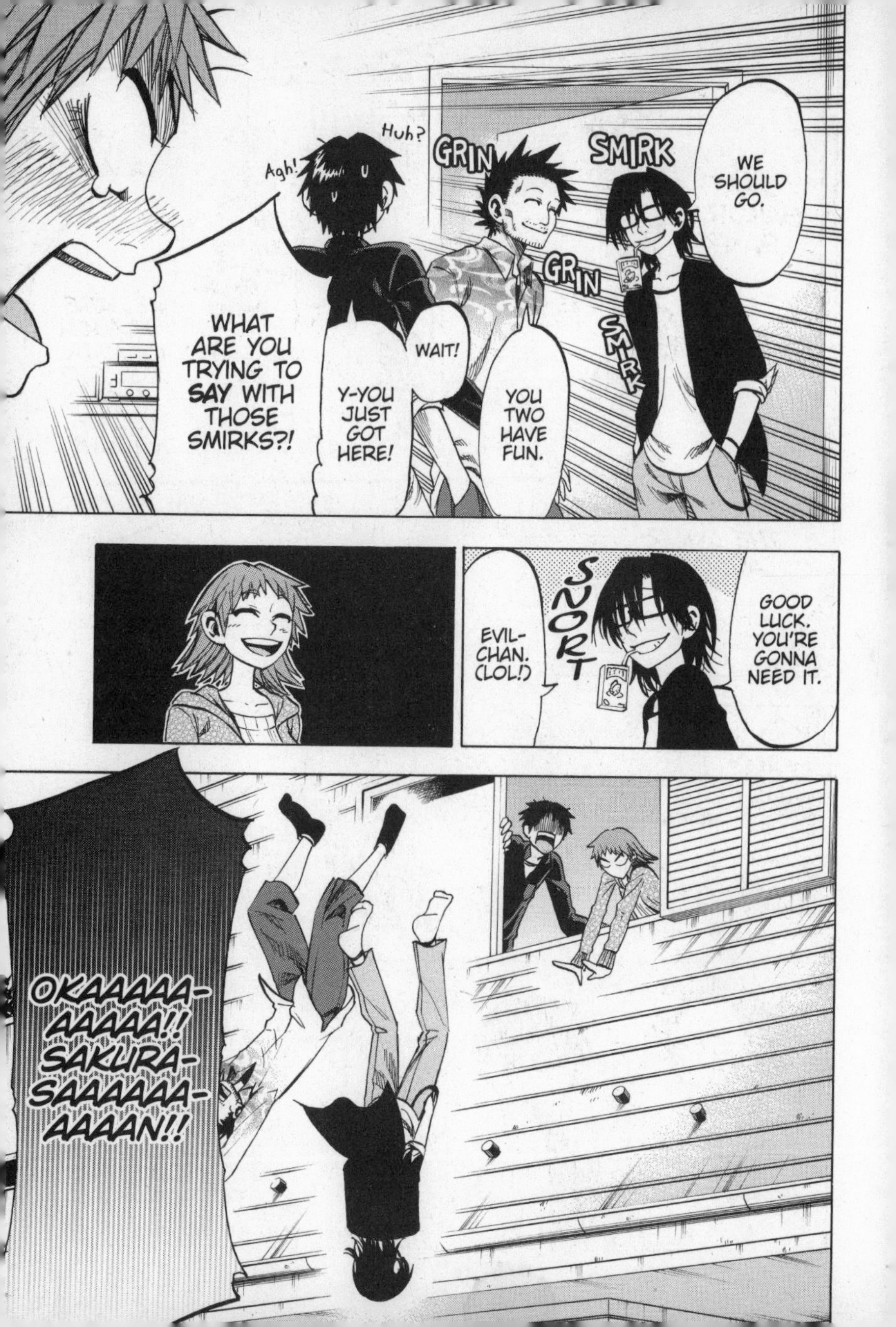
WE SHOULD GO.
SMIRK
GRIN
Huh?
Agh!
GRIN
SMIRK
YOU TWO HAVE FUN.
WAIT!
Y-YOU JUST GOT HERE!
WHAT ARE YOU TRYING TO SAY WITH THOSE SMIRKS?!
GOOD LUCK. YOU'RE GONNA NEED IT.
SNORT
EVIL-CHAN. (LOL!)
OKAAAAAA-AAAAAA!! SAKURA-SAAAAAAA-AAAAN!!

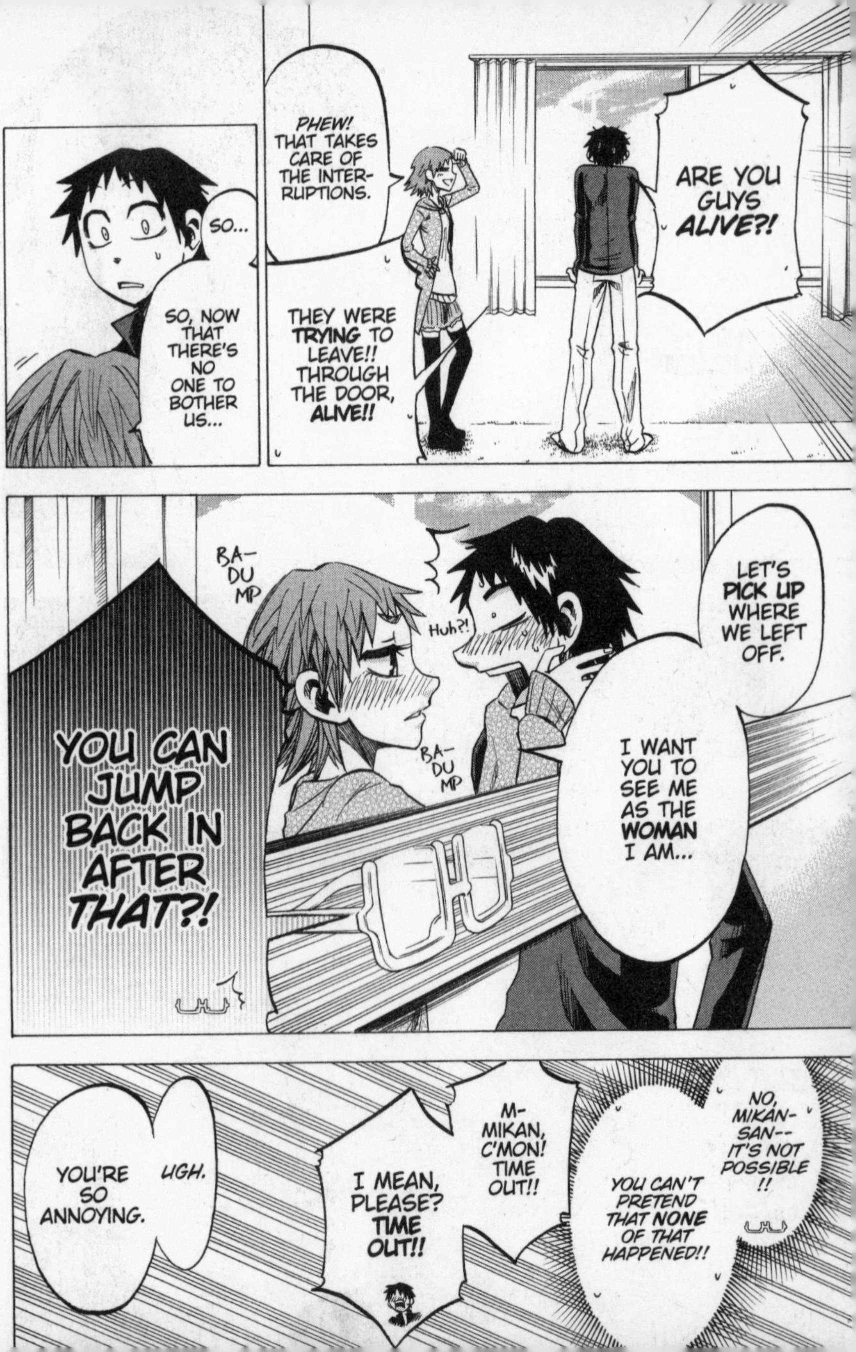
ARE YOU GUYS ALIVE?!
PHEW! THAT TAKES CARE OF THE INTER-RUPTIONS.
THEY WERE TRYING TO LEAVE!! THROUGH THE DOOR, ALIVE!!
SO...
SO, NOW THAT THERE'S NO ONE TO BOTHER US...
LET'S PICK UP WHERE WE LEFT OFF.
BA-DUMP
Huh?!
BA-DUMP
I WANT YOU TO SEE ME AS THE WOMAN I AM...
YOU CAN JUMP BACK IN AFTER THAT?!
NO, MIKAN-SAN-- IT'S NOT POSSIBLE!!
YOU CAN'T PRETEND THAT NONE OF THAT HAPPENED!!
M-MIKAN, C'MON! TIME OUT!!
I MEAN, PLEASE? TIME OUT!!
UGH.
YOU'RE SO ANNOYING.

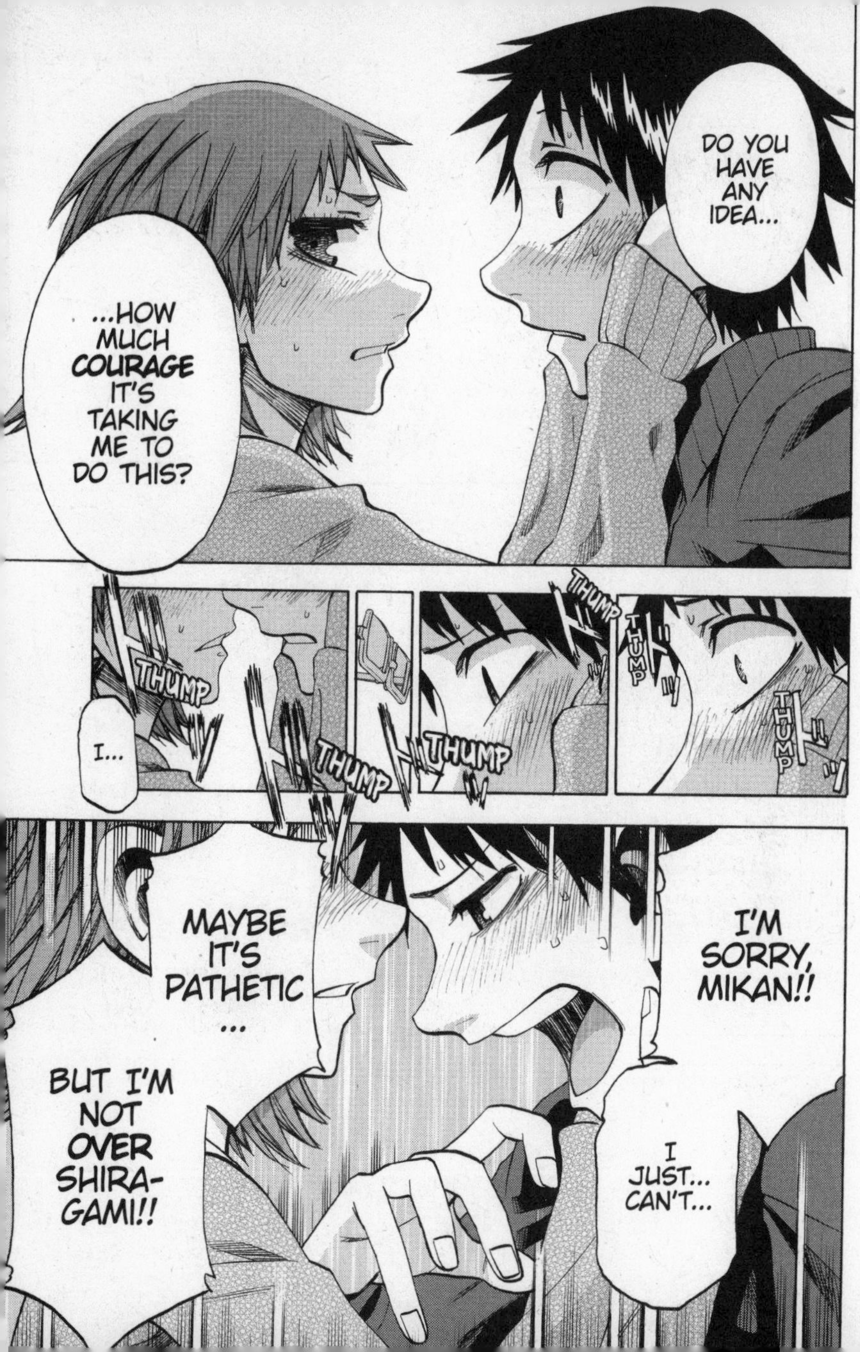
DO YOU HAVE ANY IDEA...
...HOW MUCH COURAGE IT'S TAKING ME TO DO THIS?
THUMP
THUMP
THUMP
THUMP
THUMP
THUMP
THUMP
I...
I'M SORRY, MIKAN!!
MAYBE IT'S PATHETIC...
BUT I'M NOT OVER SHIRA-GAMI!!
I JUST... CAN'T...

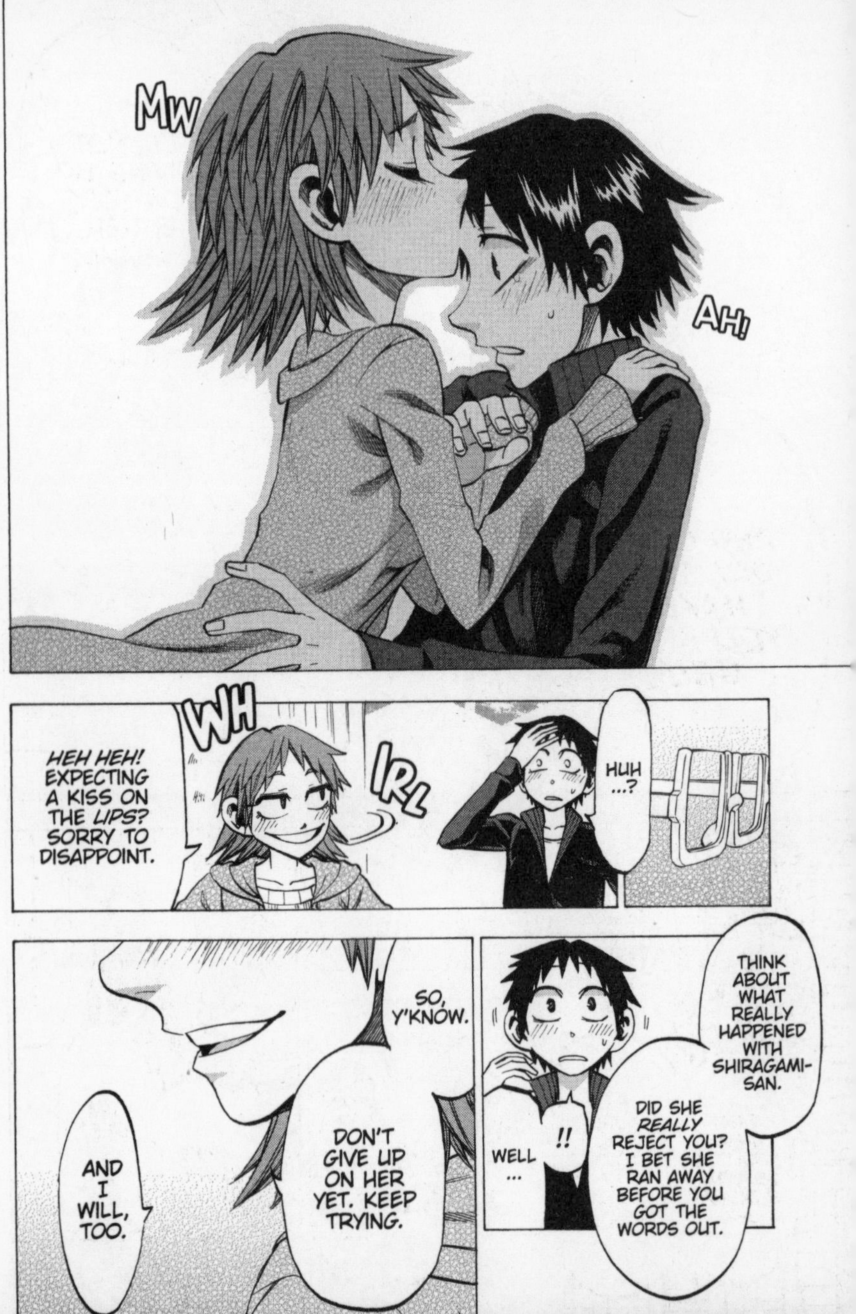
MW
AH!
HUH ...?
WHIRL
HEH HEH! EXPECTING A KISS ON THE LIPS? SORRY TO DISAPPOINT.
THINK ABOUT WHAT REALLY HAPPENED WITH SHIRAGAMI-SAN.
DID SHE REALLY REJECT YOU? I BET SHE RAN AWAY BEFORE YOU GOT THE WORDS OUT.
!!
WELL ...
SO, Y'KNOW.
DON'T GIVE UP ON HER YET. KEEP TRYING.
AND I WILL, TOO.

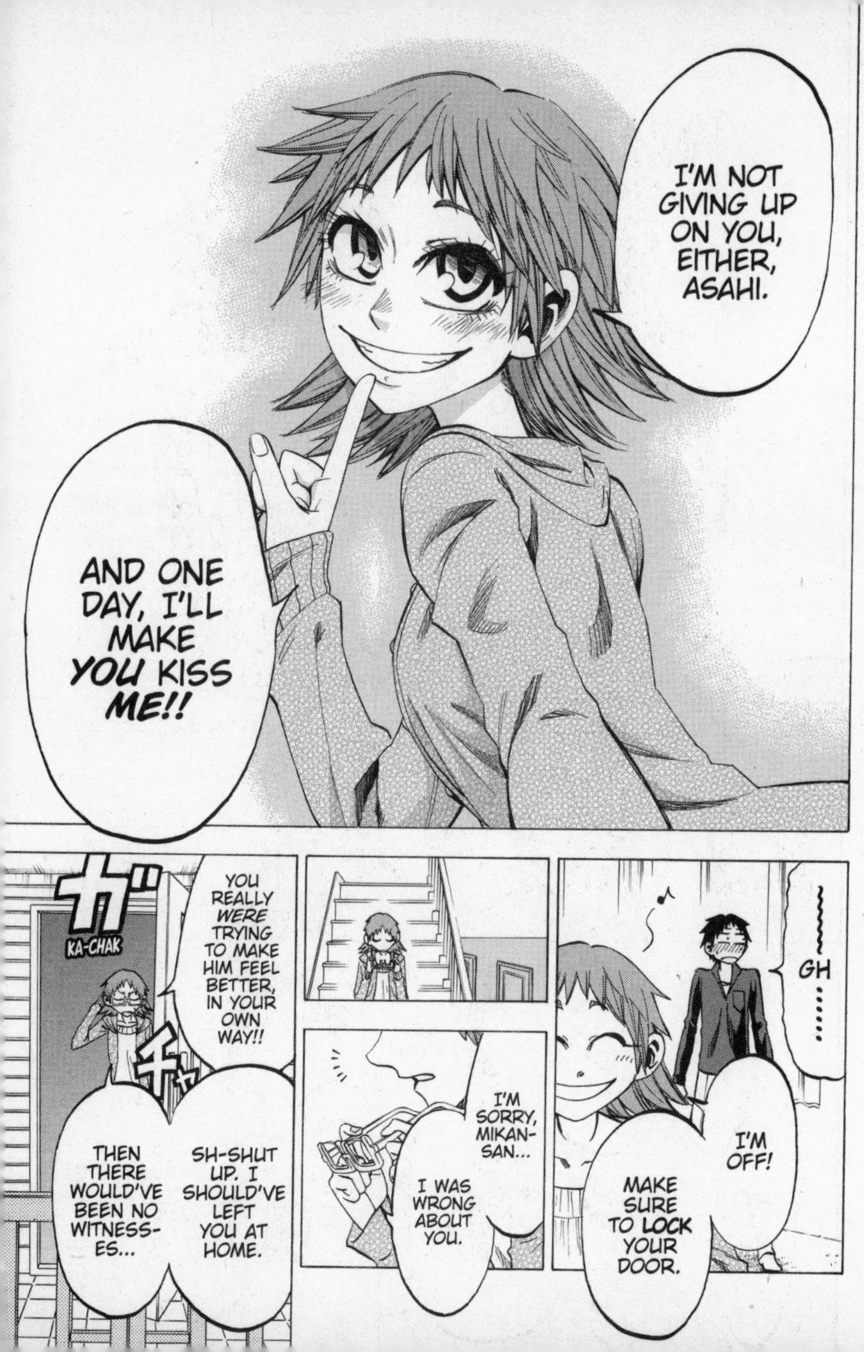
I'M NOT GIVING UP ON YOU, EITHER, ASAHI.
AND ONE DAY, I'LL MAKE YOU KISS ME!!
GH......
I'M OFF!
MAKE SURE TO LOCK YOUR DOOR.
I'M SORRY, MIKAN-SAN...
I WAS WRONG ABOUT YOU.
KA-CHAK
YOU REALLY WERE TRYING TO MAKE HIM FEEL BETTER, IN YOUR OWN WAY!!
SH-SHUT UP. I SHOULD'VE LEFT YOU AT HOME.
THEN THERE WOULD'VE BEEN NO WITNESS-ES...

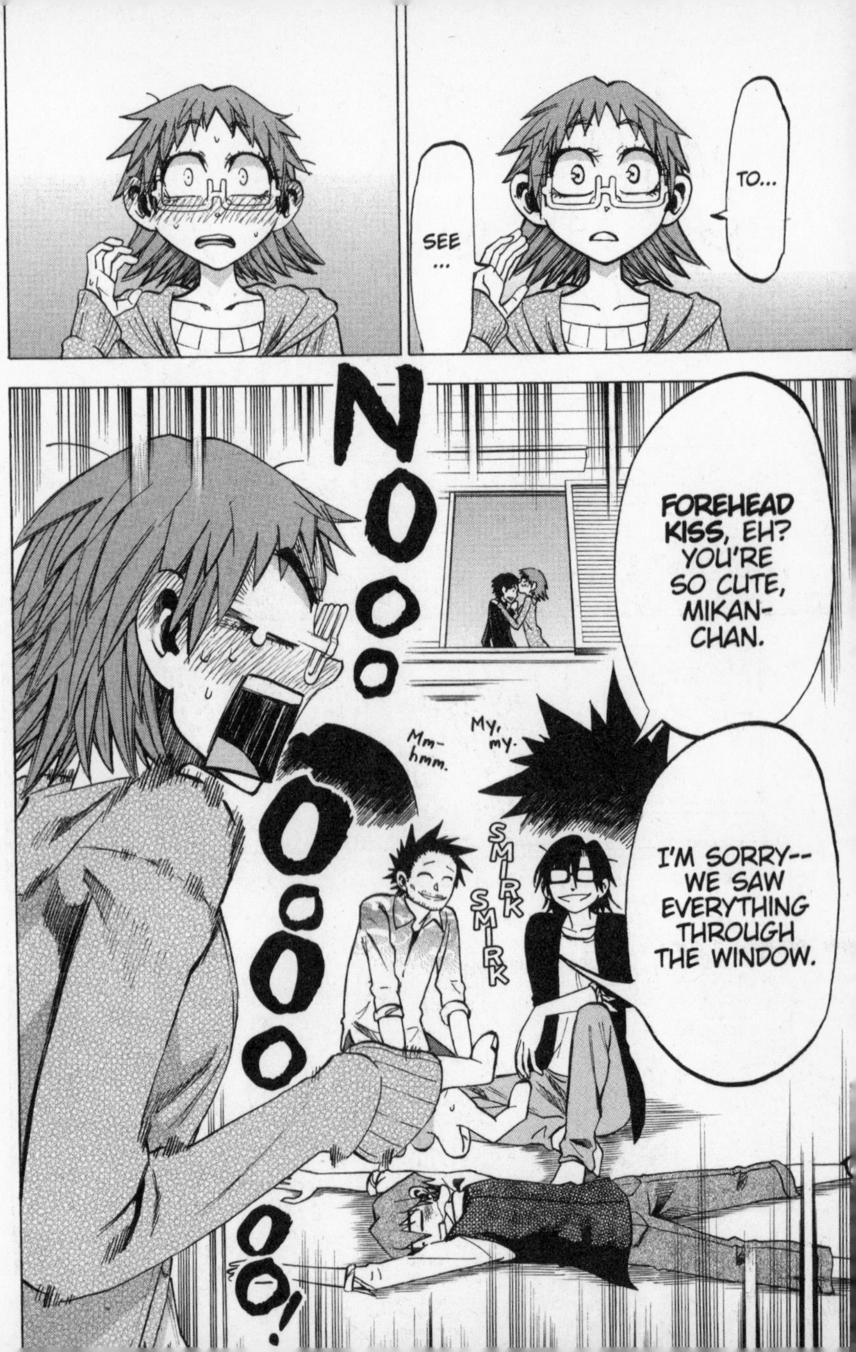
TO...
SEE ...
FOREHEAD KISS, EH? YOU'RE SO CUTE, MIKAN-CHAN.
I'M SORRY-- WE SAW EVERYTHING THROUGH THE WINDOW.
My, my.
Mm-hmm.
SMIRK
SMIRK
NOOOOOOOOOO!

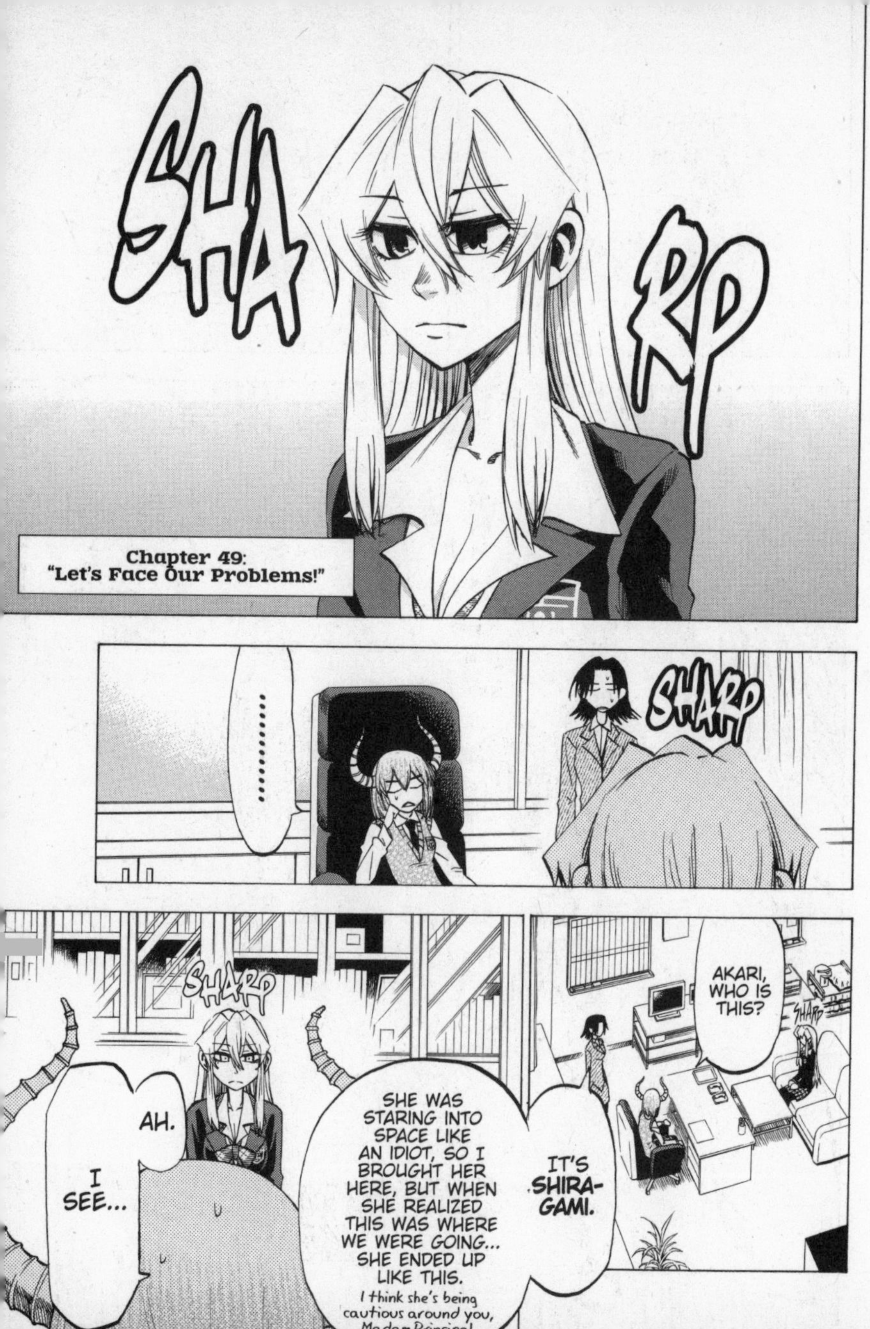
SHARP
Chapter 49: "Let's Face Our Problems!"
SHARP
......
AKARI, WHO IS THIS?
SHARP
IT'S SHIRAGAMI.
SHARP
SHE WAS STARING INTO SPACE LIKE AN IDIOT, SO I BROUGHT HER HERE, BUT WHEN SHE REALIZED THIS WAS WHERE WE WERE GOING... SHE ENDED UP LIKE THIS.
I think she's being cautious around you, Madam Principal.
AH.
I SEE...

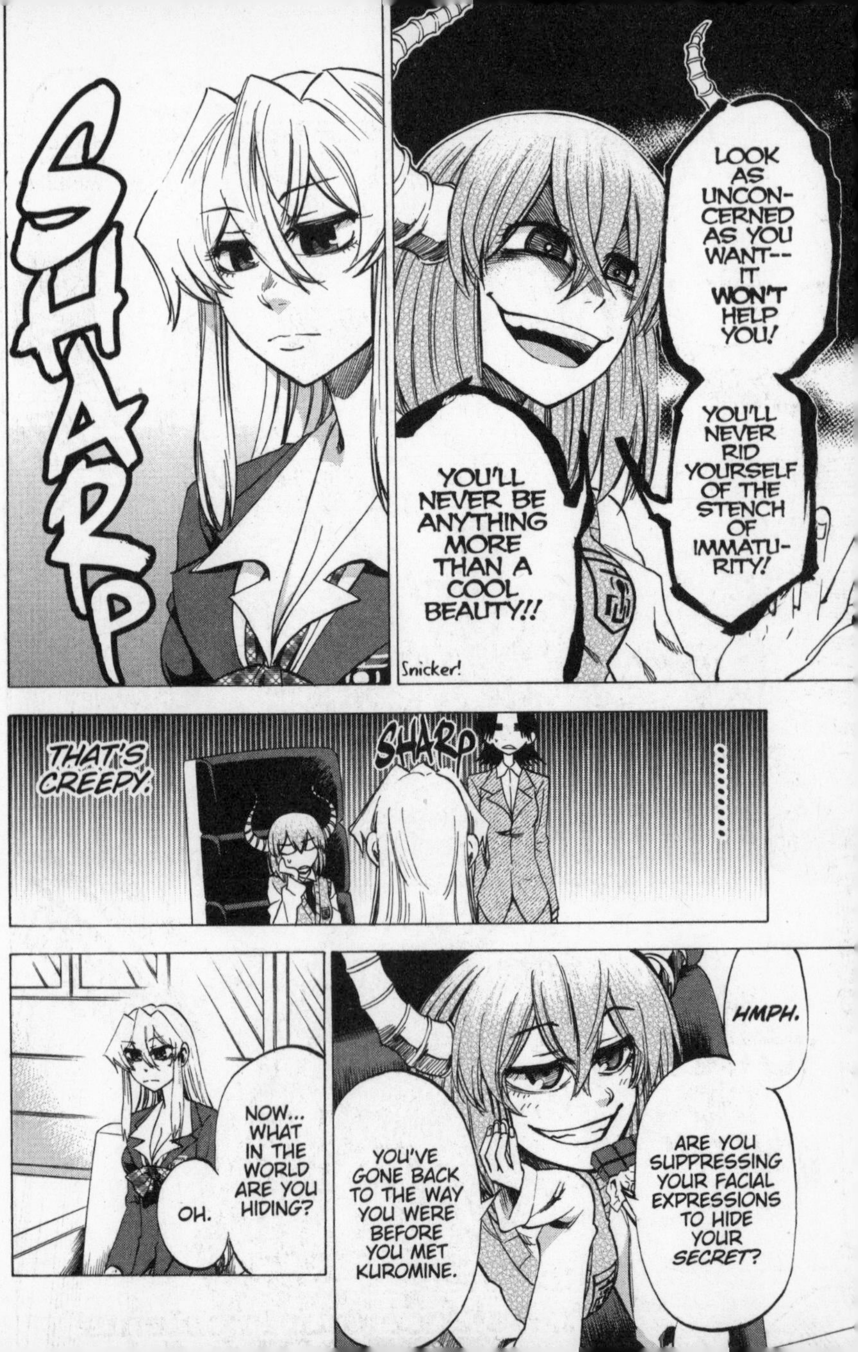
LOOK AS UNCONCERNED AS YOU WANT-- IT WON'T HELP YOU!
YOU'LL NEVER RID YOURSELF OF THE STENCH OF IMMATURITY!
YOU'LL NEVER BE ANYTHING MORE THAN A COOL BEAUTY!!
Snicker!
SHARP
....
SHARP
THAT'S CREEPY.
HMPH.
ARE YOU SUPPRESSING YOUR FACIAL EXPRESSIONS TO HIDE YOUR SECRET?
YOU'VE GONE BACK TO THE WAY YOU WERE BEFORE YOU MET KUROMINE.
NOW... WHAT IN THE WORLD ARE YOU HIDING?
OH.

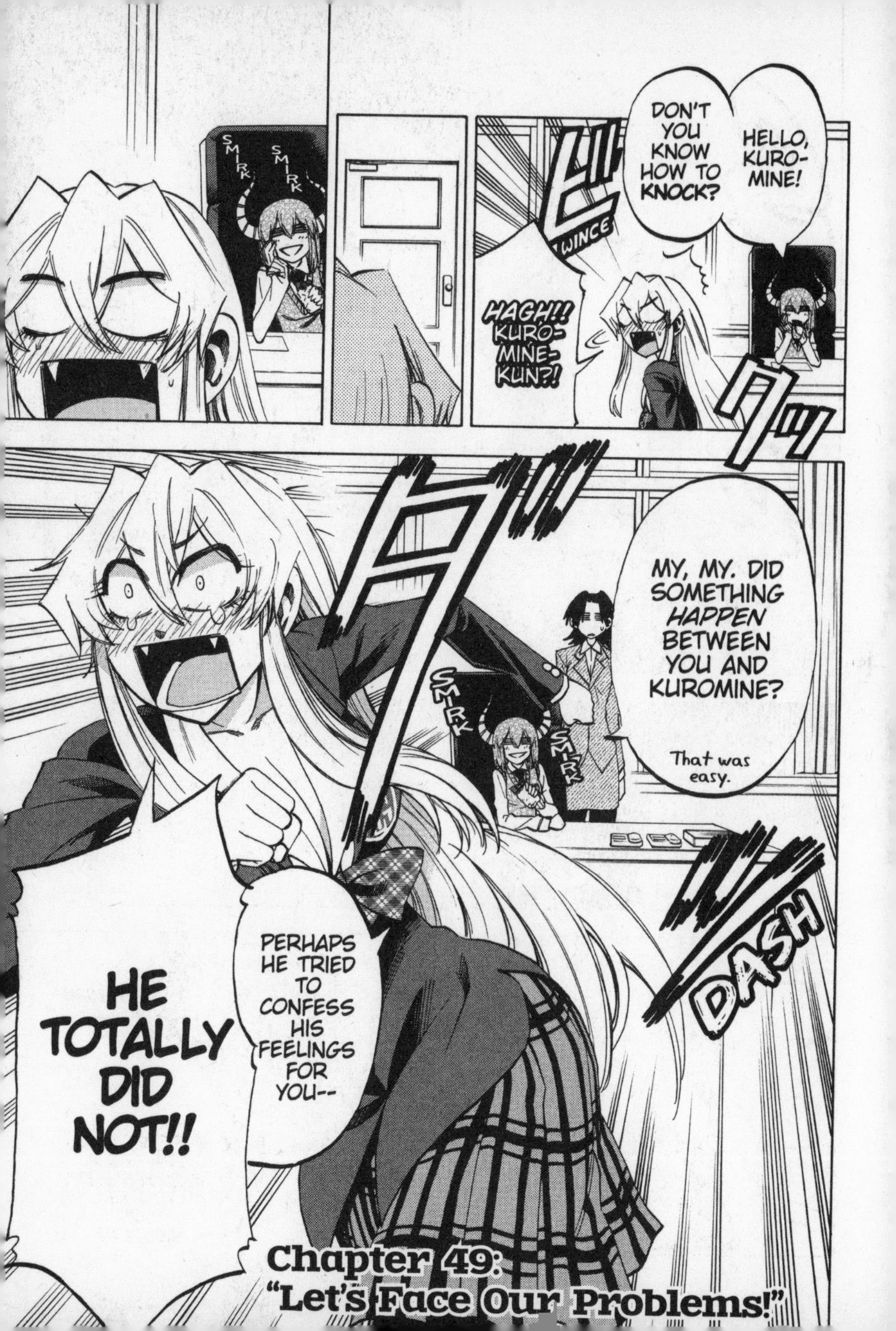
HELLO, KURO-MINE!
DON'T YOU KNOW HOW TO KNOCK?
WINCE
HAGH!! KURO-MINE-KUN?!
SMIRK
SMIRK
MY, MY. DID SOMETHING *HAPPEN* BETWEEN YOU AND KUROMINE?
That was easy.
DASH
SMIRK
SMIRK
PERHAPS HE TRIED TO CONFESS HIS FEELINGS FOR YOU--
HE TOTALLY DID NOT!!

Chapter 49: "Let's Face Our Problems!"

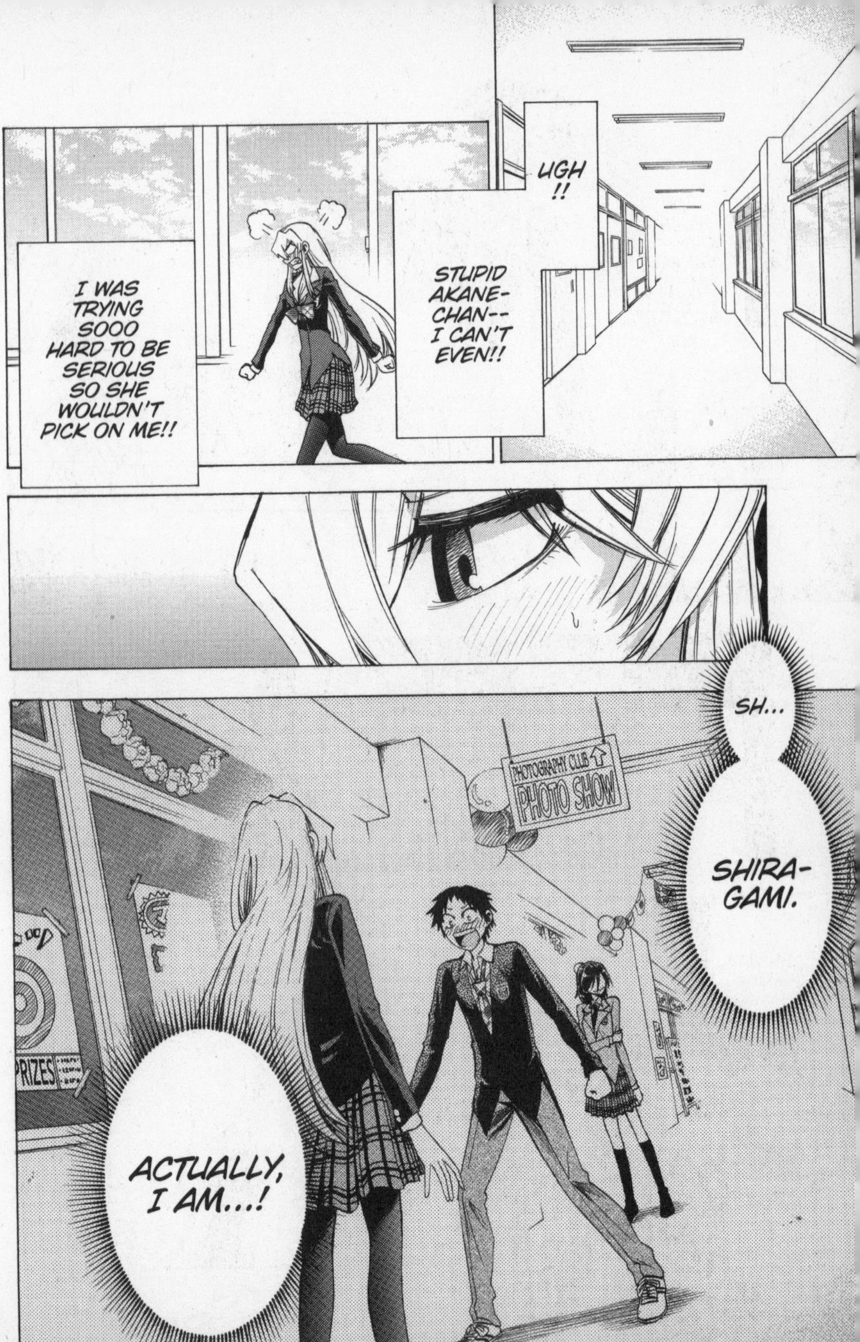
UGH !!
STUPID AKANE-CHAN-- I CAN'T EVEN!!
I WAS TRYING SOOO HARD TO BE SERIOUS SO SHE WOULDN'T PICK ON ME!!
SH...
SHIRA-GAMI.
PHOTOGRAPHY CLUB
PHOTO SHOW
PRIZES
ACTUALLY, I AM...!

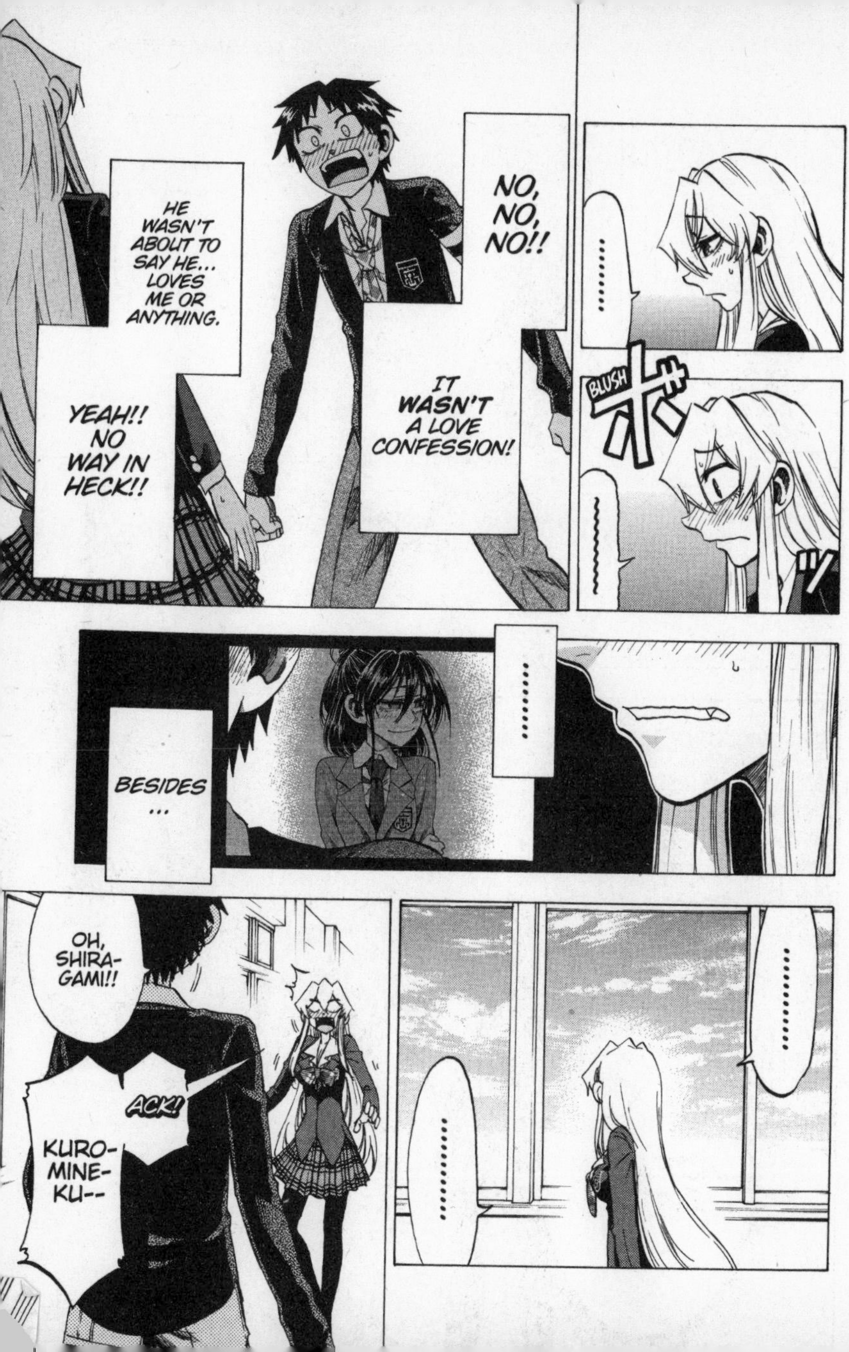
......
BLUSH
NO, NO, NO!!
IT WASN'T A LOVE CONFESSION!
HE WASN'T ABOUT TO SAY HE... LOVES ME OR ANYTHING.
YEAH!! NO WAY IN HECK!!
....
BESIDES ...
....
....
OH, SHIRA-GAMI!!
ACK!
KURO-MINE-KU--

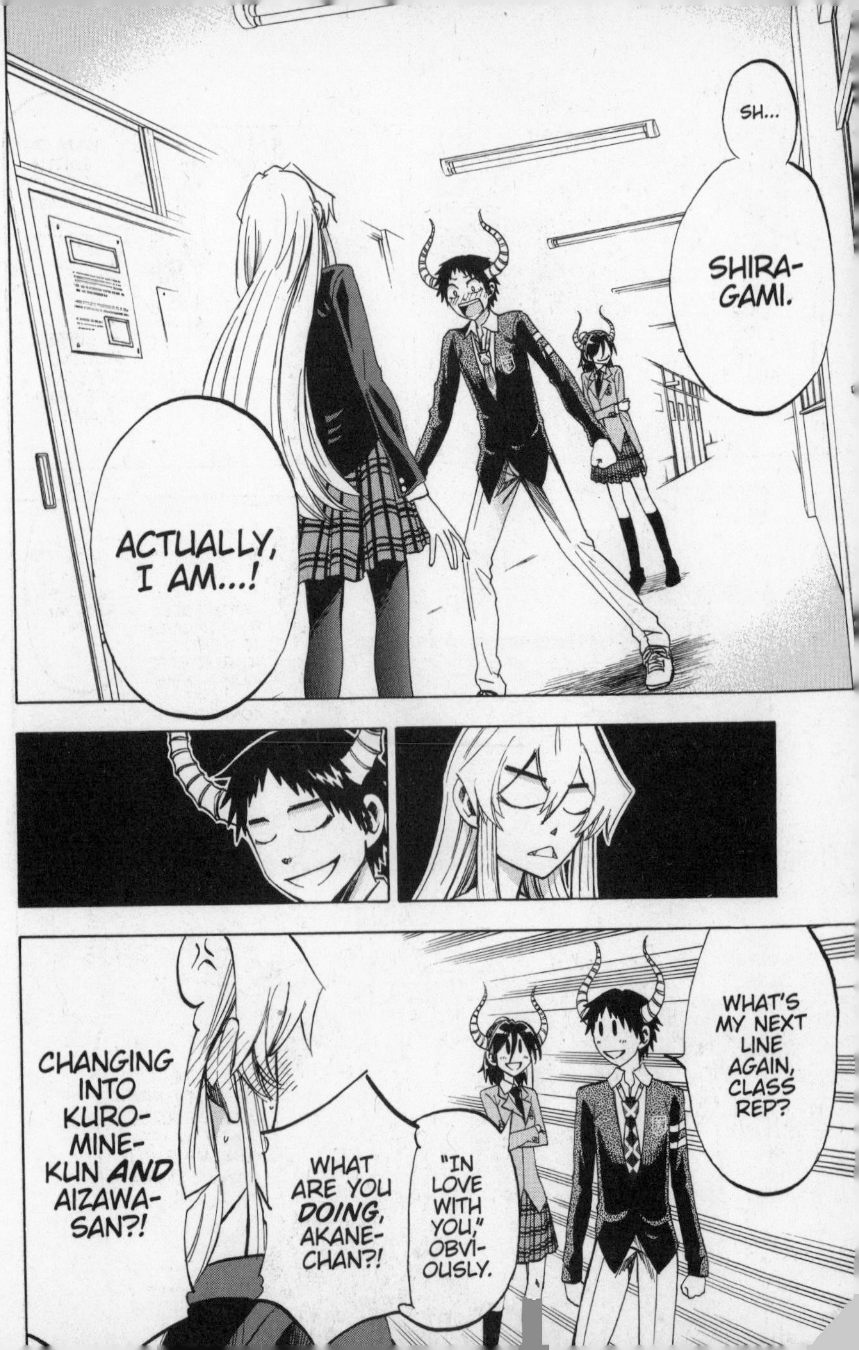
SH...
SHIRAGAMI.
ACTUALLY, I AM...!
WHAT'S MY NEXT LINE AGAIN, CLASS REP?
"IN LOVE WITH YOU," OBVIOUSLY.
WHAT ARE YOU *DOING*, AKANE-CHAN?!
CHANGING INTO KUROMINE-KUN *AND* AIZAWA-SAN?!

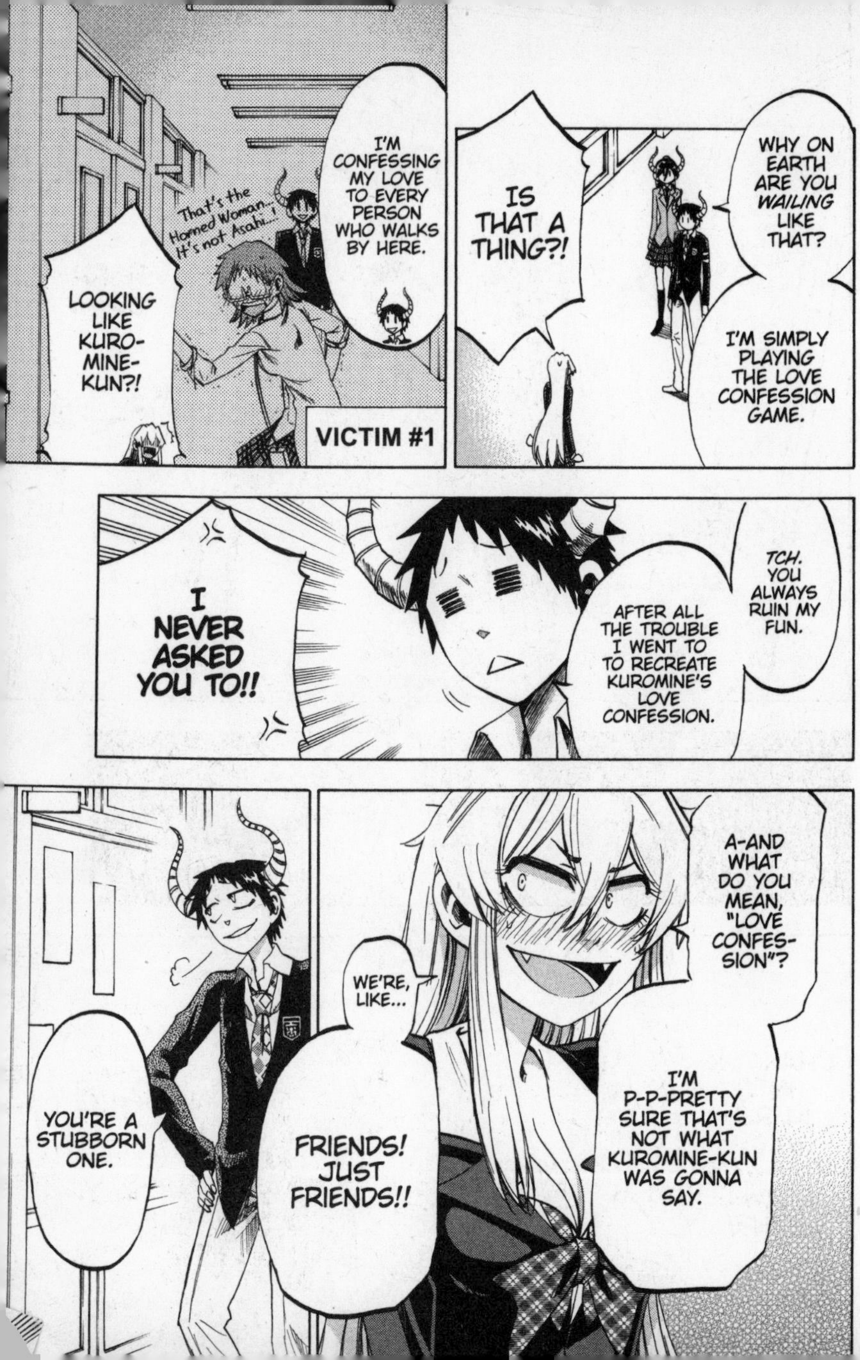
WHY ON EARTH ARE YOU *WAILING* LIKE THAT?
I'M SIMPLY PLAYING THE LOVE CONFESSION GAME.
IS THAT A THING?!
I'M CONFESSING MY LOVE TO EVERY PERSON WHO WALKS BY HERE.
That's the Horned Woman... It's not Asahi...!
LOOKING LIKE KUROMINE-KUN?!
VICTIM #1
TCH. YOU ALWAYS RUIN MY FUN.
AFTER ALL THE TROUBLE I WENT TO TO RECREATE KUROMINE'S LOVE CONFESSION.
I NEVER ASKED YOU TO!!
A-AND WHAT DO YOU MEAN, "LOVE CONFESSION"?
WE'RE, LIKE...
I'M P-P-PRETTY SURE THAT'S NOT WHAT KUROMINE-KUN WAS GONNA SAY.
FRIENDS! JUST FRIENDS!!
YOU'RE A STUBBORN ONE.

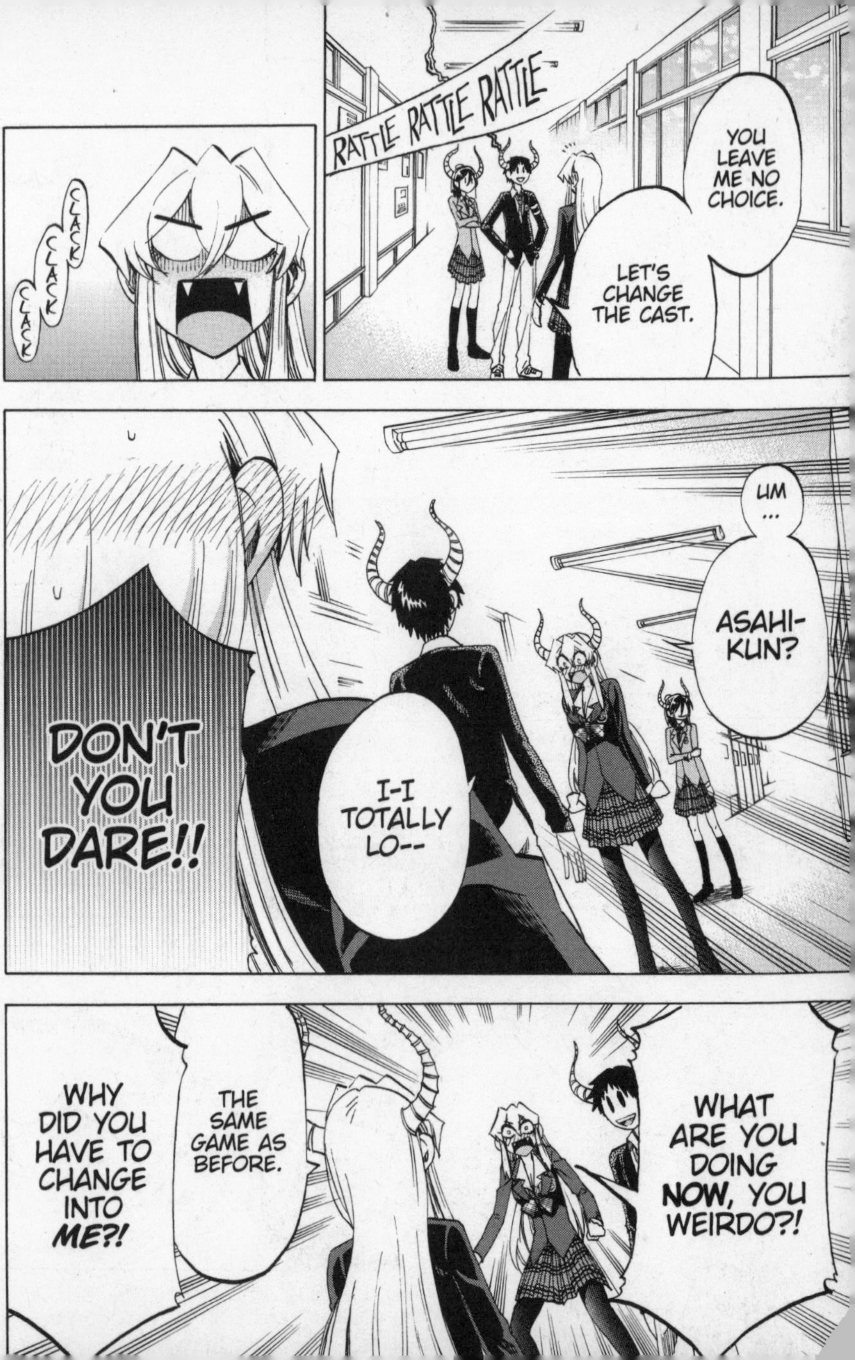
RATTLE RATTLE RATTLE
YOU LEAVE ME NO CHOICE.
LET'S CHANGE THE CAST.
CLACK CLACK CLACK
UM ... ASAHI-KUN?
I-I TOTALLY LO--
DON'T YOU DARE!!
WHAT ARE YOU DOING **NOW**, YOU WEIRDO?!
THE SAME GAME AS BEFORE.
WHY DID YOU HAVE TO CHANGE INTO ***ME?!***

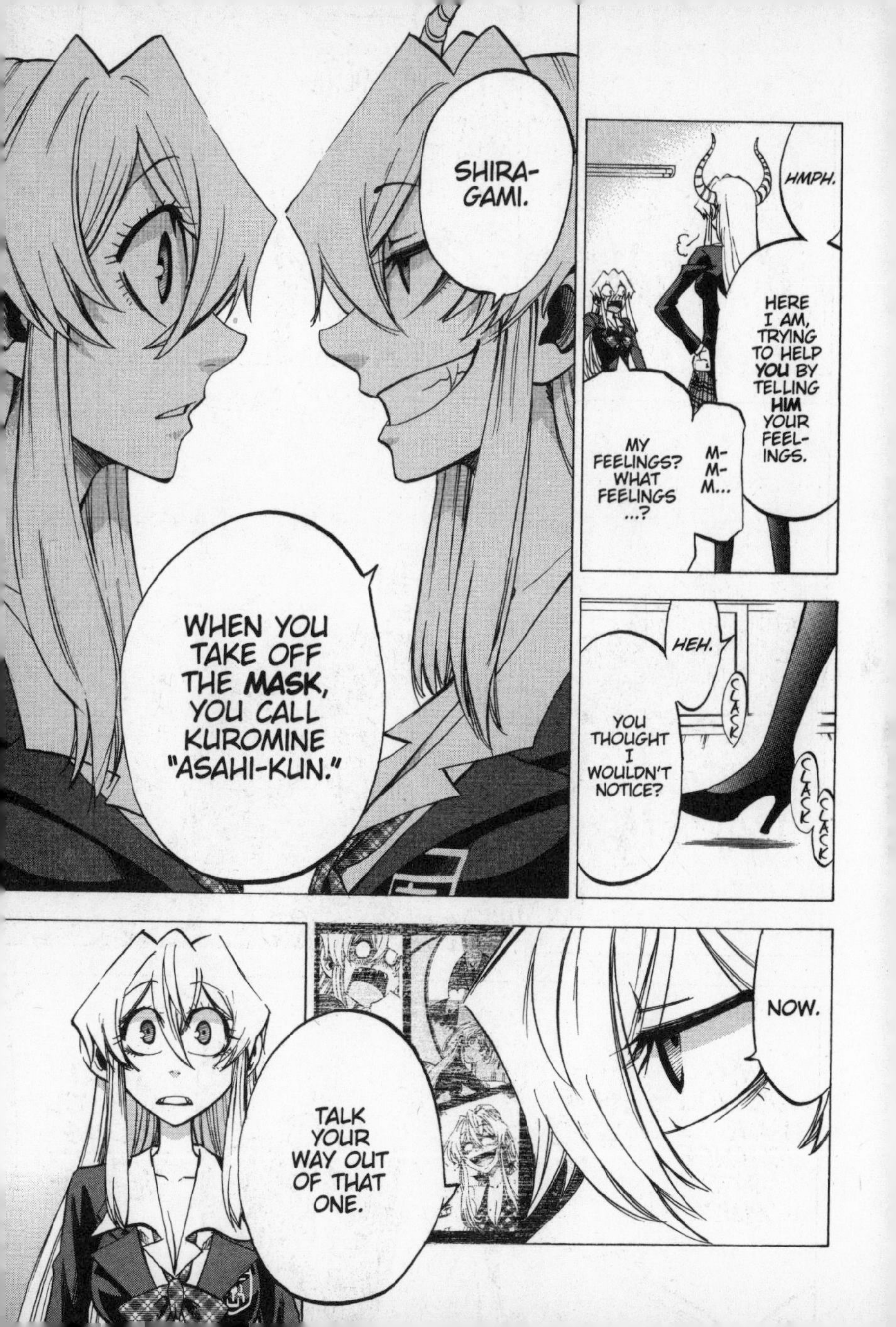
HMPH.
HERE I AM, TRYING TO HELP YOU BY TELLING HIM YOUR FEEL-INGS.
M-M-M...
MY FEELINGS? WHAT FEELINGS ...?
HEH.
CLACK
YOU THOUGHT I WOULDN'T NOTICE?
CLACK
CLACK
CLACK
SHIRA-GAMI.
WHEN YOU TAKE OFF THE MASK, YOU CALL KUROMINE "ASAHI-KUN."
NOW.
TALK YOUR WAY OUT OF THAT ONE.

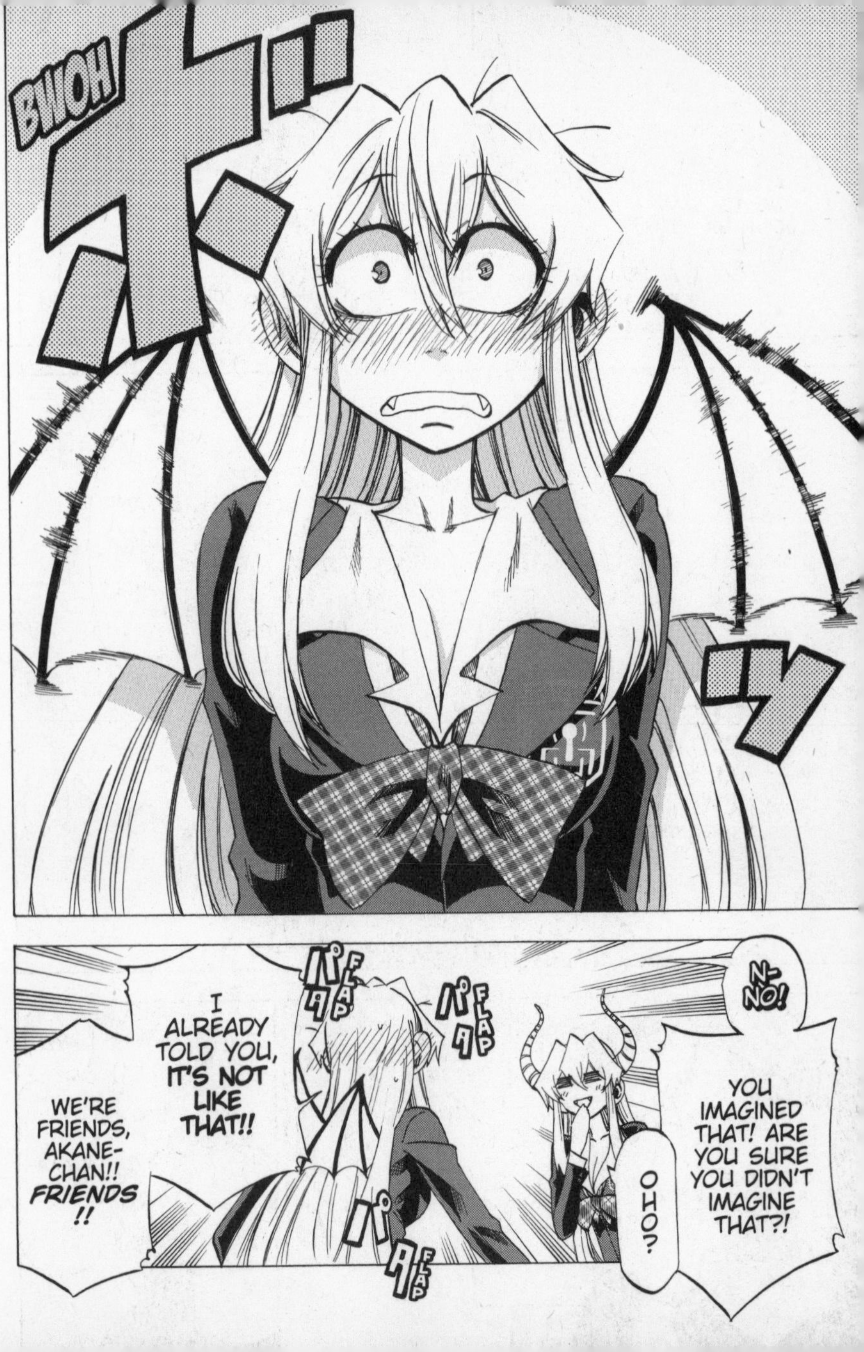
BWOH
N-NO!
YOU IMAGINED THAT! ARE YOU SURE YOU DIDN'T IMAGINE THAT?!
OHO?
FLAP
FLAP
I ALREADY TOLD YOU, IT'S NOT LIKE THAT!!
FLAP
WE'RE FRIENDS, AKANE-CHAN!! FRIENDS !!

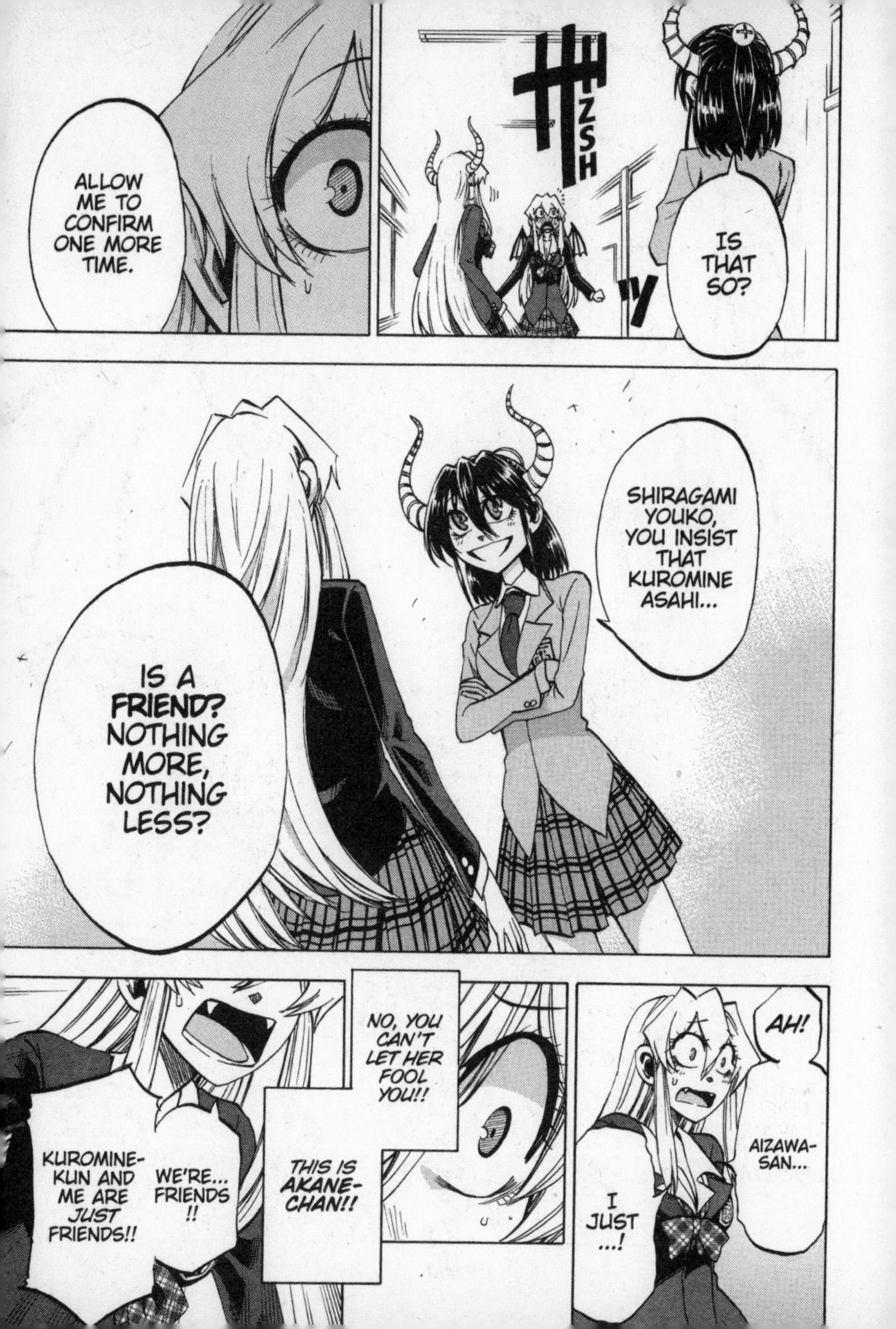
IS THAT SO?
ZSH
ALLOW ME TO CONFIRM ONE MORE TIME.
SHIRAGAMI YOUKO, YOU INSIST THAT KUROMINE ASAHI...
IS A FRIEND? NOTHING MORE, NOTHING LESS?
AH!
AIZAWA-SAN...
I JUST ...!
NO, YOU CAN'T LET HER FOOL YOU!!
THIS IS AKANE-CHAN!!
WE'RE... FRIENDS !!
KUROMINE-KUN AND ME ARE JUST FRIENDS!!

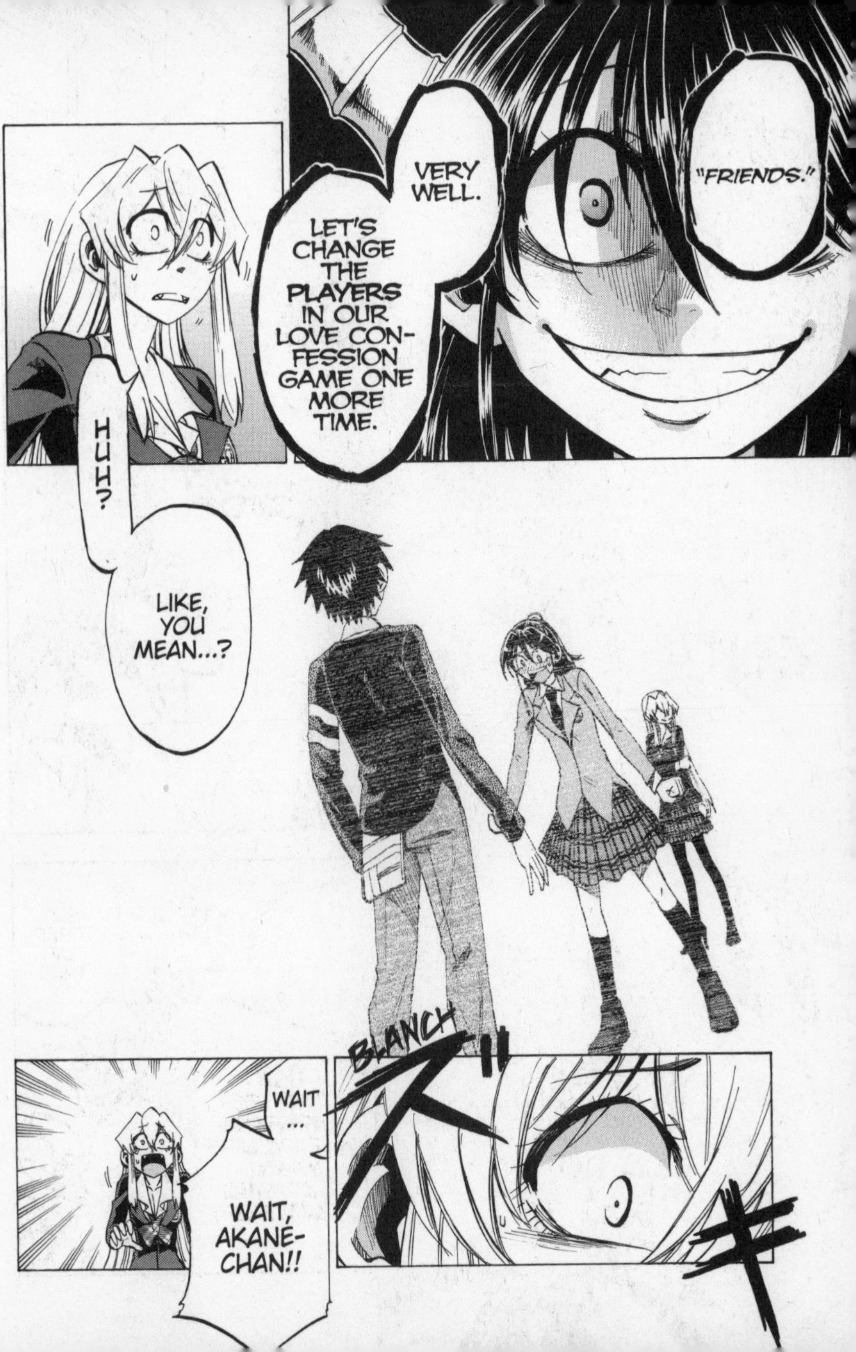

"FRIENDS."
VERY WELL.
LET'S CHANGE THE PLAYERS IN OUR LOVE CON-FESSION GAME ONE MORE TIME.
HUH?
LIKE, YOU MEAN...?
BLANCH
WAIT ...
WAIT, AKANE-CHAN!!

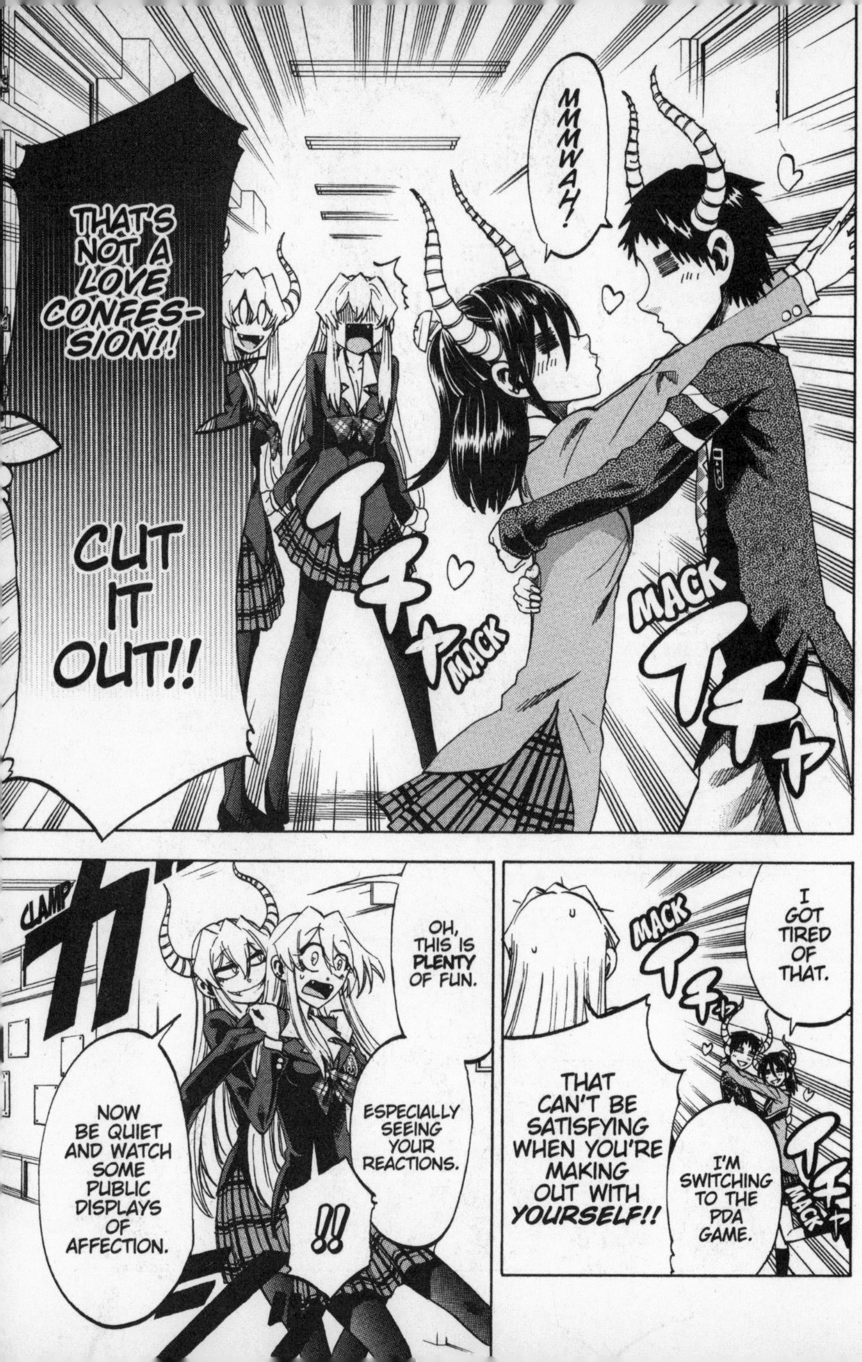
MMMWAH!
MACK
THAT'S NOT A LOVE CONFESSION!!
MACK
CUT IT OUT!!
I GOT TIRED OF THAT.
MACK
THAT CAN'T BE SATISFYING WHEN YOU'RE MAKING OUT WITH *YOURSELF*!!
I'M SWITCHING TO THE PDA GAME.
MACK
OH, THIS IS **PLENTY** OF FUN.
CLAMP
ESPECIALLY SEEING YOUR REACTIONS.
NOW BE QUIET AND WATCH SOME PUBLIC DISPLAYS OF AFFECTION.
!!

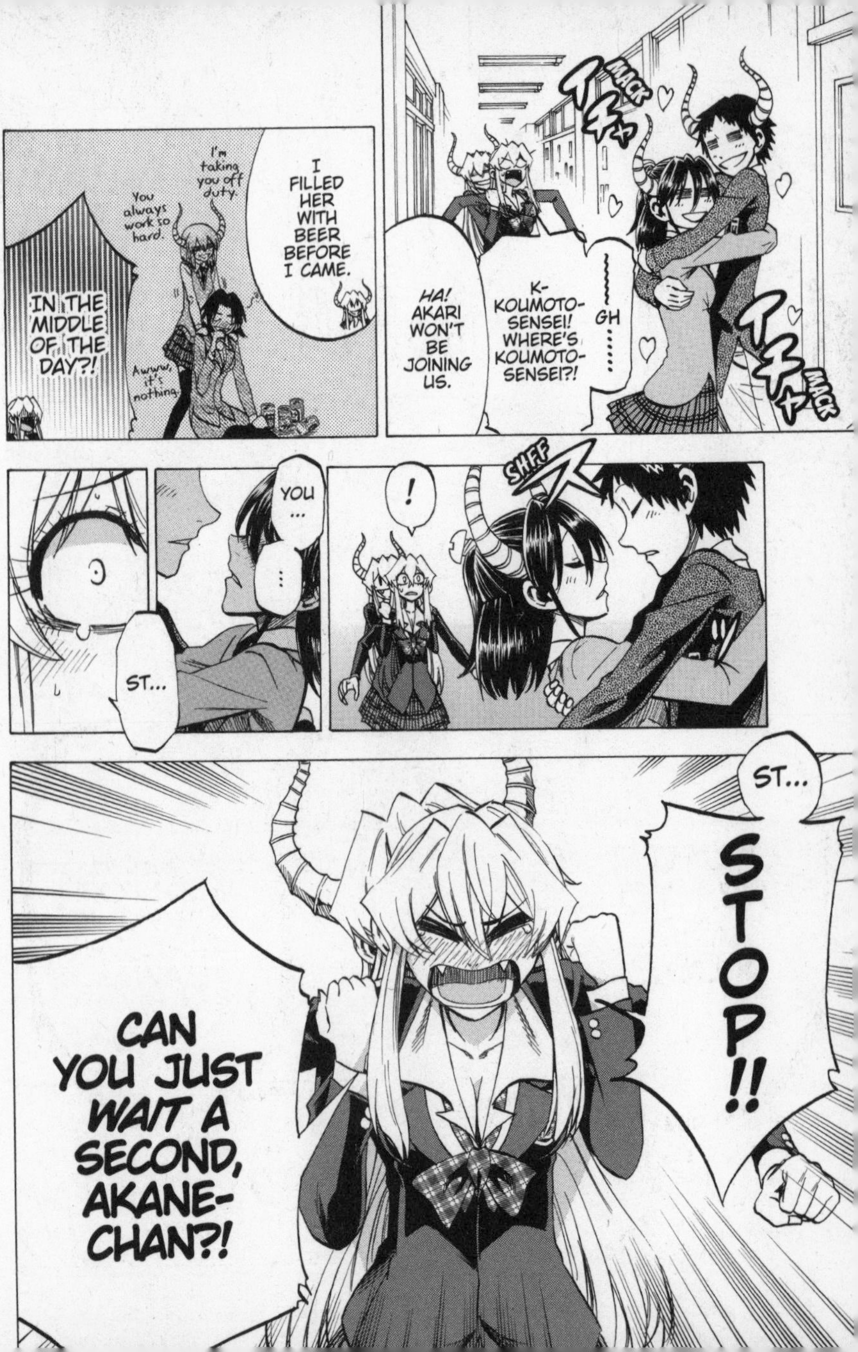
MACK
~~~~GH......
K-KOUMOTO-SENSEI! WHERE'S KOUMOTO-SENSEI?!
HA! AKARI WON'T BE JOINING US.
MACK
I FILLED HER WITH BEER BEFORE I CAME.
I'm taking you off duty.
You always work so hard.
IN THE MIDDLE OF THE DAY?!
Awww, it's nothing.
SHFF
!
YOU ...
...
ST...
ST...
STOP!!
CAN YOU JUST WAIT A SECOND, AKANE-CHAN?!
~~~~

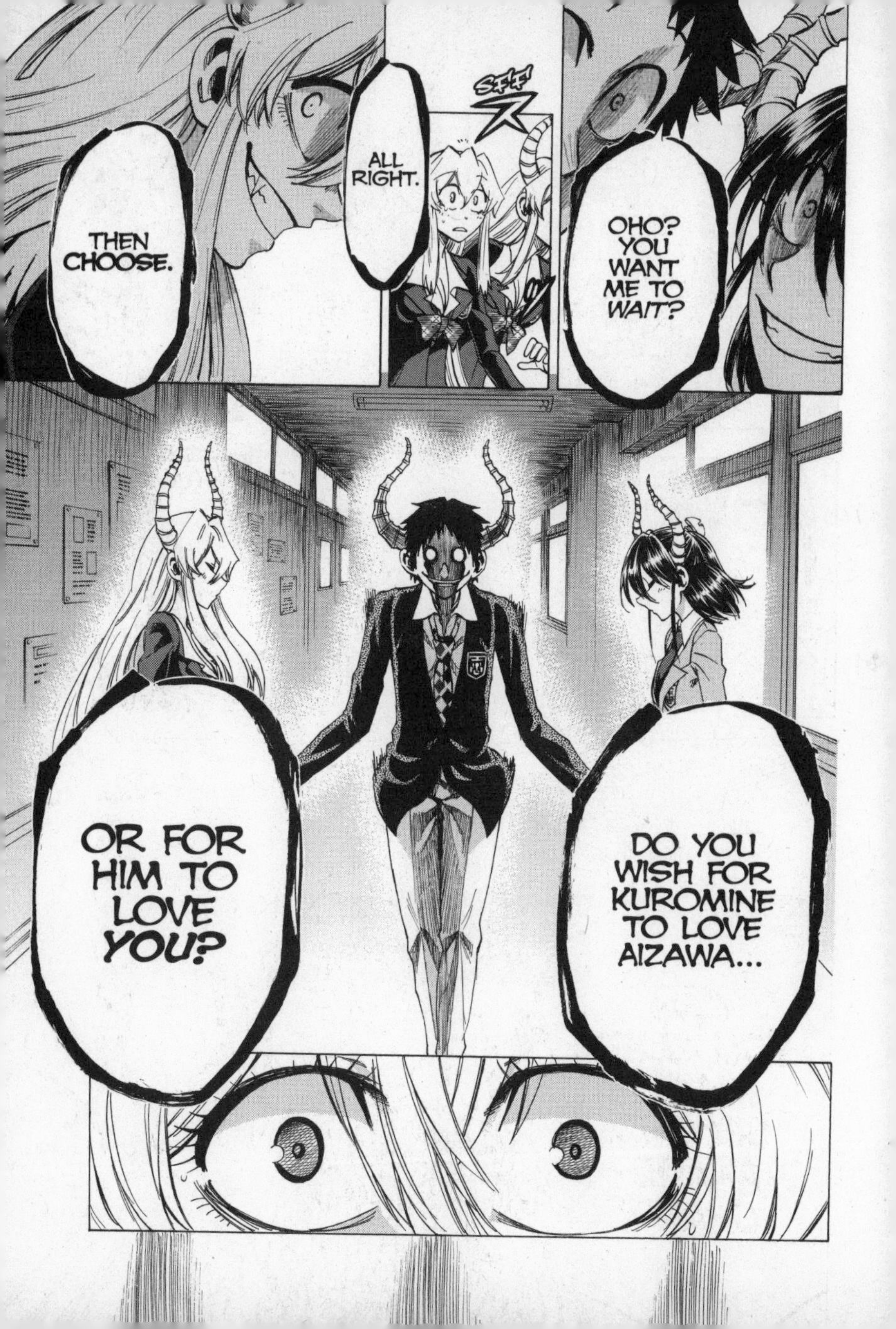
OHO? YOU WANT ME TO WAIT?
ALL RIGHT.
THEN CHOOSE.
DO YOU WISH FOR KUROMINE TO LOVE AIZAWA...
OR FOR HIM TO LOVE YOU?

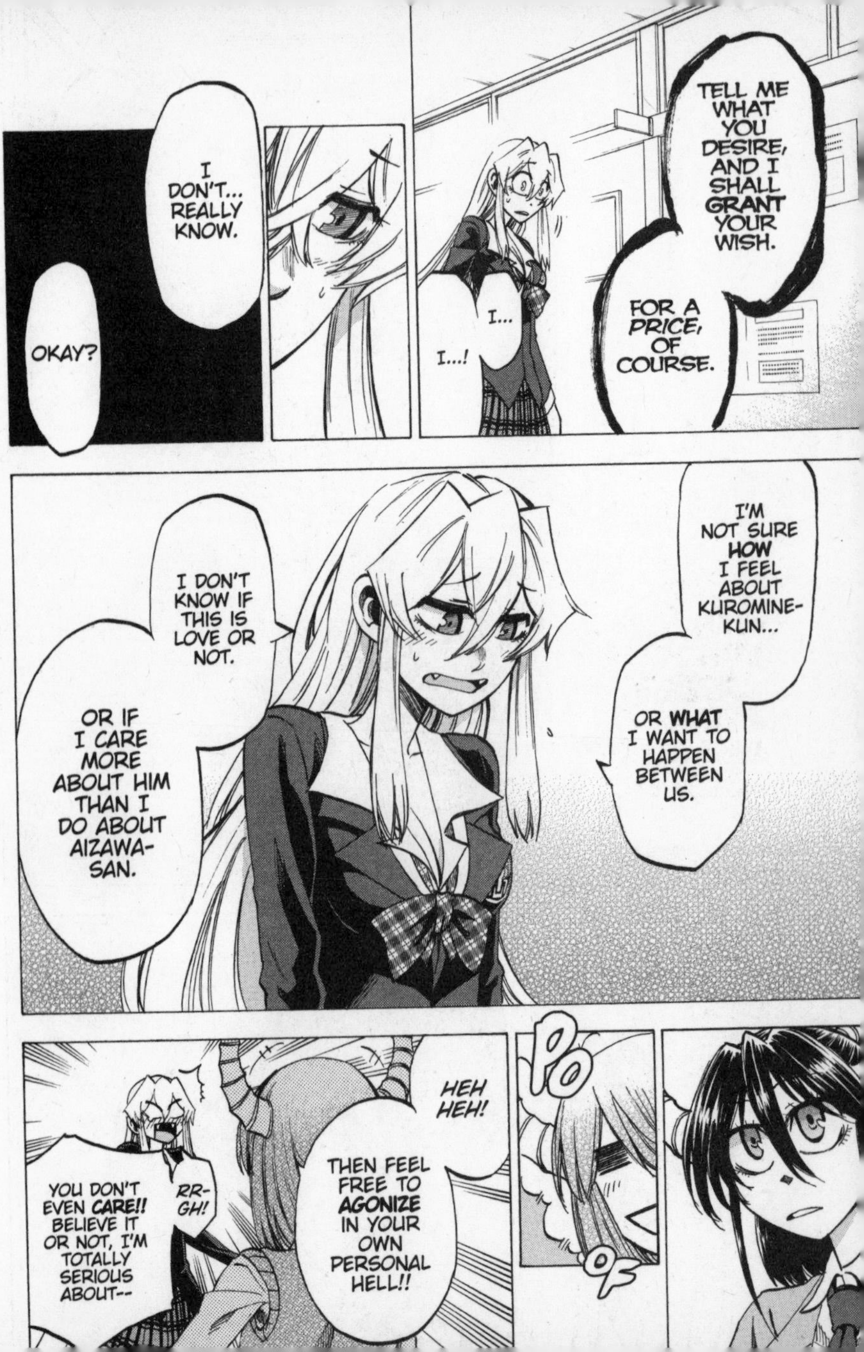
TELL ME WHAT YOU DESIRE, AND I SHALL GRANT YOUR WISH.
FOR A PRICE, OF COURSE.
I...
I...!
I DON'T... REALLY KNOW.
OKAY?
I'M NOT SURE HOW I FEEL ABOUT KUROMINE-KUN...
OR WHAT I WANT TO HAPPEN BETWEEN US.
I DON'T KNOW IF THIS IS LOVE OR NOT.
OR IF I CARE MORE ABOUT HIM THAN I DO ABOUT AIZAWA-SAN.
POOF
HEH HEH!
THEN FEEL FREE TO AGONIZE IN YOUR OWN PERSONAL HELL!!
RR-GH!
YOU DON'T EVEN CARE!! BELIEVE IT OR NOT, I'M TOTALLY SERIOUS ABOUT--

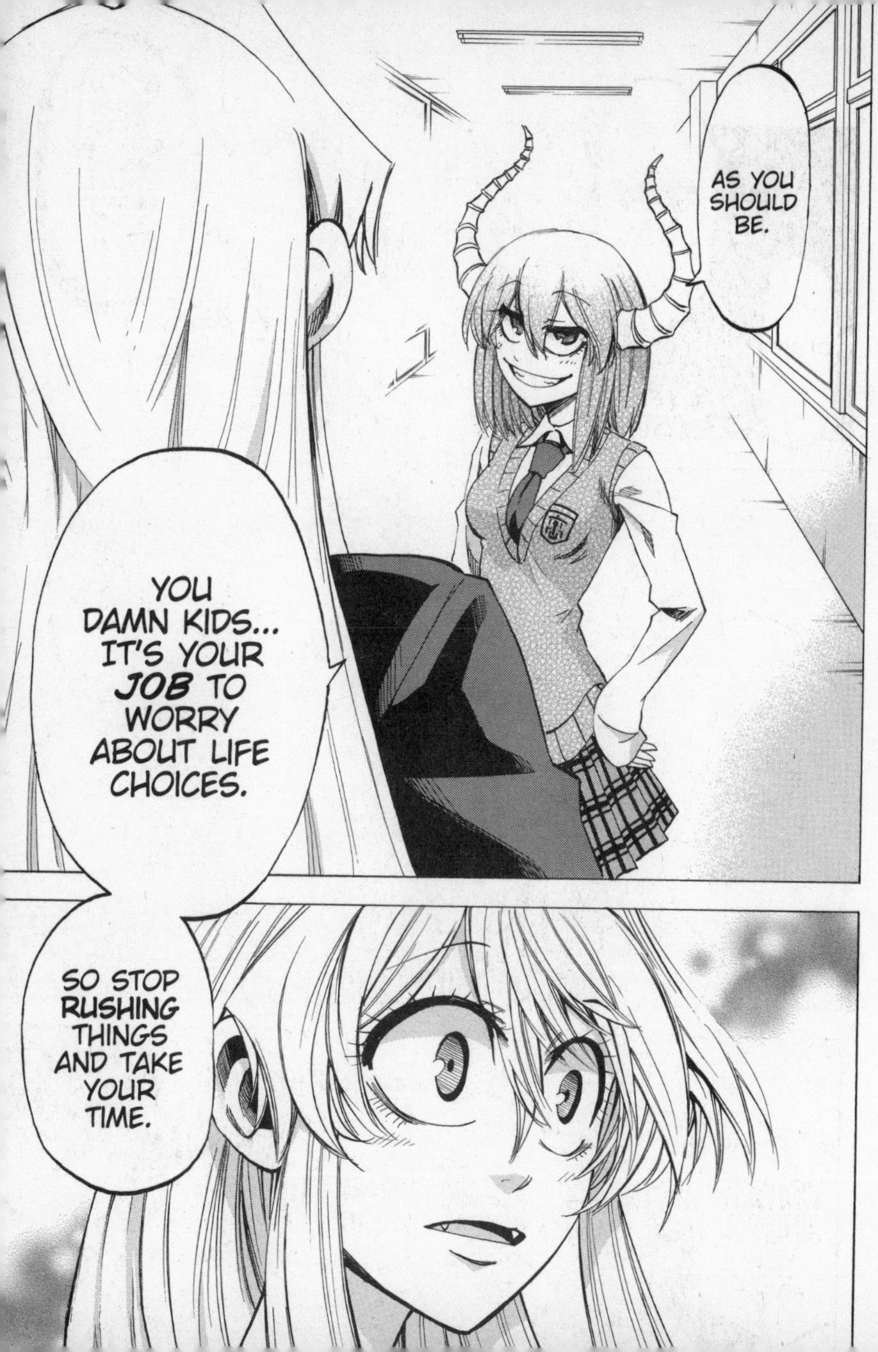
AS YOU SHOULD BE.
YOU DAMN KIDS... IT'S YOUR *JOB* TO WORRY ABOUT LIFE CHOICES.
SO STOP RUSHING THINGS AND TAKE YOUR TIME.

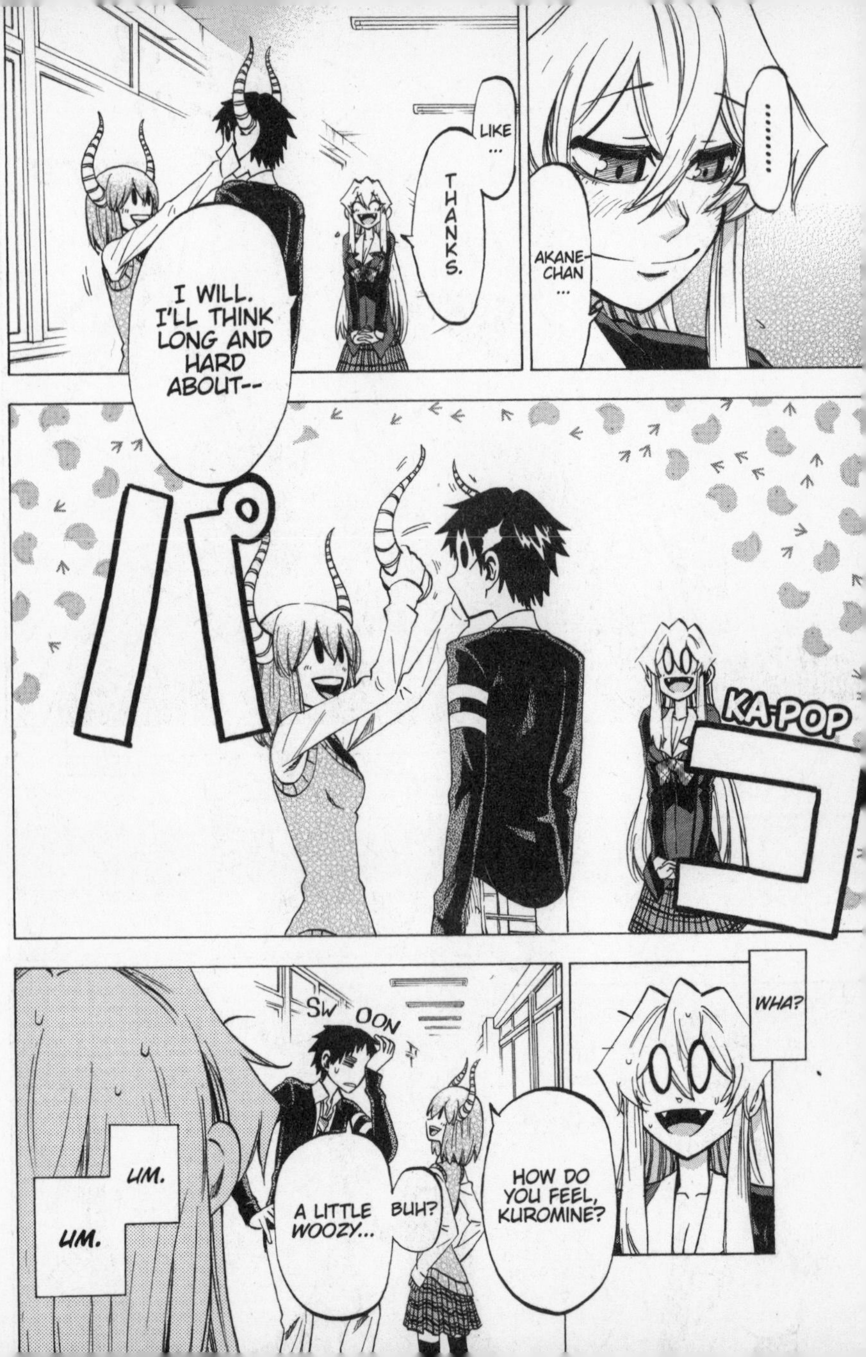
......
AKANE-CHAN ...
LIKE ...
THANKS.
I WILL. I'LL THINK LONG AND HARD ABOUT--
KA-POP
WHA?
SW OON
HOW DO YOU FEEL, KUROMINE?
BUH?
A LITTLE WOOZY...
UM.
UM.

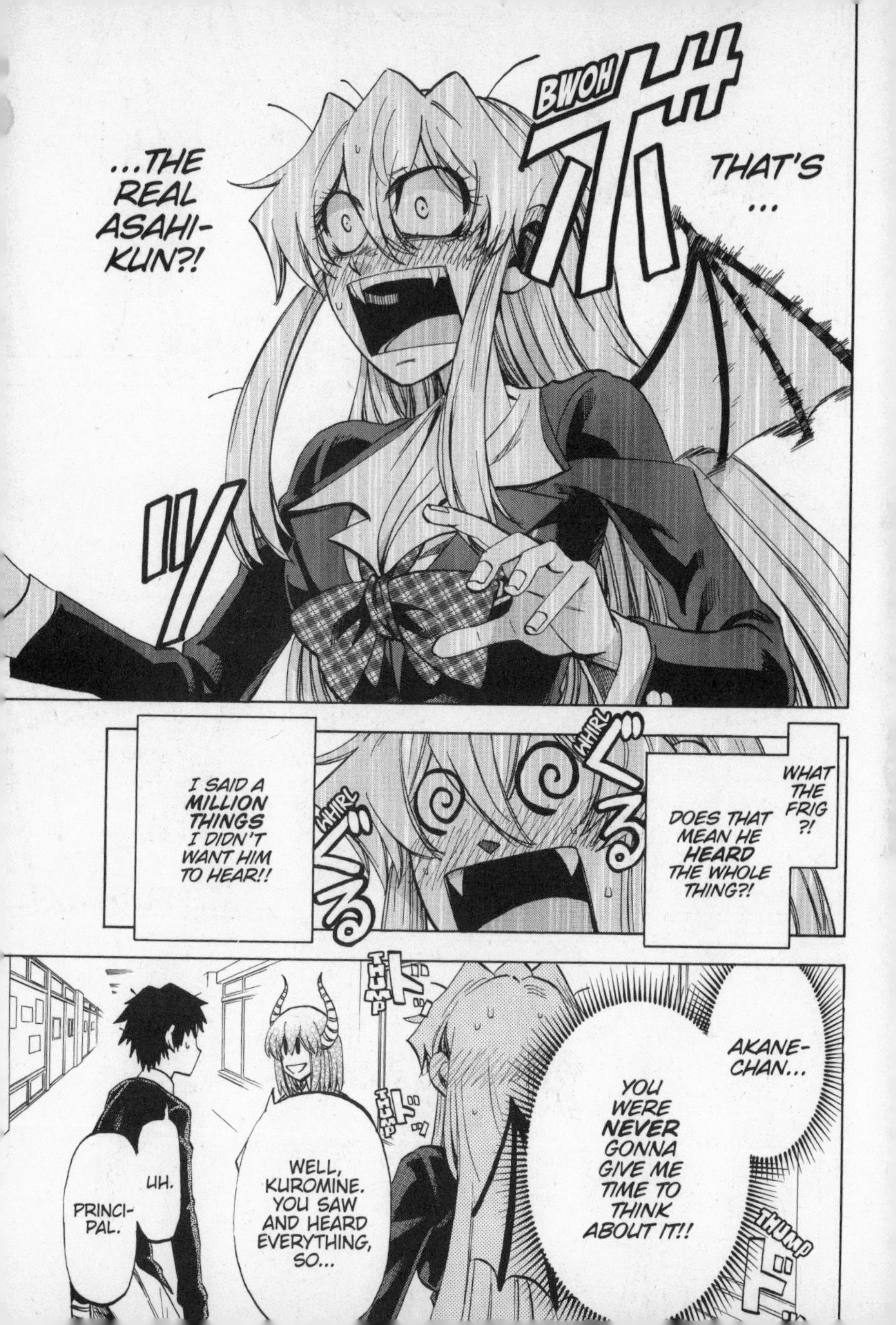
THAT'S ...
BWOH
...THE REAL ASAHI-KUN?!
WHAT THE FRIG?!
DOES THAT MEAN HE HEARD THE WHOLE THING?!
WHIRL
WHIRL
I SAID A MILLION THINGS I DIDN'T WANT HIM TO HEAR!!
THUMP
AKANE-CHAN...
YOU WERE NEVER GONNA GIVE ME TIME TO THINK ABOUT IT!!
THUMP
THUMP
WELL, KUROMINE. YOU SAW AND HEARD EVERYTHING, SO...
UH.
PRINCI-PAL.

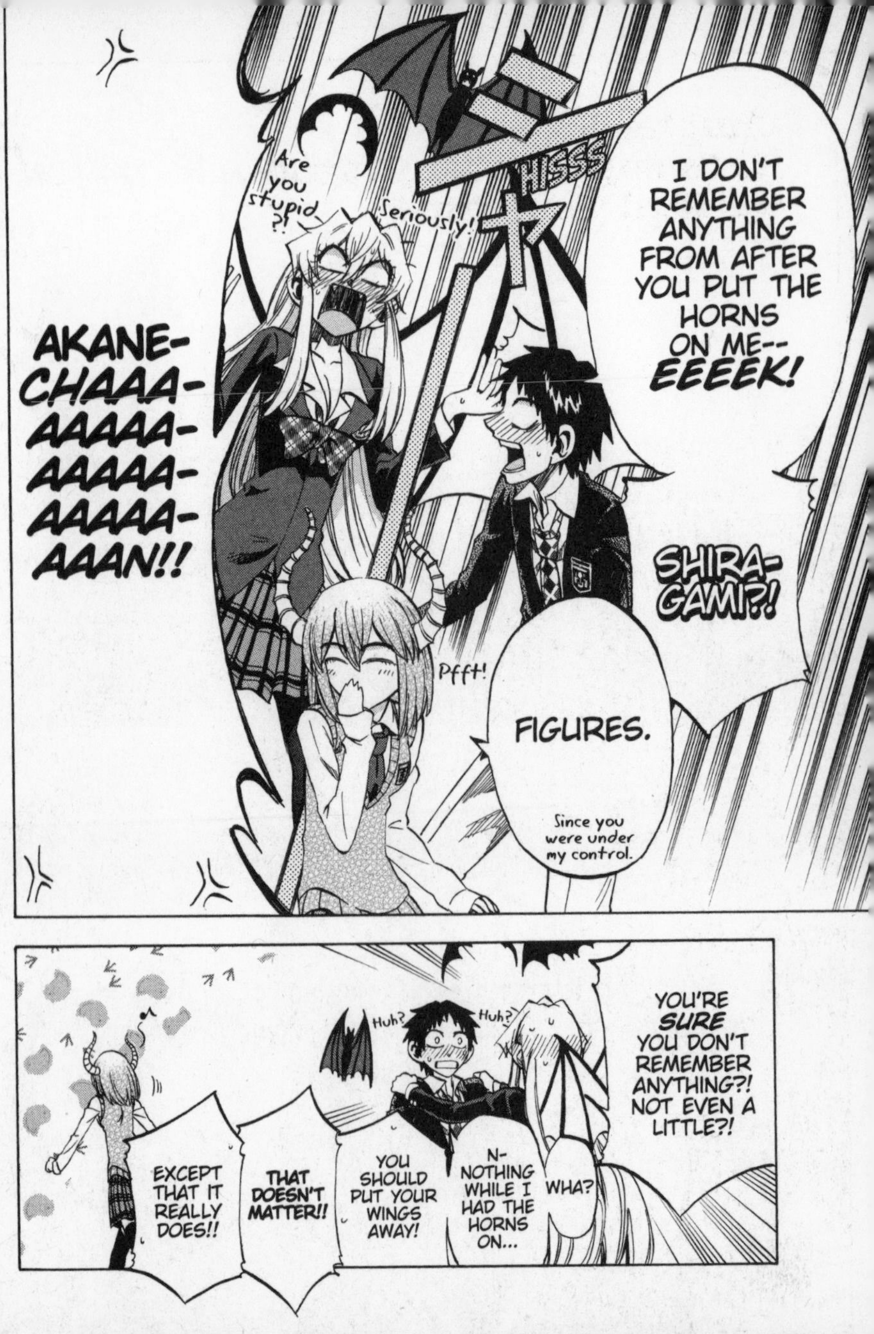
I DON'T REMEMBER ANYTHING FROM AFTER YOU PUT THE HORNS ON ME-- EEEEK!
HISSSS
SHIRA-GAMI?!
Seriously!
Are you stupid?!
FIGURES.
Since you were under my control.
Pfft!
AKANE-CHAAAA-AAAAA-AAAAA-AAAAA-AAAN!!
YOU'RE SURE YOU DON'T REMEMBER ANYTHING?! NOT EVEN A LITTLE?!
Huh?
Huh?
WHA?
N-NOTHING WHILE I HAD THE HORNS ON...
YOU SHOULD PUT YOUR WINGS AWAY!
THAT DOESN'T MATTER!!
EXCEPT THAT IT REALLY DOES!!

Chapter 50: "Let's Support Our Friends for Real This Time!"

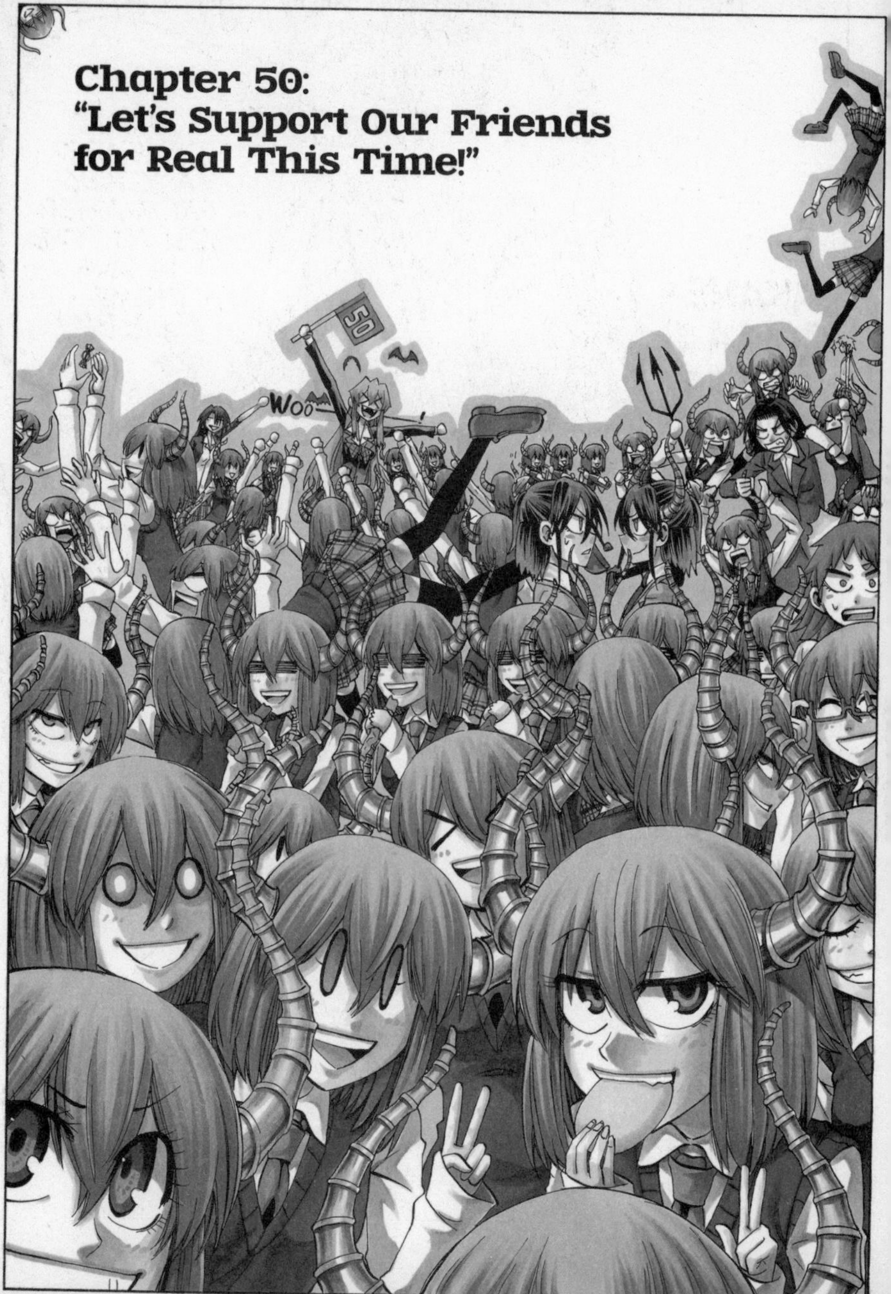
50
WOO

TOP SECRET

My Monster Secret 6

50

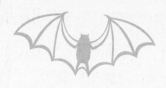

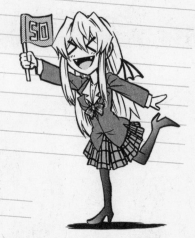

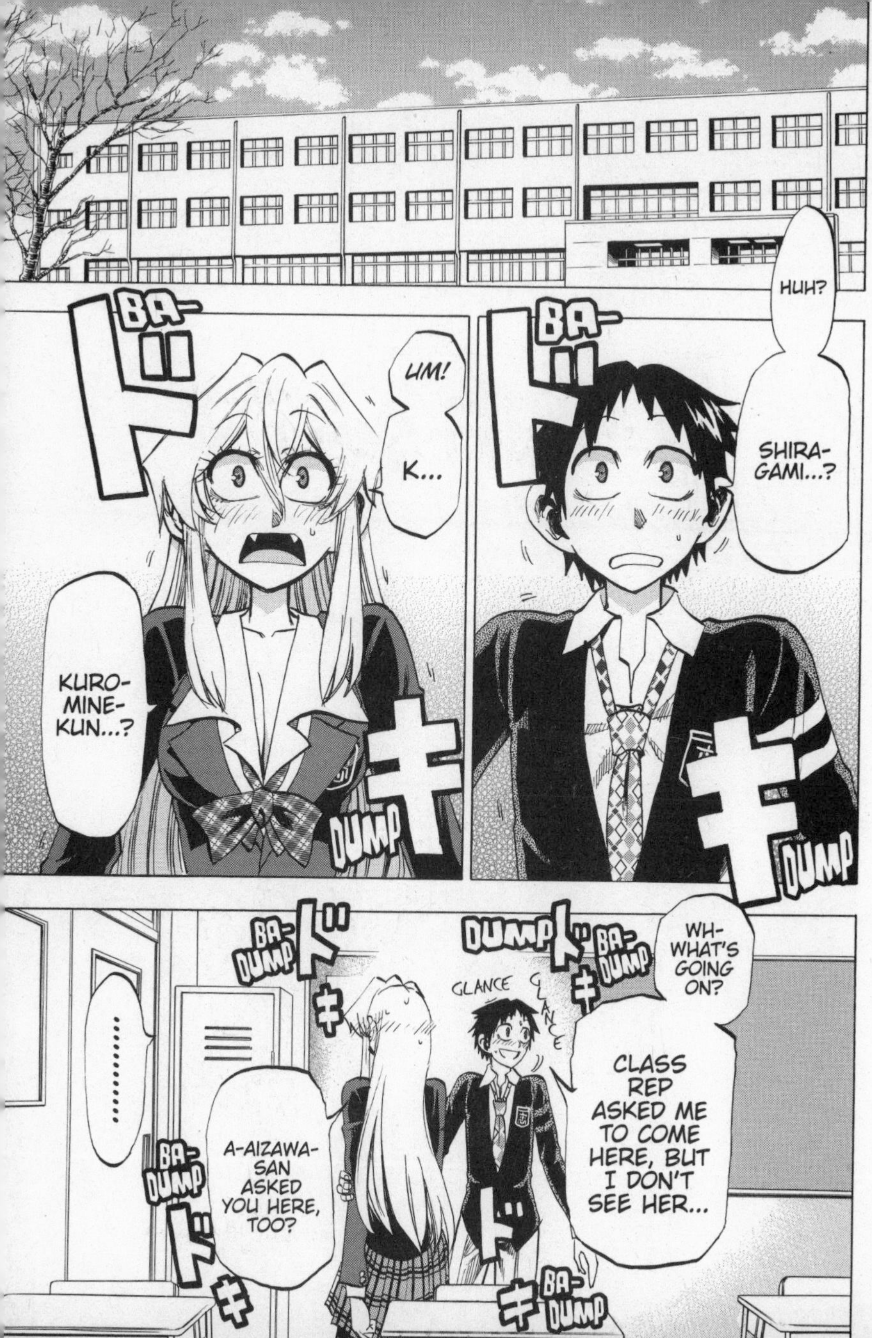
HUH?
BA-
ドキ
SHIRA-GAMI...?
DUMP
BA-
ドキ
UM!
K...
KURO-MINE-KUN...?
DUMP
WH-WHAT'S GOING ON?
BA-DUMP
ドキ
DUMP
GLANCE
GLANCE
CLASS REP ASKED ME TO COME HERE, BUT I DON'T SEE HER...
BA-DUMP
ドキ
BA-DUMP
ドキ
A-AIZAWA-SAN ASKED YOU HERE, TOO?
......
BA-DUMP
ドキ

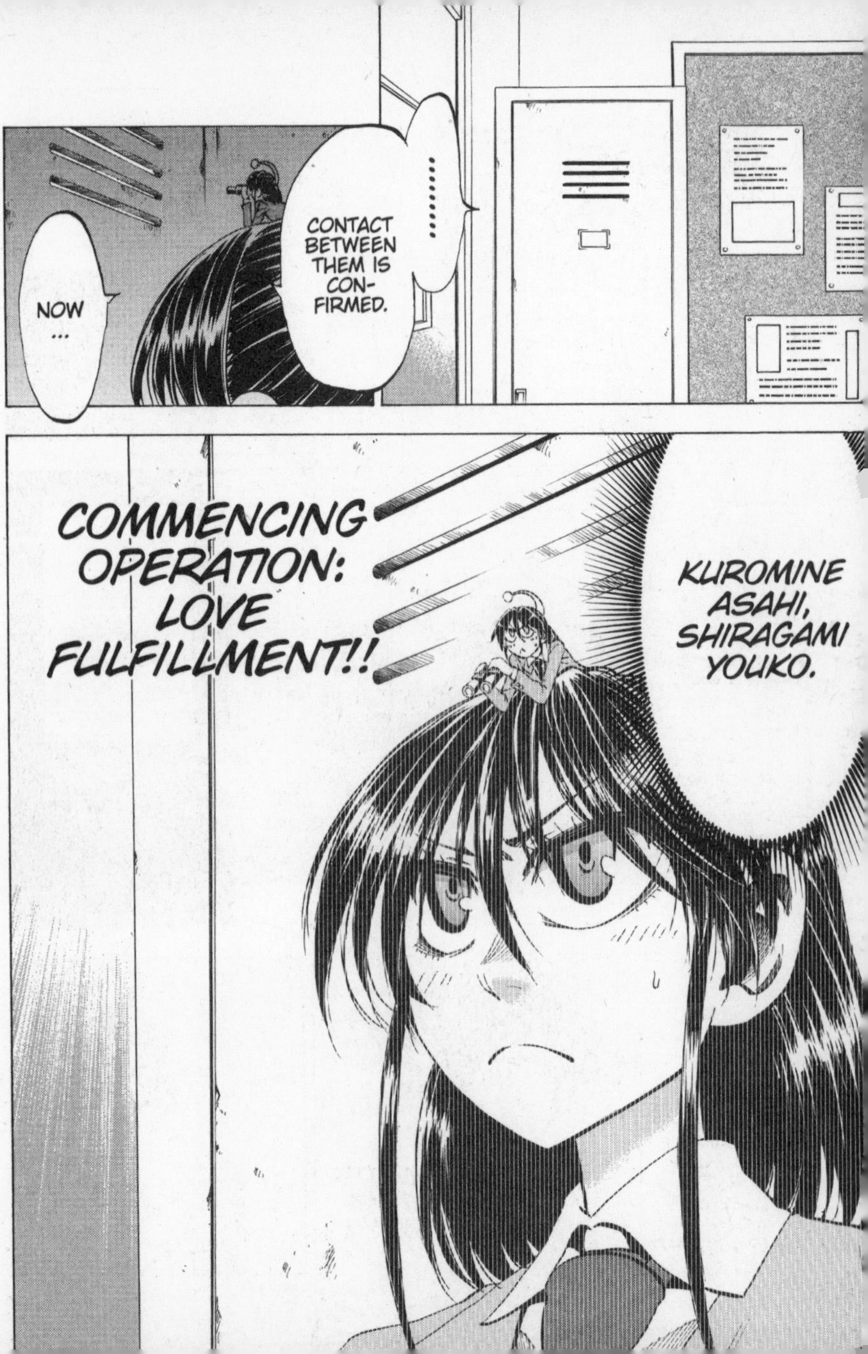
......
CONTACT BETWEEN THEM IS CON-FIRMED.
NOW ...
KUROMINE ASAHI, SHIRAGAMI YOUKO.
COMMENCING OPERATION: LOVE FULFILLMENT!!

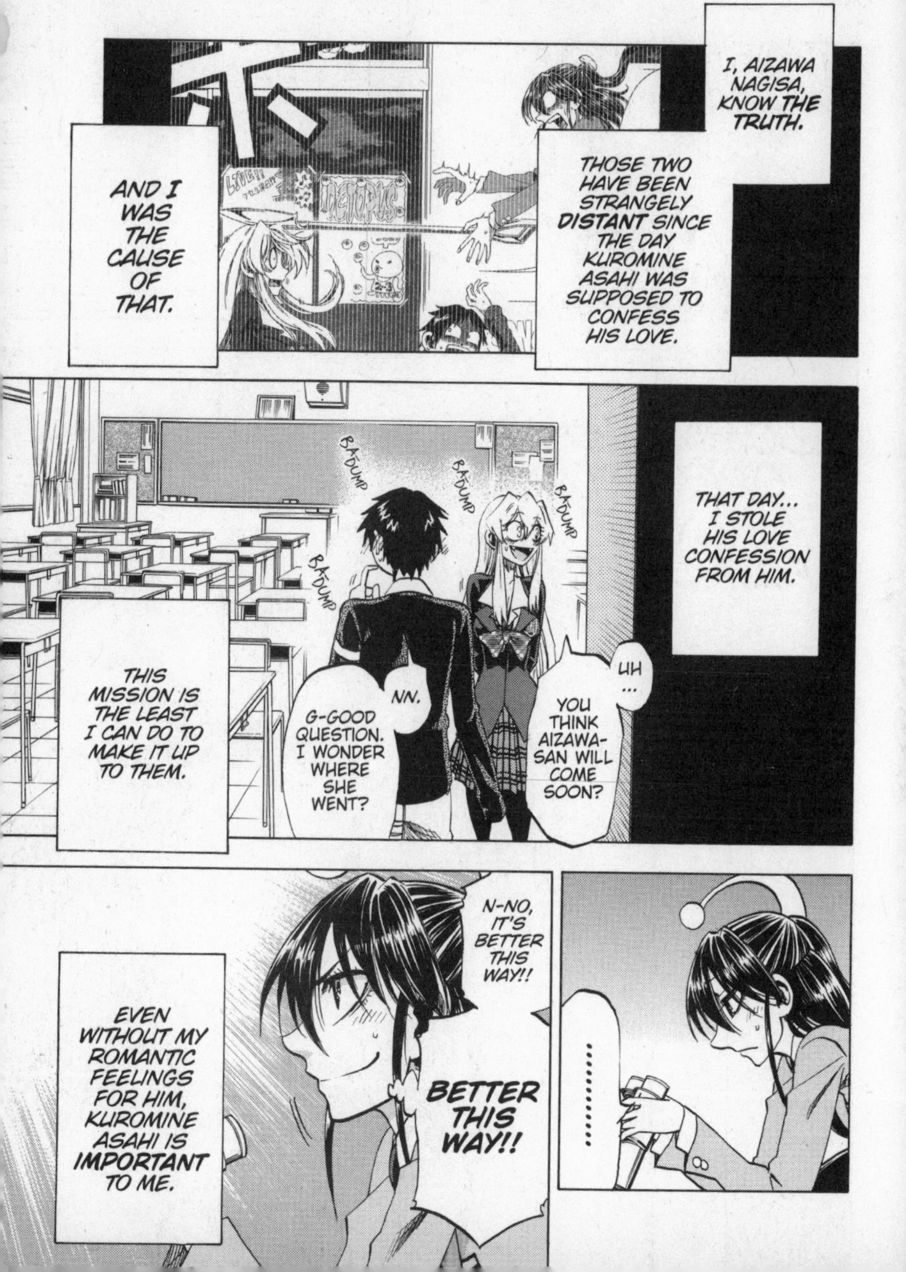
I, AIZAWA NAGISA, KNOW THE TRUTH.
THOSE TWO HAVE BEEN STRANGELY DISTANT SINCE THE DAY KUROMINE ASAHI WAS SUPPOSED TO CONFESS HIS LOVE.
AND I WAS THE CAUSE OF THAT.
THAT DAY... I STOLE HIS LOVE CONFESSION FROM HIM.
BA-DUMP
BA-DUMP
BA-DUMP
BA-DUMP
UH ... YOU THINK AIZAWA-SAN WILL COME SOON?
NN.
G-GOOD QUESTION. I WONDER WHERE SHE WENT?
THIS MISSION IS THE LEAST I CAN DO TO MAKE IT UP TO THEM.
....
N-NO, IT'S BETTER THIS WAY!!
BETTER THIS WAY!!
EVEN WITHOUT MY ROMANTIC FEELINGS FOR HIM, KUROMINE ASAHI IS IMPORTANT TO ME.

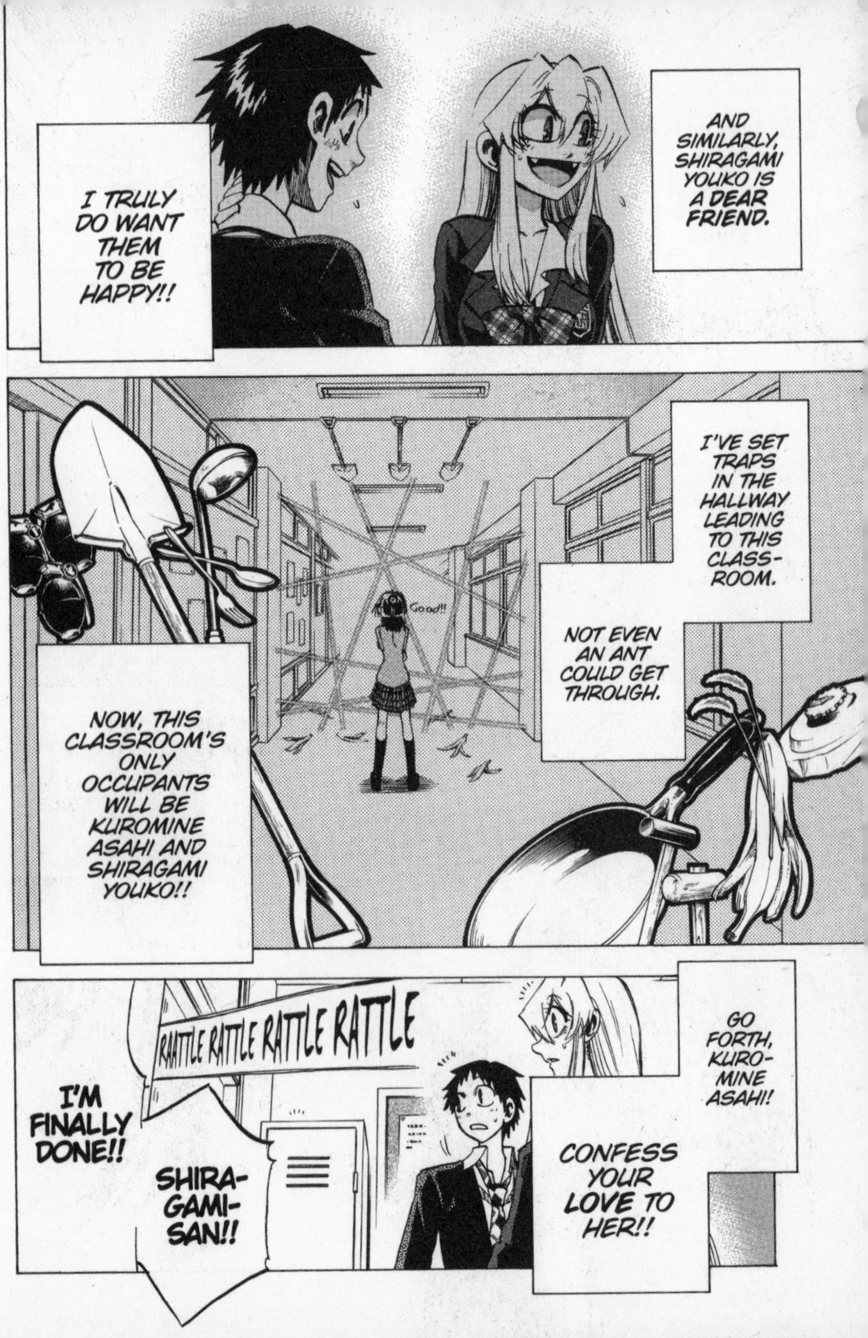
AND SIMILARLY, SHIRAGAMI YOUKO IS A DEAR FRIEND.
I TRULY DO WANT THEM TO BE HAPPY!!
I'VE SET TRAPS IN THE HALLWAY LEADING TO THIS CLASS-ROOM.
Good!!
NOT EVEN AN ANT COULD GET THROUGH.
NOW, THIS CLASSROOM'S ONLY OCCUPANTS WILL BE KUROMINE ASAHI AND SHIRAGAMI YOUKO!!
GO FORTH, KURO-MINE ASAHI!
RAATTLE RATTLE RATTLE RATTLE
CONFESS YOUR LOVE TO HER!!
I'M FINALLY DONE!!
SHIRA-GAMI-SAN!!

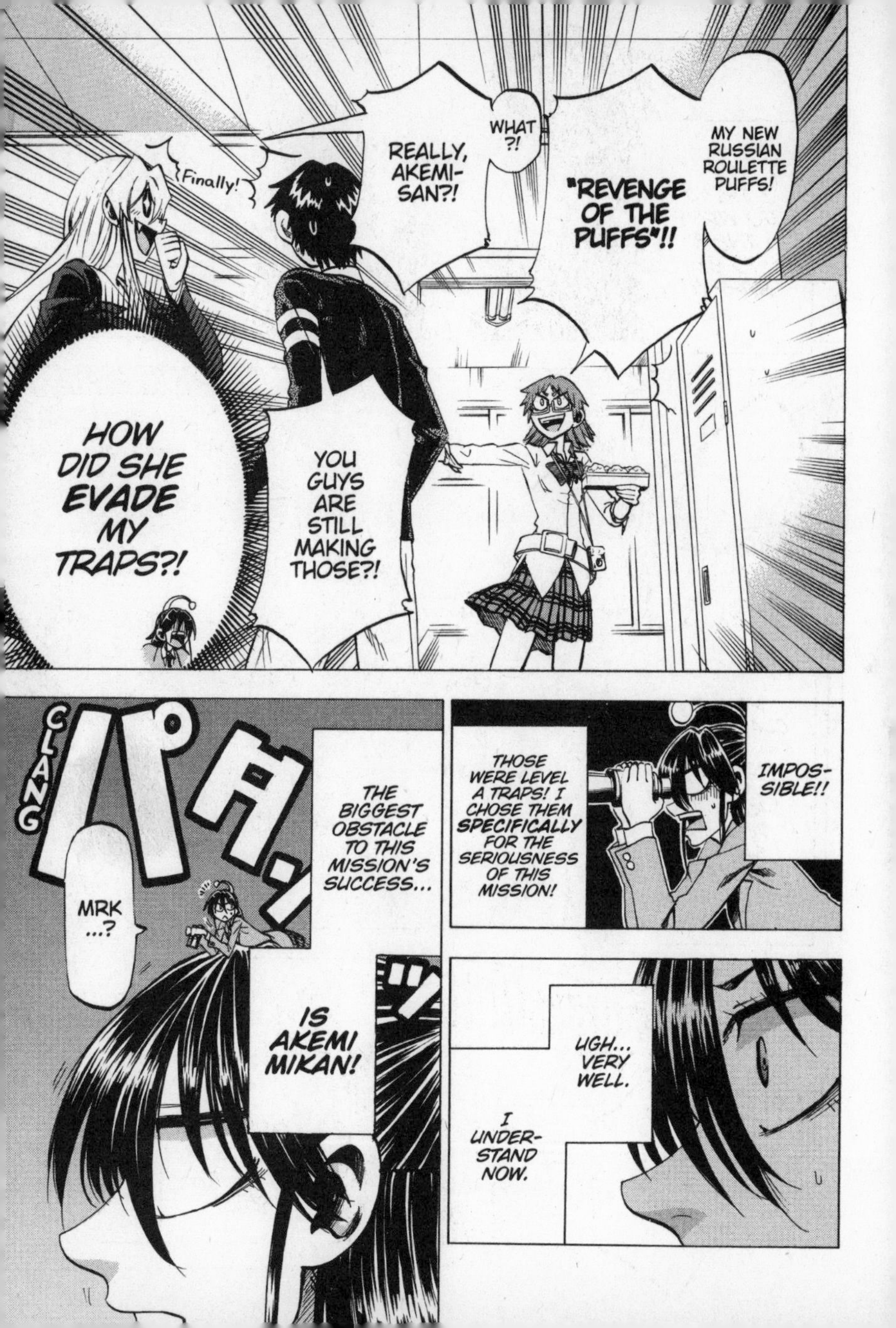
MY NEW RUSSIAN ROULETTE PUFFS!
"REVENGE OF THE PUFFS"!!
WHAT?!
REALLY, AKEMI-SAN?!
Finally!
YOU GUYS ARE STILL MAKING THOSE?!
HOW DID SHE EVADE MY TRAPS?!
IMPOSSIBLE!!
THOSE WERE LEVEL A TRAPS! I CHOSE THEM SPECIFICALLY FOR THE SERIOUSNESS OF THIS MISSION!
UGH... VERY WELL.
I UNDERSTAND NOW.
CLANG
THE BIGGEST OBSTACLE TO THIS MISSION'S SUCCESS...
MRK...?
IS AKEMI MIKAN!

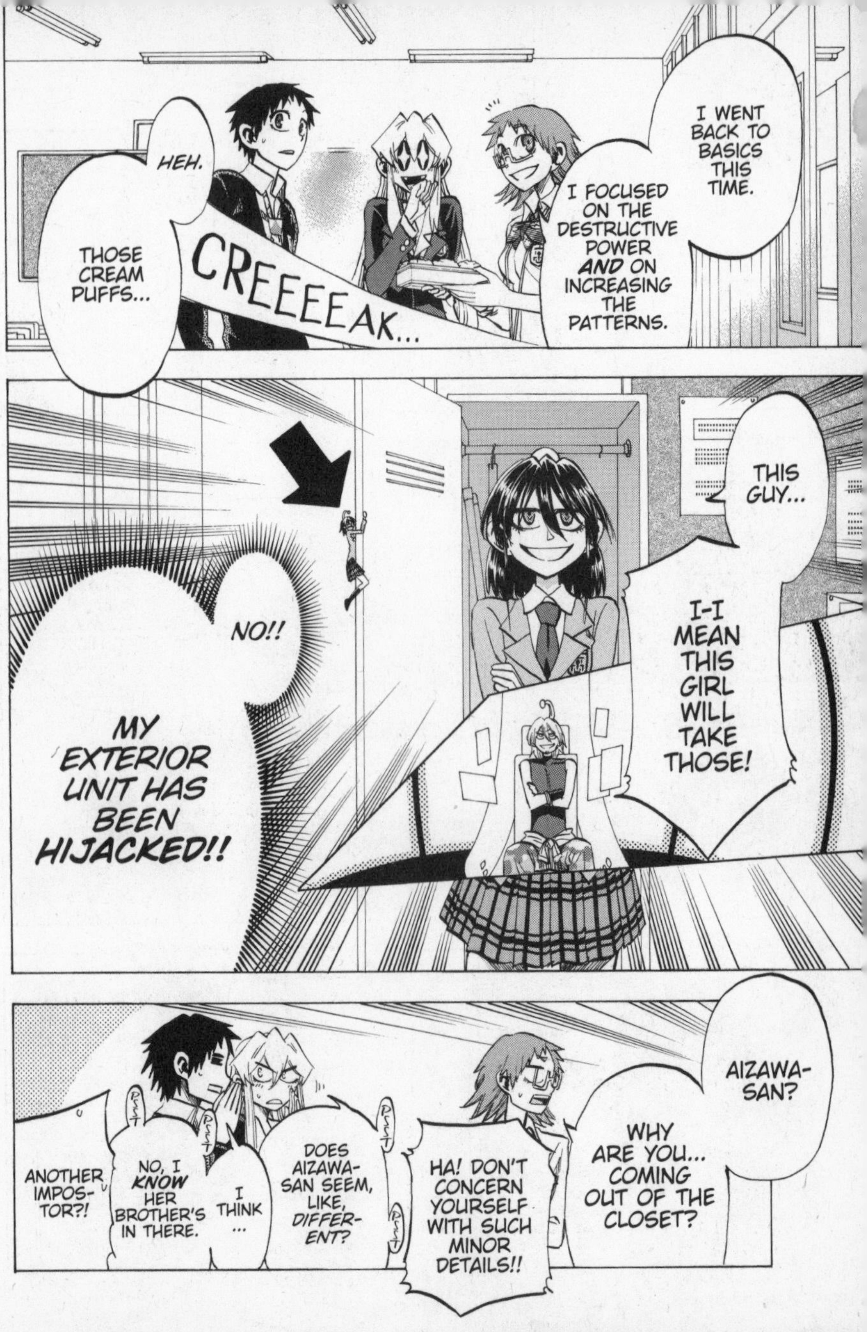
I WENT BACK TO BASICS THIS TIME.
I FOCUSED ON THE DESTRUCTIVE POWER AND ON INCREASING THE PATTERNS.
CREEEEEAK...
HEH.
THOSE CREAM PUFFS...
THIS GUY...
I-I MEAN THIS GIRL WILL TAKE THOSE!
NO!!
MY EXTERIOR UNIT HAS BEEN HIJACKED!!
AIZAWA-SAN?
WHY ARE YOU... COMING OUT OF THE CLOSET?
HA! DON'T CONCERN YOURSELF WITH SUCH MINOR DETAILS!!
DOES AIZAWA-SAN SEEM, LIKE, DIFFERENT?
I THINK ...
NO, I KNOW HER BROTHER'S IN THERE.
ANOTHER IMPOSTOR?!

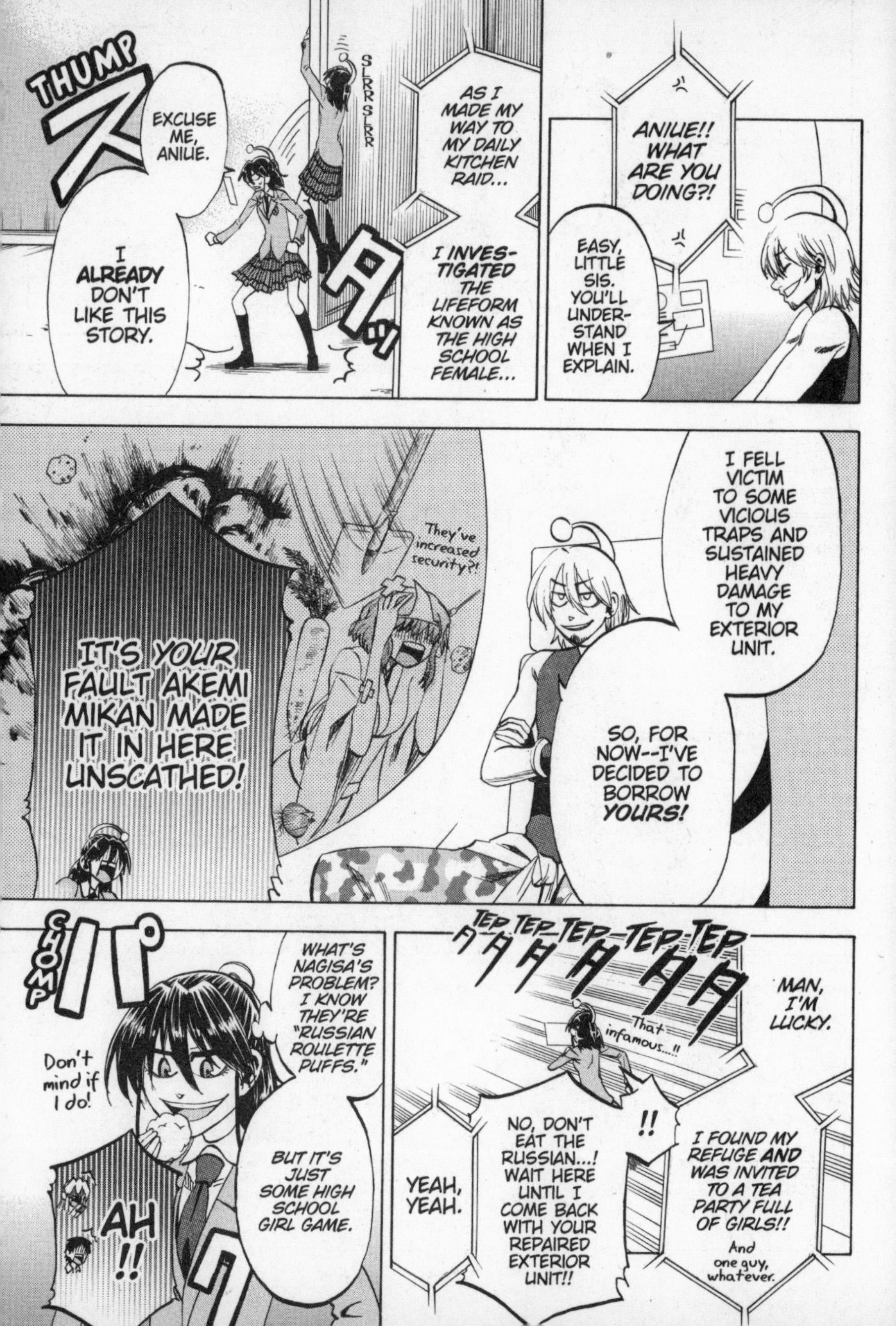
ANIUE!! WHAT ARE YOU DOING?!
EASY, LITTLE SIS. YOU'LL UNDERSTAND WHEN I EXPLAIN.
AS I MADE MY WAY TO MY DAILY KITCHEN RAID...
I INVESTIGATED THE LIFEFORM KNOWN AS THE HIGH SCHOOL FEMALE...
SLRR SLRR
THUMP
EXCUSE ME, ANIUE.
I ALREADY DON'T LIKE THIS STORY.
I FELL VICTIM TO SOME VICIOUS TRAPS AND SUSTAINED HEAVY DAMAGE TO MY EXTERIOR UNIT.
SO, FOR NOW--I'VE DECIDED TO BORROW YOURS!
They've increased security?!
IT'S YOUR FAULT AKEMI MIKAN MADE IT IN HERE UNSCATHED!
TEP TEP TEP TEP TEP
MAN, I'M LUCKY.
That infamous...!!
I FOUND MY REFUGE AND WAS INVITED TO A TEA PARTY FULL OF GIRLS!!
And one guy, whatever.
!!
NO, DON'T EAT THE RUSSIAN...! WAIT HERE UNTIL I COME BACK WITH YOUR REPAIRED EXTERIOR UNIT!!
YEAH, YEAH.
CHOMP
WHAT'S NAGISA'S PROBLEM? I KNOW THEY'RE "RUSSIAN ROULETTE PUFFS."
Don't mind if I do!
BUT IT'S JUST SOME HIGH SCHOOL GIRL GAME.
AH!!

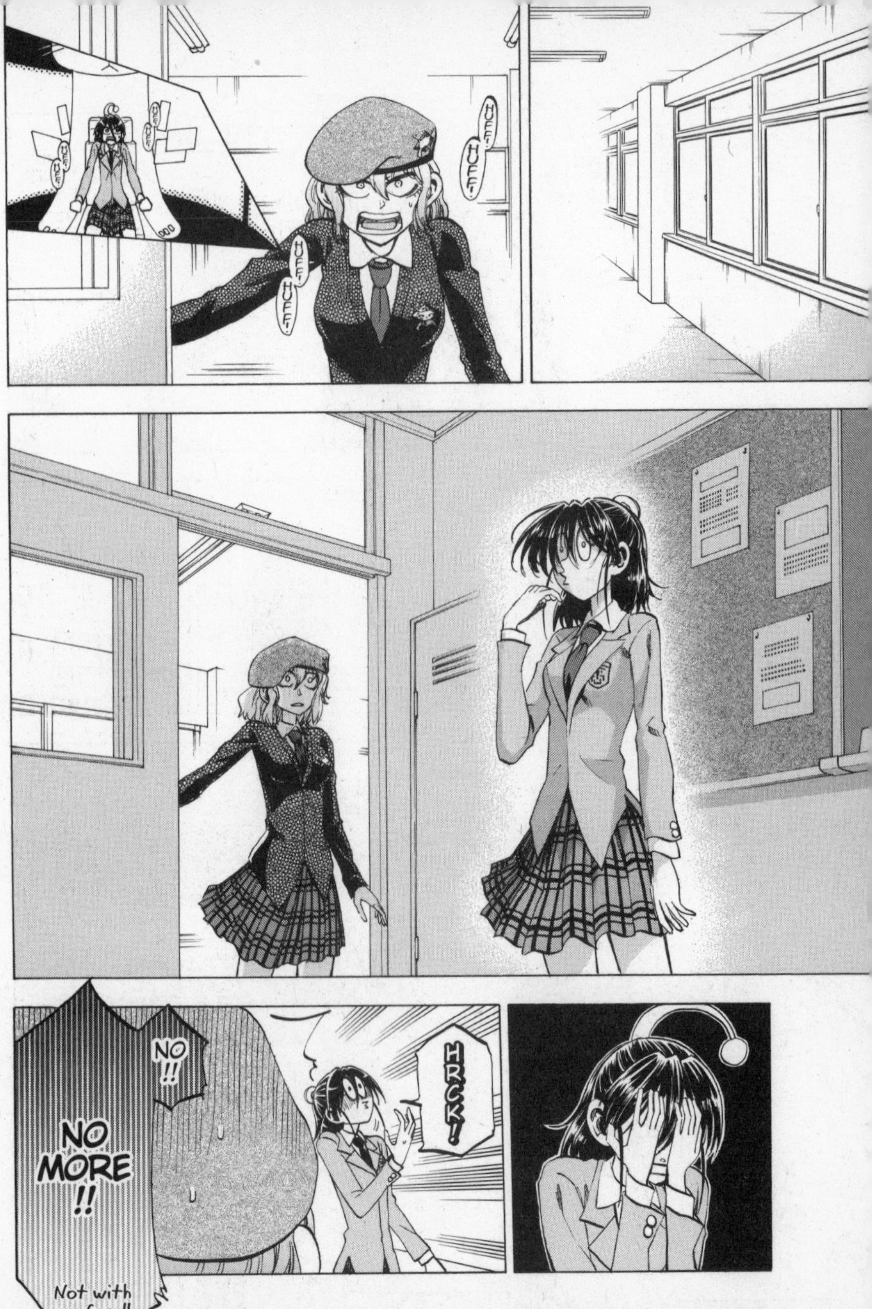
HUFF! HUFF!
HUFF! HUFF!
HEF! HEF!
HEF! HEF!
HRCK!
NO!!
NO MORE!!
Not with my face!!

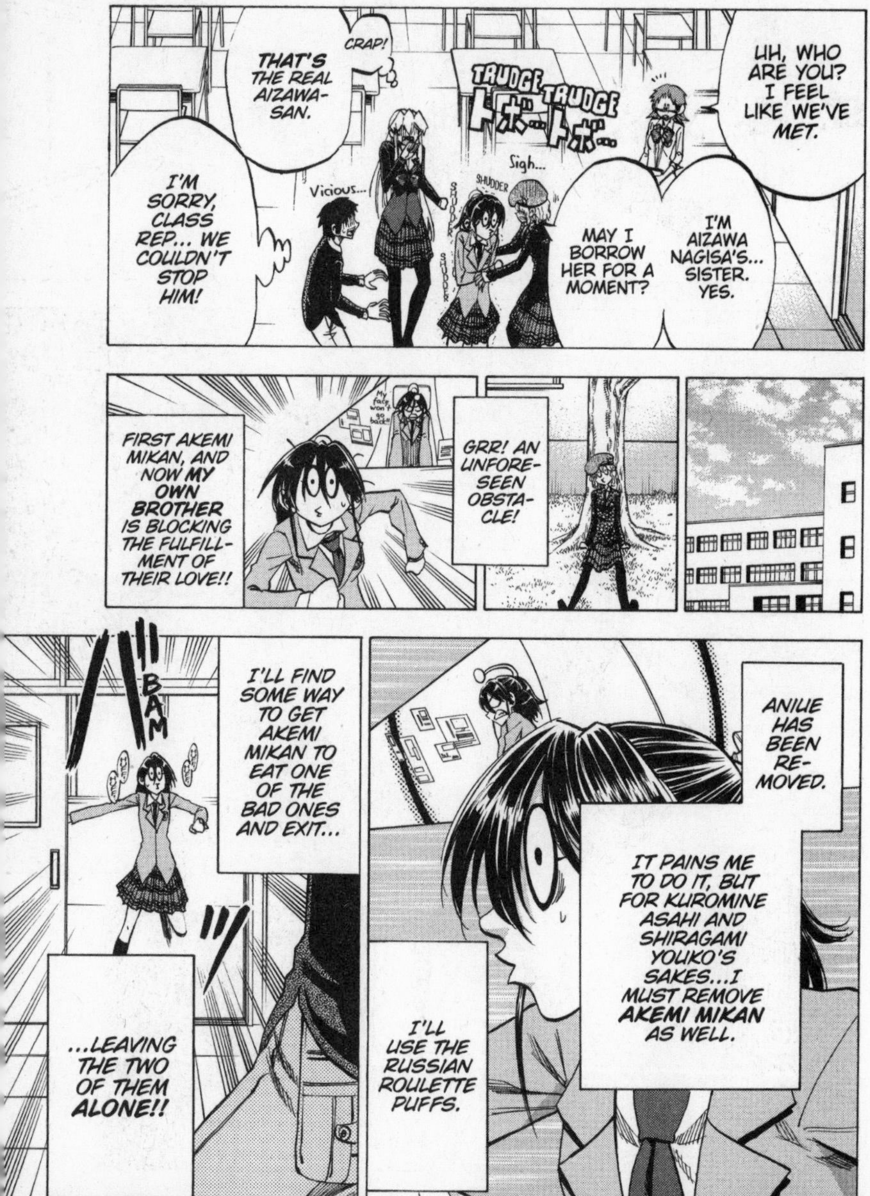
UH, WHO ARE YOU? I FEEL LIKE WE'VE MET.
I'M AIZAWA NAGISA'S... SISTER. YES.
MAY I BORROW HER FOR A MOMENT?
Sigh...
SHUDDER SHUDDER SHUDDER
TRUDGE TRUDGE
CRAP!
THAT'S THE REAL AIZAWA-SAN.
Vicious...
I'M SORRY, CLASS REP... WE COULDN'T STOP HIM!
GRR! AN UNFORESEEN OBSTACLE!
My face won't go back!!
FIRST AKEMI MIKAN, AND NOW MY OWN BROTHER IS BLOCKING THE FULFILLMENT OF THEIR LOVE!!
ANIUE HAS BEEN REMOVED.
IT PAINS ME TO DO IT, BUT FOR KUROMINE ASAHI AND SHIRAGAMI YOUKO'S SAKES...I MUST REMOVE AKEMI MIKAN AS WELL.
I'LL USE THE RUSSIAN ROULETTE PUFFS.
BAM
I'LL FIND SOME WAY TO GET AKEMI MIKAN TO EAT ONE OF THE BAD ONES AND EXIT...
...LEAVING THE TWO OF THEM ALONE!!

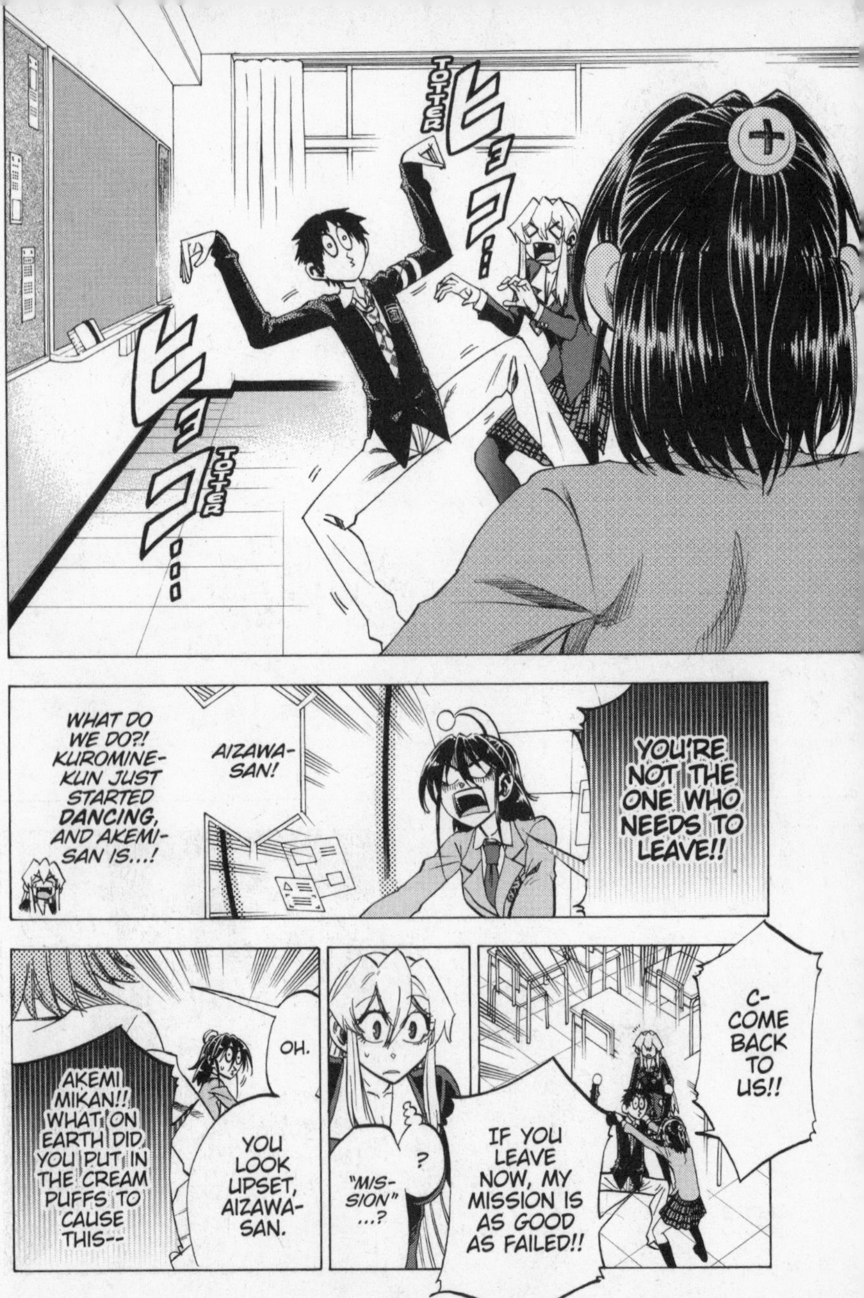
TOTTER
TOTTER
YOU'RE NOT THE ONE WHO NEEDS TO LEAVE!!
AIZAWA-SAN!
WHAT DO WE DO?! KUROMINE-KUN JUST STARTED DANCING, AND AKEMI-SAN IS...!
C-COME BACK TO US!!
IF YOU LEAVE NOW, MY MISSION IS AS GOOD AS FAILED!!
?
"MIS-SION"...?
OH.
YOU LOOK UPSET, AIZAWA-SAN.
AKEMI MIKAN!! WHAT ON EARTH DID YOU PUT IN THE CREAM PUFFS TO CAUSE THIS--

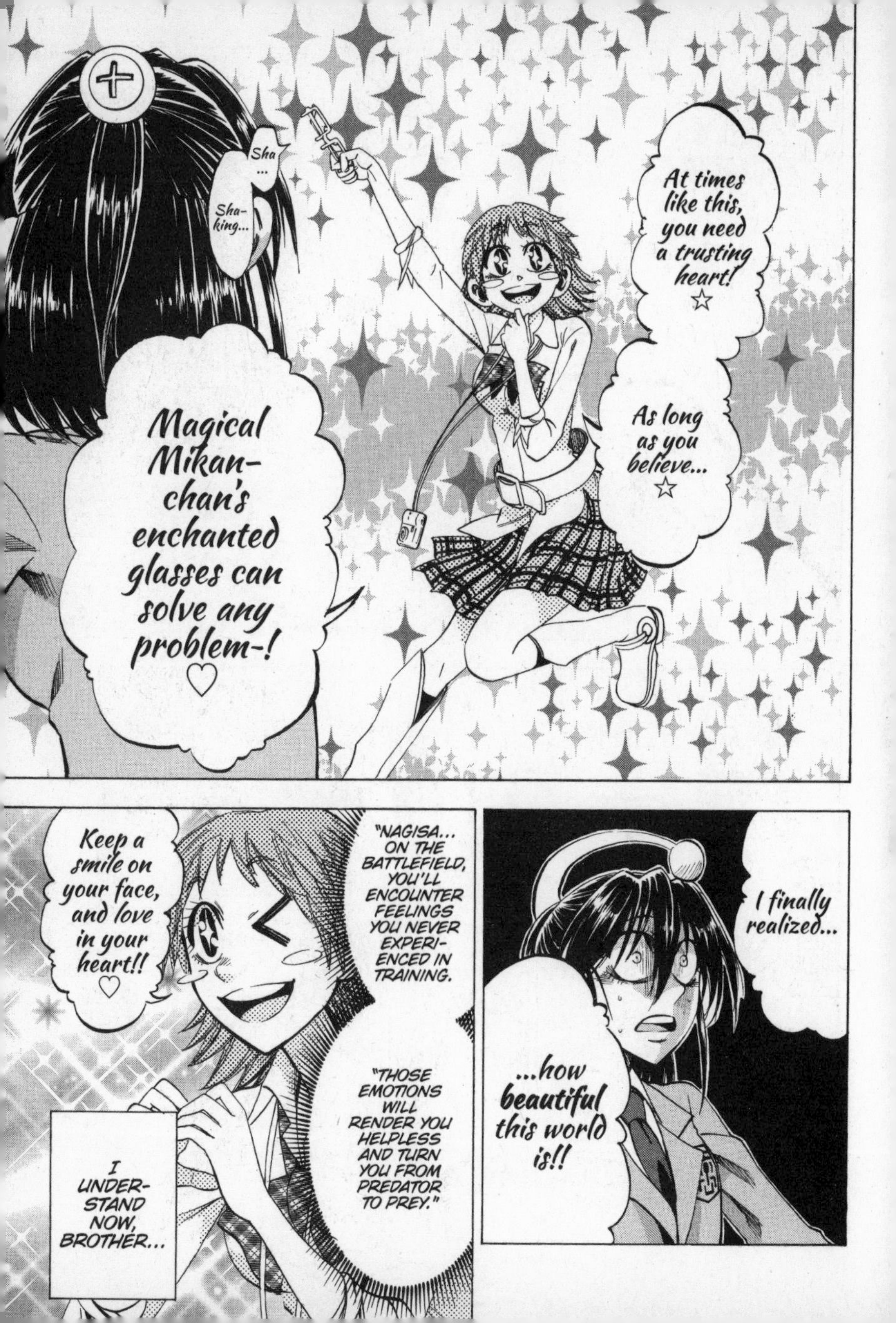
At times like this, you need a trusting heart! ☆
As long as you believe... ☆
Sha...
Sha-king...
Magical Mikan-chan's enchanted glasses can solve any problem-! ♡
I finally realized...
...how beautiful this world is!!
"NAGISA... ON THE BATTLEFIELD, YOU'LL ENCOUNTER FEELINGS YOU NEVER EXPERIENCED IN TRAINING.
Keep a smile on your face, and love in your heart!! ♡
"THOSE EMOTIONS WILL RENDER YOU HELPLESS AND TURN YOU FROM PREDATOR TO PREY."
I UNDERSTAND NOW, BROTHER...

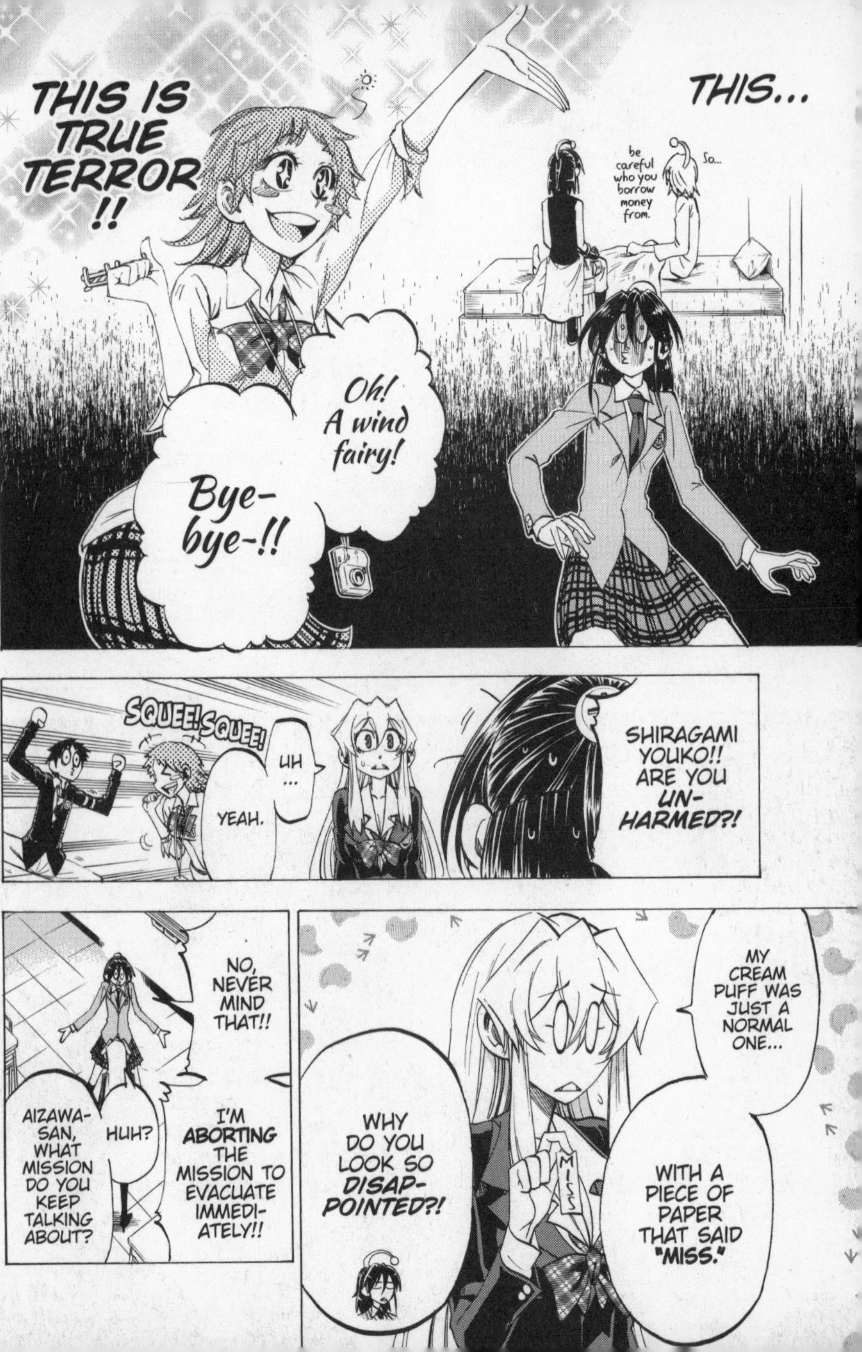
THIS...
So...
be careful who you borrow money from.
THIS IS TRUE TERROR!!
Oh! A wind fairy!
Bye-bye-!!
SHIRAGAMI YOUKO!! ARE YOU UN-HARMED?!
UH ... YEAH.
SQUEE! SQUEE!
MY CREAM PUFF WAS JUST A NORMAL ONE...
WITH A PIECE OF PAPER THAT SAID "MISS."
MISS
WHY DO YOU LOOK SO DISAP-POINTED?!
NO, NEVER MIND THAT!!
I'M ABORTING THE MISSION TO EVACUATE IMMEDI-ATELY!!
HUH?
AIZAWA-SAN, WHAT MISSION DO YOU KEEP TALKING ABOUT?

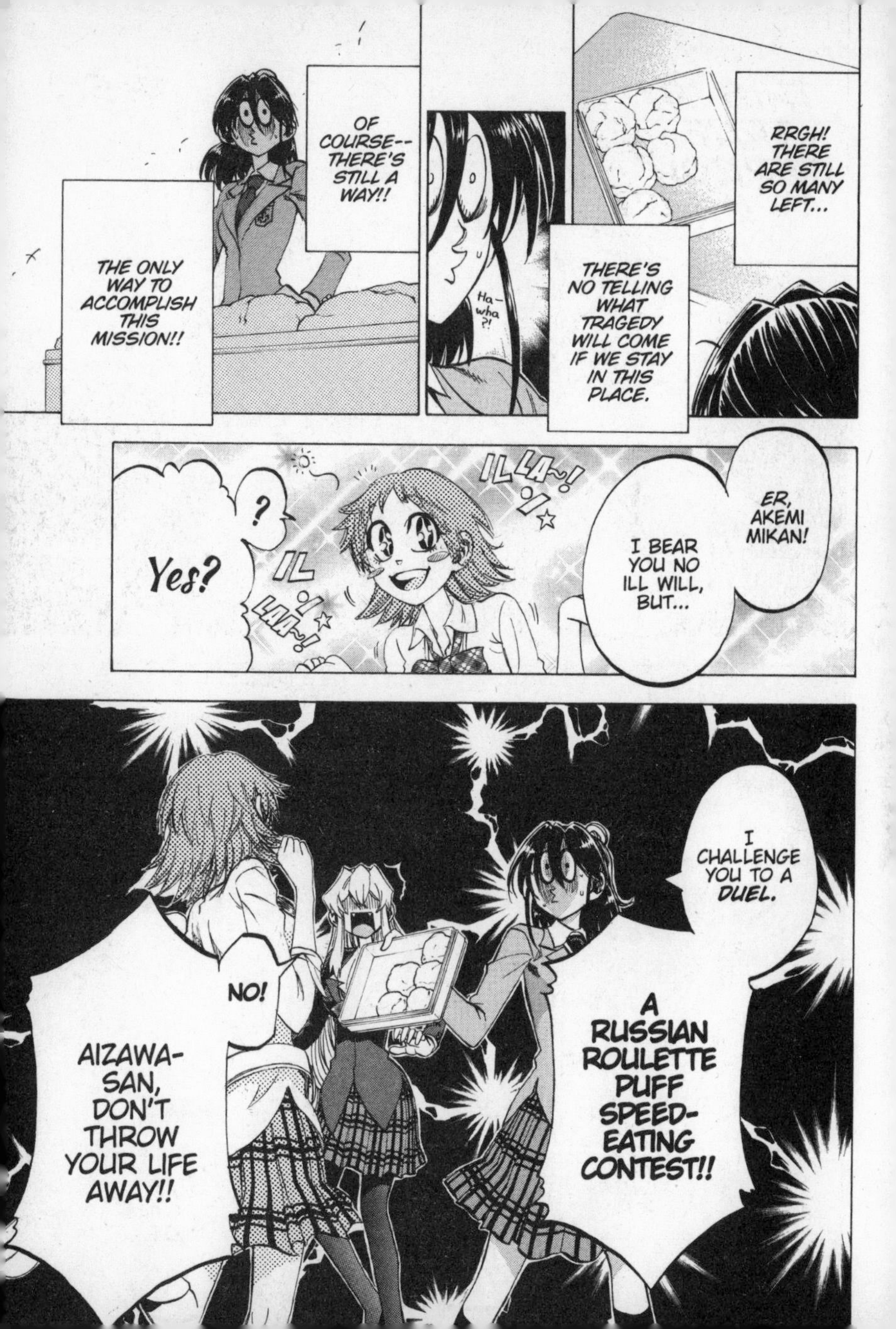
RRGH! THERE ARE STILL SO MANY LEFT...
THERE'S NO TELLING WHAT TRAGEDY WILL COME IF WE STAY IN THIS PLACE.
Ha-wha ?!
OF COURSE-- THERE'S STILL A WAY!!
THE ONLY WAY TO ACCOMPLISH THIS MISSION!!
ER, AKEMI MIKAN!
I BEAR YOU NO ILL WILL, BUT...
ILLA~!
ILLAA~!
?
Yes?
I CHALLENGE YOU TO A DUEL.
A RUSSIAN ROULETTE PUFF SPEED-EATING CONTEST!!
NO!
AIZAWA-SAN, DON'T THROW YOUR LIFE AWAY!!

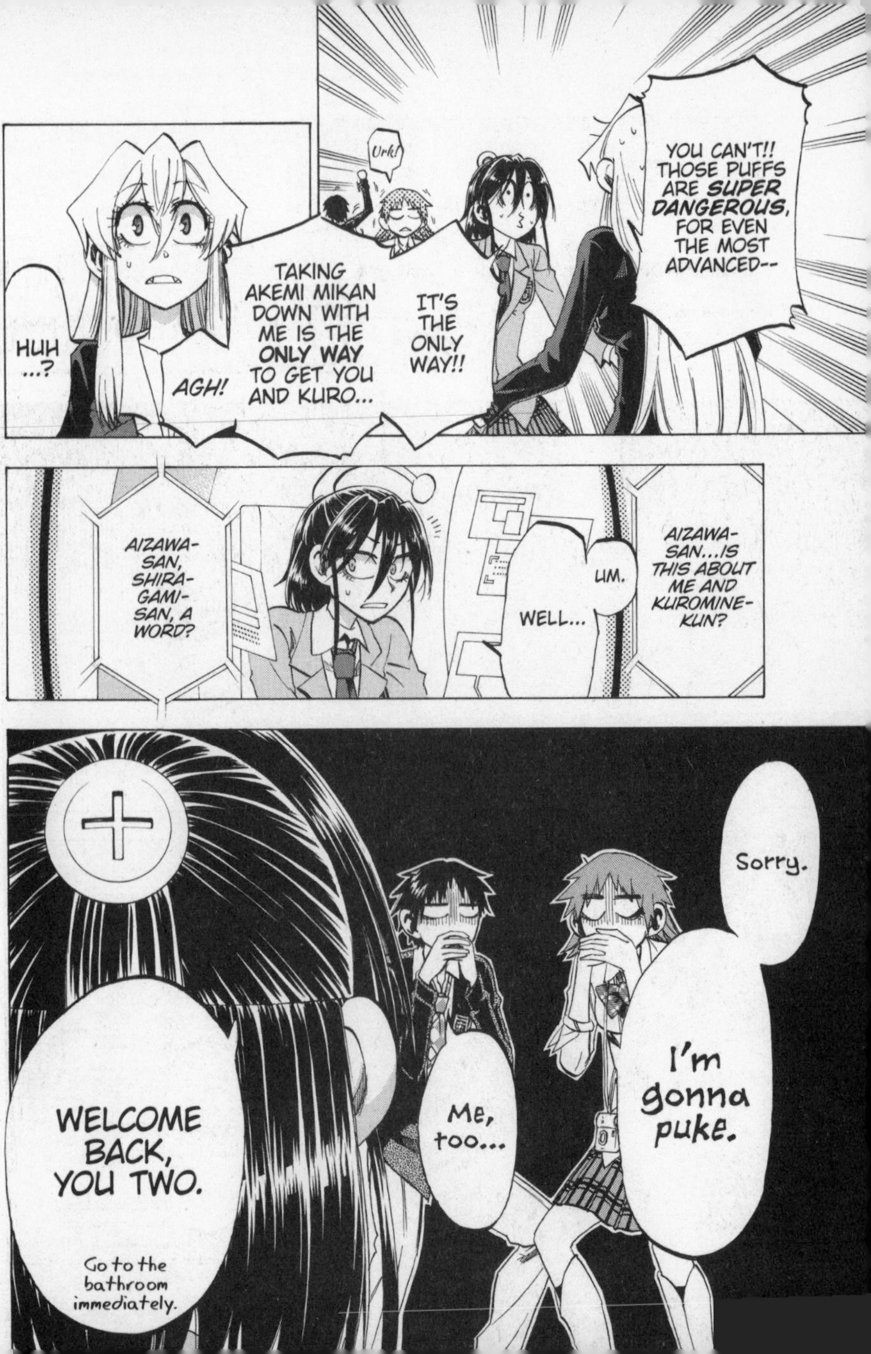
YOU CAN'T!! THOSE PUFFS ARE SUPER DANGEROUS, FOR EVEN THE MOST ADVANCED--
Urk!
IT'S THE ONLY WAY!!
TAKING AKEMI MIKAN DOWN WITH ME IS THE ONLY WAY TO GET YOU AND KURO...
AGH!
HUH ...?
AIZAWA-SAN...IS THIS ABOUT ME AND KUROMINE-KUN?
UM.
WELL...
AIZAWA-SAN, SHIRAGAMI-SAN, A WORD?
Sorry.
I'm gonna puke.
Me, too...
WELCOME BACK, YOU TWO.
Go to the bathroom immediately.

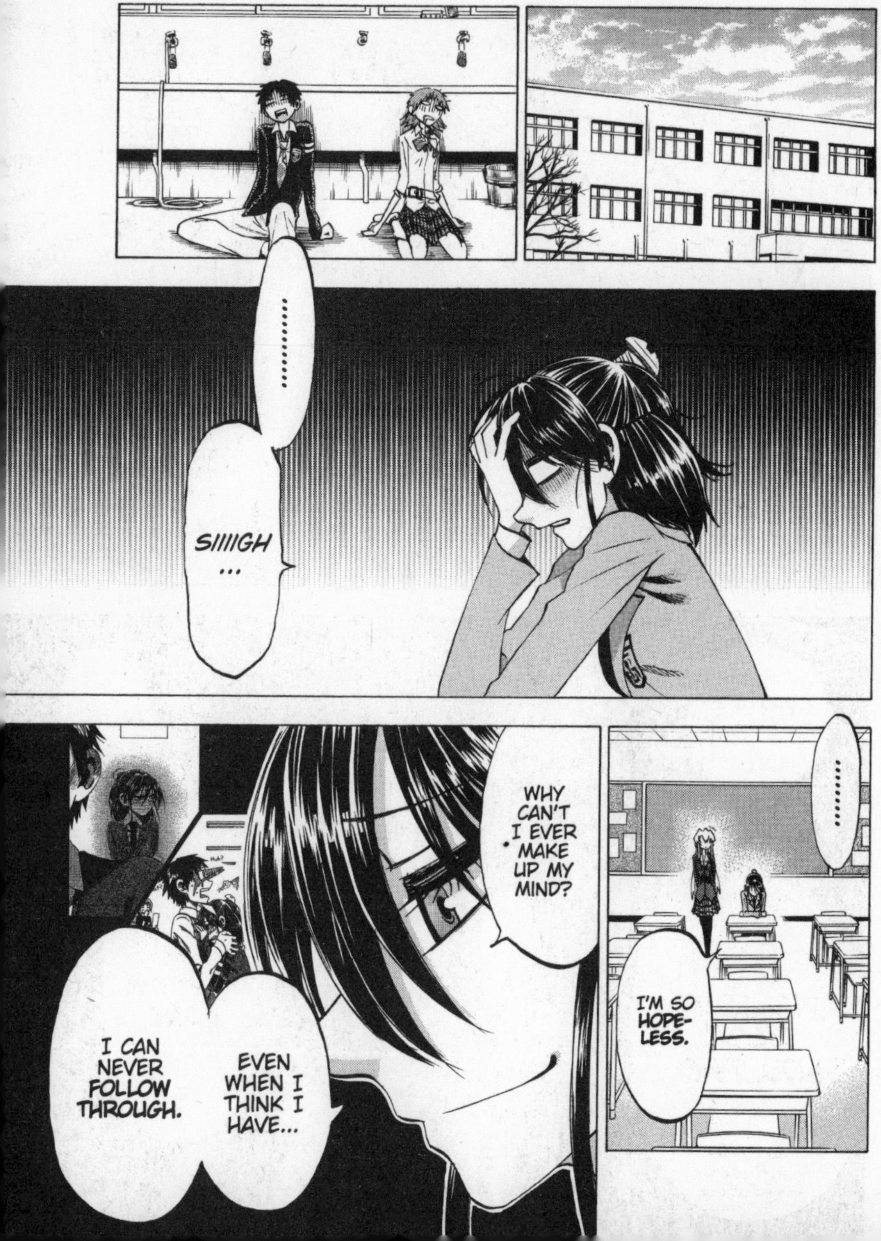
......
SIIIGH ...
......
I'M SO HOPE-LESS.
WHY CAN'T I EVER MAKE UP MY MIND?
EVEN WHEN I THINK I HAVE...
I CAN NEVER FOLLOW THROUGH.

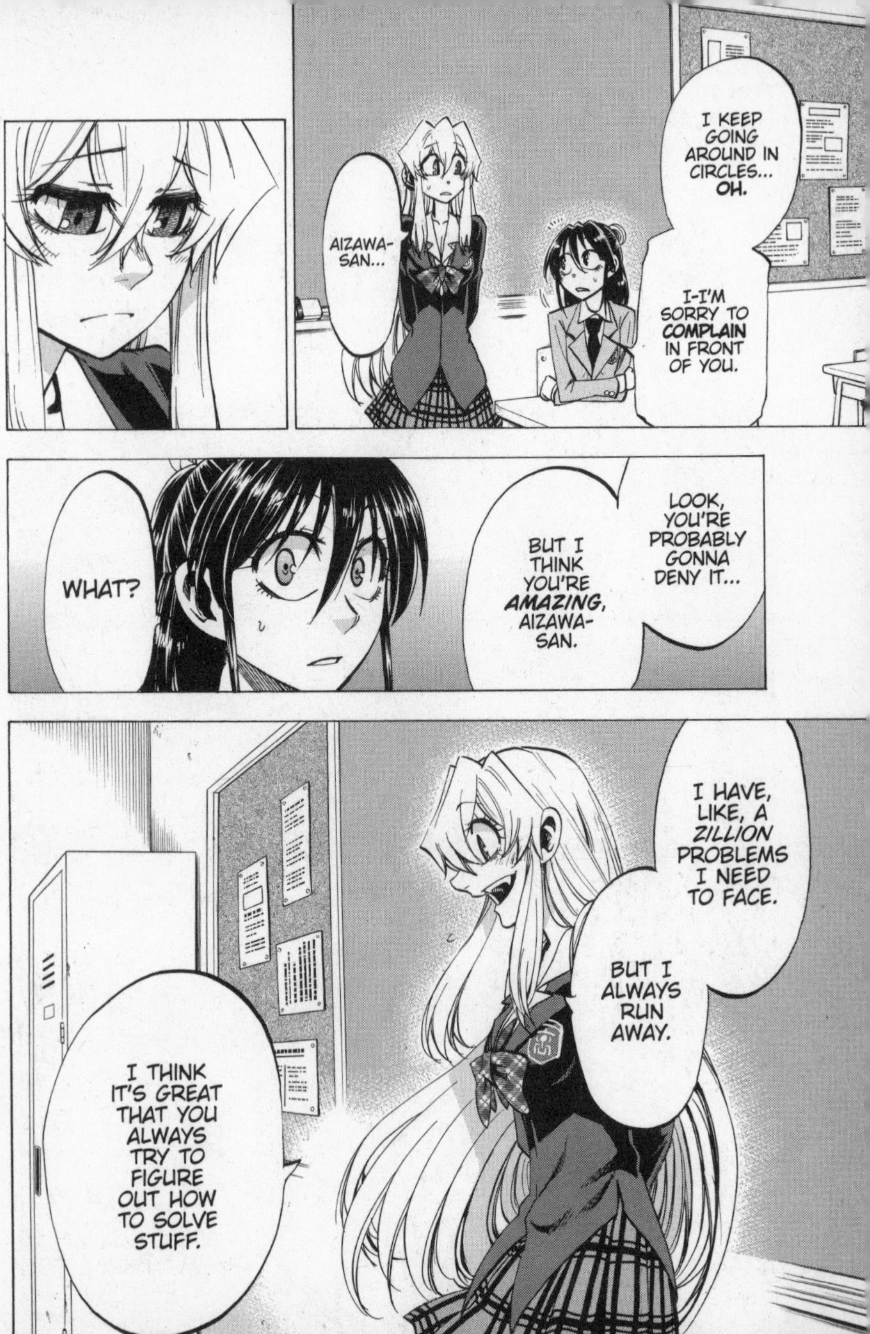
I KEEP GOING AROUND IN CIRCLES... **OH.**
I-I'M SORRY TO **COMPLAIN** IN FRONT OF YOU.
AIZAWA-SAN...
LOOK, YOU'RE PROBABLY GONNA DENY IT...
BUT I THINK YOU'RE ***AMAZING***, AIZAWA-SAN.
WHAT?
I HAVE, LIKE, A *ZILLION* PROBLEMS I NEED TO FACE.
BUT I ALWAYS RUN AWAY.
I THINK IT'S GREAT THAT YOU ALWAYS TRY TO FIGURE OUT HOW TO SOLVE STUFF.

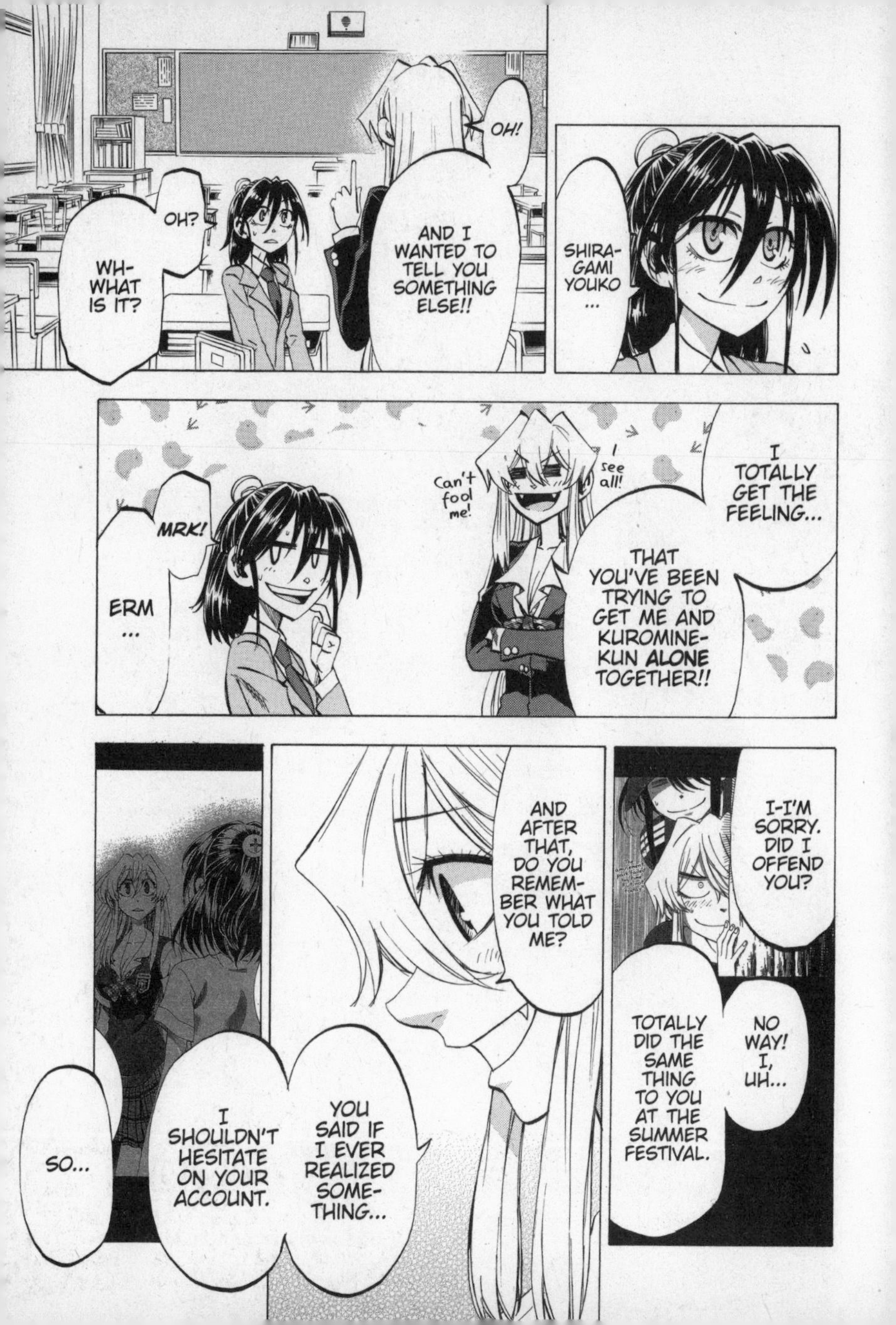
SHIRA-GAMI YOUKO ...
OH!
AND I WANTED TO TELL YOU SOMETHING ELSE!!
OH?
WH-WHAT IS IT?
I TOTALLY GET THE FEELING...
THAT YOU'VE BEEN TRYING TO GET ME AND KUROMINE-KUN ALONE TOGETHER!!
I see all!
Can't fool me!
MRK!
ERM ...
I-I'M SORRY. DID I OFFEND YOU?
NO WAY! I, UH...
TOTALLY DID THE SAME THING TO YOU AT THE SUMMER FESTIVAL.
AND AFTER THAT, DO YOU REMEMBER WHAT YOU TOLD ME?
YOU SAID IF I EVER REALIZED SOME-THING...
I SHOULDN'T HESITATE ON YOUR ACCOUNT.
SO...

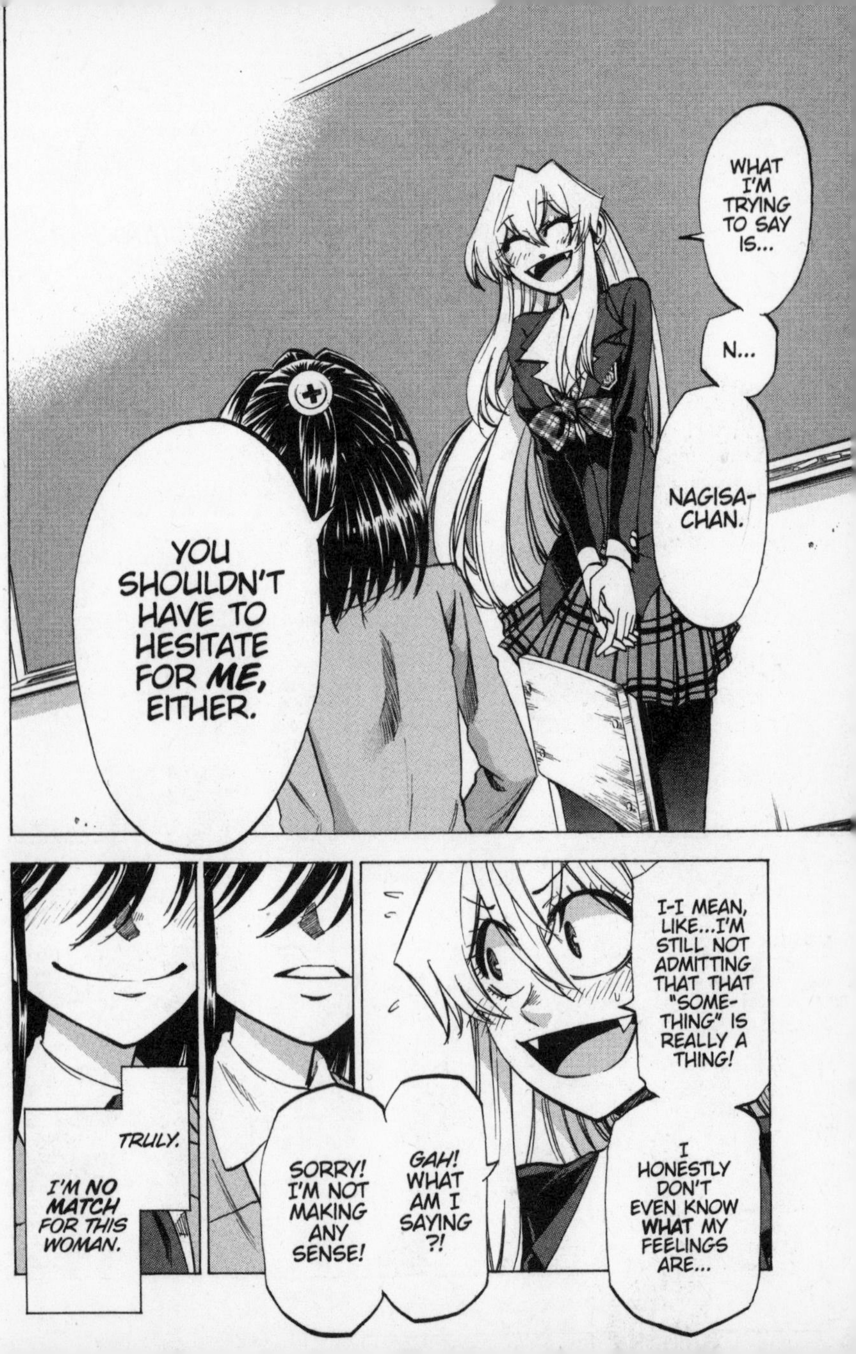
WHAT I'M TRYING TO SAY IS...
N...
NAGISA-CHAN.
YOU SHOULDN'T HAVE TO HESITATE FOR *ME*, EITHER.
I-I MEAN, LIKE...I'M STILL NOT ADMITTING THAT THAT "SOME-THING" IS REALLY A THING!
I HONESTLY DON'T EVEN KNOW **WHAT** MY FEELINGS ARE...
GAH! WHAT AM I SAYING?!
SORRY! I'M NOT MAKING ANY SENSE!
TRULY.
*I'M **NO MATCH** FOR THIS WOMAN.*

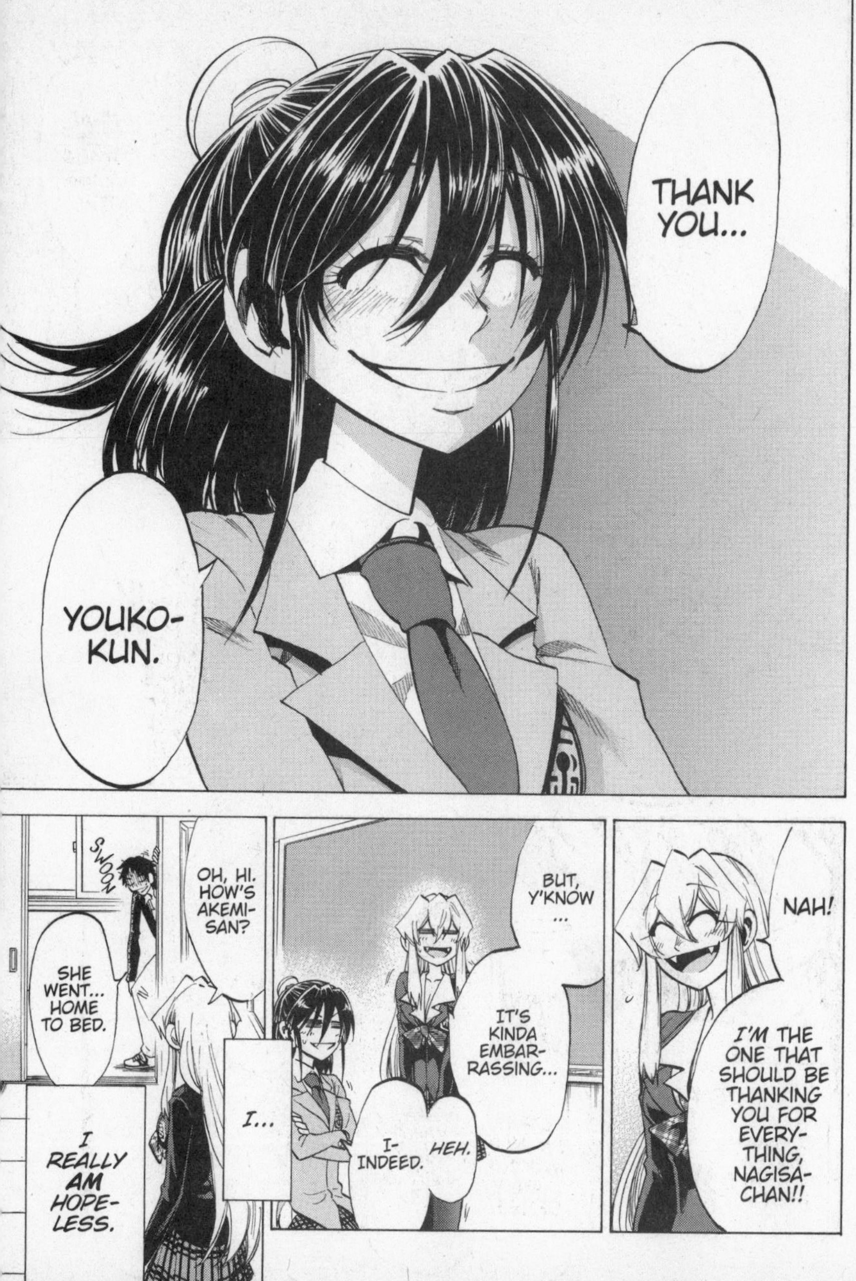
THANK YOU...
YOUKO-KUN.
NAH!
I'M THE ONE THAT SHOULD BE THANKING YOU FOR EVERYTHING, NAGISA-CHAN!!
BUT, Y'KNOW ...
IT'S KINDA EMBARRASSING...
HEH.
I- INDEED.
SWOON
OH, HI. HOW'S AKEMI-SAN?
SHE WENT... HOME TO BED.
I...
I REALLY **AM** HOPELESS.

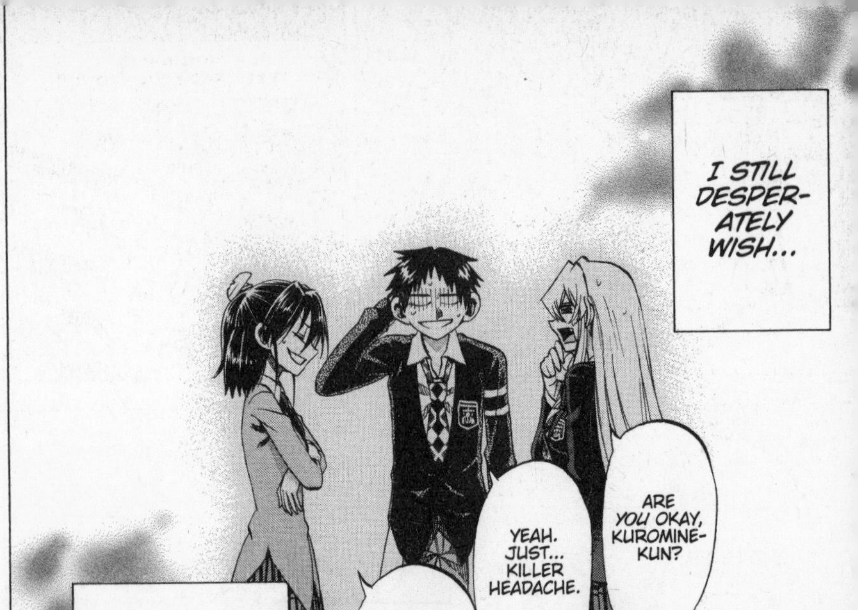
I STILL DESPERATELY WISH...
ARE YOU OKAY, KUROMINE-KUN?
YEAH. JUST... KILLER HEADACHE.
AKEMI MIKAN'S PUFFS ARE NOW WEAPONS-GRADE.
FOR THE THREE OF US TO STAY LIKE THIS FOR JUST A LITTLE LONGER.

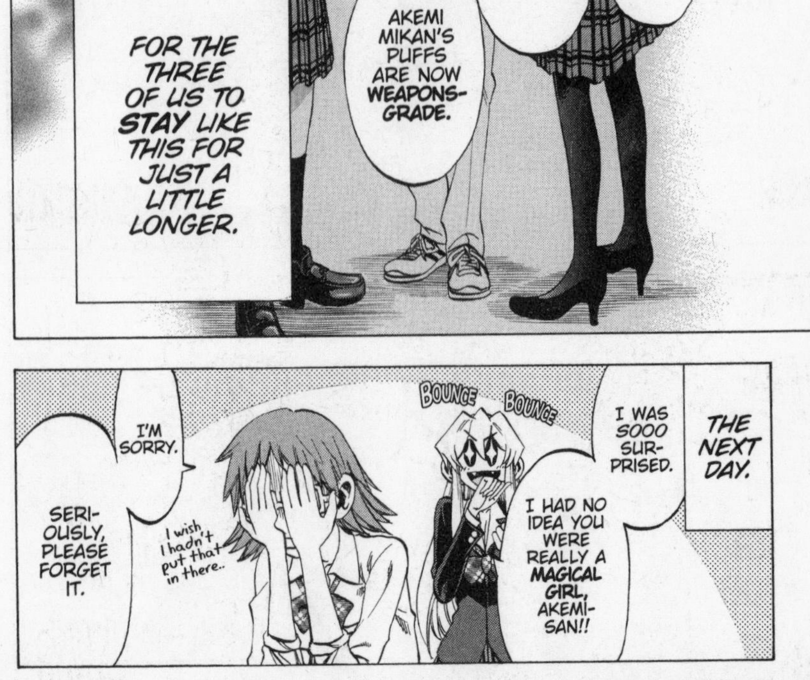
THE NEXT DAY.
BOUNCE BOUNCE
I WAS SOOO SURPRISED.
I HAD NO IDEA YOU WERE REALLY A MAGICAL GIRL, AKEMI-SAN!!
I'M SORRY.
I wish I hadn't put that in there..
SERIOUSLY, PLEASE FORGET IT.

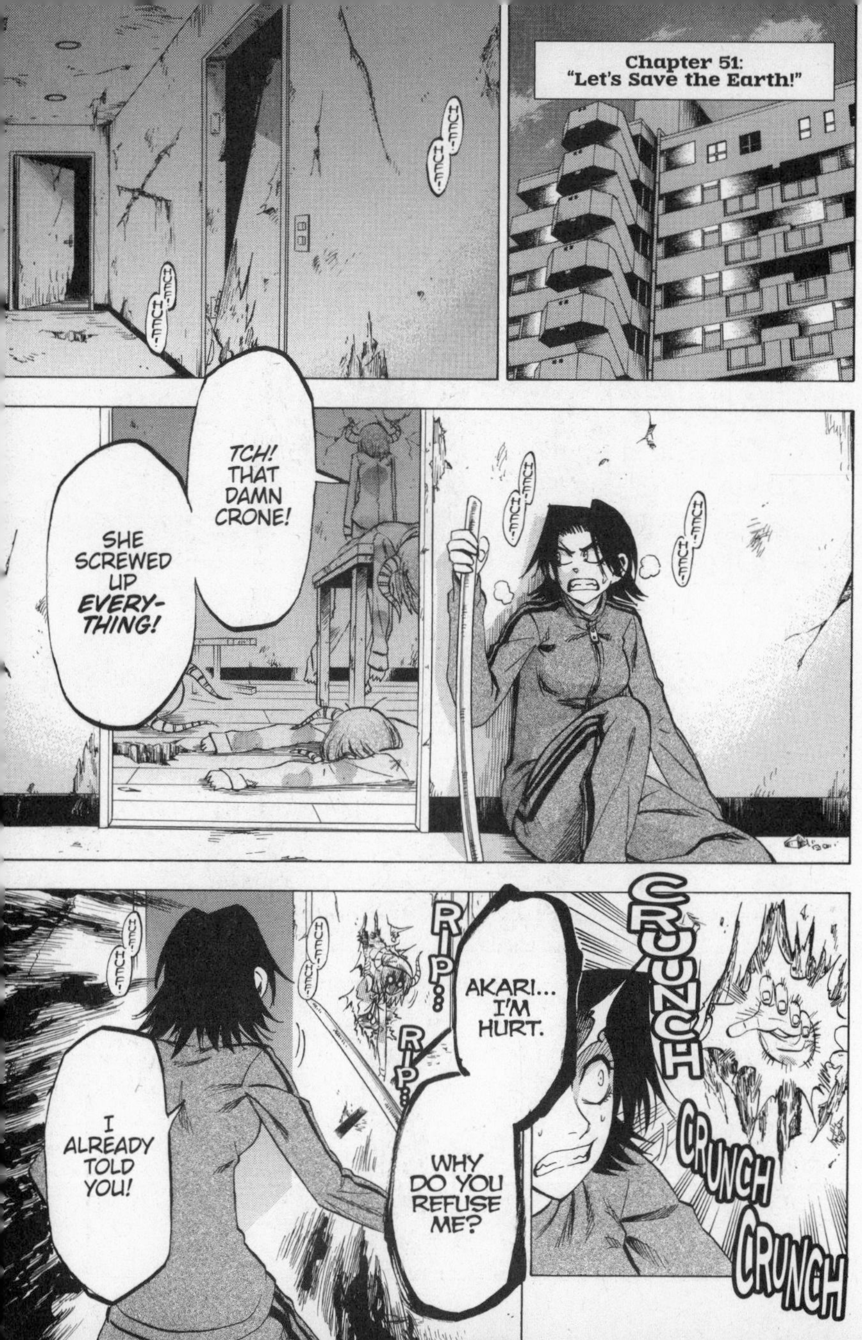
Chapter 51: "Let's Save the Earth!"
HUFF! HUFF!
HUFF! HUFF!
HUFF! HUFF!
HUFF! HUFF!
TCH! THAT DAMN CRONE!
SHE SCREWED UP EVERYTHING!
CRUNCH
CRUNCH
CRUNCH
CRUNCH
RIP...
RIP...
AKARI... I'M HURT.
WHY DO YOU REFUSE ME?
HUFF! HUFF!
HUFF! HUFF!
I ALREADY TOLD YOU!

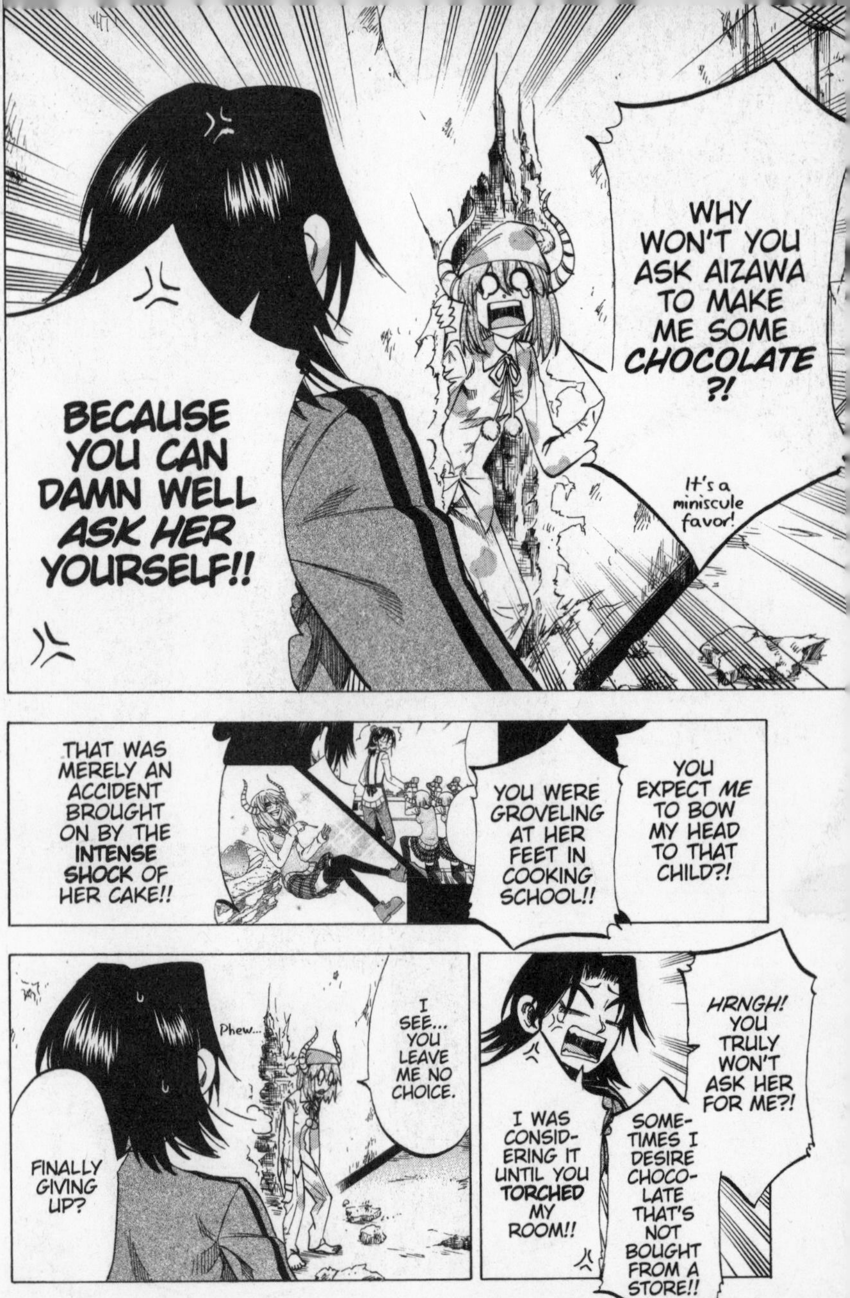
WHY WON'T YOU ASK AIZAWA TO MAKE ME SOME CHOCOLATE ?!
It's a miniscule favor!
BECAUSE YOU CAN DAMN WELL ASK HER YOURSELF!!
YOU EXPECT ME TO BOW MY HEAD TO THAT CHILD?!
YOU WERE GROVELING AT HER FEET IN COOKING SCHOOL!!
THAT WAS MERELY AN ACCIDENT BROUGHT ON BY THE INTENSE SHOCK OF HER CAKE!!
HRNGH! YOU TRULY WON'T ASK HER FOR ME?!
SOME-TIMES I DESIRE CHOCO-LATE THAT'S NOT BOUGHT FROM A STORE!!
I WAS CONSID-ERING IT UNTIL YOU TORCHED MY ROOM!!
I SEE... YOU LEAVE ME NO CHOICE.
Phew...
FINALLY GIVING UP?

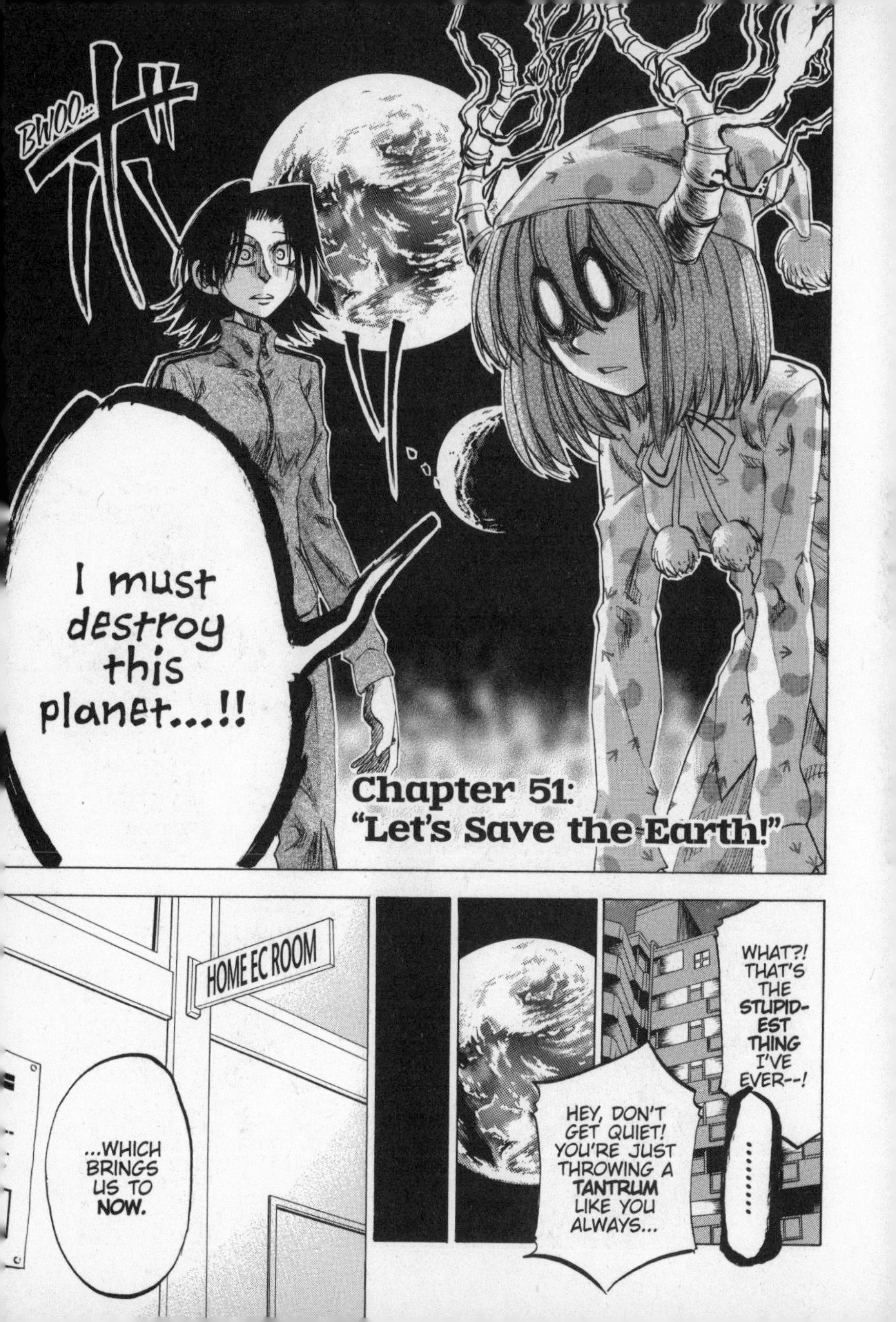
BWOO...
I must destroy this planet...!!
Chapter 51: "Let's Save the Earth!"
WHAT?! THAT'S THE STUPID-EST THING I'VE EVER--!
......
HEY, DON'T GET QUIET! YOU'RE JUST THROWING A TANTRUM LIKE YOU ALWAYS...
HOME EC ROOM
...WHICH BRINGS US TO NOW.

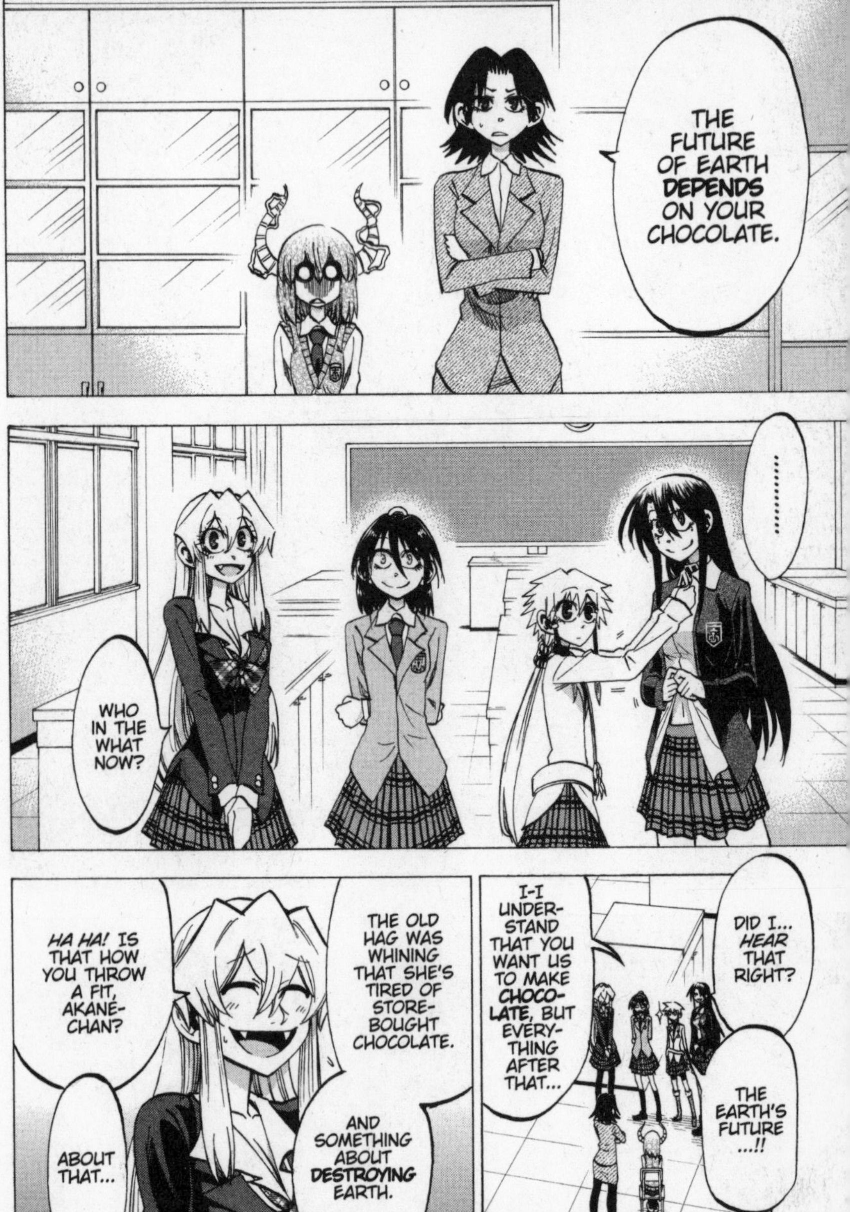
THE FUTURE OF EARTH **DEPENDS** ON YOUR CHOCOLATE.
......
WHO IN THE WHAT NOW?
DID I... *HEAR* THAT RIGHT?
I-I UNDERSTAND THAT YOU WANT US TO MAKE **CHOCOLATE**, BUT EVERYTHING AFTER THAT...
THE EARTH'S FUTURE ...!!
THE OLD HAG WAS WHINING THAT SHE'S TIRED OF STORE-BOUGHT CHOCOLATE.
HA HA! IS THAT HOW YOU THROW A FIT, AKANE-CHAN?
AND SOMETHING ABOUT **DESTROYING** EARTH.
ABOUT THAT...

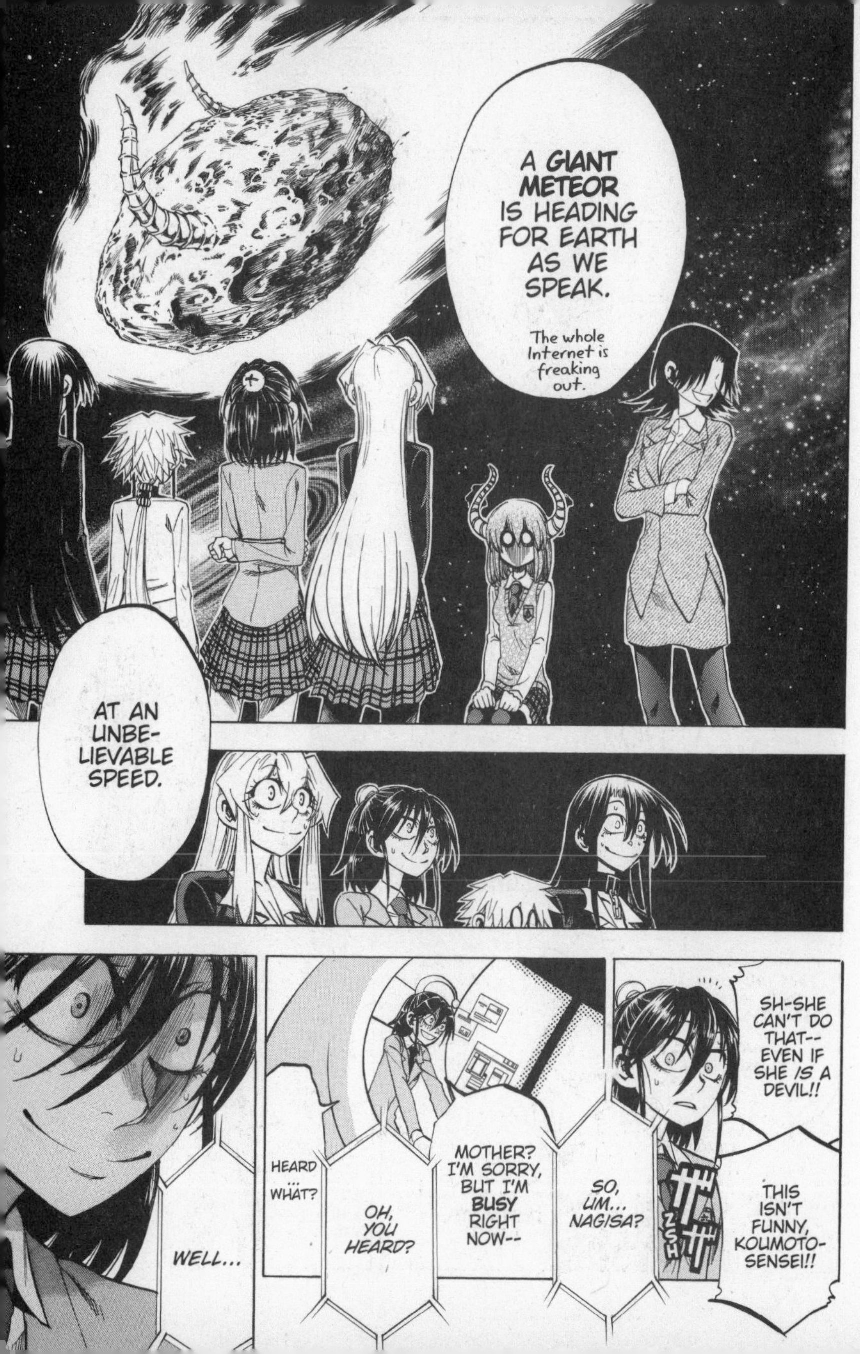
A GIANT METEOR IS HEADING FOR EARTH AS WE SPEAK.
The whole Internet is freaking out.
AT AN UNBELIEVABLE SPEED.
SH-SHE CAN'T DO THAT-- EVEN IF SHE IS A DEVIL!!
THIS ISN'T FUNNY, KOUMOTO-SENSEI!!
ZSH
SO, UM... NAGISA?
MOTHER? I'M SORRY, BUT I'M BUSY RIGHT NOW--
OH, YOU HEARD?
HEARD... WHAT?
WELL...

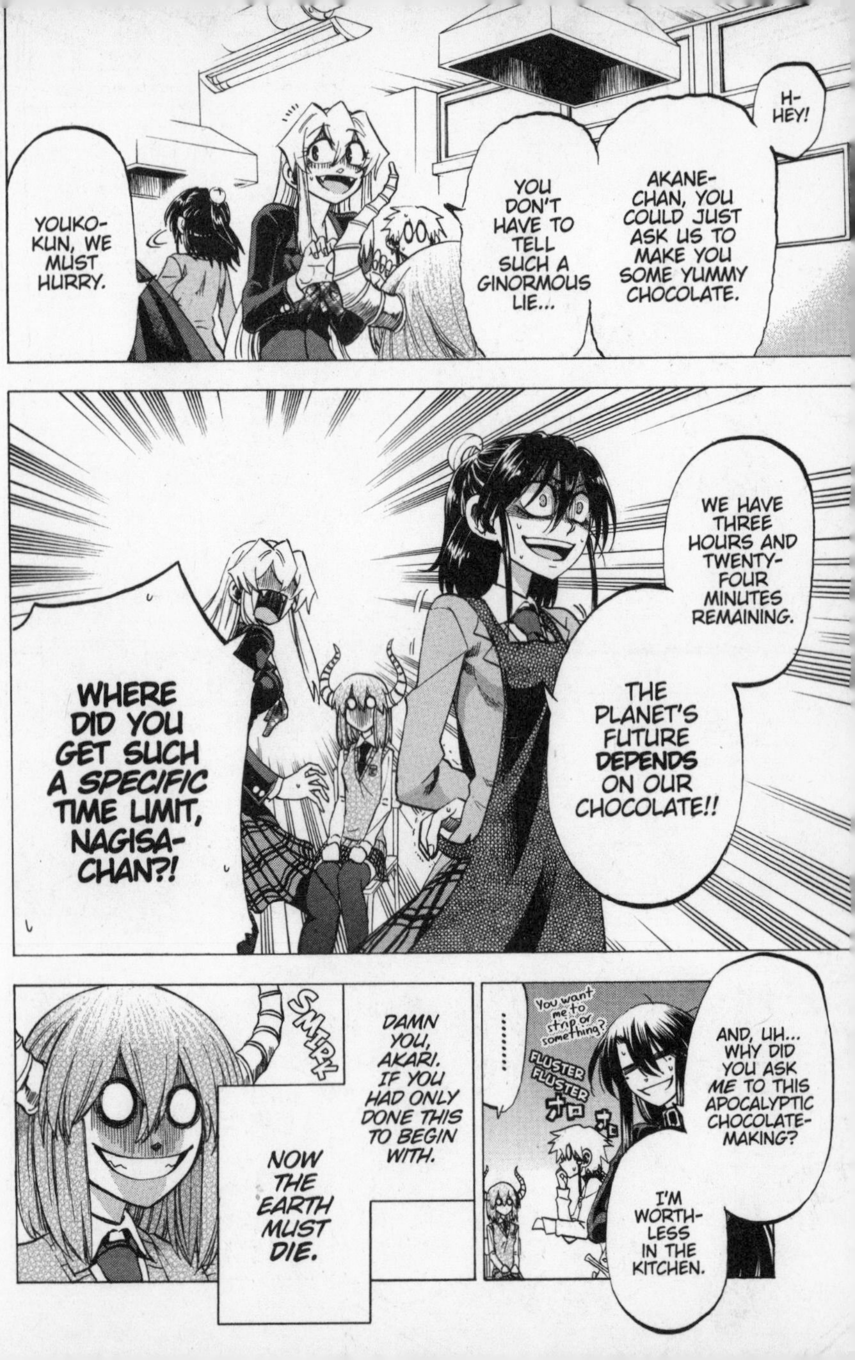
H-HEY!
AKANE-CHAN, YOU COULD JUST ASK US TO MAKE YOU SOME YUMMY CHOCOLATE.
YOU DON'T HAVE TO TELL SUCH A GINORMOUS LIE...
YOUKO-KUN, WE MUST HURRY.
WE HAVE THREE HOURS AND TWENTY-FOUR MINUTES REMAINING.
THE PLANET'S FUTURE **DEPENDS** ON OUR CHOCOLATE!!
WHERE DID YOU GET SUCH A *SPECIFIC* TIME LIMIT, NAGISA-CHAN?!
AND, UH... WHY DID YOU ASK *ME* TO THIS APOCALYPTIC CHOCOLATE-MAKING?
I'M WORTHLESS IN THE KITCHEN.
You want me to strip or something?
FLUSTER FLUSTER
......
SMIRK
DAMN YOU, AKARI. IF YOU HAD ONLY DONE THIS TO BEGIN WITH.
NOW THE EARTH MUST DIE.

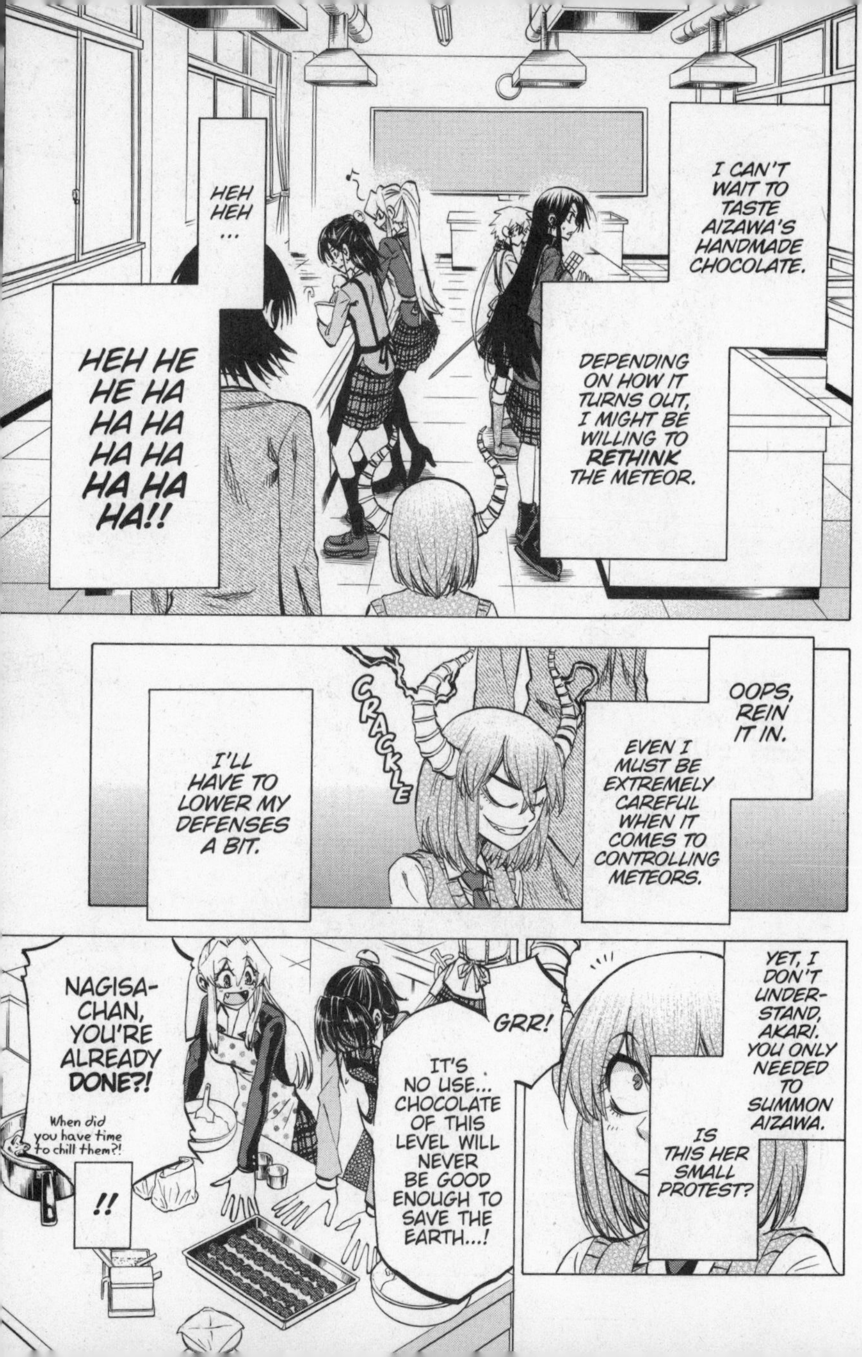

I CAN'T WAIT TO TASTE AIZAWA'S HANDMADE CHOCOLATE.
DEPENDING ON HOW IT TURNS OUT, I MIGHT BE WILLING TO RETHINK THE METEOR.
HEH HEH ...
HEH HE HE HA HA HA HA HA HA HA HA!!
OOPS, REIN IT IN.
EVEN I MUST BE EXTREMELY CAREFUL WHEN IT COMES TO CONTROLLING METEORS.
CRACKLE
I'LL HAVE TO LOWER MY DEFENSES A BIT.
YET, I DON'T UNDER-STAND, AKARI. YOU ONLY NEEDED TO SUMMON AIZAWA.
IS THIS HER SMALL PROTEST?
GRR!
IT'S NO USE... CHOCOLATE OF THIS LEVEL WILL NEVER BE GOOD ENOUGH TO SAVE THE EARTH...!
NAGISA-CHAN, YOU'RE ALREADY DONE?!
When did you have time to chill them?!
!!

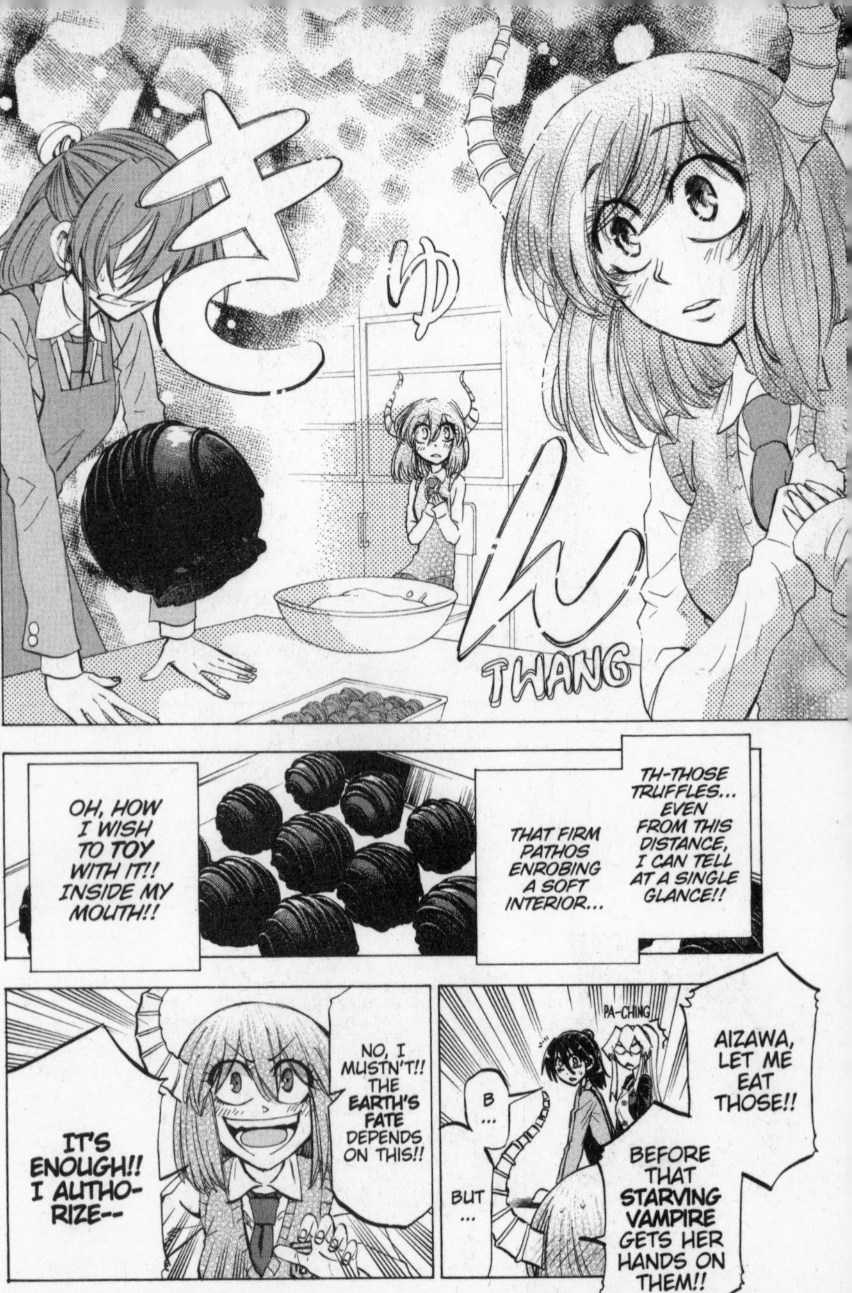
ぎゅん
TWANG
TH-THOSE TRUFFLES... EVEN FROM THIS DISTANCE, I CAN TELL AT A SINGLE GLANCE!!
THAT FIRM PATHOS ENROBING A SOFT INTERIOR...
OH, HOW I WISH TO TOY WITH IT!! INSIDE MY MOUTH!!
AIZAWA, LET ME EAT THOSE!!
PA-CHING
BEFORE THAT STARVING VAMPIRE GETS HER HANDS ON THEM!!
B ...
BUT ...
NO, I MUSTN'T!! THE EARTH'S FATE DEPENDS ON THIS!!
IT'S ENOUGH!! I AUTHO-RIZE--

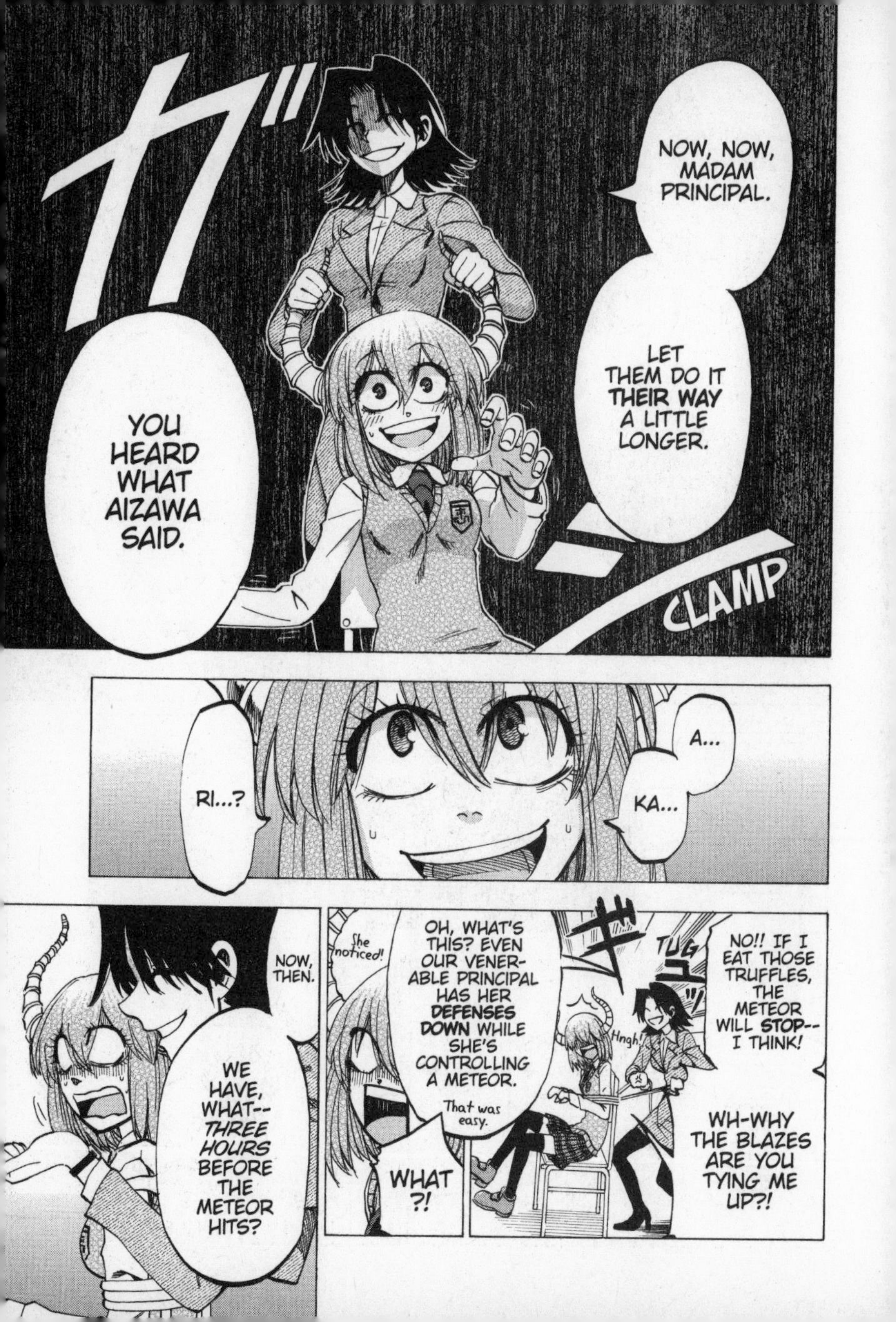
NOW, NOW, MADAM PRINCIPAL.
LET THEM DO IT THEIR WAY A LITTLE LONGER.
ガ
CLAMP
YOU HEARD WHAT AIZAWA SAID.
A...
KA...
RI...?
NO!! IF I EAT THOSE TRUFFLES, THE METEOR WILL STOP-- I THINK!
ギュッ
TUG
Hngh!
WH-WHY THE BLAZES ARE YOU TYING ME UP?!
OH, WHAT'S THIS? EVEN OUR VENER-ABLE PRINCIPAL HAS HER DEFENSES DOWN WHILE SHE'S CONTROLLING A METEOR.
She noticed!
That was easy.
WHAT?!
NOW, THEN.
WE HAVE, WHAT-- THREE HOURS BEFORE THE METEOR HITS?

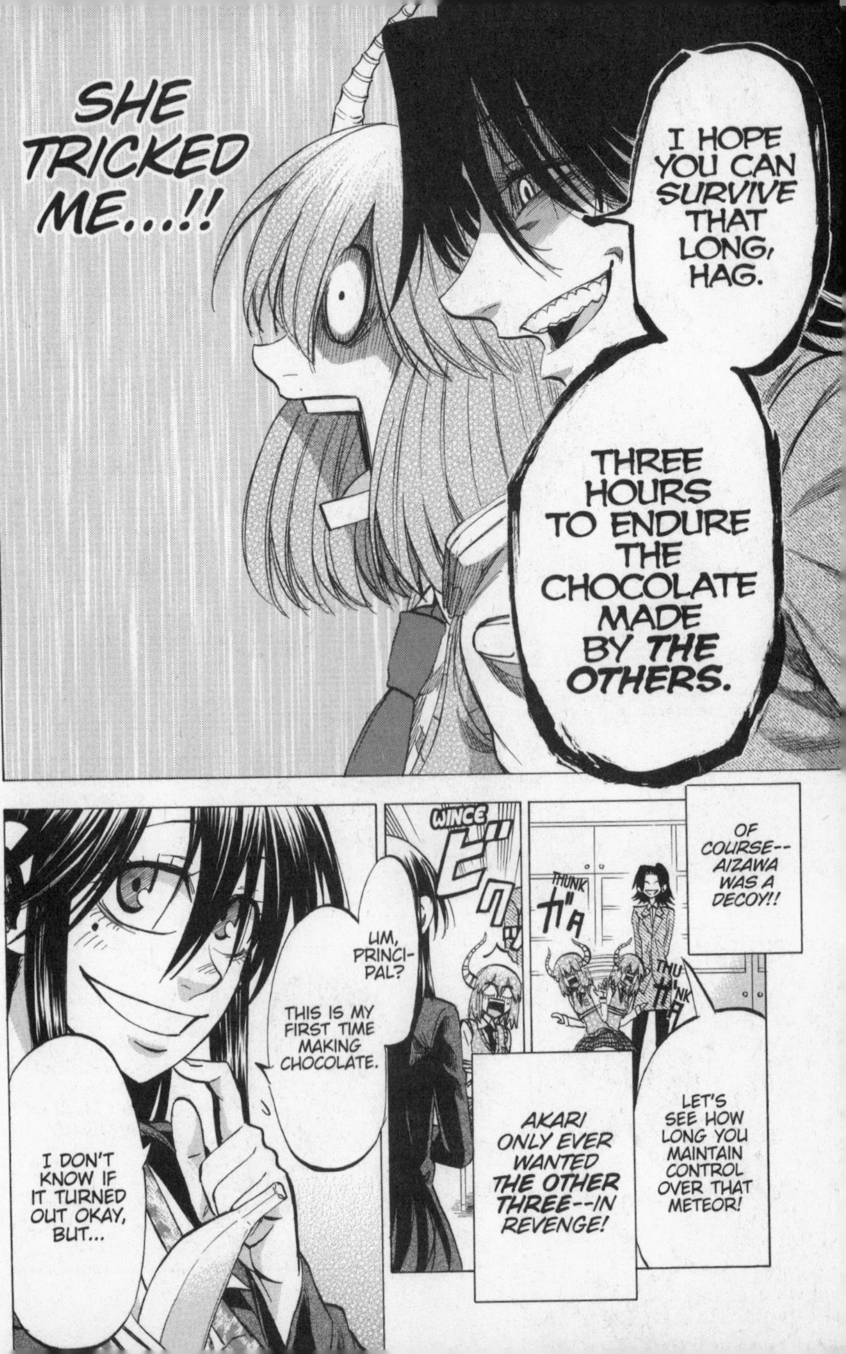
I HOPE YOU CAN SURVIVE THAT LONG, HAG.
THREE HOURS TO ENDURE THE CHOCOLATE MADE BY THE OTHERS.
SHE TRICKED ME...!!
OF COURSE-- AIZAWA WAS A DECOY!!
THUNK
THUNK
LET'S SEE HOW LONG YOU MAINTAIN CONTROL OVER THAT METEOR!
AKARI ONLY EVER WANTED THE OTHER THREE--IN REVENGE!
WINCE
UM, PRINCIPAL?
THIS IS MY FIRST TIME MAKING CHOCOLATE.
I DON'T KNOW IF IT TURNED OUT OKAY, BUT...

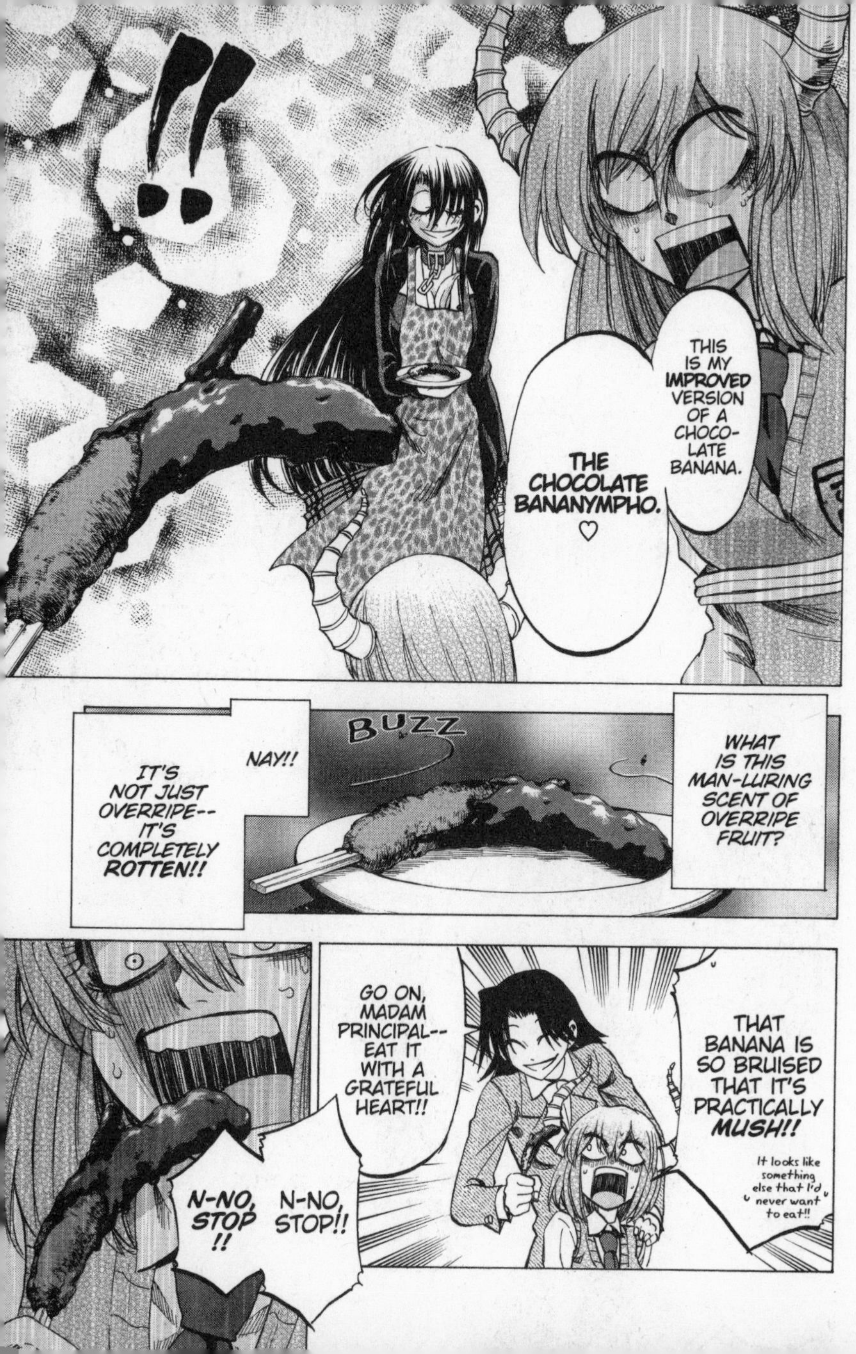
THIS IS MY IMPROVED VERSION OF A CHOCOLATE BANANA.
THE CHOCOLATE BANANYMPHO. ♡
!!
WHAT IS THIS MAN-LURING SCENT OF OVERRIPE FRUIT?
BUZZ
NAY!!
IT'S NOT JUST OVERRIPE-- IT'S COMPLETELY ROTTEN!!
THAT BANANA IS SO BRUISED THAT IT'S PRACTICALLY MUSH!!
It looks like something else that I'd never want to eat!!
GO ON, MADAM PRINCIPAL-- EAT IT WITH A GRATEFUL HEART!!
N-NO, STOP!!
N-NO, STOP !!

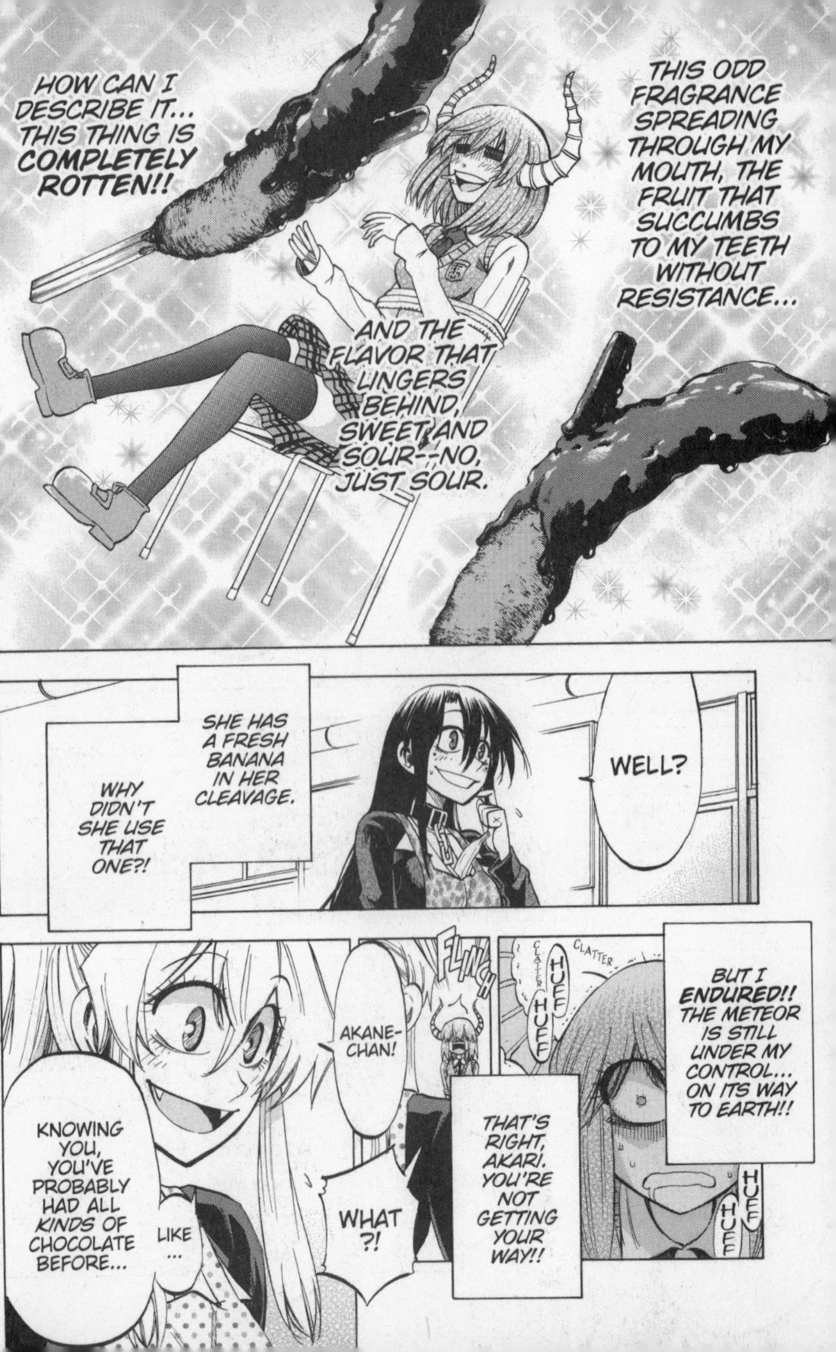
THIS ODD FRAGRANCE SPREADING THROUGH MY MOUTH, THE FRUIT THAT SUCCUMBS TO MY TEETH WITHOUT RESISTANCE...
AND THE FLAVOR THAT LINGERS BEHIND, SWEET AND SOUR--NO, JUST SOUR.
HOW CAN I DESCRIBE IT... THIS THING IS **COMPLETELY ROTTEN!!**
WELL?
SHE HAS A FRESH BANANA IN HER CLEAVAGE.
WHY DIDN'T SHE USE THAT ONE?!
BUT I **ENDURED!!** THE METEOR IS STILL UNDER MY CONTROL... ON ITS WAY TO EARTH!!
HUFF HUFF
CLATTER
HUFF HUFF
CLATTER
FLINCH
AKANE-CHAN!
THAT'S RIGHT, AKARI. YOU'RE NOT GETTING YOUR WAY!!
WHAT?!
KNOWING YOU, YOU'VE PROBABLY HAD ALL KINDS OF CHOCOLATE BEFORE...
LIKE...

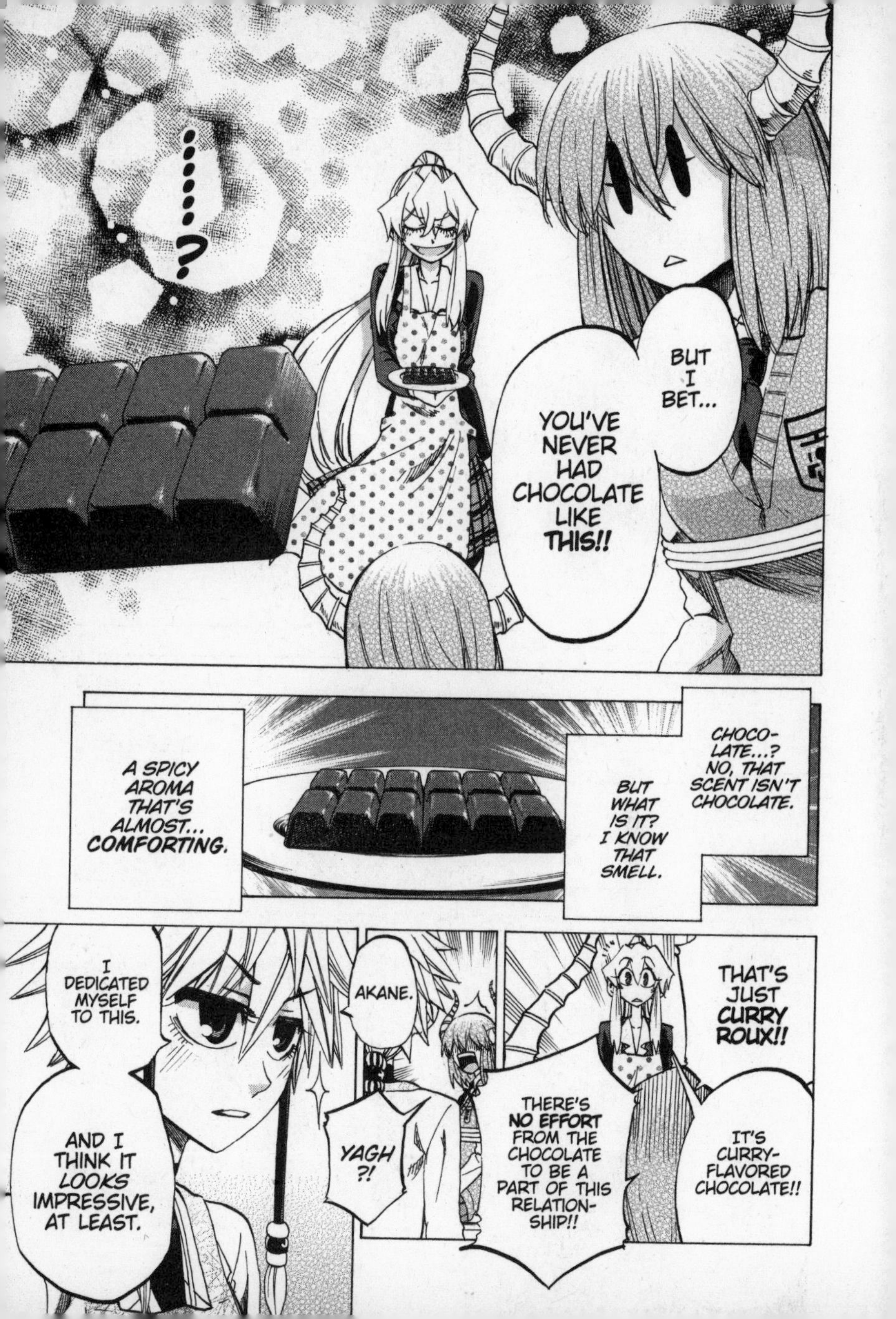

BUT I BET... YOU'VE NEVER HAD CHOCOLATE LIKE THIS!!
......?
CHOCOLATE...? NO, THAT SCENT ISN'T CHOCOLATE.
BUT WHAT IS IT? I KNOW THAT SMELL.
A SPICY AROMA THAT'S ALMOST... COMFORTING.
THAT'S JUST CURRY ROUX!!
IT'S CURRY-FLAVORED CHOCOLATE!!
THERE'S NO EFFORT FROM THE CHOCOLATE TO BE A PART OF THIS RELATIONSHIP!!
AKANE.
YAGH?!
I DEDICATED MYSELF TO THIS.
AND I THINK IT LOOKS IMPRESSIVE, AT LEAST.

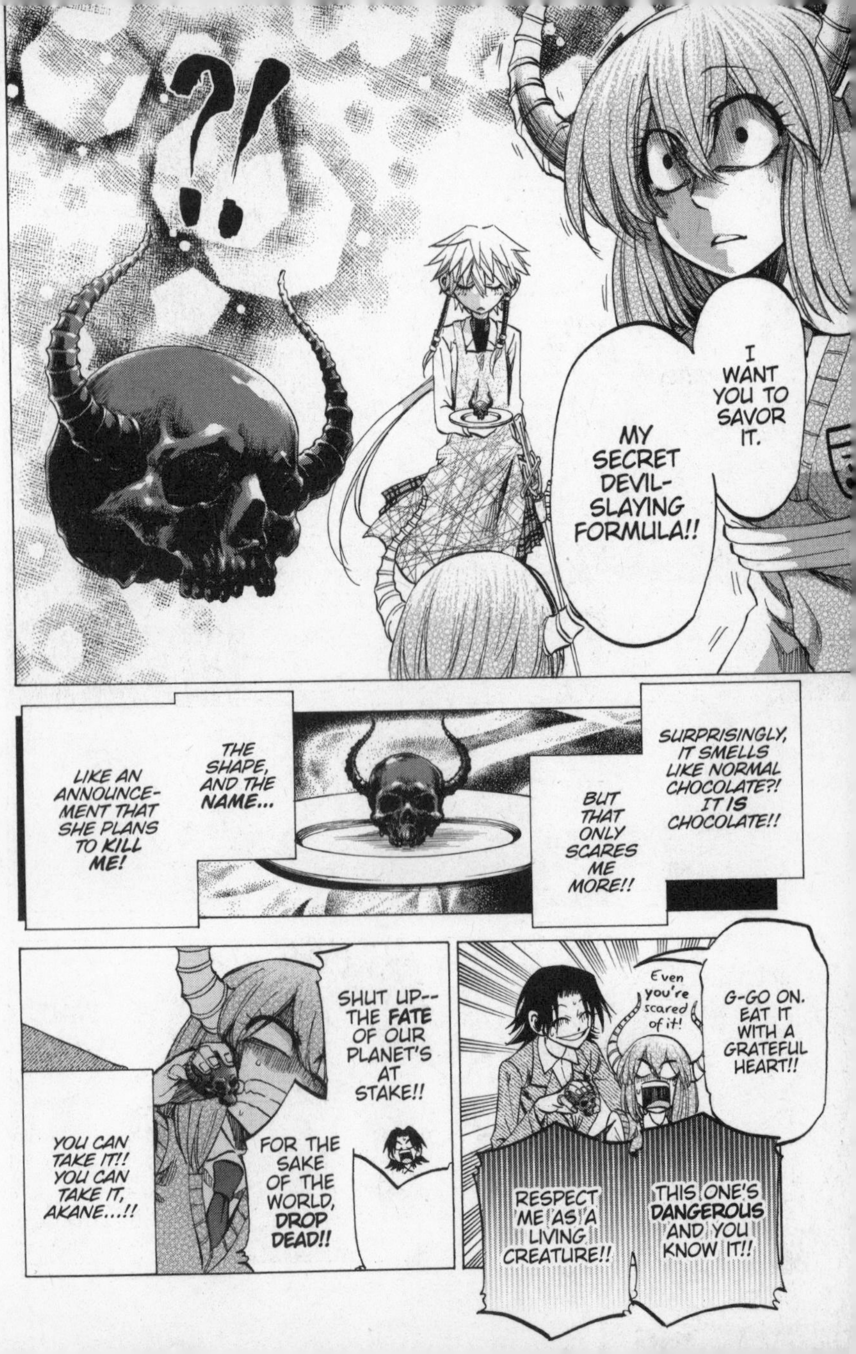
I WANT YOU TO SAVOR IT.
MY SECRET DEVIL-SLAYING FORMULA!!
?!!
SURPRISINGLY, IT SMELLS LIKE NORMAL CHOCOLATE?! IT IS CHOCOLATE!!
BUT THAT ONLY SCARES ME MORE!!
THE SHAPE, AND THE NAME...
LIKE AN ANNOUNCEMENT THAT SHE PLANS TO KILL ME!
G-GO ON. EAT IT WITH A GRATEFUL HEART!!
Even you're scared of it!
THIS ONE'S DANGEROUS AND YOU KNOW IT!!
RESPECT ME AS A LIVING CREATURE!!
SHUT UP-- THE FATE OF OUR PLANET'S AT STAKE!!
FOR THE SAKE OF THE WORLD, DROP DEAD!!
YOU CAN TAKE IT!! YOU CAN TAKE IT, AKANE...!!

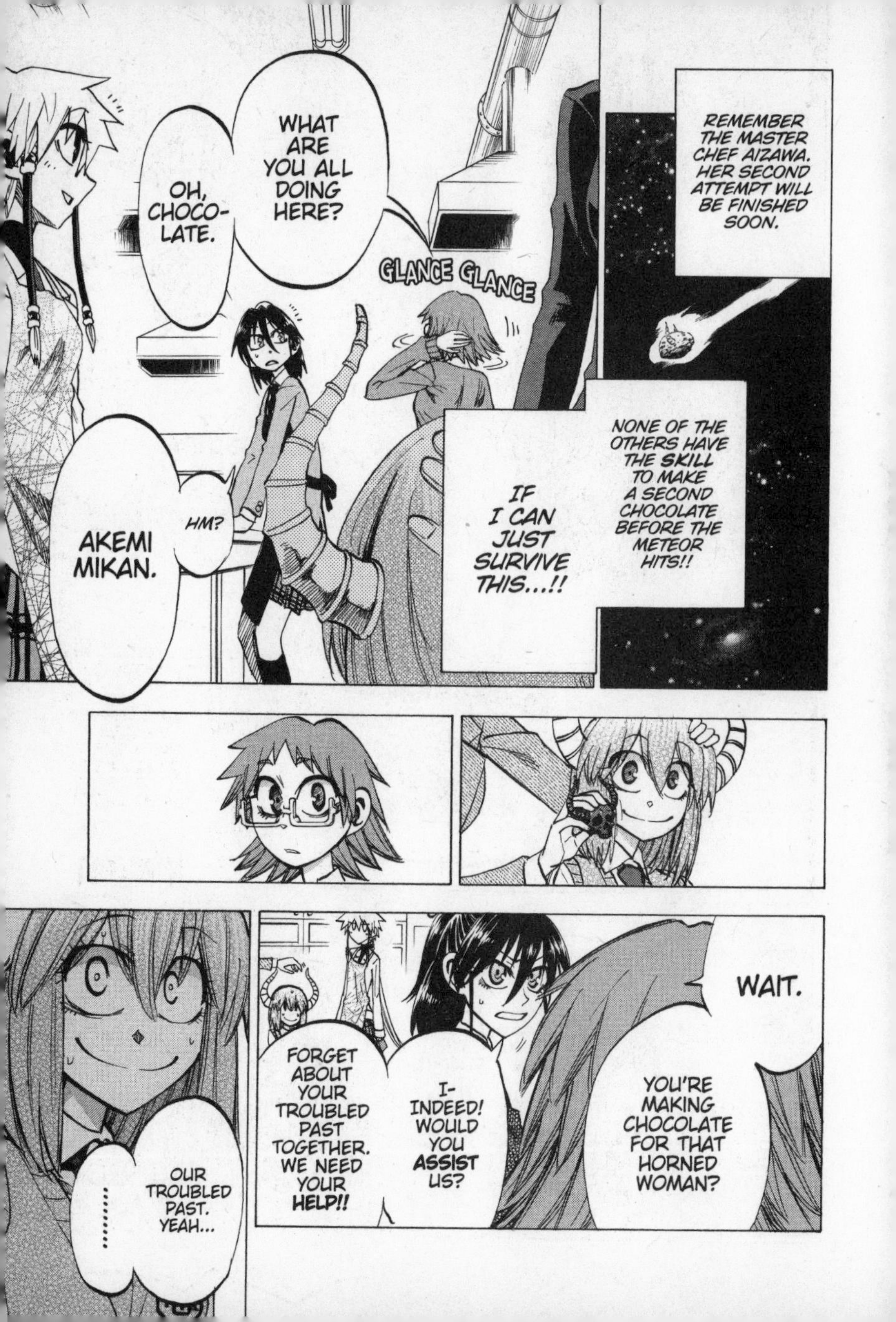
REMEMBER THE MASTER CHEF AIZAWA. HER SECOND ATTEMPT WILL BE FINISHED SOON.
NONE OF THE OTHERS HAVE THE **SKILL** TO MAKE A SECOND CHOCOLATE BEFORE THE METEOR HITS!!
IF I CAN JUST SURVIVE THIS...!!
WHAT ARE YOU ALL DOING HERE?
OH, CHOCO-LATE.
GLANCE GLANCE
HM?
AKEMI MIKAN.
WAIT.
YOU'RE MAKING CHOCOLATE FOR THAT HORNED WOMAN?
I- INDEED! WOULD YOU **ASSIST** US?
FORGET ABOUT YOUR TROUBLED PAST TOGETHER. WE NEED YOUR **HELP!!**
OUR TROUBLED PAST. YEAH...
......

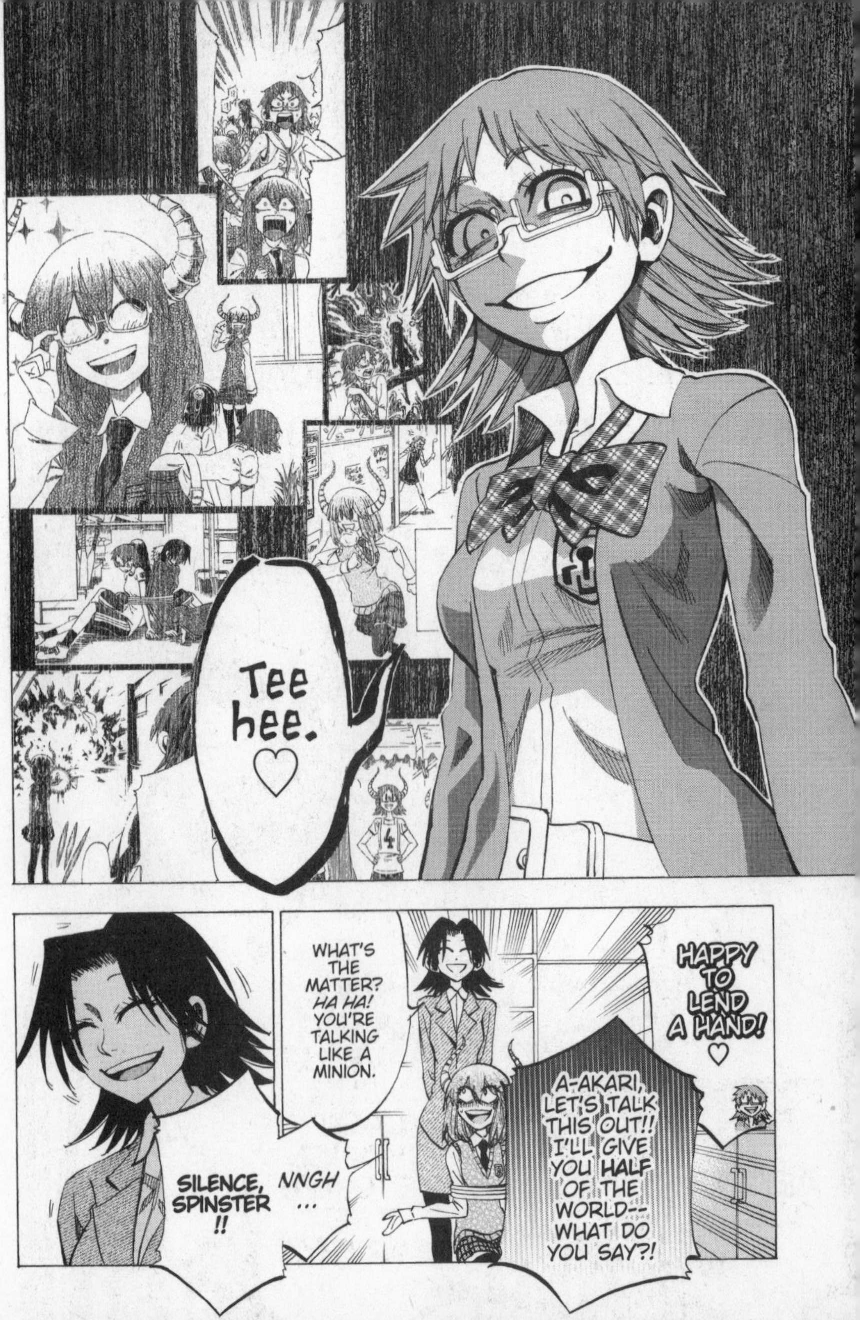
Tee hee. ♥
HAPPY TO LEND A HAND! ♥
A-AKARI, LET'S TALK THIS OUT!! I'LL GIVE YOU HALF OF THE WORLD-- WHAT DO YOU SAY?!
WHAT'S THE MATTER? HA HA! YOU'RE TALKING LIKE A MINION.
NNGH ...
SILENCE, SPINSTER !!

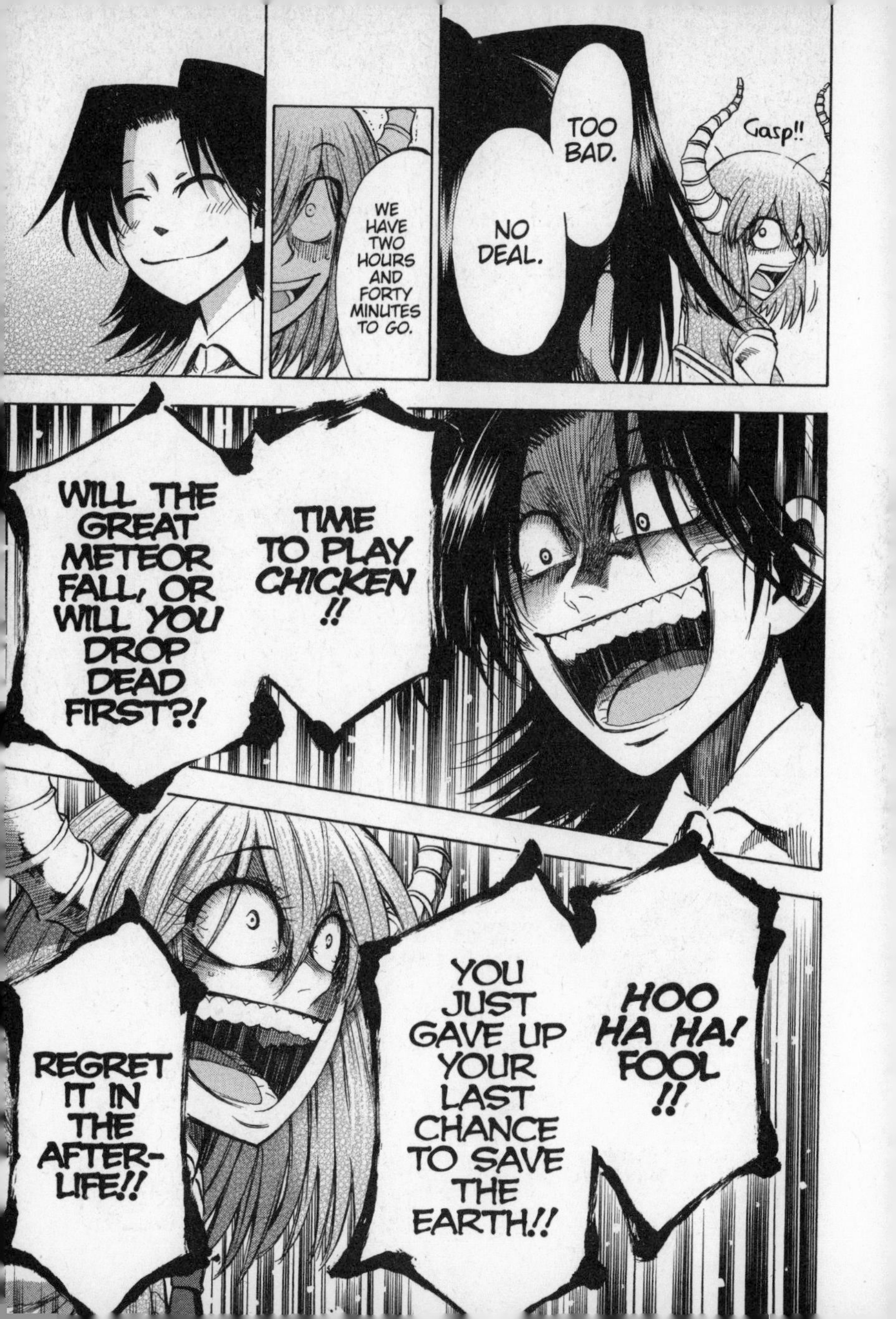
Gasp!!
TOO BAD.
NO DEAL.
WE HAVE TWO HOURS AND FORTY MINUTES TO GO.
TIME TO PLAY CHICKEN!!
WILL THE GREAT METEOR FALL, OR WILL YOU DROP DEAD FIRST?!
HOO HA HA! FOOL!!
YOU JUST GAVE UP YOUR LAST CHANCE TO SAVE THE EARTH!!
REGRET IT IN THE AFTER-LIFE!!

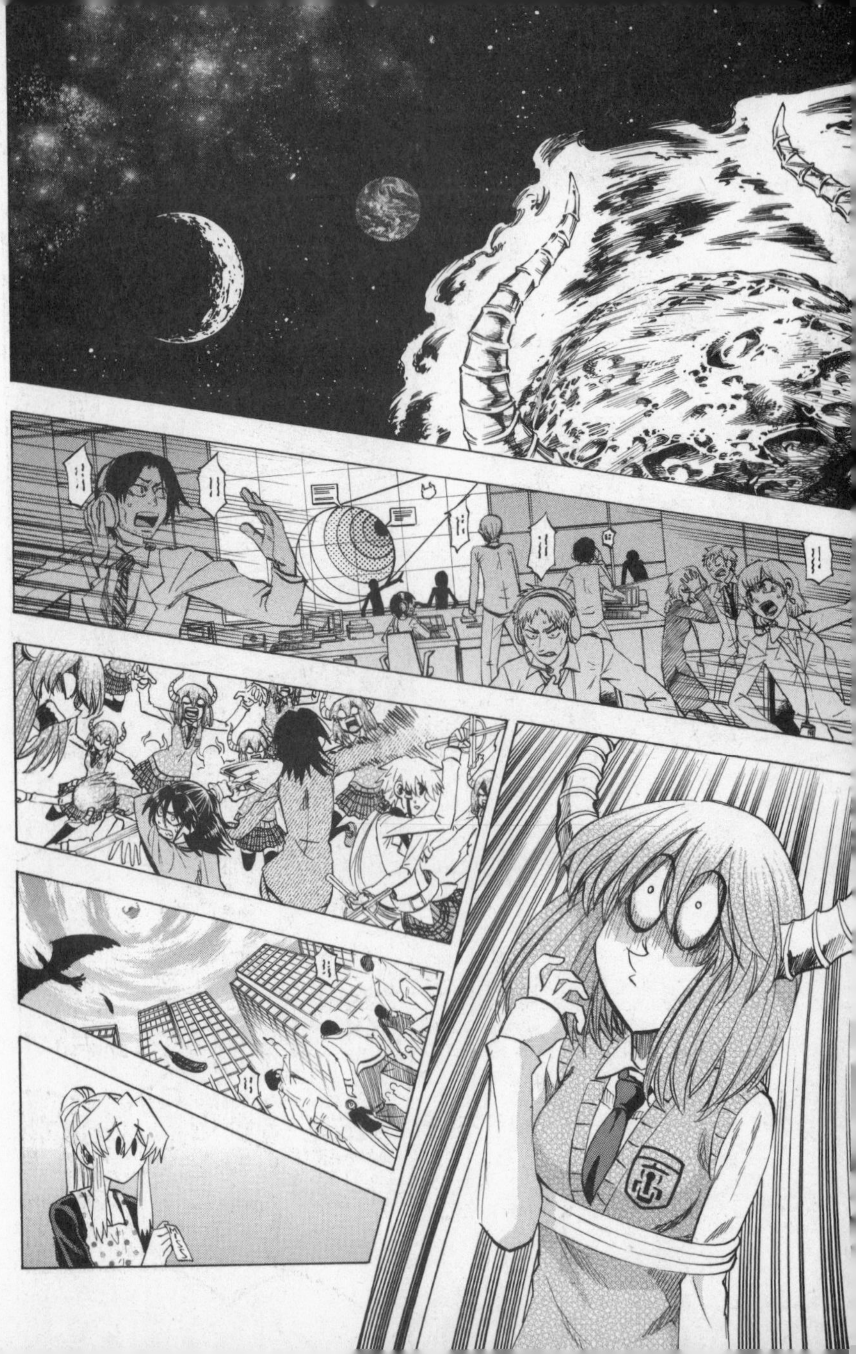

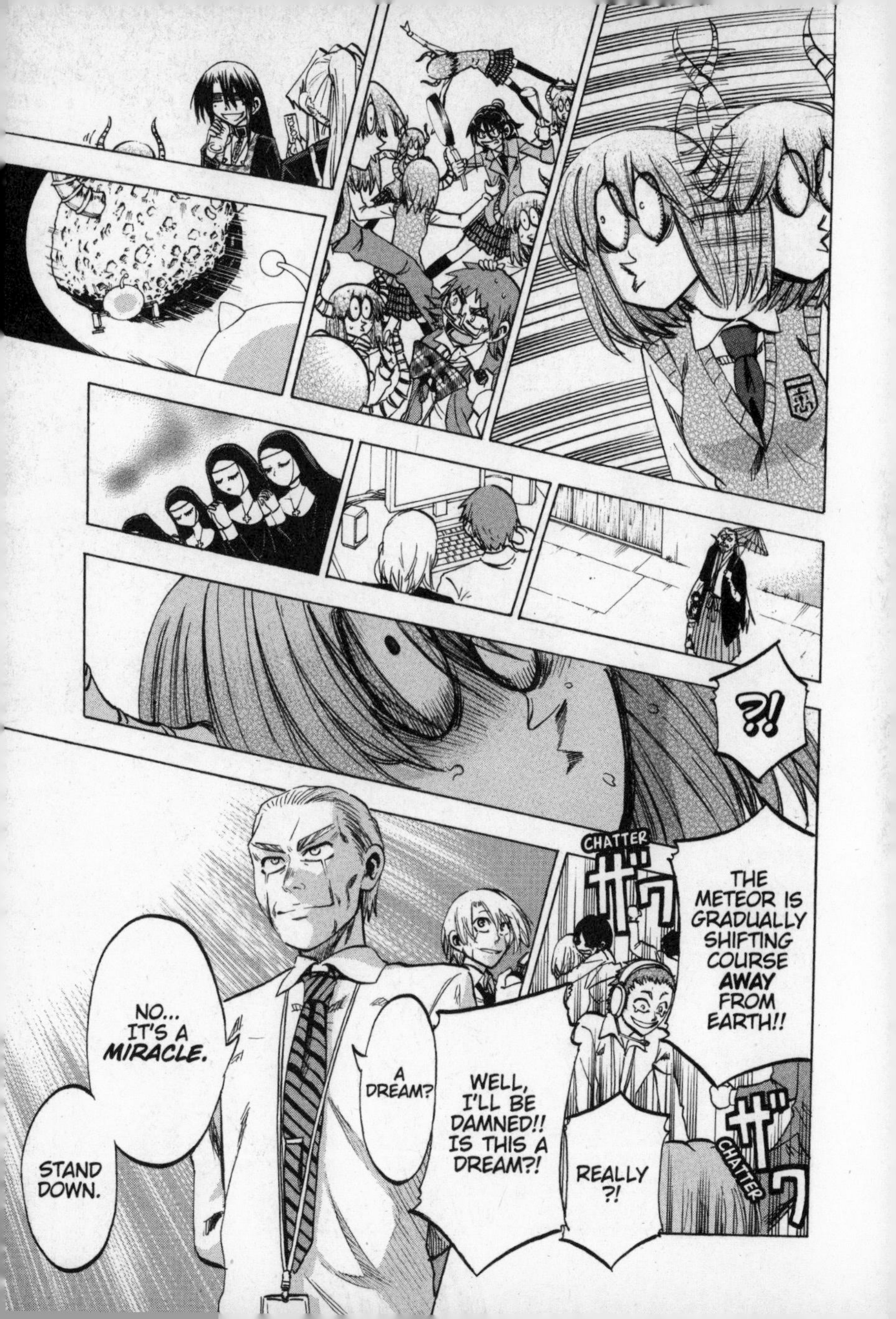
?!
CHATTER
ザワ
THE METEOR IS GRADUALLY SHIFTING COURSE AWAY FROM EARTH!!
CHATTER
ザワ
REALLY ?!
WELL, I'LL BE DAMNED!! IS THIS A DREAM?!
A DREAM?
NO... IT'S A MIRACLE.
STAND DOWN.

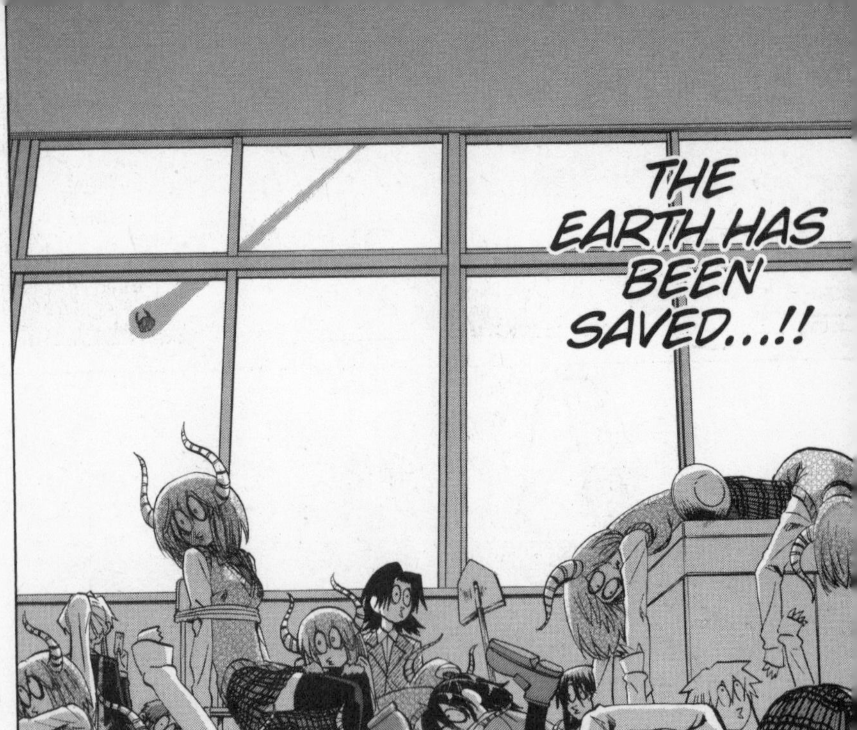
THE EARTH HAS BEEN SAVED...!!

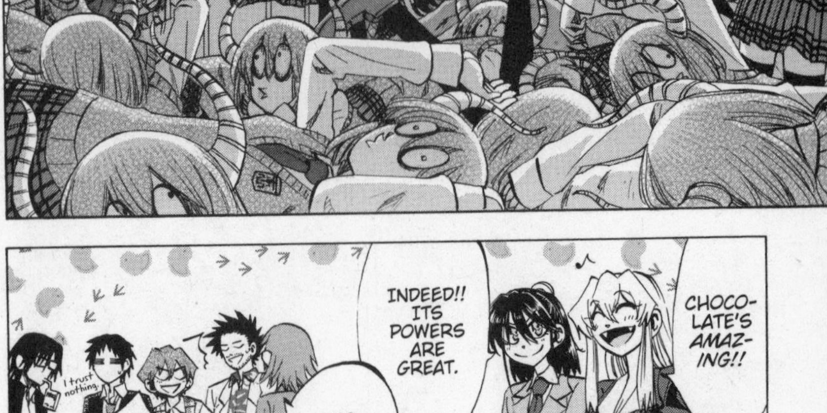
CHOCO-LATE'S AMAZ-ING!!
INDEED!! ITS POWERS ARE GREAT.
US GIRLS MADE CHOCOLATE. WANT SOME?
YOU KNOW I DO!
I trust nothing.

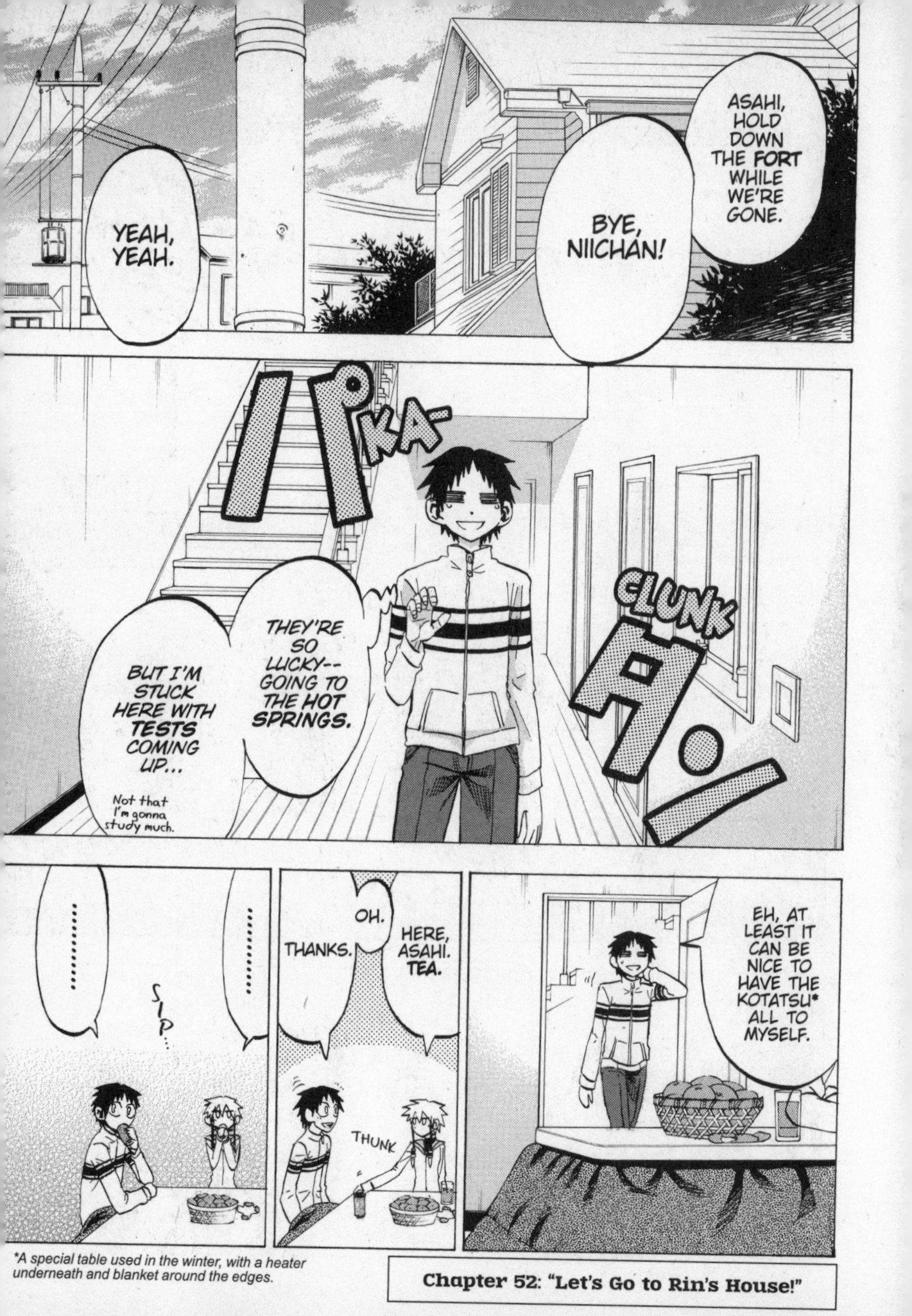
ASAHI, HOLD DOWN THE FORT WHILE WE'RE GONE.
BYE, NIICHAN!
YEAH, YEAH.
PIKA-
CLUNK
THEY'RE SO LUCKY-- GOING TO THE HOT SPRINGS.
BUT I'M STUCK HERE WITH TESTS COMING UP...
Not that I'm gonna study much.
EH, AT LEAST IT CAN BE NICE TO HAVE THE KOTATSU* ALL TO MYSELF.
HERE, ASAHI. TEA.
OH.
THANKS.
THUNK
......
......
SIP...

*A special table used in the winter, with a heater underneath and blanket around the edges.

Chapter 52: "Let's Go to Rin's House!"

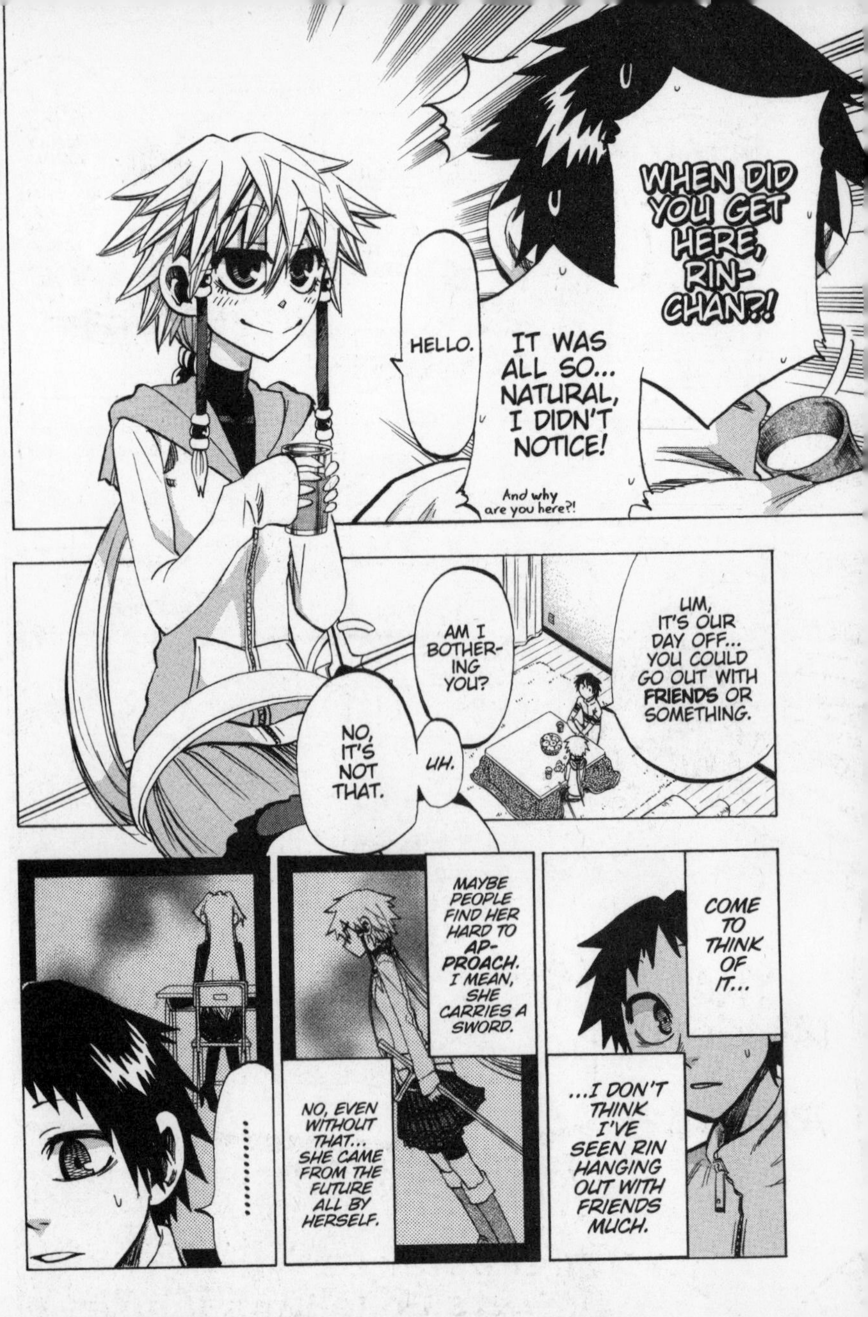
WHEN DID YOU GET HERE, RIN-CHAN?!
IT WAS ALL SO... NATURAL, I DIDN'T NOTICE!
HELLO.
And why are you here?!
UM, IT'S OUR DAY OFF... YOU COULD GO OUT WITH FRIENDS OR SOMETHING.
AM I BOTHERING YOU?
UH.
NO, IT'S NOT THAT.
COME TO THINK OF IT...
...I DON'T THINK I'VE SEEN RIN HANGING OUT WITH FRIENDS MUCH.
MAYBE PEOPLE FIND HER HARD TO AP-PROACH. I MEAN, SHE CARRIES A SWORD.
NO, EVEN WITHOUT THAT... SHE CAME FROM THE FUTURE ALL BY HERSELF.
......

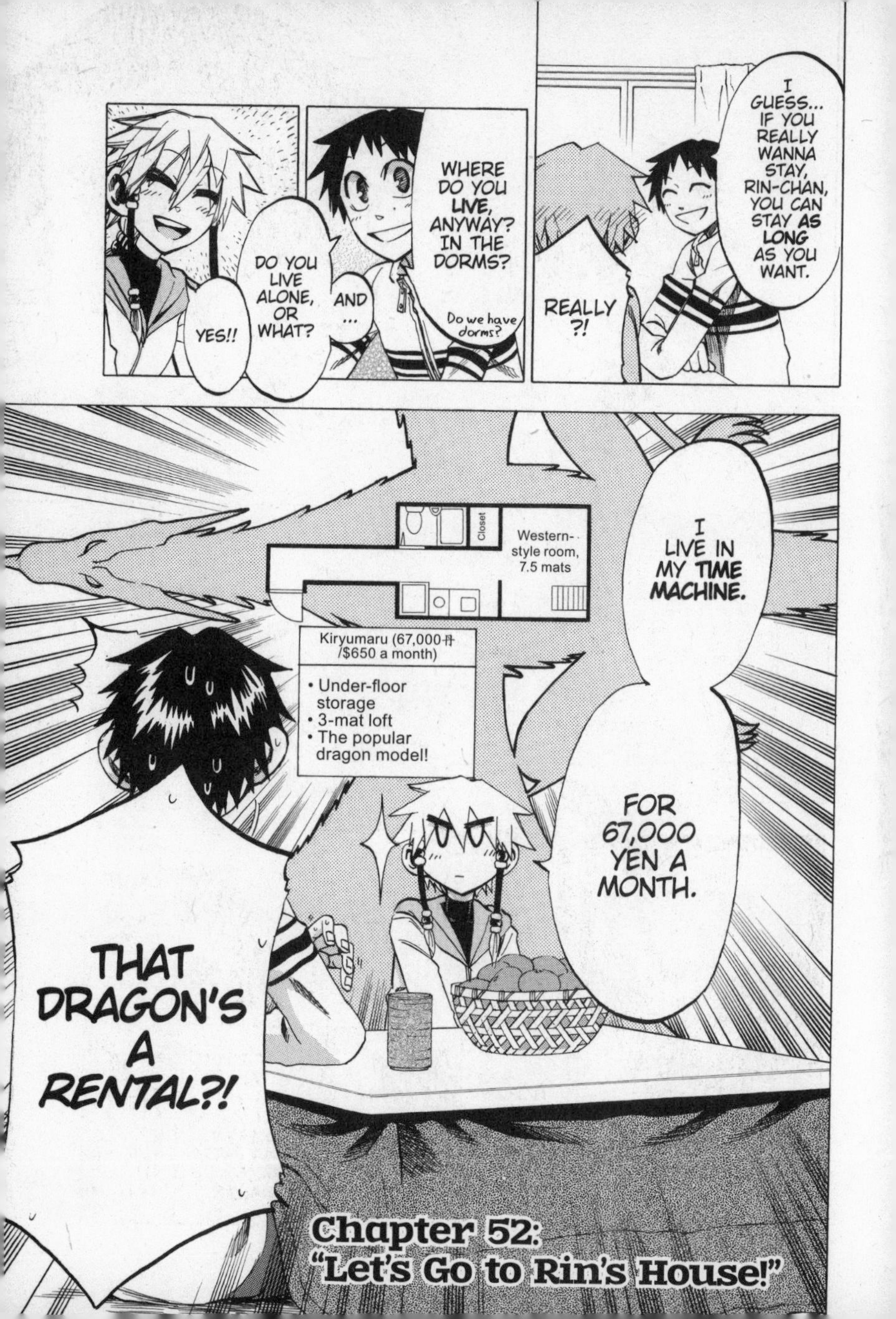
I GUESS... IF YOU REALLY WANNA STAY, RIN-CHAN, YOU CAN STAY AS LONG AS YOU WANT.
REALLY?!
WHERE DO YOU LIVE, ANYWAY? IN THE DORMS?
Do we have dorms?
AND ...
DO YOU LIVE ALONE, OR WHAT?
YES!!
I LIVE IN MY TIME MACHINE.
FOR 67,000 YEN A MONTH.
Closet
Western-style room, 7.5 mats
Kiryumaru (67,000円 /$650 a month)
• Under-floor storage
• 3-mat loft
• The popular dragon model!
THAT DRAGON'S A RENTAL?!

Chapter 52: "Let's Go to Rin's House!"

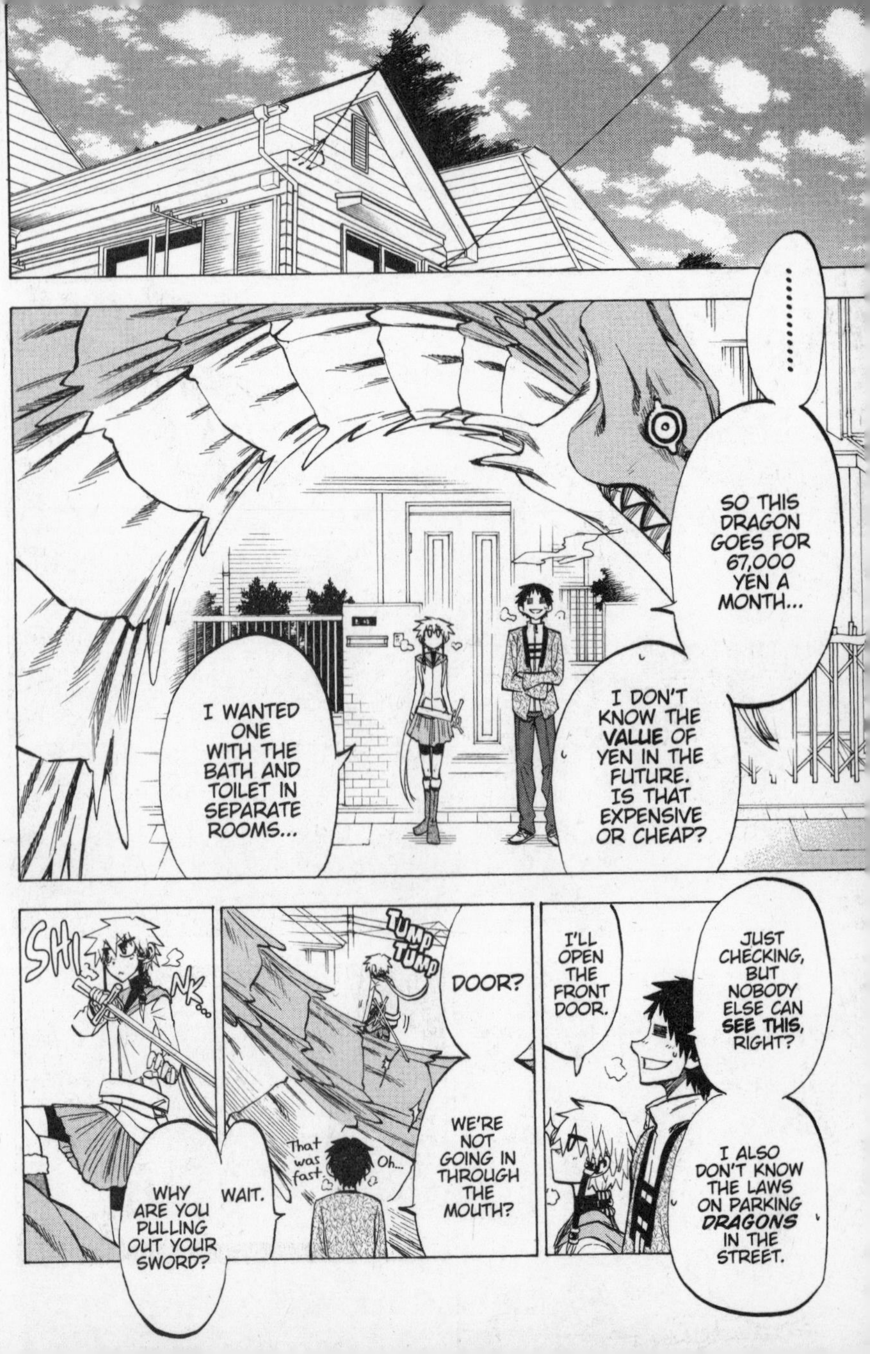
......
SO THIS DRAGON GOES FOR 67,000 YEN A MONTH...
I DON'T KNOW THE VALUE OF YEN IN THE FUTURE. IS THAT EXPENSIVE OR CHEAP?
I WANTED ONE WITH THE BATH AND TOILET IN SEPARATE ROOMS...
JUST CHECKING, BUT NOBODY ELSE CAN SEE THIS, RIGHT?
I ALSO DON'T KNOW THE LAWS ON PARKING DRAGONS IN THE STREET.
I'LL OPEN THE FRONT DOOR.
TUMP TUMP
DOOR?
WE'RE NOT GOING IN THROUGH THE MOUTH?
Oh...
That was fast.
SHINK...
WAIT.
WHY ARE YOU PULLING OUT YOUR SWORD?

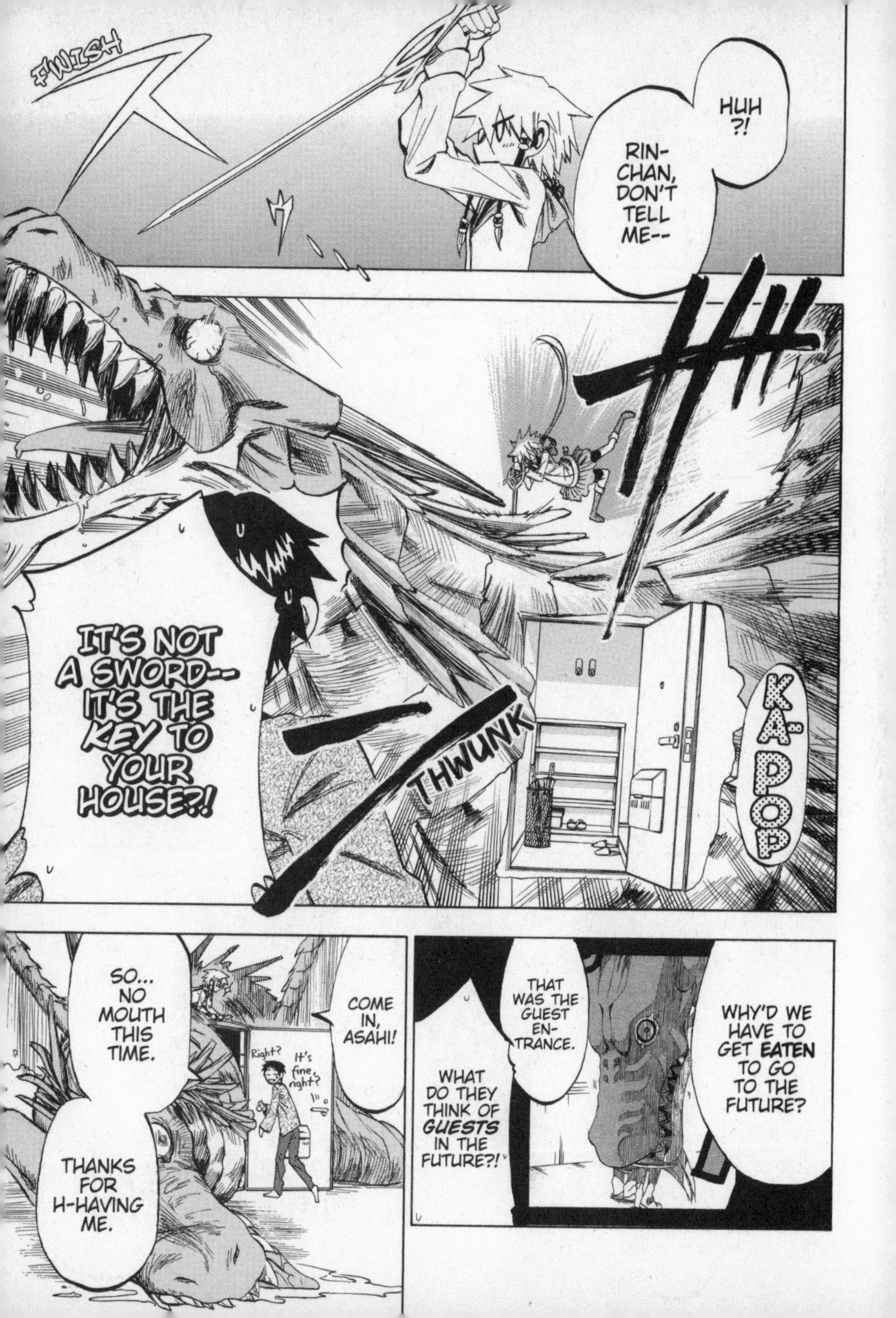
HUH?!
RIN-CHAN, DON'T TELL ME--
FWISH
KA-POP
THWUNK
IT'S NOT A SWORD-- IT'S THE KEY TO YOUR HOUSE?!
WHY'D WE HAVE TO GET EATEN TO GO TO THE FUTURE?
THAT WAS THE GUEST EN-TRANCE.
WHAT DO THEY THINK OF GUESTS IN THE FUTURE?!
COME IN, ASAHI!
Right? It's fine, right?
SO... NO MOUTH THIS TIME.
THANKS FOR H-HAVING ME.

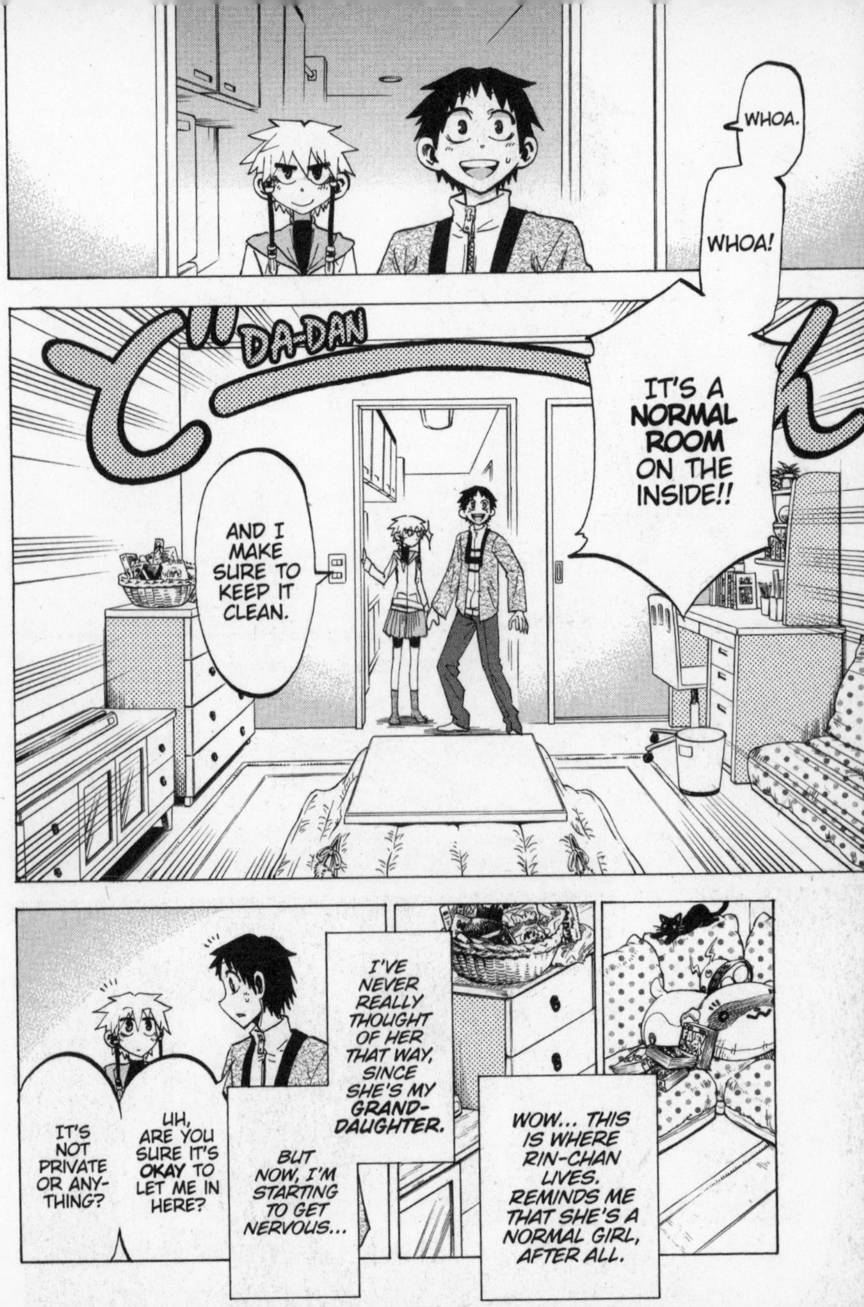
WHOA.
WHOA!
DA-DAN
IT'S A NORMAL ROOM ON THE INSIDE!!
AND I MAKE SURE TO KEEP IT CLEAN.
WOW... THIS IS WHERE RIN-CHAN LIVES. REMINDS ME THAT SHE'S A NORMAL GIRL, AFTER ALL.
I'VE NEVER REALLY THOUGHT OF HER THAT WAY, SINCE SHE'S MY GRAND-DAUGHTER.
BUT NOW, I'M STARTING TO GET NERVOUS...
UH, ARE YOU SURE IT'S OKAY TO LET ME IN HERE?
IT'S NOT PRIVATE OR ANY-THING?

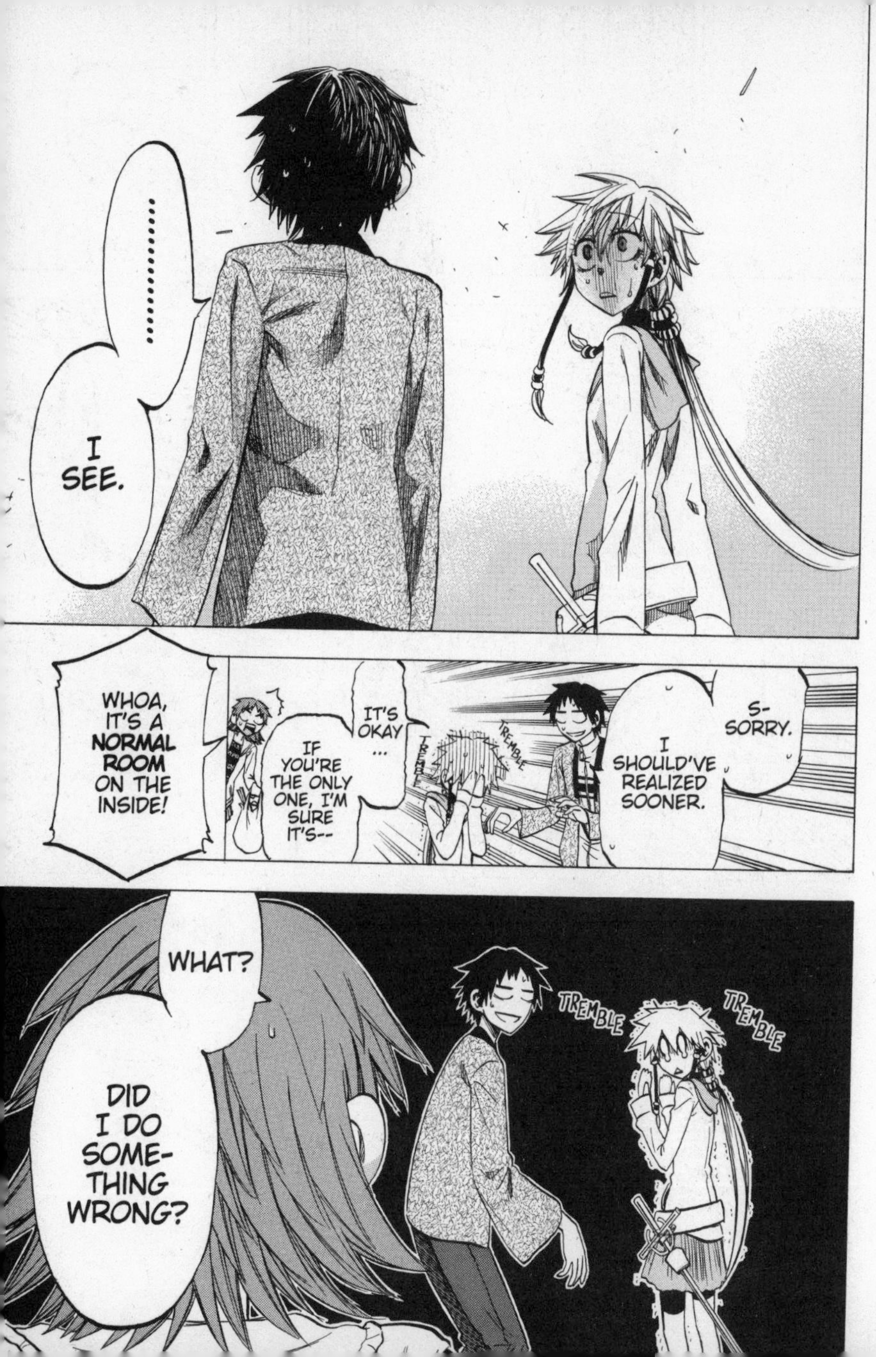
......
I SEE.
S- SORRY.
I SHOULD'VE REALIZED SOONER.
IT'S OKAY...
TREMBLE
TREMBLE
IF YOU'RE THE ONLY ONE, I'M SURE IT'S--
WHOA, IT'S A **NORMAL ROOM** ON THE INSIDE!
TREMBLE
TREMBLE
WHAT?
DID I DO SOME-THING WRONG?

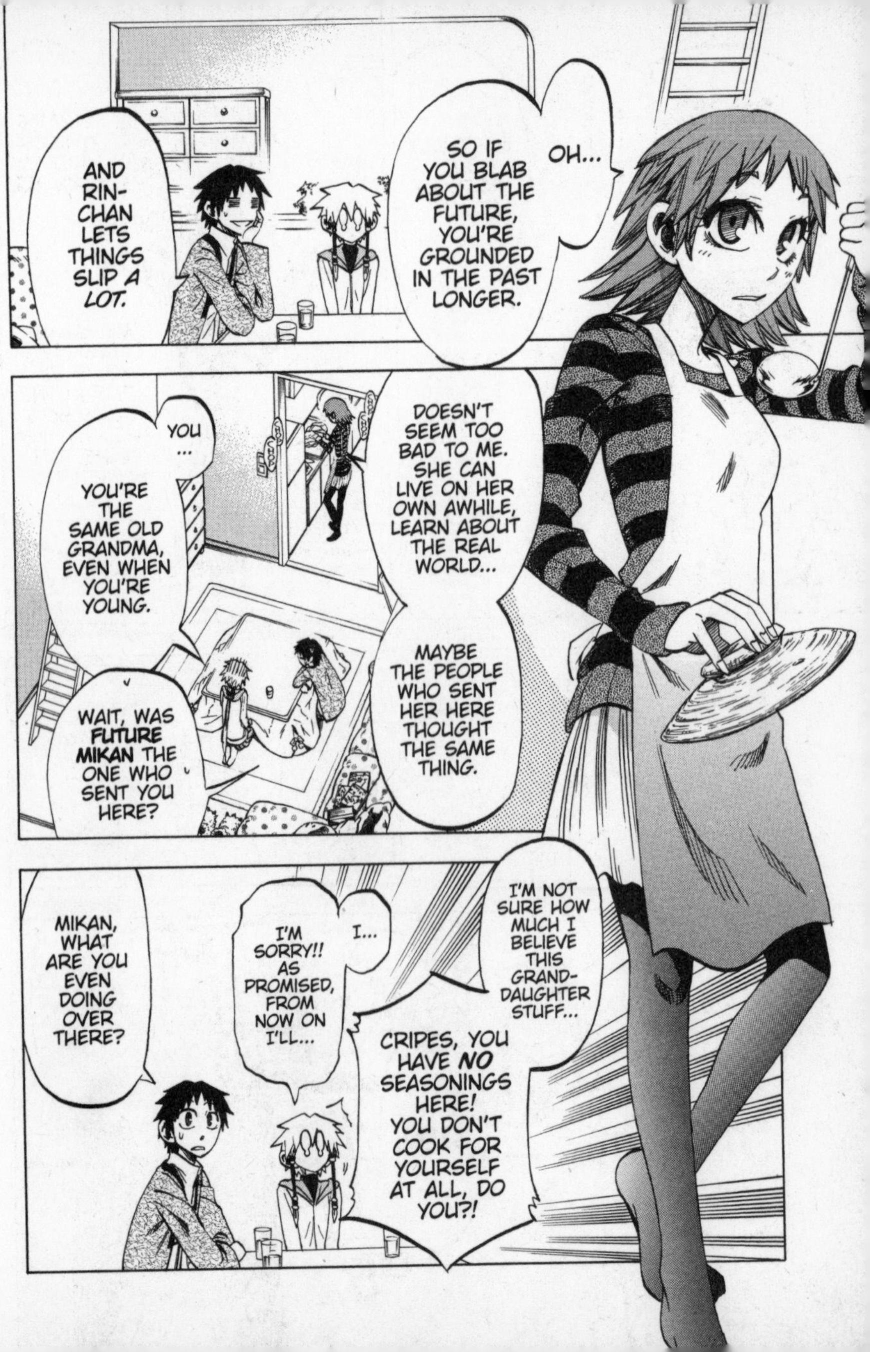
OH...
SO IF YOU BLAB ABOUT THE FUTURE, YOU'RE GROUNDED IN THE PAST LONGER.
AND RIN-CHAN LETS THINGS SLIP A LOT.
DOESN'T SEEM TOO BAD TO ME. SHE CAN LIVE ON HER OWN AWHILE, LEARN ABOUT THE REAL WORLD...
MAYBE THE PEOPLE WHO SENT HER HERE THOUGHT THE SAME THING.
YOU ...
YOU'RE THE SAME OLD GRANDMA, EVEN WHEN YOU'RE YOUNG.
WAIT, WAS FUTURE MIKAN THE ONE WHO SENT YOU HERE?
I'M NOT SURE HOW MUCH I BELIEVE THIS GRAND-DAUGHTER STUFF...
CRIPES, YOU HAVE NO SEASONINGS HERE! YOU DON'T COOK FOR YOURSELF AT ALL, DO YOU?!
I...
I'M SORRY!! AS PROMISED, FROM NOW ON I'LL...
MIKAN, WHAT ARE YOU EVEN DOING OVER THERE?

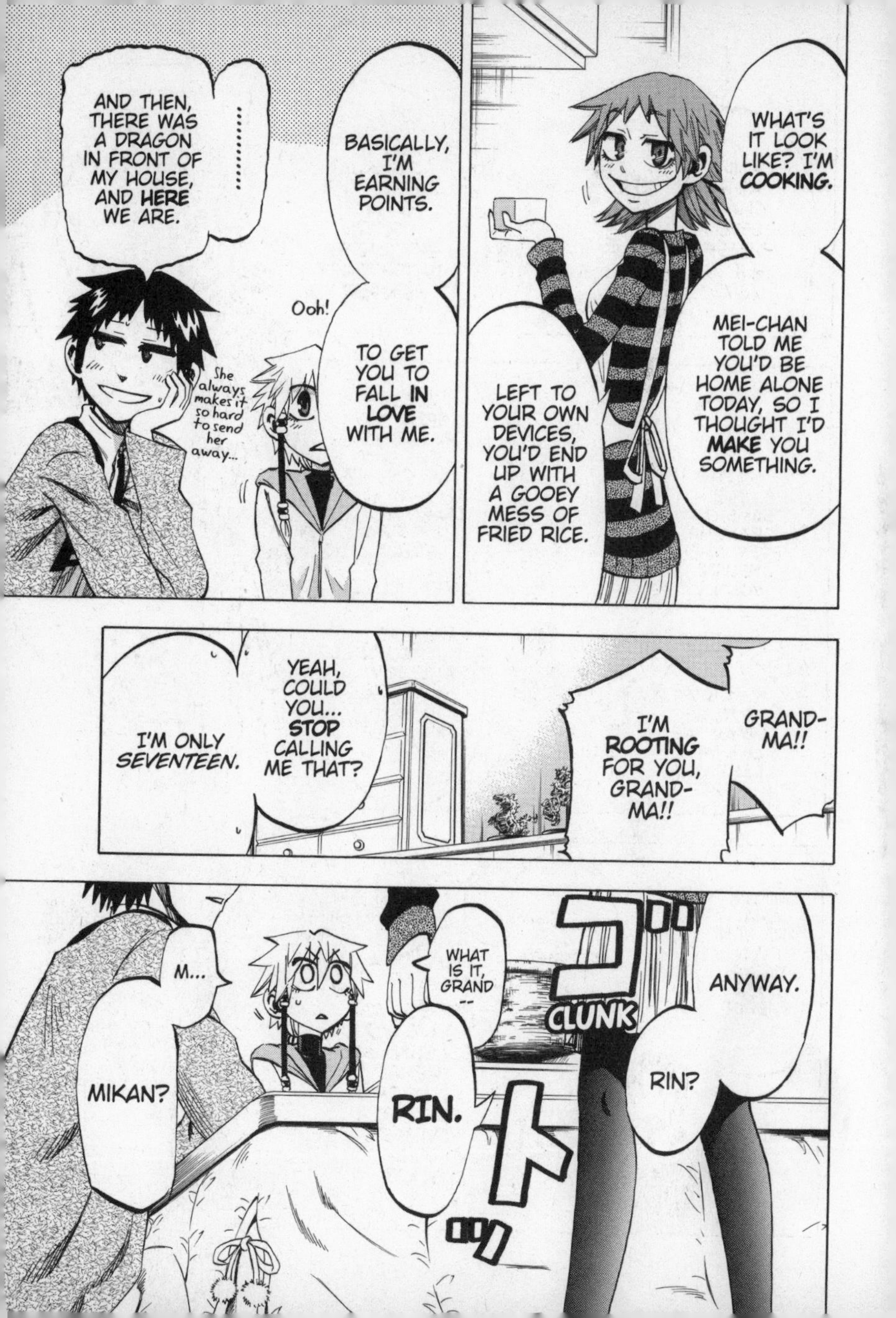
WHAT'S IT LOOK LIKE? I'M COOKING.
MEI-CHAN TOLD ME YOU'D BE HOME ALONE TODAY, SO I THOUGHT I'D MAKE YOU SOMETHING.
LEFT TO YOUR OWN DEVICES, YOU'D END UP WITH A GOOEY MESS OF FRIED RICE.
BASICALLY, I'M EARNING POINTS.
TO GET YOU TO FALL IN LOVE WITH ME.
Ooh!
......
AND THEN, THERE WAS A DRAGON IN FRONT OF MY HOUSE, AND HERE WE ARE.
She always makes it so hard to send her away...
GRAND-MA!!
I'M ROOTING FOR YOU, GRAND-MA!!
YEAH, COULD YOU... STOP CALLING ME THAT?
I'M ONLY SEVENTEEN.
ANYWAY.
RIN?
CLUNK
WHAT IS IT, GRAND --
RIN.
M...
MIKAN?

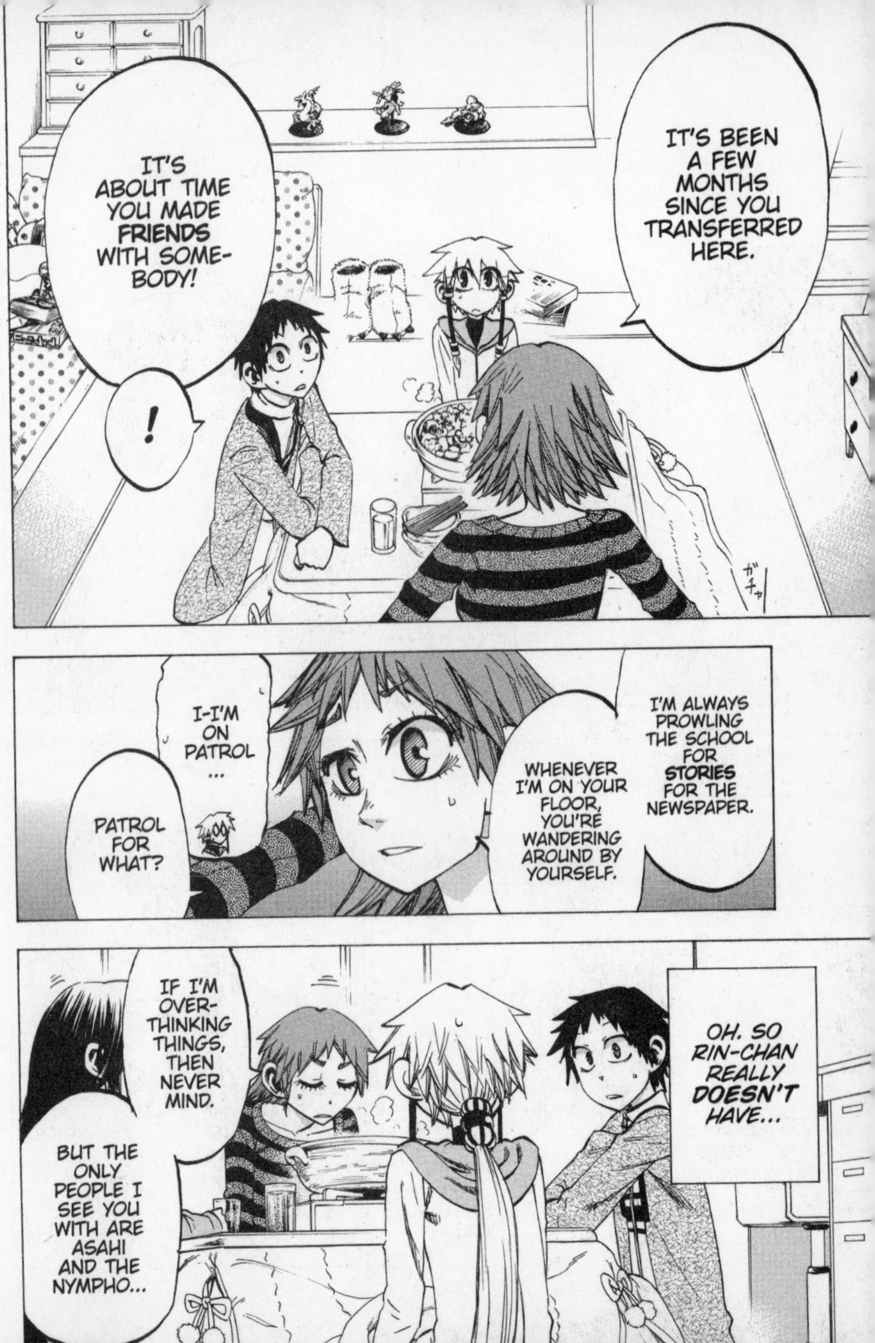
IT'S BEEN A FEW MONTHS SINCE YOU TRANSFERRED HERE.
IT'S ABOUT TIME YOU MADE **FRIENDS** WITH SOME-BODY!
!
ガチャ
I'M ALWAYS PROWLING THE SCHOOL FOR **STORIES** FOR THE NEWSPAPER.
WHENEVER I'M ON YOUR FLOOR, YOU'RE WANDERING AROUND BY YOURSELF.
I-I'M ON PATROL ...
PATROL FOR WHAT?
OH. SO RIN-CHAN REALLY **DOESN'T** HAVE...
IF I'M OVER-THINKING THINGS, THEN NEVER MIND.
BUT THE ONLY PEOPLE I SEE YOU WITH ARE ASAHI AND THE NYMPHO...

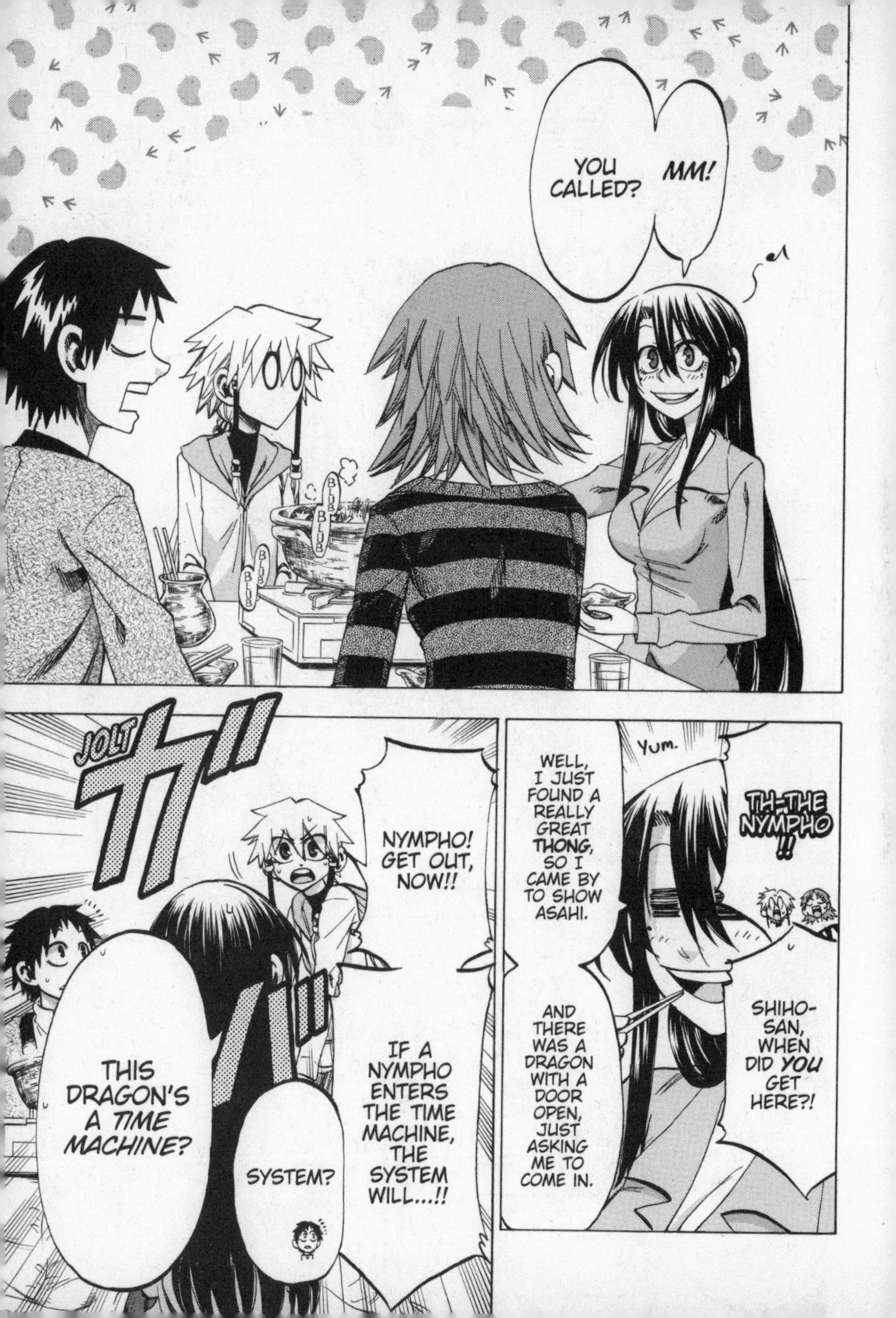
MM!
YOU CALLED?
BLUB BLUB BLUB
BLUB BLUB
Yum.
WELL, I JUST FOUND A REALLY GREAT THONG, SO I CAME BY TO SHOW ASAHI.
TH-THE NYMPHO!!
SHIHO-SAN, WHEN DID YOU GET HERE?!
AND THERE WAS A DRAGON WITH A DOOR OPEN, JUST ASKING ME TO COME IN.
JOLT
NYMPHO! GET OUT, NOW!!
IF A NYMPHO ENTERS THE TIME MACHINE, THE SYSTEM WILL...!!
SYSTEM?
THIS DRAGON'S A TIME MACHINE?

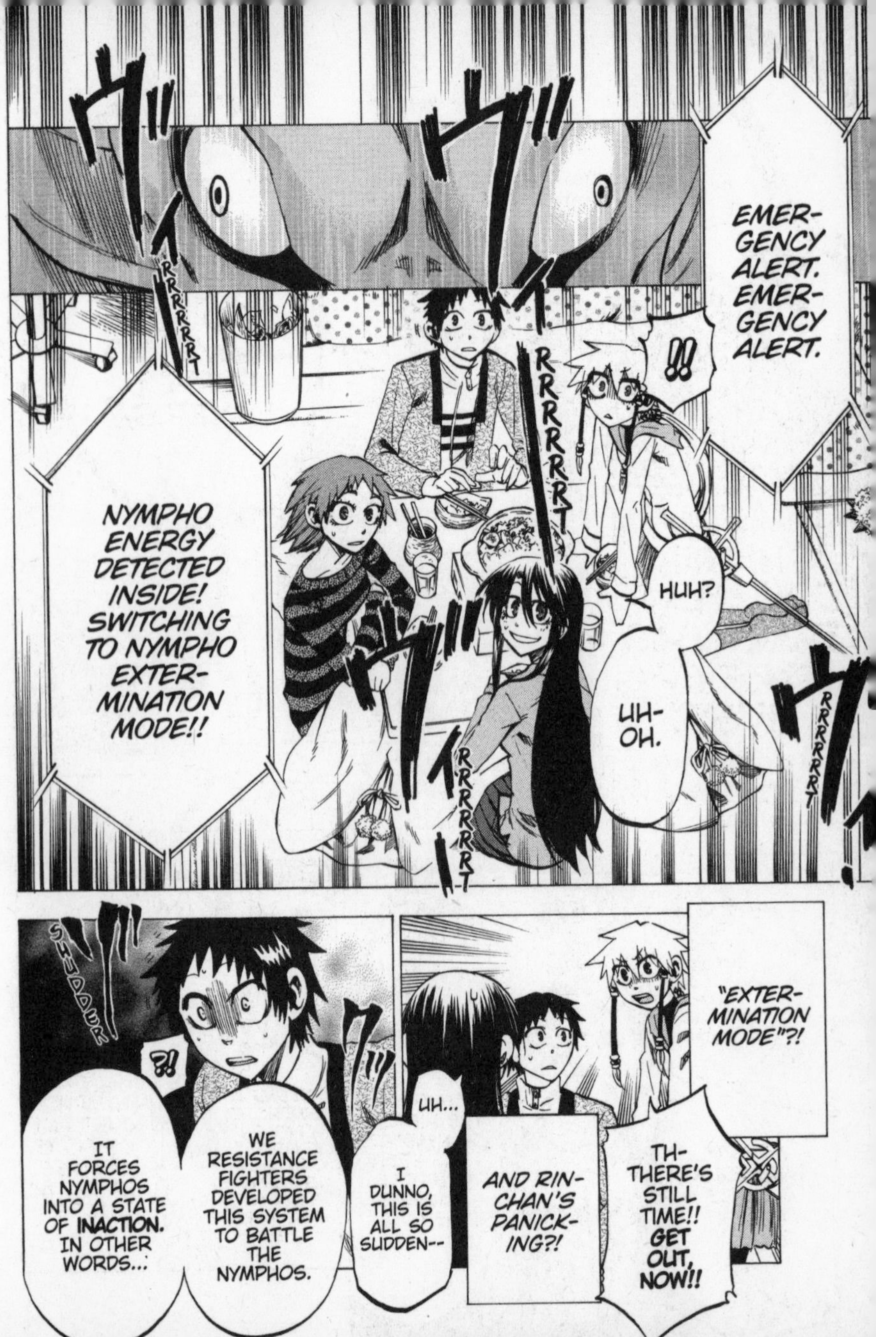
EMERGENCY ALERT. EMERGENCY ALERT.
RRRRRRRT
!!
HUH?
UH-OH.
RRRRRRRRT
RRRRRRRT
NYMPHO ENERGY DETECTED INSIDE! SWITCHING TO NYMPHO EXTERMINATION MODE!!
RRRRRRRT
"EXTERMINATION MODE"?!
TH-THERE'S STILL TIME!! GET OUT, NOW!!
AND RIN-CHAN'S PANICKING?!
UH...
I DUNNO, THIS IS ALL SO SUDDEN--
SHUDDER
?!!
WE RESISTANCE FIGHTERS DEVELOPED THIS SYSTEM TO BATTLE THE NYMPHOS.
IT FORCES NYMPHOS INTO A STATE OF INACTION. IN OTHER WORDS...

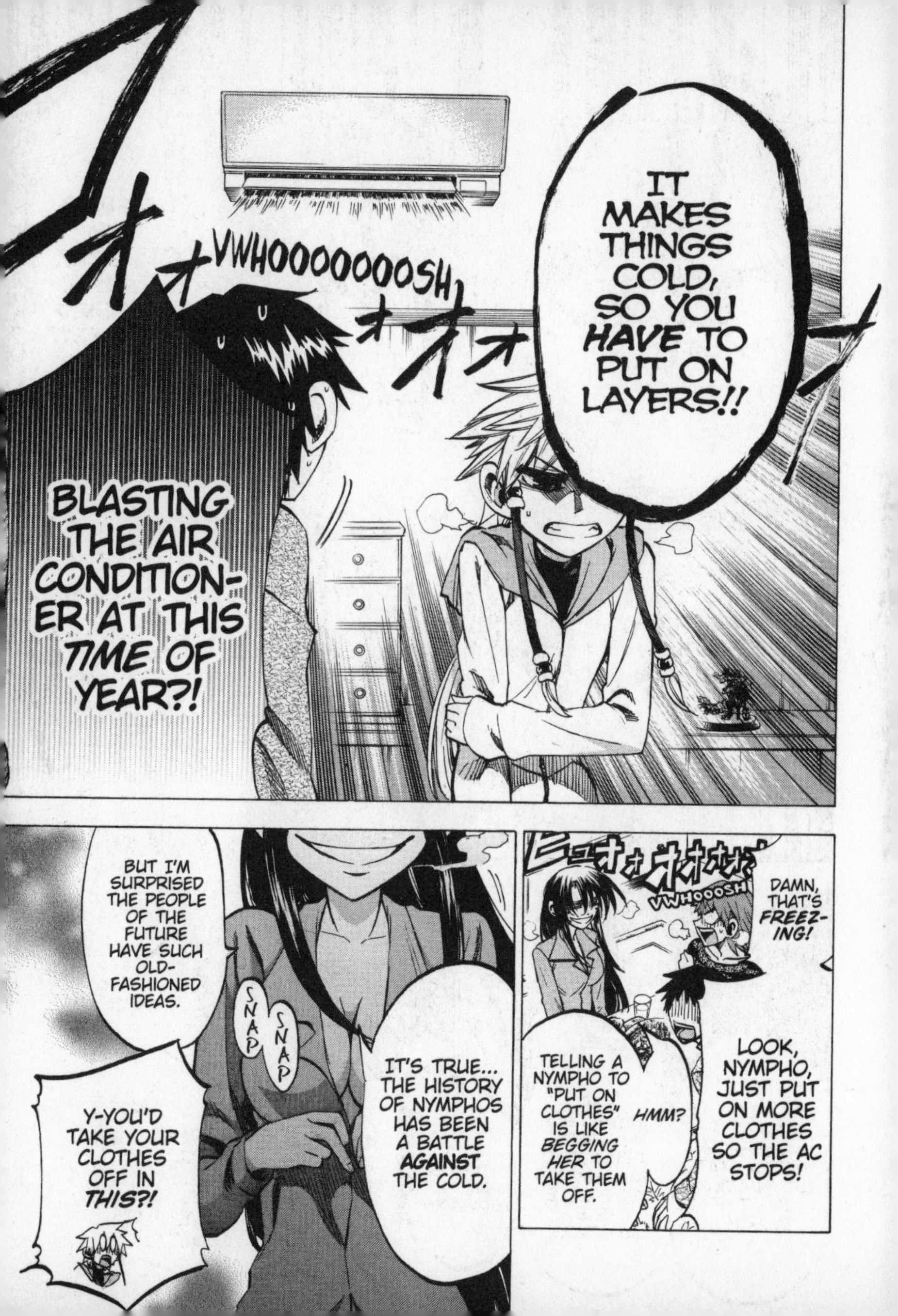
IT MAKES THINGS COLD, SO YOU HAVE TO PUT ON LAYERS!!
VWHOOOOOOOSH
BLASTING THE AIR CONDITIONER AT THIS TIME OF YEAR?!
DAMN, THAT'S FREEZING!
VWHOOOSH
LOOK, NYMPHO, JUST PUT ON MORE CLOTHES SO THE AC STOPS!
HMM?
TELLING A NYMPHO TO "PUT ON CLOTHES" IS LIKE BEGGING HER TO TAKE THEM OFF.
BUT I'M SURPRISED THE PEOPLE OF THE FUTURE HAVE SUCH OLD-FASHIONED IDEAS.
SNAP SNAP
IT'S TRUE... THE HISTORY OF NYMPHOS HAS BEEN A BATTLE AGAINST THE COLD.
Y-YOU'D TAKE YOUR CLOTHES OFF IN THIS?!

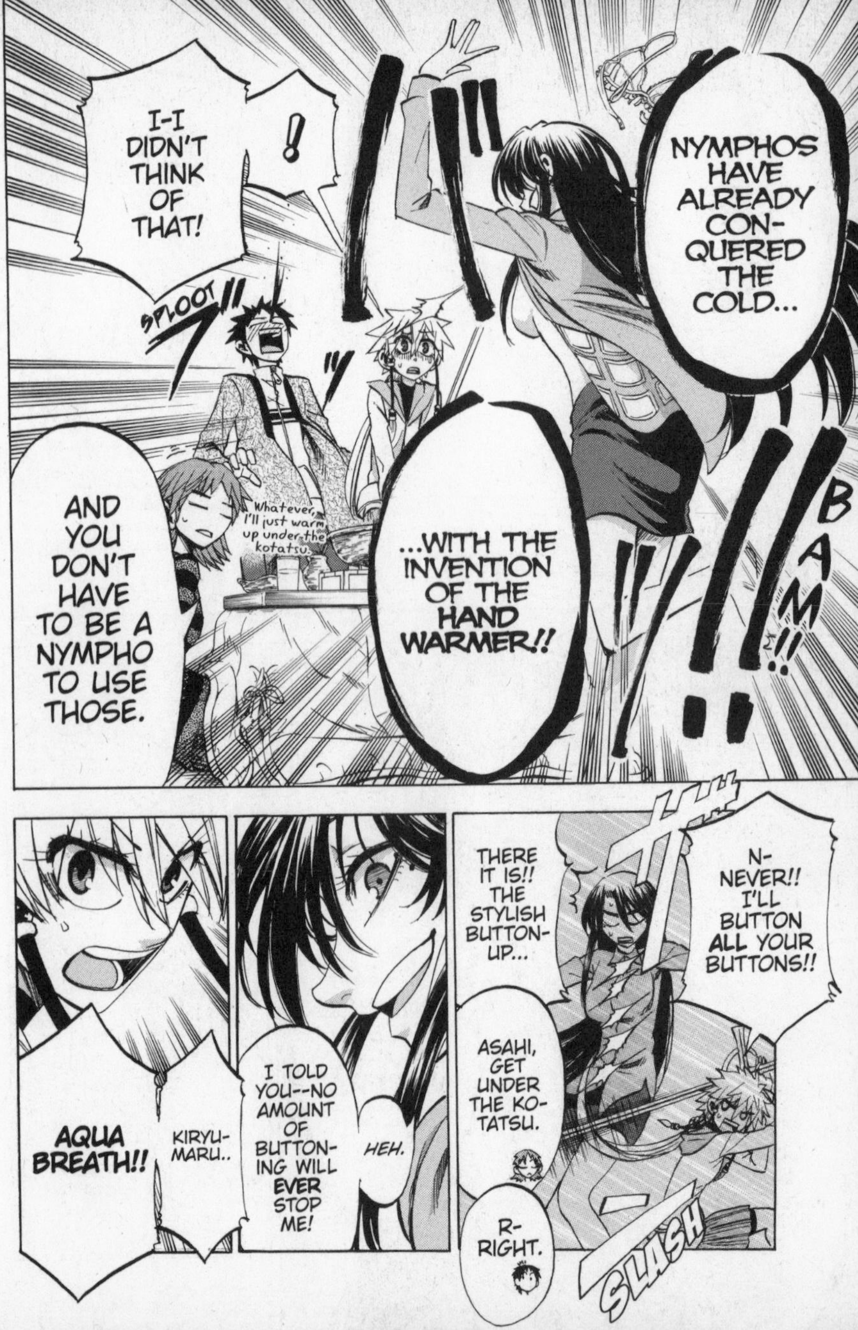
NYMPHOS HAVE ALREADY CON-QUERED THE COLD...
...WITH THE INVENTION OF THE HAND WARMER!!
BAM!!
!
I-I DIDN'T THINK OF THAT!
SPLOOT!!
Whatever, I'll just warm up under the kotatsu.
AND YOU DON'T HAVE TO BE A NYMPHO TO USE THOSE.
N-NEVER!! I'LL BUTTON ALL YOUR BUTTONS!!
THERE IT IS!! THE STYLISH BUTTON-UP...
ASAHI, GET UNDER THE KO-TATSU.
R-RIGHT.
SLASH
HEH.
I TOLD YOU--NO AMOUNT OF BUTTON-ING WILL EVER STOP ME!
KIRYU-MARU..
AQUA BREATH!!

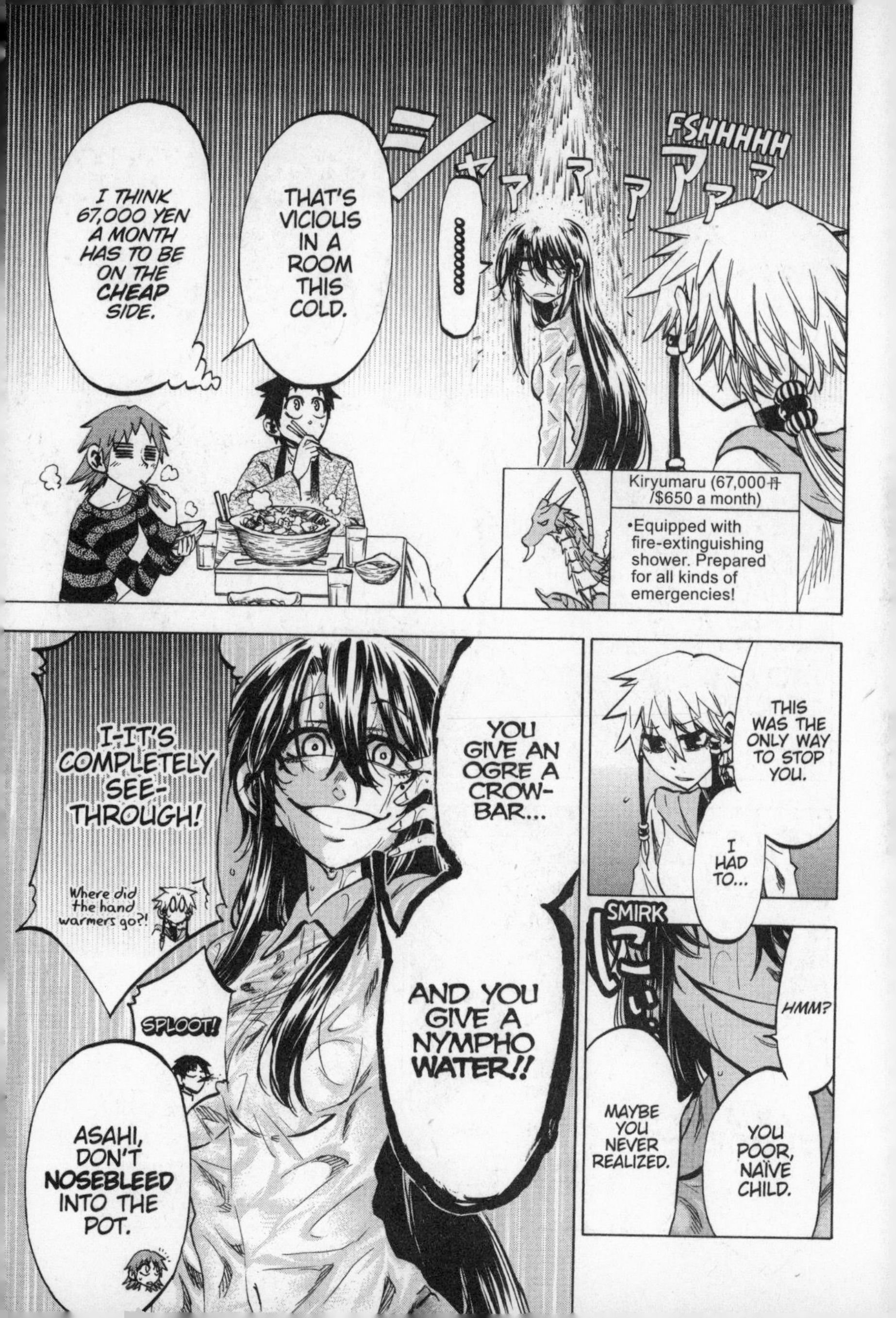
FSHHHHH
......
THAT'S VICIOUS IN A ROOM THIS COLD.
I THINK 67,000 YEN A MONTH HAS TO BE ON THE CHEAP SIDE.
Kiryumaru (67,000円/$650 a month)
•Equipped with fire-extinguishing shower. Prepared for all kinds of emergencies!
THIS WAS THE ONLY WAY TO STOP YOU.
I HAD TO...
SMIRK
HMM?
YOU POOR, NAÏVE CHILD.
MAYBE YOU NEVER REALIZED.
YOU GIVE AN OGRE A CROWBAR...
AND YOU GIVE A NYMPHO WATER!!
I-IT'S COMPLETELY SEE-THROUGH!
Where did the hand warmers go?!
SPLOOT!
ASAHI, DON'T NOSEBLEED INTO THE POT.

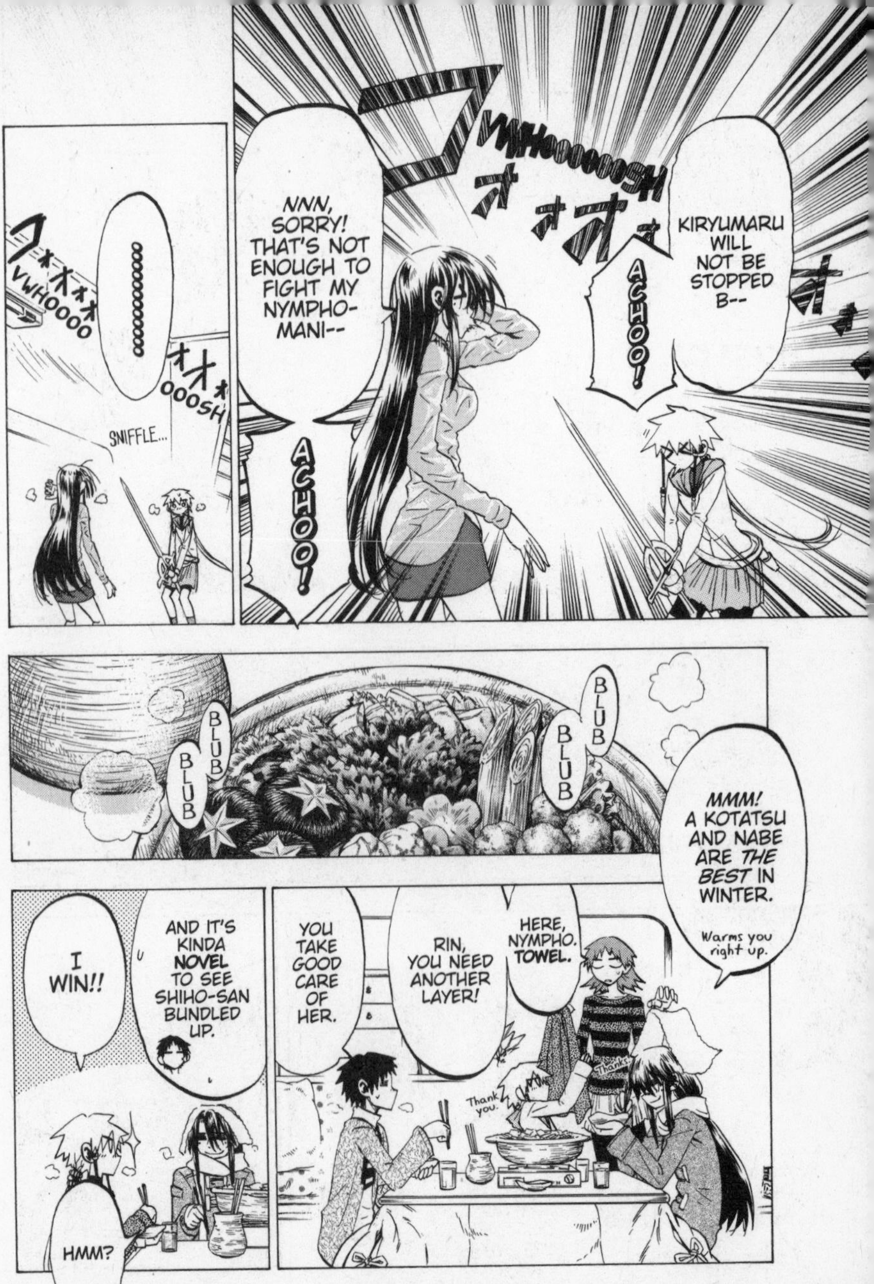
VWHOOOOOOSH
KIRYUMARU WILL NOT BE STOPPED B--
ACHOO!
NNN, SORRY! THAT'S NOT ENOUGH TO FIGHT MY NYMPHO-MANI--
ACHOO!
....
VWHOOOOOOOOSH
SNIFFLE...
MMM! A KOTATSU AND NABE ARE *THE BEST* IN WINTER.
Warms you right up.
BLUB BLUB
BLUB BLUB
HERE, NYMPHO. **TOWEL.**
Thanks.
RIN, YOU NEED ANOTHER LAYER!
Thank you.
YOU TAKE GOOD CARE OF HER.
AND IT'S KINDA **NOVEL** TO SEE SHIHO-SAN BUNDLED UP.
I WIN!!
HMM?

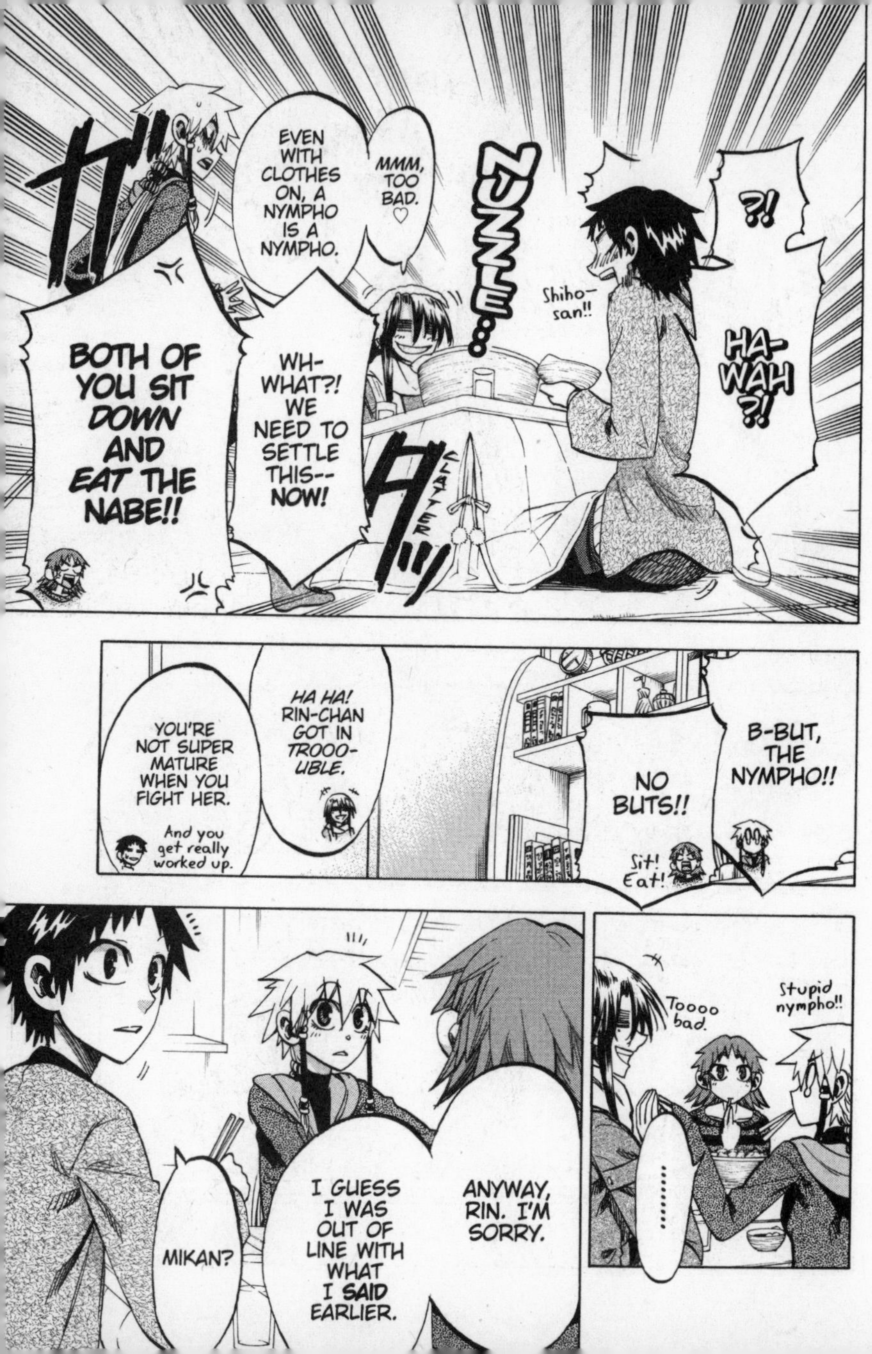
?!
HA-WAH?!
Shiho-san!!
NUZZLE...
MMM, TOO BAD. ♡
EVEN WITH CLOTHES ON, A NYMPHO IS A NYMPHO.
WH-WHAT?! WE NEED TO SETTLE THIS--NOW!
CLATTER
BOTH OF YOU SIT DOWN AND EAT THE NABE!!
B-BUT, THE NYMPHO!!
NO BUTS!!
Sit! Eat!
HA HA! RIN-CHAN GOT IN TROOOUBLE.
YOU'RE NOT SUPER MATURE WHEN YOU FIGHT HER.
And you get really worked up.
Stupid nympho!!
Toooo bad.
......
ANYWAY, RIN. I'M SORRY.
I GUESS I WAS OUT OF LINE WITH WHAT I SAID EARLIER.
MIKAN?

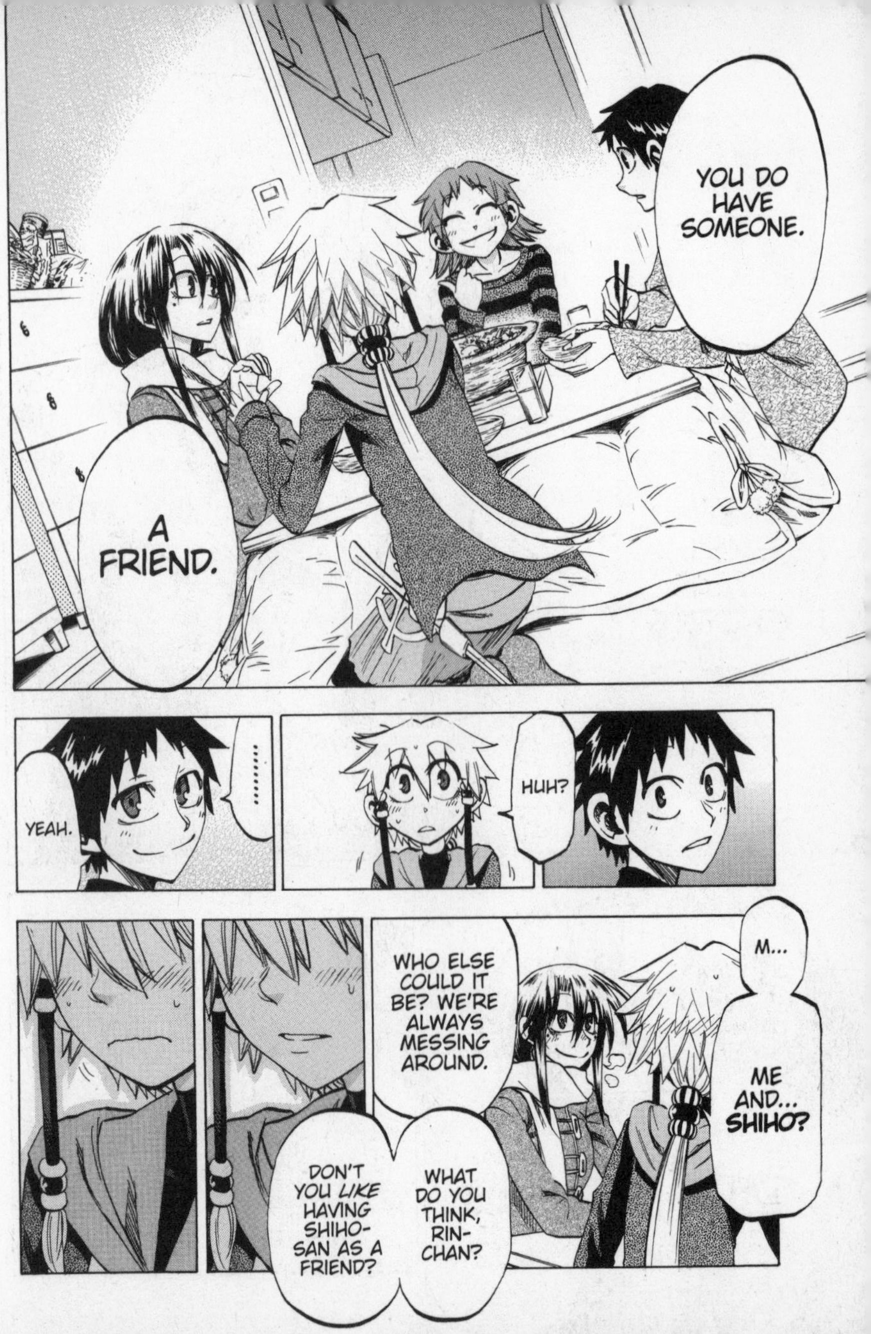
YOU DO HAVE SOMEONE.
A FRIEND.
HUH?
......
YEAH.
M... ME AND... SHIHO?
WHO ELSE COULD IT BE? WE'RE ALWAYS MESSING AROUND.
WHAT DO YOU THINK, RIN-CHAN?
DON'T YOU *LIKE* HAVING SHIHO-SAN AS A FRIEND?

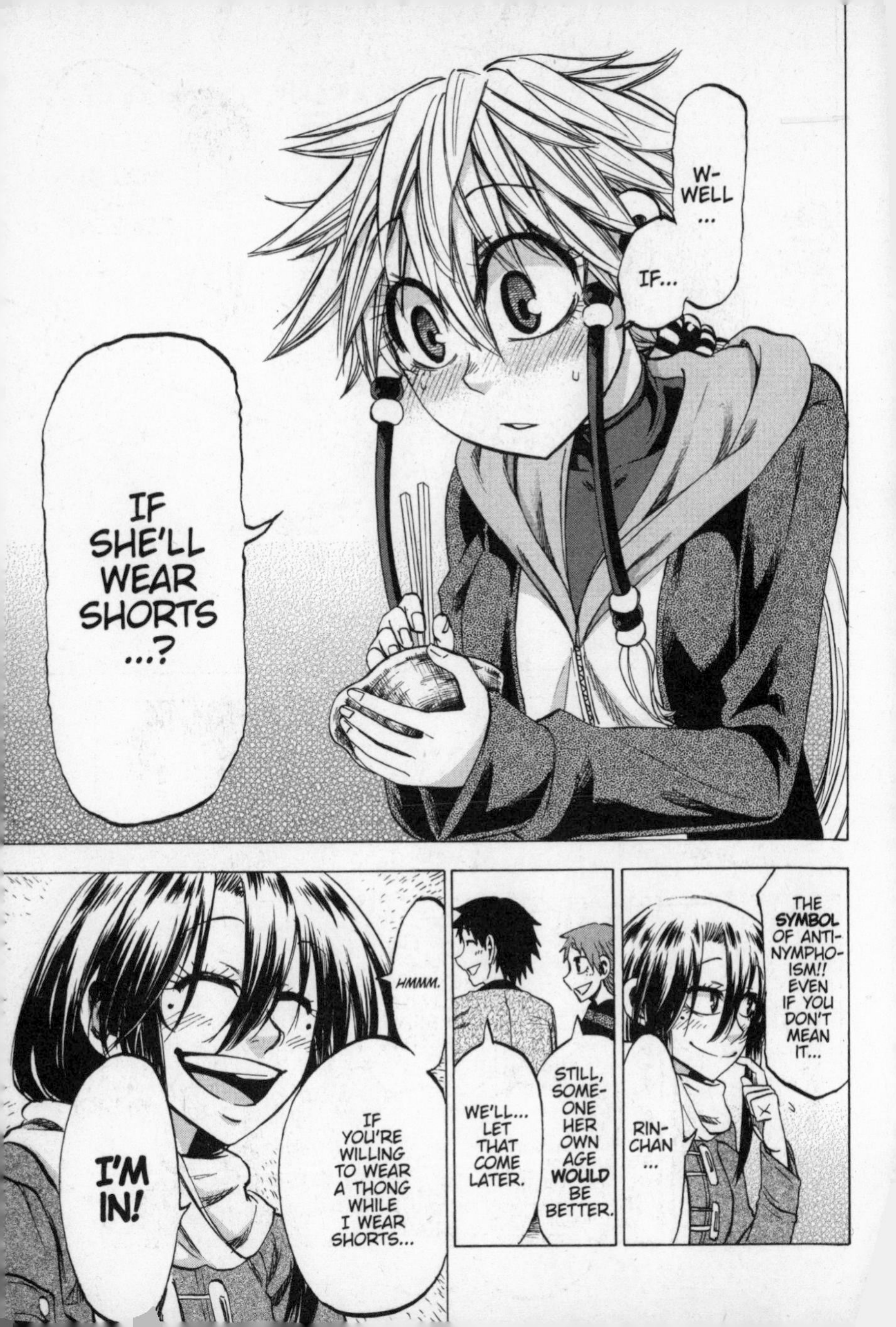
W-WELL...
IF...
IF SHE'LL WEAR SHORTS...?
THE **SYMBOL** OF ANTI-NYMPHO-ISM!! EVEN IF YOU DON'T MEAN IT...
RIN-CHAN...
STILL, SOME-ONE HER OWN AGE **WOULD** BE BETTER.
WE'LL... LET THAT COME LATER.
HMMM.
IF YOU'RE WILLING TO WEAR A THONG WHILE I WEAR SHORTS...
I'M IN!

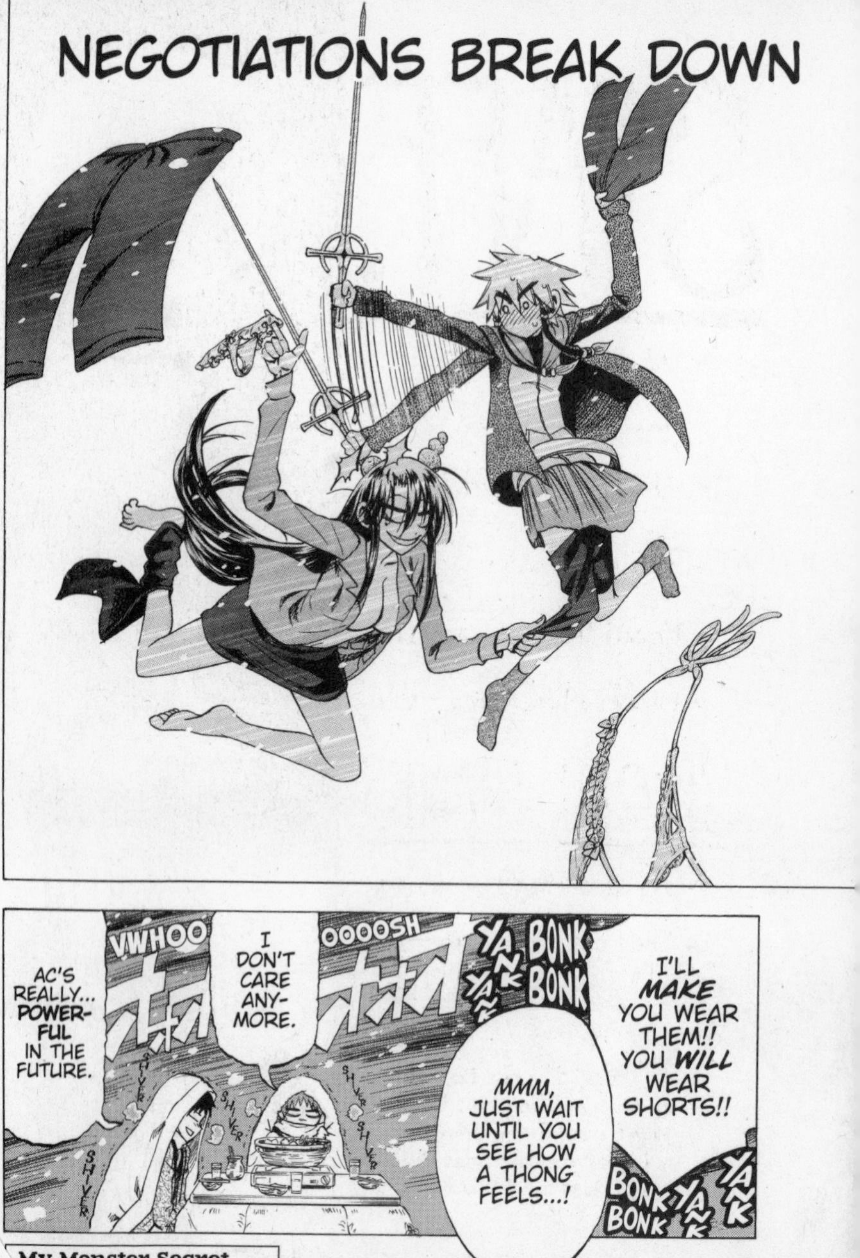
NEGOTIATIONS BREAK DOWN
BONK BONK
YANK YANK
I'LL MAKE YOU WEAR THEM!! YOU WILL WEAR SHORTS!!
MMM, JUST WAIT UNTIL YOU SEE HOW A THONG FEELS...!
BONK BONK
YANK YANK
VWHOOOOOOSH
I DON'T CARE ANY-MORE.
AC'S REALLY... POWER-FUL IN THE FUTURE.
SHIVER SHIVER
SHIVER SHIVER
My Monster Secret Volume 6 / End

STAFF.

- Akutsu-san
- Garage Okada-san
- Shuumeigiku-san
- Seijun Suzuki-san
- Kouki Nakashima-san
- Hiroki Minemura-san

(in syllabary order)

SPECIAL THANKS.

- Ayako Matsuda-san
- Editor: Mukawa-san, Otsuka-san

I give my thanks to those of you holding this book right now and everyone who let me and this work be a part of their lives.

Eiji Masuda

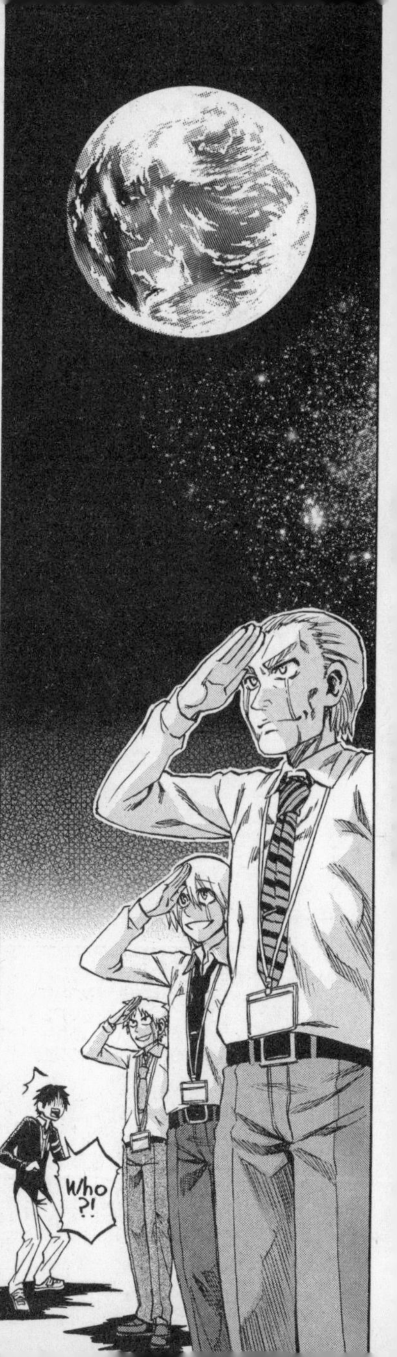

Who ?!

I am 6...

School Festival ①

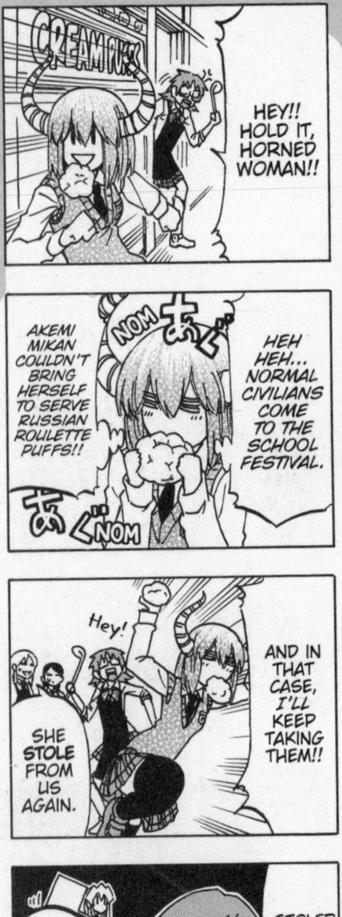
HEY!! HOLD IT, HORNED WOMAN!!
HEH HEH... NORMAL CIVILIANS COME TO THE SCHOOL FESTIVAL.
NOM あぐ
AKEMI MIKAN COULDN'T BRING HERSELF TO SERVE RUSSIAN ROULETTE PUFFS!!
あぐNOM
AND IN THAT CASE, I'LL KEEP TAKING THEM!!
Hey!
SHE STOLE FROM US AGAIN.
STOLE? NO.
I'M GETTING HER GUARD DOWN.
Growl
UNTIL SHE STUFFS WHOLE PUFFS IN HER FACE WITHOUT CHECKING INSIDE!!

School Festival ②

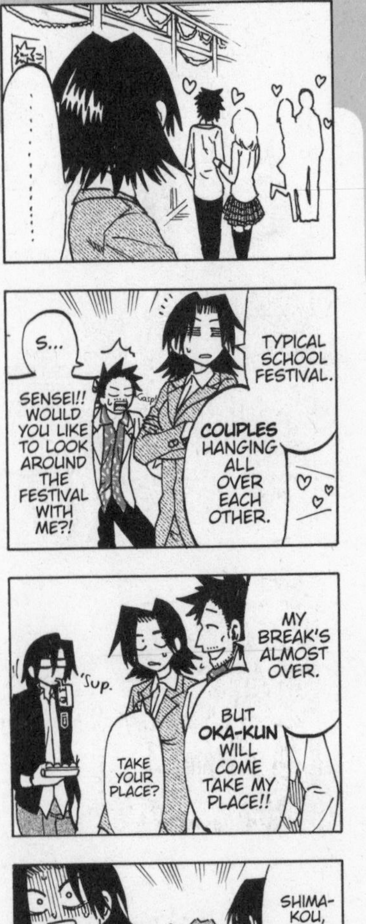
TYPICAL SCHOOL FESTIVAL.
COUPLES HANGING ALL OVER EACH OTHER.
S...
Gasp!
SENSEI!! WOULD YOU LIKE TO LOOK AROUND THE FESTIVAL WITH ME?!
MY BREAK'S ALMOST OVER.
BUT OKA-KUN WILL COME TAKE MY PLACE!!
'Sup.
TAKE YOUR PLACE?
SHIMA-KOU, THE BATON'S YOURS.
YOU GOT IT!!
I WON'T LET KOUMOTO-SENSEI BE ALONE IN HERE, NO SIR!!
AM I BEING BABY-SAT?!
Am I that bad?!